MAN'S BEST FRIEND
ON THE ROAD AG

A Selective Guide to New England's Bed and Breakfasts, Inns, Hotels, and
🐾 🐾 🐾 🐾 Resorts that Welcome You and Your Dog 🐾 🐾 🐾 🐾

ON THE ROAD AGAIN WITH
MAN'S BEST FRIEND

elective Guide to New England's Bed and Breakfasts, Inns, Hotels, and

🐾 🐾 🐾 Resorts that Welcome You and Your Dog 🐾 🐾 🐾 🐾

DAWN AND ROBERT HABGOOD

MACMILLAN • USA

Macmillan General Reference
A Simon & Schuster Macmillan Company
15 Columbus Circle
New York, NY 10023

Howell Book House
MACMILLAN is a registered trademark of Macmillan, Inc.

TX907
.3
.N35H32
1995

Third Edition

ISBN: 0-87605-705-9

Editor: Barbara M. Hayes
Interior Artwork: Glynn Brannon

Soc Su
10/3/96

Manufactured in the United States of America
10 9 8 7 6 5 4 3 2 1

To M.S.F.

for your love and support

Contents

Introduction

Like millions of others in this country, we cherish our dogs and their unique place within our family. Our two golden retrievers are an integral part of our lives, and we find it difficult to leave them for extended periods of time. From the earliest days of our marriage, we loved to pack our bags and hit the road in search of new, undiscovered terrain. Each of the regions in our country is so distinct from the next, we thrive on the new pleasures and discoveries around each bend in the road. However, our unwillingness to abandon our pets soon clashed with our questing, traveling spirits.

So twelve years ago, we started including our dogs on weekend vacations. We began compiling lists of pet-friendly accommodations. Before long, we owned virtually every regional guidebook, but had unearthed only a handful of decent lodgings. Brochures could be deceptive, and the places were not always as nice as we expected. Our dogs did not care, but we did.

Finally, we decided to solve the problem ourselves and went "on the road again" in search of a variety of accommodations that would not only appeal to us, but to other people who wanted to vacation with their dog and who were seeking quality places with character, regional flavor, and charisma.

On The Road Again With Man's Best Friend is the result — a series of regional travel guides that are both selective and comprehensive. We include listings of all accommodations that accept travelers and their dogs; however, we highlight only those that merit special attention. For over a decade, we have been traveling to, and writing about, places to stay with dogs, allowing us to provide readers with our personal, first-hand impressions. If we think a place is great, we let you know, and if there are areas that could be improved, we mention them as well. We are able to do this only because we make a point of personally visiting and revisiting each entry in each of our guides.

In looking through this book, prospective guests will discover a wide range of vacation destinations that should appeal to their senses, as well as to their pocketbooks. And remember, traveling with a dog can be a delightful experience, but it is also a responsibility that, if misused, can not only completely ruin your vacation, but can deny the opportunity for others to visit that establishment in the future.

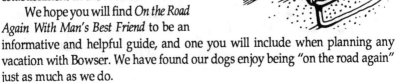

We hope you will find *On the Road Again With Man's Best Friend* to be an informative and helpful guide, and one you will include when planning any vacation with Bowser. We have found our dogs enjoy being "on the road again" just as much as we do.

How do we Select "the Best" Accommodations?

We choose our dog friendly entries by sifting through all the accommodations that welcome dogs in a given region, looking for places that exude a warmth, charm, and quality that even dog-less vacationers would find appealing. For instance, we include cottage communities that have been around for decades and, although some are rather rustic, attract a strong following of devoted patrons. Intimate B&Bs are added for their personalized attention and ambiance, while resorts are appealing for their diversity of activities. Elegant country inns and small hotels often top our list, but equally important are the family-run farms in the countryside.

Once selected, we pay an unannounced visit to the establishment, always maintaining our anonymity. This allows us, in most cases, to provide future guests with a concise overview and detailed descriptions that are not influenced by any type of special treatment. Because we accept no money from the innkeepers or owners, we can remain objective and you can feel more comfortable with our recommendations.

How to Use the Book — General Information

Each entry begins with pertinent general information about the establishment, including the address, telephone number, owner or manager's name, acceptable methods of payment, and number, type, and cost of the various guest rooms. We also describe any pet policies, and restrictions regarding children, if any. This section tells you more about each area we cover.

Types of Accommodations:

B&Bs: These are often private homes and guests should treat this experience as though they are staying with a friend. B&Bs are usually short on amenities and on-site activities, but long on personalized attention. You can expect to find comfortable guest rooms, a common area with perhaps a television and stereo, a Continental breakfast, and a warm and friendly host who genuinely enjoys having houseguests. B&Bs generally do not serve lunch and dinner.

Inns: Inns can sometimes be confused with B&Bs. Most have the same type of intimate feeling, but with just a few more rooms. One of the biggest differences is they have either a restaurant or can serve at least breakfast and dinner. Inns are more highly regulated and must meet the various state and national health and access codes. Also, they provide more activities and creature comforts than do traditional B&Bs.

Cottages: The cottage complexes we feature vary greatly in size, amenities, and activities — but even the most rustic are very clean and well maintained. Although the cabin or cottage might offer only the bare essentials, there is always plenty to do on the premises or in the nearby area. There is almost always a main lodge with a great restaurant. In some cases, all guests eat here, and in others they have a kitchenette that gives them the option of dining in their cottage or at the main lodge. We usually choose a cottage complex because it offers a picturesque setting with plenty of open space for both owner and dog to explore.

Hotels and Resorts: Smaller hotels often label themselves inns because they feel it makes them appear more intimate. We try to warn readers of this early and explain exactly what they can expect. Hotels usually have fifty or more rooms, and are located in large towns and cities. They traditionally deliver a full range of amenities, which could include an indoor or outdoor swimming pool, concierge services, multiple restaurants, a large staff, and a health club. Resorts, on the other hand, are generally located on the outskirts of popular tourist destinations or in the countryside. They offer a wide variety of guest rooms, as well as an expansive list of amenities, activities, and on-site programs.

Motels/Motor Lodges: These vary greatly in cost and features, although guests can usually expect standard rooms, a few amenities, and perhaps a restaurant either on the premises or nearby. They do not usually warrant a description, which is why we have provided our comprehensive appendix, "The Best of the Rest," which gives readers the names, addresses, and telephone numbers of these establishments.

Rooms:

Because guestrooms vary a great deal from one establishment to the next, it is important, when making a reservation, to be very specific about your requirements. Read the descriptions carefully and decide which amenities are important, whether they are a private bathroom, a bedroom with a big closet, a firm mattress, a room on the first floor, or a separate sitting room. Do you want a room that could be out of the pages of *House Beautiful,* or modern conveniences such as televisions or Jacuzzis? Please be specific.

Rates:

The range of rates listed with each description gives you a good idea of what to expect at a particular establishment. Many of these accommodations offer special discount packages, off-season rates, weekly rates, or interesting theme weekends. Always inquire about what's offered. Almost all of the accommodations listed in our books have "shoulder" seasons too — quiet times immediately before or after the busier times of the year. In addition to saving a little money, people traveling during these months will have a better choice of rooms, be able to eat out without making reservations, and enjoy sightseeing without all the usual crowds. Guests should also be careful to check if the rates are based upon single or double occupancy and if they include local taxes, fees, and so on.

Meal Plans:

We always indicate the type of meal plan offered by a given establishment.

* Bed and Breakfast (B&B) rates includes a Continental *or* full breakfast.
* European Plan (EP) does not include any meals.
* Modified American Plan (MAP) includes both breakfast and dinner
* American Plan (AP) is all-inclusive, providing breakfast, lunch, and dinner.

Method of Payment:

While most of the smaller establishments would prefer to be paid in cash or by personal check, the larger inns, hotels, and resorts accept an array of credit cards, abbreviated as follows:

* **AE** - American Express
* **CB** - Carte Blanche
* **DC** - Diners Club
* **DSC** - Discover
* **ENR** - EnRoute
* **JCB** - Japanese Credit Bank
* **MC** - Master Card
* **VISA** - Visa

More and more, small establishments do not accept credit cards for the entire balance due, but will accept them for the initial deposit and perhaps a few nights.

Children:

We provide this category to inform prospective guests about any additional rules, regulations, or benefits concerning their children. Legally, people traveling with children cannot be discriminated against; however, we have found that there are certainly places where parents with young children would be uncomfortable. When we mention appropriate ages, it is at the request of the innkeeper or manager. More often, though, there are special discounts for young children and those under the age of 12 often stay free of charge when accompanied by a parent.

Dog Policies:

This category outlines any restrictions concerning guests' canine companions. These can include size requirements, the age of the dog, and management concerns such as leaving dogs alone in the room or walking them off the property. Some establishments offer an array of doggie treats for their canine guests, which could be homemade biscuits or extra dog beds and bowls.

Opening and Closing Dates:

Seasonal openings and closings are outlined in this section. Many of the accommodations are open all year; however, during the off-season it is fairly common for B&B owners or innkeepers to shut down and go on a short vacation. Always, call ahead to make sure the establishment is open when you are planning to visit.

Planning Your Trip

In our experience, and we are sure fellow travelers agree, planning ahead of time is the best way to avoid mistakes that make for unpleasant experiences. Here are some of our time-tested guidelines.

Traveling by Car - Planning & Precautions:

If you've never traveled with your dog before, think twice about setting out on a four-day vacation together. To ease the uninitiated dog into travel mode, start with a day trip, then an overnight or weekend jaunt, then book a longer stay somewhere. If your dog has a tendency to bounce around the car, you should buy a travel crate or a car gate — something to confine him to the rear of the vehicle so that you can drive safely.

Before you set out on your trip, take your dog for a leisurely walk. This will not only give him a chance to work off a little energy, but may also coax him into sleeping during the trip. Do not feed him or give him substantial amounts of water just before leaving. Once in the car, make sure the dog's area is either well-ventilated or amply air-conditioned. Plan frequent pit stops (every two hours or so), where you can exercise your dog on a leash.

Even if the day is not hot, a car can heat up to very high temperatures in very little time. Take the following precautions to prevent heat stroke, brain damage, or even death to your dog:

* Try to park the car in the shade and leave the window open enough to provide ample ventilation.
* Do not leave your dog for long intervals of time.
* Before you leave the car, fill his bowl with cold water to ease any effects of the heat.
* *Never leave a dog in a hot car!*

Traveling by Plane - Planning & Precautions:

There are certain legal guidelines and restrictions for air travel with a dog. The United States Department of Agriculture (USDA) and the International Air Transport Association (IATA) govern air travel for pets. The airlines themselves have regulations, and they differ, so you should always contact your airline in advance to review their procedures and requirements. Regardless of your carrier, these are important guidelines to consider:

* The dog should be at least eight weeks old and fully weaned.
* The dog cannot be ill, violent, or in physical distress.
* The dog should have all the necessary health certificates and documentation.
* The travel crate must meet the airline's standards and be large enough for the dog to lie down comfortably, turn around, and stand freely in it.

Try to book a non-stop flight, and take temperature into consideration: In the summer, try to fly at night when it's cooler; in winter, fly during the day, when it's warmer.

Plan your trip well in advance and make sure you are following all the rules.

What Your Dog Needs to Enjoy the Trip:

Just as you have to pack appropriately for your vacation, your dog will need certain items to ensure he has a comfortable and enjoyable time, too. These include:

* A leash and collar with ID tags.
* A few favorite toys, chew bones, and treats.
* A container of fresh drinking water from home.
* A supply of his regular dog food.
* Food and water bowls.
* A dog "bed," whether it is a towel, mat, or pillow, or the dog's travel crate.

* Grooming aids, including extra towels for wet dogs and muddy paws.
* Any medication your veterinarian has prescribed or suggested.
* The dog's vaccination records, especially a rabies certificate or tag.

When You Arrive:

Many of the hosts and innkeepers we have met have expressed their general concerns about guests who bring their canine companions. So that your visit is an enjoyable one, we wanted to list them so you can keep them in mind.

* Dogs should be kept leashed while on the grounds.
* Dogs should not be left alone in the bedrooms unless management allows. In that case, the dog should be left in his crate or confined to the bathroom with some favorite toys.
* Always clean up after the dog, and try to walk him away from the main grounds.
* Use the dog's bedding to lessen the chance of damage to the furnishings. Never let your dog sit or lie on any of the furnishings.
* Because of health codes, dogs are generally not allowed in any area where food is made or served.

Disclaimer

Please keep in mind that the hosts, managers, and innkeepers are under no obligation to accept your dog. The management of each establishment listed in our guides has indicated to us, both verbally and in writing, that they have welcomed dogs in the past, had positive experiences, and will accept them in the future provided they are very well-behaved. Prior to publication, each of the establishments was contacted again to ensure they still welcome guests traveling with dogs. We cannot, however, guarantee against last minute changes of heart. Sometimes circumstances exist that require them to decline admitting our canine friends. They may already have a few dogs there, or be hosting a special function that would make it impractical for them to have your dog stay with you. *It is imperative you notify the establishment that you will be traveling with your dog when making your reservations.*

Connecticut

Avon Old Farms Hotel

P.O. Box 961
Junction of Routes 10 & 44
Avon, Connecticut   06001
(203) 677-1651, Fax (203) 677-0364

Manager: Ross Clark
Rooms: 160 doubles, 3 suites
Rates: Doubles $79-129 (EP), Suites $160-260 (EP)
Payment: AE, CB, DC, DSC, MC, and VISA
Children: Welcome (cribs, cots, and highchairs are available)
Dogs: Welcome in the motel units only, special rooms designated for dog owners
Open: All year

The Avon Old Farms Hotel is comprised of several different buildings erected by the North family, beginning with John North, on a parcel of land granted to him by the King of England in 1678. John's son Nathaniel built his home on this parcel in 1757, although today he would be surprised to see that it contains the hotel's foyer, lobby, dining room, and some bedrooms. In 1832, Joseph North, a blacksmith by trade, added a stone building that is now referred to as the Forge Room. It wasn't until 1923 that the homestead became the Old Farms Inn. Today, the original inn is used only for dining, while travelers stay across the street in the newer Avon Hotel.

Jack and Charlotte Brighenti first became involved with the hotel over 30 years ago, and more recently their two sons have taken over the operations. Guests have a choice of three different types of accommodations, although those traveling with Bowser will be given a choice of rooms in the motel units with separate outside entrances. These are fairly standard motel-style accommodations, although they do have a more appealing decor than most would expect. The furnishings and colors are soon going to be upgraded, so that they are in keeping with the rest of the Colonial-style bedrooms found in the main inn. Modern amenities, such as cable television, telephones, and good-sized bathrooms are also pleasant extras. During our most recent visit, the roofs of these units were being extended and dormered so they would complement the rest of the hotel. Travelers should be forewarned that some of these accommodations are subject to street noise; however, they are well soundproofed.

One of the reasons we like recommending the Avon Old Farms Hotel, is that it does offer a variety of amenities, an excellent restaurant, and attractive public areas that all guests are welcome to use. Pale peach tones are the backdrop for the atrium foyer, whose centerpiece is a sweeping staircase that rises, past a wall of windows, to the second and third-floor bedrooms. During the day this is a bright space, but it is equally appealing in the evening hours, when the enormous brass chandeliers are lighted. Chintz covered wing chairs and a comfortable sofa form a small sitting area off to one side, framed by some potted plants that seem to thrive in the atrium setting. In contrast, another equally appealing common room is furnished with burgundy sofas set upon Oriental rugs around a slate fireplace. This common area feels more like a formal living room, with a pillar and scroll clock resting on the mantel and hunt prints hanging from the walls. Guest rooms are found in the wings of this expansive building. These rather elegant spaces feature Colonial reproductions in dark woods. The two-poster finial bedsteads have Chippendale stools resting at their bases. Armoires hold televisions and brass lamps illuminate the thickly carpeted rooms. We hope that the pleasant combination of earth-toned walls and fabrics will also be recreated in the motel rooms, which would certainly enhance those accommodations.

Guests usually dine at The Seasons restaurant, which is both spacious and elegant. Beamed ceilings, painted a deep green, provide contrast to the colorful flower arrangements at each table and the assortment of potted plants placed about the room. As guests dine, they are privy to woodland views through the paned windows framed by chintz balloon shades. Lustrous hardwood floors, crisp white tablecloths, brass sconces, and chandeliers further set the mood. Appetizers include the warmed oyster, spinach and snow crab tart, roasted tomato and Gorgonzola crostini, or the crab and shrimp chowder. Entrée selections range from a grilled seafood Florentine or lamb atop cranberry and orange chutney to the braised rabbit with Sicilian olives, artichokes and creamy polenta and a pan-seared trout with crab and spinach. Those who are looking for a lighter fare can choose from the cobb or spinach salads or perhaps order fettuccine Alfredo or smoked Nova Scotia salmon from the appetizer menu. All of the desserts are made fresh daily in the hotel's own bakery.

There are plenty of human diversions on the premises, including the hotel's outdoor pool, and indoor exercise room, and sauna. There are 20 acres of open land surrounding the inn, that are ideal for walking with Bowser. Just off the property, there is a stable, a public golf course, and the opportunity for balloon rides and river inner-tubing. For those who are interested in exploring some of the nearby parks, we suggest Talcott Mountain and Pennwood. The former has a 1-1/2 mile trail that leads hikers to the summit, where those who are interested can climb Hueblein tower and enjoy what is considered one of the best vantage points in all of Connecticut (up to a 50-mile visibility). The latter is a 787-acre park that gives those hiking along the Metacomet Trail a great view of both the Connecticut and Farmington River Valleys. For guests who are in search of more civilized options, the nearby towns of Simsbury, Farmington, and Hartford offer an array of cultural diversions, shopping alternatives, and restaurants to sample.

The Inn at Chester

318 West Main Street
Route 148
Chester, Connecticut 06412
(800) 949-STAY, (203) 526-9541

Innkeeper: *Deborah Moore*
Rooms: *42 doubles, 1 suite*
Rates: *Doubles $90-95 (B&B), Suite $205 (B&B)*
Payment: *AE, MC, and VISA*
Children: *Welcome (cribs, cots, highchairs, and babysitters are available)*
Dogs: *Welcome in specific rooms*
Open: *All year*

The original clapboard farmhouse on the grounds of the Inn at Chester, was built by the Parmelee family in 1776. Over the years, the surrounding forests have been slowly timbered in order to clear land for livestock, make room for the addition of a pond, and provide space for the flowering shrubs and decorative trees that have been planted. Years later, in 1955, the Joslows (the former innkeepers) purchased the homestead for their private use. In 1983 they expanded the original farmhouse and opened it as an inn. The inn has been closed for a couple years, but has recently been purchased and has undergone another metamorphosis. Additional common areas and guest rooms, as well as a new tavern, all blend perfectly into the existing historic hostelry.

Located in rural Connecticut, the inn is set just off a country road, nestled amid twelve-acres of mature trees, lilacs, evergreens, and rose bushes. Returning guests (from the Joslow's tenure) will immediately notice a change when they enter the light and airy foyer. Sunlight streams in through the skylights past the cathedral ceiling to the formal Eldred Wheeler reproduction furnishings and comfortable sofas below. The other common rooms are equally pleasant spaces for guests to while away the time. Period antiques are interspersed with tastefully upholstered reproductions set upon Oriental rugs or wall-to-wall carpeting. Complimentary copies of *The New York Times* and the *Wall Street Journal*, as well as other periodicals, are always available.

The main building is quite deceptive, and is actually a grouping of smaller structures, that include the restored farmhouse and two newer wings. The antique barn still houses the cavernous post and beam dining room, where hardwood floors and walls surround the traditional furnishings and frame the massive stone fireplace. This comfortable setting allows patrons to turn their attention to the delicious meal. During our visit, a few of the appetizer selections included the mushroom strudel, a salmon terrine with a lemon and citrus ginger sauce, and a duck ravioli with a Roquefort, port, and wild mushroom pasta. It was difficult to choose from the varied entrées, such as the salmon filet with a fresh tomato and saffron vinaigrette, the roasted game hen, and the cinnamon cured and smoked duck with a peach apricot chutney. Anyone looking for a lighter fare, or a change in venue, will enjoy the newly completed tavern, Dunk's Landing. Cathedral ceilings, fitted with skylights, enliven the otherwise club-like atmosphere. Crimson and hunter green colors look terrific when combined with the cherrywood cabinets surrounding the wing and Windsor chairs set around small tables. A series of French doors lead outside to a flagstone patio, a particularly inviting spot in the summer months.

The inn's bedrooms are still quite spacious, with high ceilings and simple, clean lines. Each is furnished with Eldred Wheeler reproductions and a sprinkling of antiques and wing chairs, making the furnishings the centerpieces for these chambers. Four-poster canopy beds seem right at home with the tab curtains and Colonial-period inspired wallpapers. Thick carpeting is found in many rooms, and fireplaces are welcome additions in others. Individual climate controls, televisions, and good-sized private baths with an array of toiletries and soft towels, complete the list of modern conveniences.

There is plenty to do at the inn and on the acres of forests surrounding the grounds. The adjacent Cockaponset State Forest is the closest diversion for Bowser, offering plenty of hiking trails. There are also lawn games available, including bocci and croquet, or guests can play tennis. With the coming winter, the emphasis turns to ice-skating and cross-country skiing, both of which are available in nearby Pound Ridge. In addition to a handful of charming towns that are worth exploring along the Connecticut River, Bowser will surely enjoy investigating the nearby parks and forests. Selden Neck, Chatfield Hollow, Brainard Homestead, and Haddam Meadows State Parks are all within a short drive of the inn. When the day is done, or if the weather happens to turn inclement, indoor pursuits could include a game of backgammon, pool, darts, or cards. Anyone who considers this a little too sedentary, may enjoy a workout in the exercise room topped off with a sauna afterwards.

The Griswold Inn

36 Main Street
Essex, Connecticut   06426
(203) 767-1776

Innkeeper: William G. Winterer
Rooms: 14 Doubles, 11 Suites, 1 Cottage
Rates: Doubles $90, Suites $95-155 (EP), Cottage $175 (EP)
Payment: AE, MC, and VISA
Children: Welcome (cribs, cots, and highchairs are available)
Dogs: Welcome
Open: All year

Essex is undoubtedly one of the lovelier coastal towns in all of New England. It was first settled by the English in 1648, but was known by the Indians as Potapoug. Almost three quarters-of-a-century later, the town had grown substantially and began to flourish as a ship building center. The first Connecticut warship, the Oliver Cromwell, was built here in 1776, just about the same time the Griswold Inn first opened its doors to the public.

Although Essex is no longer a manufacturing and ship building center, visitors can still feel the strong heritage. This is partly because the residents of Essex have worked hard to retain the town's historic ambiance, leaving intact many of the original buildings which exemplify the classic New England architecture visitors find so appealing. One of the most well-preserved buildings in town is The Griswold Inn (often referred to as The "Gris"), which was the first three-story frame structure house to be built in Connecticut. With the exception of the removal of the second floor gallery, the inn has remained structurally intact for over 200 years. William Winterer, the innkeeper, first stumbled upon the inn in 1957, while he was an officer at the U.S. Coast Guard Academy in nearby New London. After he was released from active duty, Winterer attended business school, and subsequently became quite successful in the investment business. During his career, he continued to make frequent voyages to Essex on his ketch *Axia*, and would visit The "Gris". In 1972, he decided to actually buy the inn he had spent so many years frequenting.

Newcomers to the inn, and particularly history buffs, will want to spend time just wandering through the public rooms. The original hand-hewn beamed ceilings, hardwood floors, and wonderful old fireplaces are merely the framework for the collection of antiques and collectibles that are found throughout the inn. Brass chandeliers cast a soft glow onto the walls of bookshelves and the impressive collections of Currier & Ives and Antonio Jacobsen maritime paintings. There are ships' models, binnacles, clocks, and even a library of firearms dating back to the fifteenth century for guests to enjoy. The inn is practically a living museum, that most feel lucky to have had the chance to appreciate. There are other little gizmos placed around the inn, including an antique popcorn machine, an authentic potbelly stove, and an unusual mural in the Steamboat Dining Room that actually moves back and forth giving patrons the sensation of being at sea. The ever popular Tap Room, renowned as one of the "handsomest bar rooms in America," was originally a school house that was rolled to its current location by a team of oxen.

The "Gris" is characterized by, and well-loved for, its lack of pretense and its overall simplicity, particularly when it comes to the guest rooms. The charming bed chambers are each different, but continue to reflect the nautical theme through the paintings on the walls and other decorative items scattered about the rooms. Some have sloping floors and beamed ceilings, while others are carpeted and tucked into eaves. We saw one suite with pocket doors separating the bedroom from a living room. The four-poster bed nicely complements the Queen-Anne bedside tables, brass lamps, and Windsor chairs. The sitting room features a woodstove, adding its own unique atmosphere. Another small bedroom, just off the street, offers a brass bed covered in a Bates spread, a marble-topped dresser and matching side table. The antiques add to the antique feeling of the inn, but are certainly not museum pieces that guests are afraid to touch. Aside from being a Bowser-friendly inn, this is also a family-friendly inn. One good option is the garden suite, which not only offers a fireplace, but also a loft sleeping area and a wet bar. For families with more than two children or groups of friends, the inn also has the John Hayden House, which is outfitted with several guest rooms, as well as a sunporch, and a large living room (with the only television at the inn). The little extras to look for are the travel kits in the bathroom, or the witch hazel set out in each bedroom.

There are other restaurants in Essex, but none that offer the same ambiance found at The "Gris." With the exception of Steamboat, which is fairly large, all of the other dining rooms are quite cozy and filled with nooks and crannies. The menu is extensive, the fare hearty, and the prices are reasonable. The chefs do not use any preservatives or chemicals on their dishes, in keeping with their Yankee traditions. The dinner menu, for example, includes a lot of native seafood and the Griswold Inn's famous 1776 sausage sampler. Patrons can also dine on breast of duck with an apple Madeira sauce, tenderloin stuffed with blue cheese and wrapped in juniper smoked bacon, or the "awful, awful" New York strip steak (it's awful big and awful good). The Christmas feast is unusual, and features venison, rabbit, moose, partridge, pheasant, and goose, along with a cassoulet of game. But, even with this enticing fare, it is still the Sunday Hunt Brunch that is not to be missed. People come from all over the area to sample this repast. The menu includes selections like a grits and cheddar cheese souffle, creamed chipped beef or creamed mushrooms and ham, Nodine's juniper-smoked bacon, and homemade corn bread, muffins, and hard rolls. Fresh fruit, green salads, and baby sole or cod round out the menu. Oh yes, and a few surprise entrées often appear under the category of "whatever the chef can find at the market."

The "Gris" is located at the base of Main Street, just a short distance from the waterfront. The charming town is rather tiny and a great place for both walking Bowser and window shopping. There are an array of boutiques, eateries, and gift shops lining the back streets. The bicycling is good, although Bowser might want to stay at home for that, but he would probably be a good companion for a canoeing or fishing expedition. There are wildlife and nature preserves nearby as well as Rocky Neck, Devil's Hopyard, and Brainard Homestead State Parks for Bowser to explore. The Essex Steam Train and Riverboat are also perennial favorites for those who would like to gain a more comprehensive perspective of the picturesque countryside.

The Centennial Inn

5 Spring Street
Farmington, Connecticut 06032
(800) 852-2052, (203) 677-4647, Fax (203) 676-0685

Manager: John Kattato
Rooms: 112 suites
Rates: $85-180 (B&B)
Payment: AE, CB, DC, MC, and VISA
Children: Welcome (cribs, cots, highchairs, and babysitters are available)
Dogs: Welcome
Open: All year

Travelers passing to the west of Hartford, will surely want to know about The Centennial Inn, which opened just over six years ago. This spacious complex is located in the rural Farmington countryside, just a short distance from the well-known girls school, Miss Porter's. As guests pull into the drive, they will see the historic, brown clapboard Carriage House, which serves as the common area for the inn. Inside is a reception area, that is attractively decorated with fine antique reproductions interspersed with contemporary sofas and chairs. A pair of brick fireplaces add additional character. The traditional decor is enhanced by potted plants, brass standing lamps, and historic prints, all of which lend an air of casual elegance to this chamber.

Once outside, guests will see a handful of two-story, clapboard buildings set on the 12 acres of wooded grounds. There are five different types of suites and they all have covered porches or patios. Each suite is both tastefully decorated and cleverly designed. A standard suite offers a kitchen with an island that opens up into a sitting area with a comfortable sofabed and a corner fireplace. The two-bedroom suite provides a little more space and a pair of queen-bedded chambers located on two separate floors. Along with a sitting room, it also is equipped with a separate dining area. The beauty of these accommodations is that each building is outfitted with a different assortment of room types, allowing guests to create an array of adjoining room configurations. Travelers may request just the first floor of a two-room suite, or elect to add a connecting room, furnished with a pair of queen-size beds, to create an expansive master suite.

The decor remains much the same from one room to another. Camel or navy carpeting is accented by neutral wall treatments. Skylights in the second floor eaves add ample amounts of natural light to some rooms, while others are lit by a series of double-hung windows. Additional illumination comes from brass sconces and recessed fixtures. Floral draperies frame the windows and traditional botanical and wildlife prints line the walls. The overstuffed sofa and sidechairs in the sitting area allow guests to enjoy a crackling fire or the cable television and

VCR. Other modern conveniences include individual climate controls, ceiling fans, and shower massages. The fully-equipped kitchens are state-of-the-art, with stoves, refrigerators, garbage disposals, and dishwashers. There are also over 20 restaurants nearby that will deliver dinner to the inn. Popcorn and homemade cookies are placed in the suite each day, and in the morning, a complimentary breakfast and newspaper are also available. It is clear the Centennial Inn was designed to provide equal comfort for guests who want to stay for one day or for those staying as long as several months.

Those who are interested in a little exercise may wish to walk along the inn's trails, work out in the exercise room, or take a dip in either the swimming pool or whirlpool. There are also exhilarating hot air balloon rides, terrific horseback riding, and golfing facilities all within an easy drive of the inn. Naturalists may wish to investigate the Farmington River (canoeing and tubing facilities), the 400 acres of land in the Winding Trails Park (cross-country skiing facilities are also available), or pay a visit to the Talcott Mountain or Penwood State Parks.

Applewood Farms Inn

528 Colonel Ledyard Highway
Ledyard, Connecticut   06339
(203) 536-2022

Innkeepers: *Frankie and Tom Betz*
Rooms: *4 doubles, 1 suite*
Rates: *Doubles $115-135 (B&B), Suite $150 (B&B)*
Payment: *MC and VISA*
Children: *Not appropriate for very young children*
Dogs: *Dogs and other polite pets (horses, cats, etc.) are welcome with prior approval. The Betzes provide a set of guidelines to the "parents of all pets"*
Open: *All year*

Deacon Russell Gallup built this center-chimney Colonial in 1826 for his wife Hannah and their children. The times have changed, but the sense of the rural country setting has remained relatively the same. The main road leading to the inn is lined with mature trees and ancient stone walls. Seemingly endless faded white fences encircle fields dotted by grazing horses. Although five generations of Gallups grew up on this enormous farm, the tremendous cost of upkeep became a burden and the Gallups were forced to sell half of the land to Arabian horse breeders. Today, the Betz family owns the original house and the remaining acreage.

A long drive, leading past a kiosk, a horse paddock, and the inn, will bring visitors to a small parking area. Anyone who tries to enter the house in the traditional manner, through the front door, will have difficulty because it is swollen shut. Instead, guests will find the kitchen door, located off the brick patio, to be a more accessible entryway. Once inside, new arrivals will find a home that has been authentically preserved, and as a result, is listed in the National Register of Historic Places. The Colonial charm has been enhanced through the use of floral country wallpapers, interesting stenciling, and Williamsburg colors on the decorative wainscotings. The wide board floors, covered with braided and dhurrie rugs, creak as guests make their way through the various common rooms.

The first floor bedroom, the Ben Adam, has the largest antique bed that we have ever seen. This enormous, more than king-sized bed is fashioned from two double beds and is adorned with an eyelet coverlet. From here, guests ascend the steep twisting central staircase to reach the other bed chambers. The next two rooms are quite feminine, with the Lillian Room containing a canopy bedstead and Laura Ashley fabrics, while the Sarah Room provides a double four-poster bed that is surrounded by a delicate pink floral wallpaper. Laura Ashley-style prints and antique furnishings are in evidence throughout the inn's bedrooms. For those who are looking for a little added romance, four of the inn's six fireplaces are located in the guest rooms. Most of the bathrooms are private, but two are shared, with one found down the back stairs. Although each bedroom has its own unique charm and personality, the fireplaced parlor, with its comfortable furnishings, loom, and piano is a favorite resting place as well. Beyond the parlor is the breakfast room, where a full country breakfast is served each morning. Tom prepares a variety of interesting dishes, and Frankie prefers to serve and chat with the guests. Most people enjoy watching the menagerie of birds visiting the half dozen or so birdfeeders placed outside the breakfast room window.

Although Bowser can participate in most of the excursions in and around the inn, there is also a five-by-eight-foot kennel located behind the barn, should he decide to stay home. There are over 33 acres that are crisscrossed by trails. These are perfect for taking long walks with Bowser and observing the native wildlife. Nearby, Old Mystic provides plenty of walking tours of the town's historic homes (maps are available from the Chamber of Commerce), as well as an array of sights and attractions. Bowser might want to stay behind for the whale watching expedition or the visit to the U.S. submarine base and museum. Instead, he would probably prefer a trip to the Ft. Shantok State Park, Pachaug State Forest, or Devil's Hopyard State Park, where there are walking trails and some historic sites. Guests who prefer an experience closer to home, can investigate the adjacent Arabian horse farm, which is home to over 50 prize horses, as well as sheep and goats.

Finally, the Betzes have a very clear, and very reasonable pet policy. They welcome pets and give them the run of the house as long as they bring their human companions along. Pets are not allowed on the beds at any time, cannot be left alone, or cause any damage. If they do accidently damage something, the cost will be charged to guests' credit cards. We have found, that it often helps when the innkeepers specifically state their pet policy. In this way, there is little confusion over what is acceptable and both the hosts and guests are far more comfortable in the long run.

Tollgate Hill Inn

P.O. Box 1339
Route 202
Litchfield, Connecticut   06759
(800) 445-3903, (203) 567-4545 or 3821, Fax (203) 567-8397

Innkeeper: Frederick J. Zivic
Rooms: 15 doubles, 5 suites
Rates: Doubles $90-140 (B&B), Suites $150-175 (B&B)
Payment: AE, DC, DSC, MC, and VISA
Children: Welcome
Dogs: Welcome; owners are responsible for any damages
Open: All year except Tuesdays, November through June

The Tollgate Hill Inn was built in 1745 and was known as the Captain William Bull Tavern. It was used primarily as a way station for travelers en route between Hartford and Litchfield. In 1923, Frederick Fussenich moved this "publick house" to Tollgate Hill. Approximately 50 years later the inn was restored, with an emphasis on preserving its historic heritage. Today, the Tollgate Hill Inn holds a coveted place in the National Register of Historic Places.

The charm of the inn is quick to unfold. A narrow, wood-paneled hallway leads to the long, handcrafted cherry bar. A crackling fire warms this room. A glance into the two dining rooms reveals corner cupboards, wide pine floors, and beamed ceilings. The very narrow back stairway leads guests to the intimate second floor sitting area and bedrooms. These chambers are individually decorated with an emphasis on country elegance. Antique clocks, chintz-covered armchairs, and canopy or four-poster beds are the norm. The rooms on the top floor are perhaps the most unique as the steep eaves and original, exposed hand-hewn beams create cathedral ceilings that give the illusion that these rather small chambers seem more spacious than they actually are. Fireplaces make three of the guest rooms particularly inviting. The bathrooms are modern and bathed in a multitude of fragrances, including potpourri, bay rum tonic, handmade soaps, and Gucci colognes. For those who wish to enjoy a glass of wine in their room, a brass ice bucket and corkscrew are thoughtfully provided.

There are also four spacious rooms in the School House that offer even more privacy. Some find this an ideal choice for families traveling with a dog, or for the extra amenities they provide. The most requested suite has a small sitting area with a television and VCR. A wet bar with refrigerator sits discretely off to one side, but the focal point for the room is the wood-burning fireplace. Choose from a library of books, before climbing into the canopied bed at night. Since our last visit, the Captain W. Bull House has been completed, offering guests an additional eleven bedrooms. Before this was built, guests used to check-in with the bartender at the historic Captain W. Bull Tavern, but now everything is centralized in the newer Captain W. Bull House.

Guests check-in at an attractive reception area, illuminated by brass lamps. The walls have been papered in a blue paisley pattern and coordinated floral curtains frame the windows. A Berber carpet covers the hardwood floors and softens people's footsteps as they make their way toward the bedrooms. The resident parrot watches all the comings and goings, and provides companionship if new arrivals decide to sit and stay awhile. We liked the bedrooms in the new building, even though they lacked the antique character of those in the Captain W. Bull Tavern and School House. Even without the historic backdrop, they do offer many other benefits such as increased size, modern amenities, and very attractive furnishings. Floral wallpapers and coordinated draperies have been carefully selected to complement the reproduction writing desks, armoires, and tables that fill these rooms. Brass lamps set next to the canopy or four-poster beds, cast a pleasant light across the room. One of the largest fireplace suites is located on the first floor. Braided rugs cover the hardwood floors, and country pine antiques, an armoire containing a television and VCR, and a canopy bed fill in the rest of this space.

The inn has received a great deal of favorable press for its fine cuisine and unique setting. The original Tavern Room and more formal dining rooms are very traditional in both decor and furnishings. The fire from the large hearth usually casts a pretty reflection off the copper chandeliers and the original double-hung windows. The menu is extensive, but even more extensive is the wine list. Most people start with one of the appetizers, whether this is the baked garlic sausage en-croute, sautéed veal sweetbreads and lobster in a Chardonnay cream, or the chilled mussel vinaigrette. This could be followed by entrées such as the roast duckling with a pear almond sauce, the medallions of pork with a maple, green peppercorn and Bourbon demi-glaze, or the prime rib with natural juices and fresh horseradish root. Most diners find it difficult to pass by the traditional Tollgate shellfish pie, containing shrimp, scallops, lobster and crabmeat in a light sherry cream sauce that is all baked in a puff pastry. Desserts change daily but a sampling includes a fresh banana Napolean with chocolate sauce, warm apple torte with caramel sauce, or a chocolate bread pudding with pistachio sauce. In the morning, a Continental breakfast is served in either the bedroom, the dining room, or on the patio. It usually consists of fresh orange juice, fruit breads and muffins, and coffee or tea. Weekend guests can enjoy the Sunday brunch, which is rich in unusual offerings. Guests might want to begin this repast with something from the pastry plate, and then try the smoked turkey lasagna, pork tenderloin with orange and ginger, or one of the seafood selections which could include anything from scrod to catfish. The inn also offers more traditional brunch dishes, as well.

Bowser will enjoy a walk along the quiet, untraveled Tollgate Road which runs alongside the inn. Drive a short distance to Litchfield which, in addition to lots of grassy areas and an attractive town common, also has a variety of interesting shops. The 4,000 acres of the White Memorial Foundation and Conservation Center are also open to visitors and their dogs. There are also great trails in the nearby Burr Paugnut State Forest and the Humaston Brook State Park. The Tollgate Hill Inn is a terrific home base for people who want to visit the neighboring White Flower Farm, Haight Vineyards, and the Litchfield Auction. In the winter months, many of the state parks and forests are open for cross-country skiing, as is the local Mohawk Mountain for skiing of the downhill variety.

The Inn at Chapel West

1201 Chapel Street
New Haven, Connecticut   06511
(203) 777-1201

Manager: Melodie Pogue
Rooms: 10 doubles
Rates: $175 (B&B)
Payment: AE, CB, DC, DSC, MC, and VISA
Children: Not appropriate for small children
Dogs: Well-behaved dogs are welcome with advance notice
Open: All year

The Inn at Chapel West is a wonderful spot, particularly for those who enjoy the elegance of a traditional inn coupled with a contemporary decor and an abundance of amenities. This Victorian home was built in 1847 and is located in the center of bustling New Haven. The green clapboard exterior is particularly striking, as all the ornamental trim has been painted either white or peach, highlighting the original, intricate craftsmanship. The striking facade and equally impressive interior decor make The Inn at Chapel West one of the most desirable overnight destinations in New Haven.

The inn's front gate opens to reveal a charming garden containing a pair of teak benches. Upon entering the inn, guests will note many interesting and appealing architectural features. Two identical rooms flank the central hallway leading to the lustrous, wood-paneled reception area. One of these rooms is the parlor, which has a pair of Japanese screens, along with English antiques that look right at home alongside the fireplace. In the afternoon, tea and coffee, as well as an assortment of freshly baked breads, are served in this chamber. Across the hall from the parlor, is the elongated dining room. Each morning, a bountiful selection of granolas, cereals, muffins, pastries, and fresh fruit are placed on the sideboard in here, which guests can enjoy at the small tables placed toward the front of the room. On cold days, the fireplace adds additional warmth and atmosphere.

Each of the upstairs bedrooms varies in size, decor, and furnishings. In one bedroom, with a Southwest theme, the walls are rust-colored, the fireplace of exposed brick, and the period furnishings are of pine. Another chamber has gabled ceilings and walls that are enhanced by a cloud-laced mural, making this sun-drenched room as cheerful as it is whimsical. A brass bed, along with pine and wicker furnishings, rests on hardwood floors. Some of the accent pieces used in the other guest rooms include Art Deco mirrors, colorful handmade quilts, Victorian face masks, and original artwork. These whimsical accents are often combined with more useful furnishings such as pine sweater chests, English antique writing desks, and four-poster beds. Braided rugs often cover the inlaid floors. This eclectic assortment of furnishings, coupled with more traditional amenities such as down comforters and working fireplaces, ensures that any room selection will be a memorable one. The modern amenities such as color televisions, updated bathrooms (with cotton bathrobes provided), telephones, clock radios, and air-conditioning are certain to please those travelers who like the feeling of an historic inn, but also appreciate an array of modern conveniences. Those who are traveling with either a friend or a third person, will appreciate the chambers that are furnished with both a queen-size and a twin day bed.

In addition to the ambiance and amenities, one of the things that makes this inn particularly special is the attentive staff. They are quick to offer suggestions on where to go and what to do in both the New Haven area and beyond. For instance, many visitors enjoy spending the day visiting the local museums, galleries, and shops around town. Of course, Bowser probably would be more interested in a jaunt over to the sprawling Yale campus or perhaps a drive up the coast to some of the beaches. The East and West Rock Parks are located right in New Haven, while Sleeping Giant State Park, Chatfield Hollow State Park, and Hammonasset Beach State Park are all just a short drive away.

Silvermine Tavern

194 Perry Avenue
Norwalk, Connecticut 06850
(203) 847-4558, Fax (203) 847-9171

Innkeepers: Frank and Marsha Whitman
Rooms: 10 doubles
Rates: $80-99 (B&B)
Payment: AE, DC, MC, and VISA
Children: Welcome (highchairs and cots are available)
Dogs: Welcome in the rooms above the country store
Open: All year, except Tuesdays September to May

Even though the Silvermine Tavern is technically in Norwalk, and only a short distance from the Merritt Parkway, it feels as though it lies deep in the Connecticut countryside. Travelers meander along backcountry roads before arriving at a small bridge crossing a river. This is the site of the historic Silvermine Tavern, located on the banks of both the Silvermine River and Mill Pond. The pink shuttered Colonial inn is actually comprised of four buildings that were all built in the 1770s. Each houses a fine collection of early American antiques, as is evident immediately upon entering the inn.

A pair of common rooms with painted hardwood floors, covered by well-worn Oriental rugs, is furnished with an assortment of antiques ranging from grandfather clocks and captain's chests to writing desks and wonderful old portraits and primitive paintings. The intimate sitting areas set before the fireplaces are alluring; however, the cavernous dining rooms, with walls of windows overlooking the water, are often even more so. In keeping with the rest of the inn, each of the dining rooms is brimming with collectibles that include farm implements, weather vanes, cast iron lamps, and other memorabilia, some of which is hanging from beamed ceilings. Other items are placed in the various cupboards and on top of shelves. While the serene pond-side setting is appealing, the menu is also quite inspired. Traditional dishes such as lobster pie, garlic crusted chicken breasts, and prime rib top the "New England Favorites" menu. Some of the "Country Inn Specialties" are the crab stuffed filet of sole, grilled pork tenderloin stuffed with chorizo sausage and raisins, and the roast duckling with pecan wild rice and mulled cider sauce. In the warmer months, patrons are often seated on the tree shaded brick terrace that overlooks the tranquil pond and river. In the wintertime, diners are welcome to opt for dinner in front of one of the enormous white brick fireplaces. Whether guests are watching the ducks and swans frolic on Mill Pond or enjoying the warmth of a fire, the overall ambiance makes for a memorable dining experience.

The bedrooms are situated in both the main inn and over the country store, located just across the street. Guests traveling with a dog are welcome in the country store rooms. Upon entering this building, a rather steep staircase leads new arrivals up to their bed chambers. The overall decor is a simple, yet authentic, early American motif. Antique beds and bureaus are interspersed with harvest tables and faded, chintz-covered armchairs. Braided rugs cover painted hardwood floors. Other noteworthy features that are found in some of the rooms include a private bathroom with a claw-footed bathtub, a colorful handmade quilt adorning a bed, and a wall of built-in bookshelves. One particularly sunny, corner chamber is fronted by seven windows and boasts of a canopy bed, while another guest room has cathedral ceilings, a canopy bed, and a pair of wing chairs placed in a windowed alcove. The traditional wallpapers and color schemes maintain the feeling of the period in which the house was built.

It is difficult for guests to bypass the country store during their stay, particularly when they walk right by it on the way to and from their bedrooms. Here, American folk art reproductions, collectibles, and an assortment of foods and candies await interested browsers. Bowser will certainly appreciate being in this countryside setting. For those who are interested in exploring the area on foot, the inn has a three page walking tour of the historic Silvermine region (which includes portions of three towns). As visitors follow this walk, they can read about the history of many local houses, old stores, cemeteries, and local artists' homes. In nearby Westport, guests can go to the 234-acre Sherwood Island State Park that has large open fields and access to the Long Island Sound. By driving a few exits south on the Merritt Parkway, travelers will find the Mianus River State Park in Stamford. The Maritime Marine Museum, Nature Center/Zoo, and the Lockwood-Mathews Mansion are also good options when Bowser is napping.

Old Lyme Inn

P.O. Box 787
85 Lyme Street
Old Lyme, Connecticut 06371
(203) 434-2600, Fax (203) 434-5352

Connecticut

Innkeeper: Diana Field Atwood
Rooms: 13 doubles
Rates: $98-144 (B&B)
Payment: AE, DC, DSC, MC and VISA
Children: Welcome
Dogs: Welcome, not to be left alone in rooms
Open: All year, except for the first two weeks of January

Whether people read about the Old Lyme Inn in the _New York Times, Travel & Leisure, Town & Country,_ or _Bon Appetit,_ after visiting it they will surely understand why it has received such accolades over the years. The home was originally built by the Champlain family in the 1850s as a 300-acre working farm. Over the years, it was used as a riding academy, a hall for square dances, and was a favored site among the local impressionist painters. In the 1960s, much of the building was destroyed by a devastating fire, thus beginning the inn's "dark period" as Diana describes it. Then, in 1976, Diana Atwood discovered the old homestead and began a painstaking restoration process. She not only did a great job refurbishing the building, but also acquired, through assorted auctions and house demolitions, a number of interesting artifacts that would be used to revitalize the old place. Today, everything in the inn seems to have some sort of story attached to it. For instance, a few of the marble fireplace mantels came from a home in Wethersfield and the Victorian bar was rescued from an old tavern in Pittsburgh. Aficionados of art and fine antiques will appreciate many of the paintings and furniture Diana has acquired at auctions and now displays throughout the inn.

Today, the inn is comprised of five guest bedrooms in the main farmhouse and eight additional chambers in the north wing. A quaint mural depicting Old Lyme and a working dairy farm complete with cows, horses, and dogs has been painted on the entry wall and up the staircase leading to the second floor. The first set of guest bedrooms are rather simply decorated in a mix of Empire and Victorian furnishings. Bright colors contrast with the Bates bedspreads and comfortable wing chairs, all of which are illuminated by brass lamps. Some of the modern conveniences include clock radios and individual air conditioning units. The private bathrooms are well-equipped and offer extra amenities such as shampoos, fragrant soaps, heat lamps, thick cotton towels, and locally made witch hazel. The newer wing houses the second set of guest chambers. These rooms are all good-sized, allowing ample space for canopy beds and comfortable sitting areas. Antique marble-topped bedside tables, love seats, and armoires are just a few of the elegant furnishings. The bathrooms in this section are also more luxurious, with sinks and tubs accented by brass fixtures.

The Sassafras Library, named after the affectionate house cat, who has since passed away, is a cozy chamber enhanced by walls of bookshelves. There are a number of board games in here, along with a game table and television. The sitting area around the fireplace is particularly welcoming. From this room, guests can walk over to the reception area. This was looking very festive during our visit, with decorative wreaths, garlands, lights, and an even an electric train encircling

18

the Christmas tree. This good-sized chamber opens up into the cavernous Empire Room and the other three more intimate dining rooms. The restaurant is truly exceptional. Appetizers are unusual, including offerings such as New Zealand mussels served with a celery mousseline and an almond hollandaise, a chilled smoked salmon caviar pinwheel, and a terrine of lamb blended with roasted eggplant, roasted red peppers, and herbs. Entrées vary from the venison served over Johnny cakes with a sweet corn and sweet pepper cream sauce to the grilled Jamaican swordfish served with a sorrel cream sauce and caviar. There is also the breast of Connecticut pheasant, which has been stuffed with a mixture of dried fruits, nuts, and diced pheasant meat. It is served with a green peppercorn and port sauce. For dessert, fresh pastries are presented along with coffee or cappuccino.

The Old Lyme Inn is located in a rather busy part of Old Lyme. It is fine for walking Bowser in the morning and evening, but for other interesting excursions, travelers might want to head inland. Here, wonderful old back roads are lined with rock walls which seemingly protect the classic New England country homes and gentlemen's farms that lay behind them. Nearby Essex is a picturesque seaport town offering interesting shops to explore and a waterfront to amble along. There are many local parks (i.e., Devil's Hopyard or Rocky Neck) that are fun for picnicking or hiking through with Bowser. In addition to the Essex Train and Riverboat, adventurers may also wish to take the ferry from New London to Orient Point (the eastern tip of Long Island, New York). This is a rather rural area that has charming farms and vineyards. Although Bowser might not be interested in this sport, guests will probably be curious about the croquet sticker on the innkeeper's car. Discreet inquiries will lead to a discussion of the finer points of this ever popular sport, as well as the best local croquet matches in the area. While most have not practiced this exacting form of croquet, there is always the backyard version, which is available on the premises.

Old Riverton Inn

P.O. Box 6
Route 20
Riverton, Connecticut   06065
(203) 379-8678

Innkeepers: Mark and Pauline Telford
Rooms: 11 doubles, 1 suite
Rates: Doubles $70-90 (B&B), Suite $90 (B&B)
Payment: AE, CB, DC, DSC, MC, and VISA
Children: Welcome (cribs, cots, and highchairs are available)
Dogs: Welcome in specific rooms with prior approval
Open: All year

Jesse Ives originally opened the Old Riverton Inn in 1796. For many years thereafter, it was known as Ives Tavern, providing "Hospitality for the Hungry, Thirsty, and Sleepy." With the passage of time, and a countless number of owners, the inn has undergone many changes. The walls in the dining room were removed at one point to create a larger, more open space. The old hemlock beams supporting the ceiling were left intact, and were augmented by others taken from an old barn on the property. Years later, a wing was added, as was the Hobby Horse Bar with its Vermont slate floors. The Grindstone Terrace was constructed even more recently, and was created with grindstone that made the long trip from Nova Scotia to Connecticut by steamer, before being hauled to the inn by teams of oxen. Today, guests will find an inn that has survived almost 200 years of steady use, while retaining much of its historic character.

Knowing what was added to the inn and when it happened, makes it all the more interesting for guests when they first walk into the building. Just off the reception desk and dining room are the Grindstone Terrace and Hobby Horse Bar (with bar stools created from kegs and saddles). If there is any question about the inn's antiquity, one need only walk over the steeply sloping floors and under the hand-hewn beamed ceilings. A central staircase leads to the bedrooms. These chambers maintain the same historic character as the common rooms, with simple period furnishings set alongside well-worn upholstered armchairs and comfortable couches. Bates spreads cover both the maple and canopy beds, neither of which are antique but seem to fit in well with their historic surroundings. Much of the original black iron hardware can still be found on the bedroom doors. Colonial wallpapers combine with historic collectibles, including a spinning wheel in one room, to give these chambers additional authenticity. Present day amenities include remote control television, clock radios, and air-conditioning units. Although the bathrooms are a bit dated and small, they are nonetheless very clean and a few are outfitted with claw footed tubs. One of the most popular bedrooms is undoubtedly the spacious suite located at the end of the building. Its canopy bed, marble topped sidetable, Victorian couch and matching armchair all lend an elegant ambiance to this chamber. The refrigerator, stereo, and fireplace are also welcome amenities. Just outside the bedrooms, there is also a good-sized sitting area, which is outfitted with an assortment of games, books, and periodicals.

Guests only need to walk down the stairs to find a good restaurant. The dining room is charming, with its low ceilings, walls papered and painted in a Colonial style, and brass sconces subtly lighting the various corners of the room. A well-tended fireplace adds to the atmosphere. The menu is simple and hearty, focusing on traditional New England foods, with baked stuffed pork chops, lobster, filet mignon, and Boston cod topping off the menu. The breads are baked fresh daily, as is the ever changing selection of homemade desserts. In the morning, guests may return for a full country breakfast.

There are plenty of options in Riverton and the outlying areas to keep even the most energetic visitors occupied. The Telfords have put together an informative list, that describes both dog and human diversions. The tiny town center is within walking distance of the inn. Here, visitors will find the Hitchcock Chair Company along with the Thomaston Clock Company, a small antique store, and a sweet shoppe. The array of historic homes also makes for interesting walks along the side streets. Bowser might prefer a trip to the Peoples State Forest, which is just a two-mile drive from Riverton. A hiking trail leads walkers to a rock outcropping, where they are able to view the valley below. Those who just want to picnic, can do so amid the 200-year-old pine trees that dot Mathies Grove. Back roads also wend their way to cross-country and downhill skiing areas, as well as to great picnic spots and secluded fishing holes in the summer months. Some might also be interested in a drive to the Granville State Forest or, perhaps, investigating one of the two local dams, Saville and the Charles A. Goodwin dams. Guests are also welcome to take advantage of the nearby recreational diversions that include tennis, horseback riding, bicycling, and golfing.

Simsbury 1820 House

731 Hopmeadow Street
Simsbury, Connecticut   06070
(800) 879-1820, (203) 658-7658, Fax (203) 651-0724

Innkeeper: Wayne Bursey
Rooms: 28 doubles, 6 suites
Rates: Doubles $85-125 (EP), Suites $125-135 (EP)
Payment: AE, CB, DC, DSC, MC, and VISA
Children: Welcome (cribs, cots, highchairs, and babysitters are available)
Dogs: Welcome in the three carriage house rooms
Open: All year

The Simsbury House was originally constructed in 1820 by Elisha Phelps, a deeply patriotic man who served in Congress and brought his more urban sophistication to Simsbury. The two-story brick house took more than two years to build, but when it was finally completed it was one of the nicest homes in town, containing ten spacious bedrooms and a lean-to-kitchen. Years later, the house was passed down to his granddaughter Lucy Eno, who added several porches, purchased a cottage, as well as an additional 90-acres of land. Upon her husband's retirement, they added a three-story wing, another porch, and converted the old kitchen into a formal dining room. After the Enos' died, their daughter inherited the property. She began refurbishing the grounds by adding life-size eagles to the gate posts flanking the entrance to the driveway. She then converted the roof to a gambrel style, constructed Colonial arches and a cupola, and installed Palladian windows. As if this were not enough, she made the property a showplace by building elaborate walks, bridges, and gazebos, and planting a variety of shrubs, bushes, and trees. Unfortunately, after her death in 1930, the mansion and grounds fell into disarray. The years of vacancy, vandalism, and neglect which followed finally ended in 1985, when the town of Simsbury decided it was in their best interests to restore the building and the property. Today, the inn is proudly listed in the National Register of Historic Places.

After ascending the winding drive that leads up to the mansion, new arrivals may wish to unload their belongings under the porte-cochere. Upon entering the cozy foyer, guests will be struck by the rich crimson wall treatments and the intricately carved cream colored moldings. Up the stairway, and along the hallways, lovely formal portraits are illuminated by crystal chandeliers. While the leather wing chairs, placed along the hallways, are decidedly a comfortable place to read the paper, most guests will be anxious to see their bedrooms.

The upstairs chambers are all good-sized and are furnished with 18th- and 19th-century antiques or reproductions. The four-poster beds are covered with floral spreads that are coordinated with the deep blue or crisp yellow walls. Some bedrooms have a small attached sitting room, while others are corner chambers that are privy to a good deal of afternoon sunlight. Even though the guest chambers on the second floor have small decks containing wicker chairs, some of our favorite bedrooms are located on the third floor. Here, cathedral ceilings are made all the more intriguing with dormers and window seats. Guests will be pleased to find that some rooms offer additional amenities, which might include a fireplace and a wet bar. The private bathrooms are tiled and outfitted with an assortment of soaps and creams, as well as thick bath towels. Separate sinks are located outside the bathrooms. Guests who are traveling with Bowser although not permitted in the main house's bedrooms, will be equally pleased with their bed chambers in the refurbished Carriage House, which is located just across the parking area from the main inn. The same elegant decor and furnishings appear in these bedrooms; however, they have the added benefit of increased size and a separate outside entrance. Most offer a four-poster king-size bed, along with attractive sitting areas that contain sofas and wing chairs. A partner's desk provides ample space for those who have work to do during their stay. The large modern bathrooms are identically appointed to those at the main inn. We liked having a private patio as well. Anyone who especially enjoys spacious accommodations may wish to reserve Room 403. The sitting area is located down a few steps from the bedrooms, making it seem very separate from the sleeping area. The color scheme in these chambers is slightly more subdued than the blues and yellows found in the inn rooms, centering instead around hunter green and chocolate or sponge painted wall treatments.

After getting settled, many choose to explore the rest of the inn. Most soon discover a wonderful veranda, which is a popular gathering place on warm summer days. A sitting room is the best bet for colder days, as there is usually a fire crackling in the hearth and small sitting areas for relaxing. In the evening, guests need only walk down a flight of stairs and through a brick arch to a series of intimate dining rooms. The tables are covered with burgundy table cloths and white overlays, and set with fine china and fresh flower arrangements. The atmosphere is very intimate and the service is first rate. Some patrons decide to start with the proscuitto tart with a fig cabernet jam and blue cheese, the Maine crab and tuna cake seasoned with sweet potato and served with a sesame ginger mayonnaise, or with the grilled shrimp wrapped in pancetta pepato and served with a cognac, tomato, and oregano butter sauce. A salad and sorbet provide a brief interlude before the entrées are served. The pasta choices are appealing, and might include lobster, capers, and sun-dried tomatoes served over a tortiglioni pasta or the grilled duck risotto served with asparagus, roasted shallots, basil, chives, crimini and shiitake mushrooms. Other options include the tournedos of beef served with blue cheese, eggplant and a red bell pepper sauce or the salmon with savoy cabbage, citrus and a creamy pink peppercorn vinaigrette. Lighter fare can be enjoyed on the veranda during the summer, and Sunday brunch throughout the year in either the indoor dining rooms or outside.

There are plenty of things for Bowser to do in the area. There are walks in and around the town of Simsbury, where many visitors also find a variety of interesting shops to investigate. Hikers and walkers will enjoy exploring the nearby state parks that include Pennwood and Talcott Mountain (see Simsbury Inn for further details). Nepaug State Forest offers almost 2,000 acres of unspoiled woodlands, and Massacoe State Forest has an additional 4,500 acres for Bowser to explore.

The Simsbury Inn

P.O. Box 287
397 Hopmeadow Street
Simsbury, Connecticut 06089
(800) 634-2719, (203) 651-5700, Fax (203) 651-8024

Manager: Jan Losee
Rooms: 91 doubles, 7 suites
Rates: Doubles $119-139 (B&B), Suites $175-350 (B&B)
Payment: AE, DC, MC, and VISA
Children: Welcome (cribs and cots are available)
Dogs: Welcome with a $250 refundable deposit
Open: All year

The Simsbury Inn is set on a hillside, just a short distance from the charming town of Simsbury. The expansive brick main building mixes traditional eaves and gables, with clean, contemporary lines. The three separate wings contain the guest rooms, a few dining rooms, and an assortment of comfortable sitting areas. The cavernous foyer, is made a little more intimate by the use of small sitting areas. One popular common area features camelback sofas and Chippendale sidechairs placed around the large stone fireplace, which is flanked by walls of bookshelves. As guests walk through the building, they begin to understand the philosophy behind the creation of the inn. The owner's goal was to create an attractive environment in which guests' needs are quickly attended to and their overall comfort a foremost priority.

To this end, guests will find the staff at the Simsbury Inn to be very friendly and helpful. Additionally, the guest room decor is appealing and the amenities are extensive. The bedrooms are located on multiple levels at the inn. Each is quite spacious, bright, and has been furnished with both traditional reproductions and white-stained pine furnishings. These usually include writing desks, wing chairs, and armoires concealing televisions and refrigerators. Subtle earth tones combine with the brass light fixtures and the colorful quilts placed on the beds, to further set the tone for the chambers. The large bathrooms also have brass fixtures and are equipped with thick bath towels, hairdryers, and scented soaps and lotions. The suites offer the same amenities, but are decorated in a Victorian motif. Complimentary newspapers and a Continental breakfast are just two more thoughtful additions.

Guests can certainly drive to Simsbury to eat, but most prefer the spacious Evergreens restaurant. The lovely dining room has beamed ceilings, intimate seating arrangements, and walls of windows overlooking the grounds. The menu selection is varied, with appetizers ranging from a wild mushroom ragout to scallops layered in tortillas with a black bean cilantro pesto, avocado, and a papaya tomato salsa. The entrées include such selections as the roasted breast of pheasant, grilled rib eye au poivre, or salmon filled with smoked shellfish and honey roasted shallots on a lobster bordelaise. After dinner, some make a stop at the Twigs lounge to enjoy the nightly entertainment amid a tranquil setting. During the daytime, the less formal Nutmeg Cafe is often the preferred dining option.

The inn also has some indoor athletic diversions. The swimming pool is always a popular spot, as is the Jacuzzi, sauna, and health club. For those who want to venture outdoors, there is tennis right on the premises, as well as good hiking on the property. Bowser will enjoy visiting the various state parks that surround Simsbury. Penwood State Park, Talcott Mountain State Park, and the Massacoe State Forest are three good choices. Penwood is a 787-acre park that is a part of the Connecticut Blue Trail, and even has its own trail system called the Metacomet Trail. The 557-acre Talcott Mountain Park is home to the Heublein Tower. Climb to the top on a clear day and visitors can see as far as 50 miles. Other nearby people attractions include horseback riding, golf (traditional and miniature), hot air balloon rides, canoeing, and cross-country and downhill skiing. Whatever reason brings travelers to this lovely region, the inn's numerous amenities and comfortable accommodations, coupled with the array of activities, make The Simsbury Inn a wonderful destination.

Hickory Ridge

1084 Quaddick Town Farm Road
Thompson, Connecticut   06277
(203) 928-9530

Hosts: Birdie and Ken Olson
Rooms: 2 doubles
Rates: $80-90 (B&B)
Payment: Personal checks
Children: Welcome
Dogs: Welcome with prior approval
Open: All year

In the northeast corner of Connecticut, in the rural town of Thompson, there lies a wonderful post and beam B&B on the shores of Quaddick Lake. The Hickory Ridge is an expansive home situated at the end of a circular driveway. When we arrived, Ken was outside hanging lights on the trees in preparation for the holidays, and stacking the wood to be used for the upcoming winter season. From the exterior, the home appears rather rustic; however, once inside we were pleasantly surprised by the beamed cathedral ceilings and walls constructed of large pine logs. The cavernous entry leads directly into the living room and its wonderful views through the wall of windows and doors. Guests can either enjoy the views from indoors, or walk out to the deck, to take in the vistas of stands of trees and sparkling lake waters. The rather open-air floor plan leads guests from the living room to an adjoining dining area, kitchen, and den. The Olsons have decorated the B&B with an array of country collectibles, including a selection of duck decoys and ships' models. Dried flower arrangements and wreaths are placed on shelves, side tables, and hang from the walls.

Although the Olsons have a state-of-the-art kitchen, the rest of the house is decorated with more of a casual country elegance. In the morning, guests dine at the elongated breakfast table, where they will enjoy the views of the lake through the stands of trees. Because the B&B is small, Birdie can fix breakfast for her guests when they are ready for it. She offers an array of choices for the morning meal, ranging from a simple bowl of cereal to something more elaborate. The breakfast breads are homemade, and Birdie fills a decorative basket with the leftovers and leaves it out so that guests can continue to nibble on them throughout the day.

The two guest rooms are located downstairs on the garden level, just off the enormous family room. This is a light and airy space, with a sense of coziness from its oatmeal colored wall-to-wall carpeting and natural knotty pine walls. The array of family photographs hanging from the walls, coupled with country collectibles, gives guests the impression that they are staying with old friends rather than at a traditional B&B. Guests traveling with Bowser will enjoy the easy access they have to the outdoors through the many doors. A comfortable sofa and a pair of side chairs are set around a sled that has been converted into a coffee table. A television and a VCR provide some entertainment diversions. The two bedrooms are clean and comfortable. One offers a queen-size bed and another has a pair of twin beds. A refrigerator, located in the rear storage room, is made available to guests for storing their drinks, snacks, or other perishables.

There is an array of activities available to visitors while staying at Hickory Ridge. The house has almost 320 feet of lake frontage, along with three acres of property for Bowser to investigate. There is both a canoe and a rowboat available for use on the lake, for both fishing or more informal expeditions. Others prefer to test their angling skills from the shore, or wait until the winter months for ice fishing. Winter visitors might also consider bringing their ice skates and cross-country skis, as both activities are popular options in this region. There are also 17 acres of land adjacent to the B&B, as well as the local Quaddick State Park which Bowser will undoubtedly enjoy investigating. The fire roads that are cut into parts of the forest are ideal for those who would like to try a little cross-country skiing. We found Hickory Ridge to be a terrific B&B that travelers and their canine cohorts would thoroughly enjoy.

A Taste of Ireland Bed and Breakfast

47 Quaddick Road
Thompson, Connecticut 06277
(203) 923-2883

Hosts: Elaine Murphy-Chicoine and Jean Chicoine
Rooms: 3 doubles
Rates: $60-70 (B&B)
Payment: Personal checks
Children: Welcome (cribs and cots are available)
Dogs: Welcome
Open: All year

The northeast portion of Connecticut is known as the "Quiet Corner" of the state. There are no large cities, sprawling commercial outlet centers, or majestic mountain ranges. There are instead, small rural towns, quiet country roads, and plenty of old-fashioned bed and breakfasts. One of the "Quiet Corner" towns is Thompson, and just down the road from its charming common is one of the more noteworthy B&Bs in the area — A Taste of Ireland. Travelers will know they have reached it when they see an Irish flag flying alongside the B&B signboard. Look just beyond the flag and find an attractive single-level home with yellow clapboards and black shutters.

Before entering the house, it is important to know something about Elaine and her husband, Jean. Like many other B&Bs owners, they decided to open their home to guests after their children had grown up and moved away. It was easy to develop a theme for the B&B, as Elaine had strong spiritual and family ties to Ireland. She has made many trips to Ireland over the years, researching her family tree, finding long lost relatives, and purchasing unique items for her import business.

Step inside the refurbished cottage, portions of which date back to 1780, and discover pleasant spaces, which very subtly reflect an Irish theme. The living room has light coral pink walls with pale green accents. Brass and antique lamps cast a soft light over the camelback sofas, harvest table, and wing chairs. Potted plants rest on stands and sheer tab curtains frame the windows. A pair of duck prints hang over a sofa, a barometer rests against another wall, and a collection of Irish china lines still another wall. The beamed ceilings and wide board floors lend additional historic authenticity to this inviting room. Guests can often be found reading in front of the fireplace, while Irish melodies play softly in the background.

The guest rooms are located throughout the house. The first one most new arrivals will encounter is the simply furnished Kilkenney Room, located just off the intimate foyer. This delightful bedroom has a homey decor, and is often reserved by people traveling on business. It contains a half bath — a full bath is located in another part of the house. As guests walk to the other bedrooms, they will head down a hallway which is lined with photographs taken by Jean. The Galway Room is a spacious queen-bedded chamber, featuring a glass door leading to a small deck, that overlooks the backyard and gardens. Anyone who wants a private outside entrance and pretty views should consider reserving this room. Elaine's family originally comes from the Galway region in Ireland, and hence the room's name. This is an ideal space for families because it can be combined with another chamber located at the top of the adjacent staircase. As guests ascend the stairs, they emerge into the Leprechaun Room, which has a low ceiling and a double bed set under the eaves. The shared downstairs bathroom is equipped with both a shower and a Jacuzzi bathtub, as well as thick cotton towels and fragrant soaps from Ireland.

Each morning a hearty breakfast is served atop the white Irish linen covering the large dining room table. A gilded mirror hangs over the sideboard, and a hutch is filled with a variety of teas, imported jams, and preserves. The attractive decor is accentuated, once again, with photographs of both the family and of Ireland. There are also many collectibles in here that Elaine and Jean have gathered during their travels abroad. Some guests prefer to eat in the sitting room where skylights, coupled with a wall of windows, provide a sunny space for the morning meal. The shingled wall in here reminds us that it was once an outside porch; however, the television, VCR, stereo, and bookshelves now make this an inviting interior room.

Guests are treated to a substantial meal, that is reminiscent of what one would be served in an Irish B&B. An adjacent screened-in porch is another favorite gathering spot, either after breakfast or at the end of a busy day.

Before guests leave, they will probably want to look over the array of Irish literature and Celtic music, as well as the lovely assortment of handcrafted jewelry from Ireland. Elaine has a small gift shop filled with unusual items that reflect rural Ireland. Her interests run far beyond the import/export business; she also is a wealth of knowledge on genealogy research, trip planning, and Gaelic translation.

It might be hard to leave this charming abode, but we recommend that guests do explore the area at some point during their visit. Bowser will enjoy the short walk up to the charming Thompson Common. There are also boating and picnicking options available at the nearby Quaddick State Park. Thompson is located near the Massachusetts and Rhode Island borders, where visitors can easily access their state parks. Some of the more popular options are The George Washington Memorial Forest, Walls Reservation, and Webster Lake.

House on the Hill

92 Woodlawn Terrace
Waterbury, Connecticut   06710-1929
(203) 757-9901

Hostess: Marianne Vandenburgh
Rooms: 2 doubles, 2 suites
Rates: Doubles $75 (B&B), Suites $75-125 (B&B)
Payment: Personal checks
Children: "Well-behaved children with their well-behaved parents are welcome"
Dogs: Welcome with advance notice and prior approval provided they are not left
*   unattended*
Open: All year except mid-December through mid-January

While downtown Waterbury might not appeal to the typical tourist, we have no doubts that the House on the Hill will. Travelers can find the bed and breakfast by driving through the town center and up a hill to Woodlawn Terrace. Here, they will be pleasantly surprised by the charming residential neighborhood filled with elegant homes. The House on the Hill is a grand old 1880s' Victorian mansion, fronted by four-foot rock walls that are topped by large evergreen bushes. Stone pillars flank the steep, winding driveway that cuts into a grassy hillside leading up to the inn. From its lofty perch, the 20-room house overlooks grounds shaded by huge trees and covered with lovely gardens of flowers, mature plantings, and decorative grasses.

The exterior of the mansion is painted in many subtle tones of coffee and gray, with green and red accents. The house is listed on the National Register of Historic Places, and once guests step inside it is easy to understand why. The original hand-carved moldings, built-in shelves, and leaded glass windows remain beautifully intact, as does the woodworking which glows with a rich patina. The sitting rooms are two of the most delightful spaces in the mansion and contain high ceilings, which are accentuated by the detailed moldings and additional cherry and mahogany woodwork. They are literally filled with collectibles, with guests finding something interesting in every corner and on every table. The Victorian antique furnishings are set on Oriental rugs, and walls of glassed-in shelves are filled with books. Both dried and fresh flower arrangements are artfully set on the tables. Another cozy, beamed-ceiling sitting room has grass wallpaper, and more Oriental rugs set with wing chairs. A piano rests in one corner and an antique baby buggy containing a handmade quilt is in another. The crimson walls are an attractive backdrop for the huge formal living room. The sofas and side chairs have been covered with lovely fabrics, and are set around a brick fireplace.

This house is truly a treasure, including the kitchen, and although we don't normally wax poetic about these typically utilitarian rooms, this one deserves special mention. This is a true commercial kitchen that would delight any chef. A pair of enormous refrigerators hold the food, which is then prepared on the large marble-topped work stations. The commercial stove is a gourmet chef's delight with multiple burners that could easily handle the demands of any caterer. The pressed-tin ceilings in here are accented by a vast array of cooking utensils, mallets, ladles, pottery pitchers, and other accoutrements hanging from the shelves or from hooks. An assortment of dried herbs and flowers also line the kitchen walls. The day we visited, Marianne was in the final stages of preparing for an elaborate wedding.

Just as the first floor rooms don't disappoint, neither do the bedrooms. These are found on the second and third floors of the mansion, which guests can reach by way of the elegant, curved mahogany staircase. Most of these are suites, or can be converted into them. One chamber is furnished with a four-poster bed fitted with a tailored canopy, and covered with a floral quilt set against a backdrop of many pillows. There is a small sitting area in here, as well as a private bathroom with many antique fixtures. Another bedroom on the same floor, has a double bed covered in a colorful patchwork quilt. On the third floor, guests will find the most requested suite, also known as the turret room. In here, a queen bed and sitting room are enhanced by a fireplace. Another room offers a double bed and the modern amenities of a kitchenette and television. One particularly sunny chamber, occupies a corner of the house which overlooks the grounds through Palladian windows framed by lace curtains. As one might imagine, each of these charmingly decorated rooms is furnished with a mix of lovely antiques and period furniture.

Guests awake each morning to a fabulous gourmet breakfast that Marianne can either serve inside the house or on the flagstone terrace. Anyone who has heard about the inn, is also familiar with her delicate cornmeal pancakes that are made from corn ground by her family on their farm in Ohio. These might be accompanied by gourmet meats, fresh fruit and juice, and English teas or freshly brewed coffee. Later in the day, guests can also enjoy a formal tea on the wonderful wraparound porch that overlooks Marianne's lovely gardens.

While Waterbury is not exactly a tourist mecca, there are a variety of things to do in the nearby area that would certainly please Bowser. Walks along the quiet back roads will lead visitors past lovely homes and gardens. Others, who are unfamiliar with this part of Connecticut, may wish to drive northwest to the picturesque town of Litchfield, or northeast to Farmington or Simsbury. Hikers may decide to take Bowser north to the Black Rock State Park. Here, they can follow a trail which connects with the Mattatuck State Forest and provides a long walk that everyone should enjoy. Rumor has it there are still arrowheads to be found in this forest setting as well. South of Waterbury, travelers will find the 3,300-acre Naugatuck State Forest Reserve, which will provide some additional outdoor recreational opportunities for guests and their canine cohorts.

Rhode Island

The Blue Dory Inn

P.O. Box 488
Dodge Street
Block Island, Rhode Island   02807
(800) 992-7290, (401) 466-5891

Innkeeper: Ann Loedy
Rooms: 10 doubles
Rates: $95-225 (B&B)
Payment: AE, MC, and VISA
Children: Welcome (cribs and babysitters are available)
Dogs: Welcome with prior notification
Open: All year

The charming hamlet known as Block Island has had many names over the years, but the one that ultimately stuck was derived from the Dutch explorer Adrae Block, who visited the island in 1614. Some years later in 1661, Colonists arrived and settled in the Old Harbor area. Until the 19th Century, the island lay virtually undeveloped; however, visitors slowly discovered this picturesque spot and the word quickly spread. Block Island is situated 13 miles off the Rhode Island coastline. These days, some people arrive by air, but most make their way to this remote enclave by ferries originating in Connecticut, Rhode Island, or New York. Block Island is just eleven miles long, and it can become extremely busy during the height of the summer. Thus, those who can wait until the shoulder or off-season will be thoroughly delighted by a much more peaceful vacation experience.

One of the island institutions is the Blue Dory Inn, which is nestled in the historic district at the head of Crescent Beach. Originally built in 1898 by a local fisherman, the recently refurbished blue shingle building has wonderful views of the water and town from the bedrooms and the three cottages built around a central deck. Ann has done a wonderful job refurbishing the rooms and decorating them in a delightful Victorian manner. From the moment people enter the intimate inn, they will find lovely reproductions and antiques set amid delicate floral wallpapers. A charming sitting room has pretty blue-gray walls, accented with an array of flower arrangements and brass lamps set on the various tables. A secretary is brimming with books, and a cozy seating arrangement is situated around a Victorian marble-topped coffee table. We like the large, windowed alcove as much for its views as for the sunlight that streams in past the sheer curtains. Guests will also find an array of board games and puzzles, along with periodicals and newspapers in here. A television and VCR provide electronic entertainment in the evenings or if the weather forces guests indoors. In the afternoon, Ann provides an assortment of baked goodies and drinks that should ease any hunger pangs until dinner. A basket of local restaurant menus makes it easy for people to choose where they will be going that night.

The bedrooms are decorated and furnished in the same manner as the common areas and reflect a strong Victorian theme. Delicate floral wallpapers, ranging from pastel yellows to lavender, are coordinated with the fabrics draped over the sidetables and the coverlets placed on the twin-, double-, and queen-size beds. Lace or floral curtains frame many of the windows, and vases of flowers are placed on the marble-topped bed side tables. The beds are backed with wicker, carved oak, or brass headboards, and the floors are covered with wall-to-wall carpeting. Each of the rooms has a nicely refurbished private bathroom, as well.

Each morning guests are invited to partake in a substantial Continental breakfast which may be enjoyed on the patio or deck, weather permitting. After a filling repast, many are anxious to investigate the island. While some may be interested in bringing their cars over to Block Island, we suggest that cars be left on the mainland and visitors plan on walking or bicycling instead. After investigating the eclectic assortment of shops and restaurants, we recommend visiting the North Light at Sandy Point or one of the island's five wildlife refuges. Others enjoy gaining a dramatic perspective of the surrounding ocean from the 150-foot high Mohegan Bluffs. The Clayhead Nature Trails are quite popular, as are the many beaches. Another delightful area known as the Maze, is found off Corn Neck Road. Here, visitors can meander along the grassy trails that wend past small ponds and eventually cut through to the sandy inlets and the ocean.

Larchwood Inn

521 Main Street
Wakefield, Rhode Island 02879
(401) 783-5454

Innkeepers: Francis and Diann Browning
Rooms: 19 doubles
Rates: $45-100 (EP)
Payments: AE, CB, DC, DSC, MC, and VISA
Children: Welcome (cribs and cots are available)
Dogs: Welcome with a $5 fee, provided they are not left alone in the room
Open: All year

For over 150 years, the Larchwood Inn has stood in a quiet residential section of Wakefield. It is comprised of the three-story manor house and the Holly House, both of which were built during the same era but are sited at different locations. The twelve guest bedrooms located in the main inn, and seven across the street in the Holly House, overlook three acres of grounds dotted with mature oak, cherry, maple, pine, and dogwood trees. Most of the landscaping and plantings were completed in the mid-1800s by the Stephen Wright family. Today, guests are able to enjoy this peaceful setting, just as the Wright family once did, from the white wicker chairs on the expansive front porch.

The Larchwood Inn has been in our book for many years, and little has changed in that time. As guests enter the inn, they will still find a living room off to one side and a series of dining rooms on the other. The living room is a very inviting space, complete with sofas and side chairs arranged around the fireplace, and an array of mantel clocks, ship models, and portraits filling the corners. A television provides some modern diversion, although many find the resident parakeet to be more engaging. The center hall leads to the three intimate dining areas that were formerly the home's original living rooms. Assorted Scottish artifacts and collectibles, as well as writings by the poet Robert Burns, can be found throughout many of the inn's common areas. Each year, on the poet's birthday, the Brownings celebrate with a festive party. They import a piper and offer traditional Scottish dishes such as "Haggis." Birthdays aside, the traditional fare sounds more mainstream but is no less interesting, consisting of broiled swordfish, several lobster entrées, roasted chicken, and prime rib of beef. In the summer months, the Larchwood Inn is a favorite stop for visiting yachtsman, who dock their boats in nearby Point Judith Pond and make the short journey to the inn for dinner. Before heading back to their boats, many like to visit the Tam O'Shanter Lounge, which is decorated in a Scottish motif.

As guests ascend the central staircase, they will find the sloping and creaking hardwood floors lead to the individually furnished bedrooms. Antique four-poster or canopy beds are covered with white Bates spreads. Decorative fireplaces and comfortable, well-worn sofas and wing chairs grace some of the larger rooms, while antique tables, mirrors, and bureaus are standard features in the others. Full-length, floral-patterned draperies overlap sheer lace curtains at the windows. We particularly like the ell-shaped corner room on the second floor (Room 1), not only for its brick fireplace, but for the wonderful views of the sprawling front lawn. Many of the guest rooms are ideal for families because of the double and single bed configurations. Most of the chambers contain private, tiled baths that may be a little dated but are extremely clean. Those who want greater privacy may request a room in the Holly House. The furnishings and decor in these chambers are similar to those in the main inn. Regardless of choice, guests are certain to feel the Larchwood Inn is reminiscent of an old-fashioned summer home.

The area around the inn offers a good number of interesting activities. There are the local public beaches which are worth investigating both in the summertime and in the crisper off-season months. Dogs are allowed on the beaches in the morning and evening hours, and anytime during the off-season. Two good choices are the Scarborough State Beach and the Roger Wheeler Memorial Beach. Point Judith also seems to attract visitors. Historic Jamestown is accessible by way of a number of bridges. In Jamestown, the original Beaver Tail Lighthouse and a few historic homes (the British burned much of the town in 1775) are just a few of the wonderful old treasures. Locally, the Fisherman's Memorial State Park provides some interesting walking options. In addition, Wakefield is centrally located and provides easy access to such destinations as Newport, Watch Hill, Block Island, and Mystic, Connecticut.

The Villa

190 Shore Road
Westerly, Rhode Island 02891
(800) 722-9240, (401) 596-1054

Host: Jerry Maiorano
Rooms: 7 suites
Rates: $75-175
Payment: AE, MC, and VISA
Children: Those over the age of five are welcome
Dogs: Welcome with advance notice and prior approval
Open: All year

Anyone who is familiar with southern Rhode Island will probably have heard about Misquamicut Beach, a popular destination for those who enjoy relaxing in the summer sun. Situated near the crossroads leading to this beach and the renowned Watch Hill area, travelers will find The Villa. The two buildings that make up the complex are tucked unobtrusively behind a large hedge; however, once guests enter the grounds, they are quickly transported to a more Mediterranean atmosphere. The facade resembles an Italian villa, with porticos and verandas overlooking a patio that is shaded by umbrella tables. The surrounding flower gardens provide colorful accents to the sparkling pool and hot tub. Once inside, the mood changes ever so slightly to combine the antique charm of New England with an array of bright Italian colors and fabrics.

A portico marks the entrance to the main house and opens into a large, fireplaced common room. The bedrooms are found either upstairs, off one of the patios, or in the other two-story building. Each of the chambers is distinctive, varying in size and conveniences. La Sala di Roma, for instance, offers a double brass bedstead covered in a floral spread. The color scheme is complemented by the rose colored carpeting, and emerald green and alabaster accents. The kitchenette and small dining area are added creature comforts. Best of all, the private bathroom is equipped with a Jacuzzi. La Sala del Cielo, on the other hand, is tucked away on the third floor and can be reached by way of a low-ceiling staircase. A number of skylights make this one of the brightest chambers at The Villa, and also reveal distant ocean views. This elongated room features a sitting area with a sofa bed, a queen-size bed, and a kitchenette. The Rosa Maiorano Room is located just off the patio, which fronts the house. A four-poster canopy bed, covered in a muted pink and blue chintz, is set diagonally in one corner of the room. The dark, country wood paneling is enhanced by the beamed ceiling and the brick fireplace that makes this a truly cozy space.

Anyone who is looking for a little more space and privacy, should reserve La Sala di Verona. Situated on the second floor of the adjacent house, this expansive chamber gains an additional sense of openness from the skylights set into the cathedral ceiling. The brass bed is placed in one corner of the room, and on the opposite side, there are a pair of white sofas grouped around an entertainment center, outfitted with a stereo and television. A short flight of stairs leads to the modern bathroom containing a European bidet. Glass doors open out onto the balcony, which overlooks the pool and grounds. There are many accommodations to choose from at this inn, and each offers modern conveniences such as small refrigerators, televisions, and telephones.

Every morning, a hearty Continental breakfast is served buffet style, in the dining room, alongside the pool, or in one's suite. Afterwards, some choose to revel by the pool, while others decide to explore a bit with Bowser. The Misquamicut Beach is just a short drive from The Villa. During the season, guests may walk Bowser here either in the early morning or in the evening, when the beach activity has thinned out. If they visit during the off-season, Bowser can explore the beaches anytime. Watch Hill is an exclusive, yet charming, beach-side community that is also well worth investigating. Anyone who is interested in exploring Rhode Island's State Park system should consider visiting the Burlingame State Park, Acadia State Park, or Scarborough State Beach, the latter being located near the Narragansett Pier.

Massachusetts

Andover Inn

Chapel Avenue
Andover, Massachusetts   01810
(800) 242-5903, (508) 475-5903, Fax (508) 475-1053

Innkeeper: Henry Broekhoff
Rooms: 17 doubles, 6 suites
Rates: Doubles $95, Suites $110-130
Payment: AE, CB, DC, MC, and VISA
Children: Welcome (cribs, cots, highchairs, and babysitters are available)
Dogs: Welcome, smaller dogs are preferred
Open: All year

The Andover Inn was built in 1930 on the picturesque, 600-acre campus of Phillips Academy. Today, this traditional brick building is surrounded by mature trees, rock walls, and well-manicured lawns. The facade is inset with a two-story portico, where patio chairs and window boxes filled with flowers create an inviting space in the summer months. Step inside and guests emerge into a large common area, which is tastefully appointed with camelback sofas, matching armchairs, and reproduction and antique furnishings set around a central fireplace.

A tiny elevator transports new arrivals to their bedrooms. Our first stop was the second floor rooms, which have subtle floral and grass wallpapers contrasting with wood paneling and wainscotings. Finial beds are the focal points, and are accented by Queen Anne-style furnishings that include writing desks and leather side chairs. Modern conveniences such as color televisions, air conditioning, radios, and private telephones are also provided. There are a few guest bedrooms that do not have their own private bathroom. These chambers either share an adjoining bathroom or a separate facility is available down the hall. The guest rooms on the third floor are somewhat larger and have gabled or arched ceilings. One of the most requested suites is Number 24, which has an expansive sitting room that adjoins an equally spacious master bedroom. The carpeted sitting room is furnished with a desk, and the sofa and chairs are grouped around a mahogany cabinet that houses a television. This is a bright space, where natural sunlight from the many windows and the light from the brass lamps casts a warm glow across the wood paneling and recessed alcoves around the fireplace. Each of these charming bedrooms has lovely views of the campus, Cochran Chapel, or the arts building.

The intimate, dark wood-paneled bar is a favorite gathering place before and after dinner. The four-star dining room is clearly one of the inn's more noteworthy chambers. Glass chandeliers illuminate the box-beamed ceilings, and full-length draperies frame the floor-to-ceiling windows. On weekends and on special occasions, a pianist frequently plays soft background music on the grand piano. On Sunday nights, a traditional Indonesian Rijs*ttafel* is presented. This is a multi-course extravaganza, which encompasses over 20 festive dishes. Anyone familiar with Indonesian foods, might recognize items such as Babi Ketjap, Kroepoek, and the potent Sambal Badjak. Those who prefer less exotic fare, will enjoy the standard dinner menu. Appetizer selections include escargôts á la bourguignonne, oysters on the half shell, and lobster bisque. The specialties of the inn are roast duck, red curry shrimp, lobster fricassée, and veal scallops with cognac shallot butter. The kitchen is also happy to pack a box lunch for guests to enjoy on their wanderings throughout the surrounding New England countryside.

Phillips Academy has a beautiful campus that is perfect for leisurely walks and invigorating runs with Bowser. Just a short drive away are the coastal towns of Beverly Farms, Manchester-by-the-Sea, and Annisquam—three good examples of New England's classic coastal communities. Others may enjoy partaking in a favorite seasonal pastime, which could include maple sugaring in the spring or apple picking in the fall. Bowser is also welcome in many of the area's state forests, including the Harold Parker, Georgetown Rowley, or Willowdale.

Honeysuckle Hill

591 Main Street
West Barnstable, Massachusetts   02668
(800) 441-8418, (508) 362-8418

Hosts: Barbara and Bob Rosenthal
Rooms: 3 doubles
Rates: $95-110 (B&B)
Payment: AE, DSC , MC, and VISA
Children: Not appropriate for children under 5 years of age (cots are available)
Dogs: Welcome with advance notice and prior approval ($7 daily fee)
Open: All year except Christmas week

Cape Cod has long been a favorite getaway for vacationers visiting Massachusetts. While the Cape's southern coast is well-traveled, the northern side is quieter and less developed. Barnstable is one of the quaint villages here, one that is not only filled with historic charm, but also provides easy access to the many attractions found on Cape Cod.

The Honeysuckle Hill Bed & Breakfast is a wonderful destination for anyone who wants to be on the Cape, but slightly off the beaten path. The B&B is a weathered shingle house set at the end of a gravel drive, edged by flower gardens and protected by privacy hedges. The original home was built in 1810 by Josiah

Goodspeed and is listed on the National Register of Historic Places. Although an addition or two have expanded much of the farmhouse's exterior, the historic interior remains much the same. The Rosenthals have also maintained the home's New England antique flavor, but the furnishings and overall decor are probably more along the lines of an "English country" motif.

Guests will undoubtedly be greeted by the hosts' dog, Chloe, as they enter the house. She often enjoys accompanying new arrivals as Barbara gives them a tour of the first floor. Just beyond the reception area, which is tucked into a large hall closet, guests will come to the expansive post-and-beam Great Room. On sunny days, the bright light streams in through a wall of French doors and windows topped by a single Palladian window. Shades of blue and cinnamon set the color scheme of the large braided rug and the couch and chairs which encircle it. A woodstove creates additional warmth in the winter months, while the grandfather clock ticks away unobtrusively in the corner. An entertainment center provides a little diversion in the evenings. Guests are also certain to note the array of collectibles and knickknacks that line the exposed beams and shelves. More likely than not, Chloe will end her tour here, and curl up in front of the stove for an afternoon nap. As guests walk out the French doors they will find a pretty garden, complete with a small pond and waterfall. Birds flit all around the feeders, and a hammock swings invitingly in the breeze.

Each of the guest bedrooms is individually decorated. The Peter Rabbit Room, which is situated off the screened-in porch, is particularly appealing. This lavender chamber offers an antique four-poster bedstead, with a mattress softened by a featherbed and a down comforter covered by a handmade quilt. The pine floors are covered with a pretty blue-gray carpet. In addition to the mix of Peter Rabbit memorabilia stored in the china cabinet, guests will also appreciate the lovely antique furnishings and the sunny alcove opposite the foot of the bed. The Rose Room is decidedly less whimsical, and is most often reserved for romantic getaways. The queen-size bed is tucked into an alcove, which is backed by a wall of windows framed by rose-patterned chintz curtains. The box-beamed ceiling and hardwood floors provide just the right setting for the Victorian furnishings and working fireplace. A pair of wine glasses displayed on a side table are waiting to be filled. The large Cape Cod Room is located on the second floor and not only offers the charm of gabled ceilings, but also the comfort of a king-size bed. As with the other bedrooms, this chamber also has an interesting array of carefully selected antiques, as well as a colorful handmade quilt draped over the bed. In the summer months, fresh flower arrangements grace each bedroom and all year long there are delicious homemade cookies. The private bathrooms are made more luxurious by the addition of fragrant soaps and shampoos, along with thick terry robes.

In the morning, guests are invited to the dining room, where they will be served a full breakfast. During our visit, Barbara had an assistant in one of the guests, who was happily flipping Johnny cakes in her country kitchen. The repast varies, but includes a variety of fresh fruits to start, which are generally followed by omelets, souffles, or French toast. A lighter fare might consist of homemade muffins, and coffee or tea. Those who cannot finish this hearty meal should not be concerned about their food going to waste as Barbara gives any leftovers to the resident "boufant" (more commonly known as a skunk).

There are plenty of ways for guests to stay busy here. A walk on Sandy Neck beach is the first stop on Barbara's "to do" list. Borrow one of their bicycles, or bring your own, and ride up Meadow Lane to the salt marshes. Once guests have visited the neighboring towns, explored the quiet beaches, and taken long walks with Bowser, they might want to hop on a ferry for a short ride over to Martha's Vineyard. Very few inns on the island welcome guests traveling with a dog, so a day trip is a good way to visit without having to book one of the few rooms available.

At the end of a busy day, guests look forward to their afternoon tea. Barbara often serves this on the cool, wraparound, screened-in porch, which is filled with white wicker furniture along with hanging and potted plants.

The Lamb & Lion

P.O. Box 511
Route 6A - Main Street
Barnstable, Massachusetts   02630
(508) 362-6823

Innkeepers: Joanne and David Rice
Rooms: 4 doubles, 1 suite, 2 cottages, and 3 efficiencies
Rates: Doubles $65-85 (B&B), Suite $95-110 (B&B), Efficiencies $70-85 (B&B),
*   Cottages $80-600 (B&B)*
Payment: MC and VISA
Children: Welcome in certain rooms at the inn
Dogs: Quiet, well-trained dogs are welcome in certain areas
Open: All year

The Lamb & Lion is located on the more tranquil northern side of Cape Cod, yet it is only a few minutes from bustling Hyannis and the ferry boats taking visitors out to Martha's Vineyard and Nantucket. The inn consists of several buildings, each offering unique accommodations. The most authentic part of The Lamb & Lion is the original Colonial homestead, which was built in 1740. Although this building faces the road, most of the guest rooms are located to the rear of it, and encircle the outdoor swimming pool. That each of these chambers is bright and airy is due as much to the light pouring in from the many windows as to the cheerful floral prints on the coordinated bedspreads and slipcovered chairs. Country antiques and white wicker furniture are also found in each of the rooms. Modern amenities include private bathrooms, air conditioning, and color television.

The standard bedrooms usually provide everything the average guest might need; however, those who require more space or the conveniences of a kitchenette or a living room, will be pleased with some of the larger accommodations. The honeymoon suite is one of our favorites with a cozy fireplace in the living room and sunken tub in the bathroom. The private deck creates additional outdoor living space. Families or groups of friends might opt to reserve the converted barn, which was also built in 1740. These accommodations are decidedly a little more rustic, although they still have Colonial overtones. Here, guests will find multiple bedrooms, along with a full kitchen, living room, and a private patio. Finally, there is the one-bedroom cottage with a sleeping loft, kitchenette, living/dining room combination, and a separate entrance leading to a small deck. Joanne and David go out of their way to make sure that guests are matched with just the right type of room, so that one's stay is as relaxing as possible.

There are plenty of ways to unwind at the inn. One popular place to rest is in the sun-drenched solarium. This is a great retreat any time of day, although it is particularly welcoming after a swim in the pool. The solarium also doubles as a game room, as it contains a substantial collection of interesting board games. From the vantage point provided by the white wicker couches and chairs there are also nice views of the gardens and the swimming pool through the floor-to-ceiling windows. In the morning, this chamber is the gathering place for a light Continental breakfast.

The Lamb and Lion is an ideal destination for anyone who wants a tranquil low-key Cape Cod setting. It is well situated for antiquing forays along rural Route 6A, as well as for playing golf or tennis. Beachcombing with Bowser is another pleasant pastime on several of the nearby coves. Sandy Neck Beach is also close to the inn, and there are plenty of quiet lanes to take leisurely walks with Bowser. The nearby Cape Cod Potato Chip Factory is a popular attraction, that offers self-guided tours and plenty of samples.

The Jenkins House
Bed and Breakfast Inn

P.O. Box 779
Routes 122 & 32 on Barre Common
Barre, Massachusetts   01005
(800) 378-7373, (508) 355-6444, Fax (508) 355-6449

Innkeepers: David Ward
Rooms: 5 doubles
Rates: $70-120 (B&B)
Payment: AE, DSC, MC, and VISA
Children: Not appropriate for children under the age of five (highchairs and cots are
*   available)*
Dogs: Welcome with advance notice
Open: All year

As travelers venture along back country roads in central Massachusetts, they might stumble upon the small town of Barre. Just 30 minutes northwest of Worcester, but seemingly hundreds of miles from any large city, there lies a small town common surrounded by sprawling farms and dense woods. On the common, travelers will discover a pair of churches, some historic New England homes, a library, a handful of stores, and The Jenkins House. Originally built in 1834, by local entrepreneur James W. Jenkins, the Victorian house has been carefully refurbished over the years so that its character has remained intact. Today, the good-size house lies at the intersection of two rural routes. Its white clapboards and blue-gray shutters, as well as a wraparound porch, are surrounded by well-kept English gardens and the grassy common.

As with many New England homes, new arrivals enter The Jenkins House by way of the side door. A hallway leads into an intimate sitting room and a small tearoom and coffee house that are drenched in sunlight pouring in through three walls of windows. When we visited, the sitting room was decked in Christmas finery, making the sofas and armchairs that normally occupy the room look all the more inviting. A brick hearth was laid with a fire. Just across the hall, a staircase leads up to the bedrooms. One of these chambers has a pair of twin beds, which can be combined to form a king-size bed, and a rocking chair set on a green rug. A white bureau also doubles as a stand for the television and VCR. A remote control is conveniently laid out next to the clock radio on the bedside table. Step up into the small bathroom, with its stall shower. The rather bold masculine wallpaper gives the room an additional sense of warmth. One of the most popular chambers is set above the tea room. Eleven paned windows are set into three walls, allowing a great deal of sunlight to pour into this space, enhancing the pale floral and striped wallpaper. The queen-size canopy bed is positioned perfectly against one wall to take maximum advantage of the setting. A rocking chair and a small desk also occupy the room. The private bathroom has a shower/tub combination. The three other bedrooms are also eclectically yet attractively furnished as well, and offer either queen or king beds.

Breakfast is served each morning in the sunny, fireplaced tearoom. This meal varies daily, with creations that could include French toast (made with homemade bread), light and fluffy pancakes accompanied by spicy sausage, apple cinnamon waffles, and a variety of farm fresh egg dishes. Homemade breads, scones, and muffins are also favored breakfast items. Anyone who needs to depart early, can request a Continental breakfast the night before, or for those with late night munchies, there is a short list of items that can easily be sent to the room. There is also a small lunch room, where diners can choose from a variety of tasty, and often organic, dishes. The menu has a number of unusual treats, including Buffalo burgers, strawberry-date tea, and mozzarella, pesto, and tomato spread sandwiches. The spinach lasagna is also a popular offering. In addition to this menu, patrons can select from more than three dozen herbal teas, a dozen varieties of coffee, and an ever changing assortment of delectable desserts.

This is a rural region that Bowser will definitely enjoy. The Quabbin Reservoir is the largest body of water in the area; however, Bowser would probably prefer forays into the nearby Wachusett Mountain State Reservation, or to the Leominster State Forest. The latter offers hiking and canoeing opportunities in the summer, and cross-country skiing in the winter months. An Audubon sanctuary is also close to the B&B. Antique buffs will be anxious to make the twice yearly trips to nearby Brimfield, the site of one of the largest antique fairs in the country. Visitors can also check out the country's oldest agricultural fair in the summer, pick apples in the fall, and watch the sap run in the spring. Best of all, Bowser should enjoy the rural setting and expansive areas for running and exploring.

Boston Harbor Hotel
at Rowes Wharf

70 Rowes Wharf on Atlantic Avenue
Boston, Massachusetts 02110
(800) 752-7077, (617) 439-7000, Fax (617) 330-9450

General Manager: Paul Jacques
Rooms: 230 doubles and suites
Rates: Doubles $195-390 (EP), Suites $350-600 (EP)
Payment: AE, DC, MC, and VISA
Children: Welcome (cribs, cots, highchairs, and babysitters are available)
Dogs: Welcome
Open: All year

Boston's waterfront has always held a great deal of appeal for tourists and locals alike. It is a hub of activity, reminding visitors that this is indeed a seacoast city. There are only two hotels on the waterfront, and of the two, the Boston Harbor Hotel stands out as a premier property. It is popular for business travelers because it is close to the financial district, plus they can easily take the water shuttle directly from the hotel to the airport. It is also a terrific weekend destination as it lies within walking distance of Faneuil Hall and Quincy Market, the Freedom Trail, the North End, and the Aquarium. Finally, anyone arriving by yacht will be pleased to know the hotel has access to 30 marina slips.

We are always warmly greeted by everyone at the hotel, from the doormen to the front desk staff. The soft colors in the intimate lobby are accented by Italian marble arches and floors covered with thick Oriental carpets. As guests walk toward the rear of the hotel, they will see an array of nautical paraphernalia. The highlights are the two model ships, which are housed in glass cases, and the impressive collection of antique maps which line the walls. We are told the maps belong to the owner of the hotel, Mr. Laventhal, who shares them with the public but maintains them as a private collection. Massive fresh flower arrangements are set on the English antique barrel tables and sideboards.

The guest rooms do not contain antiques; however, they are formal. Their varying color schemes usually combine deep green, gold, or copper with a neutral camel backdrop. These tones reveal themselves in the full-length chintz draperies and the coordinated fitted bedspreads. The furnishings are equally traditional, with armoires containing televisions and mini-bars, writing desks topped with brass lamps, and small sitting areas. The bedrooms vary in size, but even the standard ones are spacious enough for guests with a dog. The tiled bathrooms are equally well-appointed with cotton robes, slippers, hair dryers, Swiss soaps and shampoos, and even a telephone. We were impressed with the generous number of thick cotton towels. Our favorite chambers are those facing the water, as guests feel suspended over the harbor and can also enjoy the twinkling lights at night.

Although the view from the waterside guest rooms is beautiful, guests should also consider dining in the Rowes Wharf Restaurant. Their Executive Chef is Daniel Bruce, who continues to win accolades both locally and nationally. The restaurant itself is impressive, with dark wood paneling, royal blue wall treatments, and well planned seating arrangements. Needless to say, the most coveted tables are those with picturesque views of the Boston Harbor. Menu items change frequently, but appetizers from the autumn menu included the sea scallop ravioli with a spinach butter sauce, the maple smoked Atlantic salmon on lacy potato cakes, and the Maine lobster sausage over lemon pasta. Entrée selections included the charred duck breast with red onion jam and sautéed watercress, fricasseé of lobster and chorizo with sweet corn pudding, and the mustard roasted rack of lamb or the spinach and cheddar cheese cannaloni with a wild mushroom and roasted pepper sauce. The restaurant is also dedicated to offering heart healthy selections for every meal, including their famous Sunday brunch.

Guests may work off their excesses in the hotel's luxurious health club. Here, a 60-foot lap pool is complemented by a spa, sauna, whirlpool, and a variety of aerobic equipment. Guests may also reserve time for a massage or beauty treatment, as well. This is a city hotel, so Bowser will be more comfortable if he is used to the commotion of the city streets. Guests might want to ask for the "Doggie Kit" provided by the hotel and try one of the many recommended walks. In addition to these pleasant routes, there are a myriad of other routes along the harbor front, through Faneuil Hall, and up through Beacon Hill. Once walkers cross over the hill they can find grassy areas on the Boston Common and in the Boston Public Gardens. They might also want to head over one of the footbridges leading to the Esplanade, where there are miles of riverside walks to enjoy.

The Copley Plaza

138 St. James Avenue
Boston, Massachusetts   02116
(800) 822-4200, (617) 267-5300, Fax (617) 267-7668

General Manager: Nicolas de Segonzac
Rooms: 373 rooms
Rates: Singles $160-245 (EP), Doubles $180-270 (EP), Suites $350-1250 (EP)
Payment: AE, CB, DC, DSC, ENR, MC, and VISA
Children: Welcome (cribs, cots, highchairs, and babysitters are available)
Dogs: Welcome
Open: All year

Boston is a popular destination for those who not only enjoy the splendid shopping and dining opportunities, but also the array of museums, art, and theater alternatives that can be found in and around the city. Set in the heart of Back Bay, The Copley Plaza is not only convenient to renowned Newbury Street, but is also just a short distance from Copley Place, the Charles River, Beacon Hill, The Boston Public Gardens, and a host of other noteworthy diversions and attractions. Those travelers who are both interested in a central location and in accommodations that exude an old world charm and elegance, will want to consider staying at The Copley Plaza.

The seven-story gray stone building is a landmark dating back to 1912. The main entrance to the hotel opens into Peacock Alley, a magnificent domed-ceiling hallway that is accented with crystal chandeliers. It leads to the equally impressive lobby. Anyone who has visited The Plaza Hotel in New York City will be quick to recognize its design themes in its sister hotel, here in Boston. Architect Henry Hardenbergh was responsible for the design of both buildings. Here, large yellow marble columns support the frescoed blue sky ceilings trimmed with ornate gilded moldings. Near the reception desk, mirrored Palladian faux windows give the impression that the lobby is even more cavernous than it actually is.

The recent restoration of both the common areas and guest rooms is immediately apparent as guests are escorted to their rooms. The darkly finished doors, elegant decor, and impressive furnishings are sure to please most travelers. Subtle wall treatments are enhanced by crimson chintz coverlets and coordinated draperies and valances in many of the chambers. Wing chairs are set next to couches in some sitting areas, while an elegant writing desk or a barrel table fills a corner in others. Armoires and low cabinets contain televisions and refrigerators. Many guests prefer the corner suites, which combine good-sized living rooms with king-bedded master bedrooms. These not only have overstuffed sofas and side chairs set around a fireplace, but some also offer commanding views of Trinity Church and the plaza.

Although the guest rooms are beautifully appointed, it is the common areas, restaurants, and bars that are the real draw to this Grande Dame of Boston. The highly regarded Plaza Bar is one such congregating place. It is elegant with dark paneled walls, deep leather chairs, and an impressive bar flanked by statues of lions. These components, combined with the subdued lighting, evoke images of a private club. There is usually evening entertainment in here, where jazz reigns supreme on most nights. Copley's Bar, on the other hand, is a more casual place to gather. The Plaza Dining Room is an excellent choice for hotel dining. The impeccable service combined with the handsome setting produces a superior dining experience. The varied menu ranges from a roasted cornish game hen in a mustard and herb marinade and veal with asparagus, lobster claw meat and bernaise to roast prime rib of beef and the lamb porterhouse. During their stay, guests should also take a little time to look at the stately Grand Ballroom, Oval Room, and Venetian Room, which have hosted many Presidents, political figures, and foreign dignitaries over the last eighty years.

In addition to enjoying the full complement of exercise equipment available on the premises, guests also have free use of the Le Pli Spa, as well. Bowser will appreciate the ease of access to many dog-friendly attractions. The Copley Plaza is just a two-minute walk to Newbury Street, where there is an array of great shopping and dining alternatives. The Esplanade along the Charles River, the picturesque Beacon Hill neighborhoods, and the Boston Public Gardens and Common are other interesting walking options that Bowser is sure to appreciate. Best of all, there is a well-versed concierge who is more than happy to assist guests in finding a variety of entertaining things to do during their visit to Boston.

Four Seasons Hotel

200 Boylston Street
Boston, Massachusetts 02116
(800) 332-3442, (617) 338-4400, Fax (617) 423-0154

General Manager: Robin Brown
Rooms: 288 doubles and suites
Rates: Doubles $160-355 (EP), Suites $450-2,600 (EP)
Payment: AE, CB, DC, MC, and VISA
*Children: Welcome. There are extensive children's amenities and programs available,
including cribs, cots, and babysitters.*
*Dogs: Smaller dogs are welcome (dog beds, pet menus, feeding bowls, bones, and assorted
toys are available)*
Open: All year

Comparatively speaking, the Four Seasons Hotel is one of the more recent additions to the Boston hotel scene. Ideally located across from the Boston Public Gardens and close to the theater district, Copley Place, and the Newbury Street shops, the Four Seasons Hotel will delight both travelers and their canine companions. From the outside, the hotel is attractive, with clean, contemporary lines. But once inside, guests immediately are enveloped in its elegance and tradition. Sitting areas are inviting, with deep sofas and comfortable side chairs, accented by fine English antiques and reproductions. Lavish indoor plantings and floral arrangements add colorful touches to these spaces.

The bedrooms are almost as lovely as the public areas, yet a little less opulent. Neutral wallpapers complement the English chintz bed coverlets and coordinated draperies. Formal wing chairs, marble-topped coffee tables, and Sheraton-style writing desks are accented by brass standing lamps. There are a number of guest room configurations from which to choose, ranging from adjoining rooms to expansive suites. The Four Seasons rooms have comfortable parlors separated from the bedroom by folding doors, allowing guests and their dogs to have separate sleeping areas. We prefer the accommodations with picture windows overlooking the Boston Public Gardens. All of the rooms have been designed with windows that actually open, an unusual feature for a city hotel. Some of the largest rooms are the garden suites, which include parlors that are approximately 700 square feet and adjoin up to three spacious bedrooms. Those who wish to spend a longer period of time at the hotel should inquire about the condominiums that are located on the floors above the main hotel. Regardless of room choice, all guests will have the benefit of five-star amenities. The remote-control televisions are concealed in mahogany armoires and the small refrigerators open to reveal well-stocked mini-bars. Of course, the bathrooms have a full array of toiletries, although the staff will supply most anything guests might have forgotten, along with terry bathrobes, hair dryers, and one of the room's three telephones. They have not overlooked Bowser either, and include an array of dog-oriented provisions. These range from dog beds and bones to dog bowls and play toys. They also have a list of activities that may be of interest to canine travelers, as well. Should Bowser need a late night snack, there is also a pet menu which includes items such as "shepherd's pie."

Of course, we recommend the extensive restaurant menu for the guests, and the Four Seasons happens to have an award-winning one. Aujourd'hui is the premier restaurant in the hotel, and has continued to win accolades over the years. In addition to the lovely decor and picturesque views of the Boston Public Gardens, guests will enjoy an ever-changing entrée selection. Chef Jamie Mammano might offer such appetizers as a grilled portabello mushroom carpaccio with balsamic vinegar and pecorino ricotta, the white bean and lobster soup, or the buttermilk biscuits with apple-cured salmon and Ossetra caviar. Next, diners may wish to sample the peppered saddle of venison with a spiced acorn squash timbale and Cape cranberries; the herb-roasted red snapper, gulf shrimp, artichoke and truffle risotto, or the veal tenderloin in pancetta, sweet onion and fennel seed roesti.

The hotel's spa, located on the eighth floor, is open from 6:00 a.m. to 9:00 p.m., just in case someone feels a need to work off a few extra calories. The adjacent 51-foot lap pool, also has a terrific view of the Boston Public Gardens. Further rest and relaxation can be found in either the whirlpool or sauna. A professional massage is another delightful option, particularly for those who have had a full day seeing the sights. Bowser will enjoy a stroll in the Boston Public Gardens any time of year. During the summer months strollers will see the famous swan boats quietly circling the pond, and ice skaters spinning and twirling throughout the long winter months. Other noteworthy excursions bring walkers to the Boston Common, Beacon Hill, and along Newbury Street, as well as on the Esplanade (also a great place to ride bicycles and roller-skate) that parallels the Charles River (where sailboats may be rented). A quick ride on the "T" will bring travelers and their canine companions over the hill to Faneuil Hall Marketplace and Quincy Market.

Le Meridien

250 Franklin Street
Boston, Massachusetts 02110
(800) 543-4300, (617) 451-1900, Fax (617) 423-2844

General Manager: Hugues Jaquier
Rooms: 326 doubles and suites
Rates: Doubles $210-235 (EP), Suites $400-790 (EP)
Payment: AE, CB, DC, JCB, MC, and VISA
Children: Welcome (cribs, cots, highchairs, and babysitters are available)
Dogs: Small, very well-behaved dogs are welcome with prior approval
Open: All year

Le Meridien, housed in the old Federal Reserve Bank building, lies in the heart of Boston's financial district. It is also close to Faneuil Hall Marketplace and the Boston waterfront. The hotel has been deemed an historic landmark, thus the exterior facade cannot be markedly altered. When it was being renovated, this presented some interesting architectural problems, but they have been beautifully and creatively resolved. The area across from the hotel used to be rather nondescript, but a few years ago a lovely park was built here which will undoubtedly intrigue Bowser. The interior design of Le Meridien, on the other hand, remains just as beautiful as ever. Le Meridien has well earned its reputation as being one of Boston's more elegant hotels. Guests are often struck by the intimacy of the lobby where low, recessed ceilings are accented with crystal chandeliers that reflect a soft light off the rose-colored walls and traditional furnishings. As guests walk further into the hotel, they will encounter walls of glass, open spaces that rise six floors, and intimate sitting areas.

There are two restaurants at Le Meridien, each having an equally distinct ambiance. Julien is the premier restaurant. Diners might begin their evening in the classic sitting room just above the dining room, where the elegant furnishings are complemented by the grand mahogany bar and the carved gold inlaid ceilings. The restaurant's cuisine may be primarily Nouvelle, but the classic architecture is old world. The narrow windows were formerly gun ports guarding the entrance to the building. Today, the old vault, once reserved for precious valuables, is now the pastry pantry. The huge mirrors, inset into the carved block on one wall, reflect the light from the enormous crystal chandeliers and small table lamps. The menu changes frequently, with appetizers such as a salmon souffle, breast of Muscovey duck in a terrine with baby vegetables, and the Maine lobster on a saffron pasta. The entrées include a lamb loin stuffed with a spinach mousse, a breast of duckling with apples and huckleberries, and sautéed medallions of venison loin.

The adjacent Café Fleuri is an equally striking space, but for different reasons. It is located at the base of a six-story atrium filled with plants and natural light. The Cafe's Sunday brunch is extravagant, with ten stations serving an array of foods. Guests can try the Far East corner, where platters of sushi and stir fry are waiting or head over to the French Country area, with the pâtés, fresh breads, and dozen or so different kinds of luscious salads. One table contains a long wooden boat filled with huge shrimp, mussels, smoked salmon and capers. Anyone who can save enough room for dessert will be able to select from at least 30 different confections, that are as beautifully presented as they are tasty. It is no wonder that Café Fleuri consistently is voted as serving one of the best brunches in Boston. They now have another award to be proud of, the "Best Indulgence" in Boston. This is for their Chocolate Bar, where chocoholics can indulge in chocolate éclairs, crêpes, light and dark chocolate mousses, pies, fondue, and an array of other delectables.

Le Meridien is not all about eating though, they also have equally impressive guest chambers. These are not cookie cutter rooms, where each one resembles the next. Out of over 300 chambers, each is unique architecturally as well as in terms of its interior design. Some of these bedrooms are ell-shaped and many of the exterior walls (where the old building meets the new) are of sloping glass. Many of the small suites have bedroom lofts and first floor sitting rooms that are naturally lit by floor-to-ceiling windows. Other spaces have intimate nooks and alcoves into which are tucked comfortable sofas or canopy beds. The hotel plans to renovate all of the bedrooms starting in 1995. For the next few years though, guests will still find sophisticated black lacquered and mahogany furnishings that are reproductions of classic French and English antiques. Chintz draperies are coordinated with the quilted bedspreads, which are done in rich chocolate, coffee, and taupe color schemes. Live plants and flower arrangements further enhance the effect. At night, guests return to find their beds turned down, French chocolates placed on the pillows and Evian water set upon the bedside table. As would be expected in a hotel of this caliber, there is a mini-bar, clock radio, and telephone in the room. The tiled bathrooms contain marble sinks and are stocked with a vast array of European toiletries, a bathroom scale, hair dryer, and terry robe. Mirrors on the closet doors make even the smallest chambers appear quite spacious.

Before either breakfast or one of the delicious brunches, energetic souls might like to visit Le Club Meridien, where they will find a spa and swimming pool, along with state-of-the-art workout equipment. Bowser might prefer a quick walk in any number of nearby parks. Later, guests can walk a few blocks to Faneuil Hall and then perhaps over to the waterfront, where there is another attractive waterside park to investigate. A five minute walk in another direction will bring guests over the hill and into the Boston Common and the more formal Boston Public Gardens and perhaps down along Commonwealth Avenue. Just as Boston has been named the most livable city in the country, Le Meridien continues to maintain its reputation as one its premier hotels.

The Ritz-Carlton

15 Arlington Street,
Boston, Massachusetts   02117
(800) 241-3333, (617) 536-5700, Fax (617) 536-9340

Manager: Sigi Brauer
Rooms: 278 doubles and suites
Rates: Doubles $260-385 (EP), Suites $325-1,495 (EP)
Payment: AE, CB, DC, DSC, ENR, JCB, MC, and VISA
Children: Welcome (cribs, cots, highchairs, and babysitters are available)
Dogs: Welcome with a $25 deposit
Open: All year

The Ritz-Carlton is one of Boston's many great traditions, having developed a reputation for impeccable service, fine food, and elegant accommodations over the last six decades. An extensive renovation was completed in 1985, when guest rooms were stripped down to the bare walls. Windows, wall moldings, plumbing, and ventilation systems were all updated. Even with extensive refurbishing, the charm and character of the grand old hotel remains intact. This is evident upon entering the lobby, where the elegant decor and furnishings can still transport one back to the days of Brahmin opulence. The ornate woodwork glows with renewed life and, of course, every piece of brass has been polished to a brilliant luster. This is one of the few hotels left in the United States where white-gloved elevator operators and a butler on every floor are still fashionable.

As guests walk along the halls to their rooms, they will most certainly cross from the original building into a newer one, completed in the early 1980s, but even the most practiced eye will be hard-pressed to know the difference. The same dove gray walls framed by white moldings, and crystal chandeliers give the entire hotel an old world elegance. Although each guest room maintains its own character, all have been decorated in what the management calls a French Provincial style. We found the overall effect to be quite formal. Most often, teal green and rose chintz frames the windows and covers the fitted bedspreads, while cut glass and brass lamps illuminate the dressing tables and oversized beveled mirrors. As one would expect at The Ritz, modern amenities such as televisions, fully-stocked honor bars, and refrigerators have been discreetly tucked away in the armoires. The closets lock, as does the safe inside each one. The marble bathrooms are well-appointed, with fine European toiletries, immense towels bearing the cobalt blue Ritz insignia, and terry robes. Some of the accommodations in the new addition have sunny window alcoves outfitted with chintz covered armchairs set around a side table. The guest rooms in greatest demand overlook either the Boston Public Garden or the twinkling lights of Newbury Street. Our favorites are the corner suites that offer views of both. Perhaps the most unusual aspects about the hotel are the woodburning fireplaces found in many of the suites. For those who require a little more pampering, there is also the Club Level, which not only offers a little more privacy and comfort but also complimentary food, beverage, butler and concierge services. On all floors, the morning newspaper awaits on the credenza by the elevator, so that guests may take a copy with them to breakfast. Whether one is staying in a single bedroom or the Presidential Suite, guests will find that with well over 500 staff members, the service and attention to detail is impeccable.

The hotel offers many enticing excuses for venturing out of the lovely bedrooms. High Tea is served every afternoon in The Lounge. Guests often stay for hours, indulging on scones and intriguing sandwiches while sipping imported teas in a traditional English fashion. Just across from the Lounge is the formal main dining room, where enormous windows offer pretty views of the Boston Public Gardens. Fine crystal and china are set on linen covered tables, including their trademark blue cobalt glasses. The unobtrusive staff is adept at catering to patrons in virtually flawless style. The menu is in French, although for those unfamiliar with the language there is a translation just below each description. Guests might want to start with a lobster bisque laced with armagnac, escargots, or the Beluga caviar served the traditional way, of course. The changing Continental menu offers everything from lobster in a delicate whiskey sauce and scallops and calamari in a lime and ginger sauce to a broiled veal chop with rosemary honey sauce and the sautéed beef tenderloin served with duck liver and wild mushrooms. Lastly, after a delicious meal, many gravitate to the fireplace in the Ritz Bar. This is the epitome of old Boston, with a dark wood paneled room that lends itself to quiet conversation. The actual bar is exceptionally complete, containing fine, aged whiskeys, unusual aperitifs and cordials, and a variety of ports; however, the 13 varieties of martinis are also quite a draw for both locals and visitors alike.

The Ritz is indeed a special spot, consistently and conscientiously making an effort to put its guests needs above all else, which is why it has been able to develop such a loyal clientele over the years. The Ritz also happens to be centrally located to most of Boston's cultural and scenic attractions, allowing guests to leave their car behind and walk everywhere. Bowser will certainly enjoy a stroll down any one of the lovely residential streets in the Back Bay and Beacon Hill areas. Commonwealth Avenue is especially enticing for leisurely walks, as there is a central sidewalk lined with plenty of grass and shade trees. He may also enjoy accompanying his two-legged friends along the Freedom Trail that meanders through many of Boston's historic districts. The Esplanade along the Charles River is a short hop from the hotel as are the Boston Public Gardens and Boston Common.

High Brewster

964 Satucket Road
Brewster, Massachusetts 02631
(800) 203-2634, (508) 896-3636

Innkeeper: Frances Herman
Rooms: 2 doubles, 4 cottages
Rates: Doubles $80-100 (B&B), Cottages $100-190 (EP)
Payment: AE, MC, and VISA
Children: Welcome
Dogs: Welcome in the cottages
Open: April through December

Brewster is an historic village, located on the quiet, north side of Cape Cod. Driving along rural Route 6A, travelers will discover a host of 200-year-old sea captain's houses, country stores, and antique shops. The back country roads also wend by scenic ponds and salt marshes, all of which reflect an idyllic and unspoiled part of the Cape. High Brewster, fortunately enough, also maintains this kind of ambiance. Tucked away on a rock and grass studded knoll overlooking Lower Mill Pond, High Brewster has been around for years. It has not only built a strong reputation for its fine food and intimate dining, but also for its unique accommodations. The restaurant and a few guest rooms are housed in the main inn, which retains an antique atmosphere, along with assorted cottages placed discreetly about the grounds. Three houses were actually built here in 1738, on land granted to Nathaniel Winslow by the King of England. For the next 200 years the Winslow family retained control of the property. Over the years, two of the buildings were dismantled and the overall acreage reduced, but guests will still feel a strong sense of history associated with High Brewster.

We loved the feeling of High Brewster from the moment we drove onto the gravel drive. The three and a half acres are encircled by rock walls, studded with mature trees, and dotted with lawns that are made all the more private with mature plantings. As we walked around the property, we would come across small gardens framed by rock walls, where a chair or bench had been placed to take advantage of the private and pretty setting. The largest expanse of lawn is perhaps the most picturesque, with benches set on a point overlooking the trees and pond below.

The cottage that offers the best vantage point in this bucolic setting is called, appropriately enough, Pond Cottage. It, like all of the other cottages, is a gray weathered-shingle building with barn red trim. Its one room is furnished with a white wicker bed and country antiques. There is nothing fancy here, the pine board walls are painted white and the kitchenette is retro-1950s, but it is attractive in a very casual sort of way. The high ceilings make it almost seem spacious, and the crowning glory is the screened-in porch, which is accessed through a wall of sliding glass doors. The porch has even more wicker chairs, and guests are often quite content to just visit, read, or watch the wildlife around the pond. Just behind Pond Cottage is the smallest cottage, but what it lacks in size it more than makes up for in character. The vaulted ceilings have exposed handhewn beams. Once again, the natural board walls have been whitewashed, as has the bedstead. An antique oak armoire, nicely complements the country cottage decor. A pair of Adirondack chairs have been placed upon the small deck, which overlooks the grounds and the inn.

Anyone who is searching for more spacious accommodations, should consider either the Barn Cottage or Brook House. The former was built on the site of the original barn, and has roughhewn walls and high ceilings. We especially liked this cottage, as it was furnished with beautiful country antiques. A pretty table was placed in front of a set of windows to take advantage of the southern exposure. The comfortable sofa and armchairs were gathered around the fireplace. The white kitchen was another sunny space, and even though it had old-fashioned cupboards, the refrigerator and other fixtures were quite modern. A room with a queen-size bed is found downstairs, while a bunk room is located upstairs. The slate patio is an ideal spot for some impromptu entertaining and summertime barbecuing on the Weber grill. Finally, there is the Brook House, which is more contemporary in appearance and feeling. The living room is the focal point for this house, with hardwood floors that are covered with area rugs. A floral patterned sofa and a rocking chair draped with a blanket face the big brick fireplace. Once again, the dining room table is placed in a sunny corner, allowing guests to peek through the surrounding trees and see the glimmering waters of the pond. A full kitchen is an added convenience as well. We liked the idea of sitting out on the private deck and taking an afternoon nap. The two bedrooms are furnished with country antiques and reproductions. One contains a four-poster natural pine bed that is backed by a decorative windowpane mirror. The other room has a bureau and double bed that are painted in matching colors. Guests will thoroughly enjoy the fact that nothing is overdone or too new, but is instead attractive, extremely comfortable, and very inviting.

Even though most of the cottages have kitchen facilities, guests would be remiss if they did not sample at least one dinner at the inn. There are three intimate dining rooms in here, where barnboard walls and low-beamed ceilings create the perfect backdrop for the small tables lit by oil lamps and graced with flowers. The varied menu offers such entrées as rack of lamb with a dried black current demi-glace, an oven roasted salmon covered with herbs and a spicy rouille, and a tenderloin of beef served on a bed of spinach with carmelized onions and boursin cheese.

There is plenty for Bowser to do at High Brewster, as well. Just below the inn, is the historic Grist Mill and Herring Run. In the spring, guests can take their canine cohort over to the run, and watch the herring make their way along it. There is also an extensive bike trail that runs close to the inn, which is a terrific place to take a walk with Bowser. Nickerson State Park is within easy driving distance of High Brewster, and visitors will find many hiking trails to explore. Although the National Seashore is off limits to dogs, there are still plenty of salt marshes and other beaches within an easy drive of the inn. Just ask, and one of the staff will be more than happy to offer an array of suggestions that would appeal to guests and their dogs.

The Bertram Inn

92 Sewall Avenue
Brookline, Massachusetts   02146
(800) 295-3822, (617) 566-2234, Fax (617) 277-1887

Manager: Erin Clairmont
Rooms: 12 doubles
Rates: $69-154 (B&B)
Payment: MC and VISA
Children: Not appropriate for children under seven years of age (cots are available)
Dogs: Welcome provided there are not more than two dogs per room
Open: All year

Brookline, just outside of Boston, is a wonderful mix of quiet residential neighborhoods and interesting shops and restaurants. This gives visitors the feeling of being in the suburbs, yet with close access to the excitement and diversity of the city. While Boston accommodations are limited to large hotels, Brookline and its environs offer more intimate accommodations. We found just the right spot, on a quiet tree-lined street, in a residential part of Brookline. The Bertram Inn is a turn-of-the-century Victorian that offers an array of attractively decorated guest rooms with a charming ambiance.

A cobblestone walk leads guests to an elongated front porch, where the walls of paned windows that protect it from the cold in the winter months are replaced each spring with screens to allow the cool air to circulate. This is just one of the many pleasant living spaces at the inn, with a pair of hunter green benches and a handful of rocking chairs set upon a braided rug. Upon entering the wood paneled foyer, we couldn't help but be drawn to the grand staircase which dominates this space. Antiques, Oriental rugs, and an array of collectibles set the decorative tone for this, and many of the other common areas. A good-size living room offers more Oriental rugs set on hardwood floors, along with a comfortable green velvet couch and armchairs that are gathered around the fireplace. The Victorian antiques fit in well with the equally Victorian architectural features in here. Some of the more noteworthy aspects are the window alcove backed by leaded glass, the dark wood paneling around the fireplace, and the intricate moldings across the ceiling. This is a well-utilized space, as it is also the site for a hearty Continental breakfast each morning. This is served on a large buffet table at the far end of the room. Next to it there is a small closet, fronted by a curtain, containing a refrigerator, in which guests may store any snacks or perishables. The morning meal includes an array of fresh fruit, juices, muffins, bagels, morning breads, and hot and cold beverages.

The guest bedrooms are located on all three floors of the inn. One of our favorites is a wonderful wood paneled chamber off the foyer with a king-size bedstead set on an Oriental rug. The fireplace lends the room even more character, and the television is an added convenience. The wonderful, old-fashioned bathroom completes the setting. As guests ascend the staircase, they will pass by old portraits and paintings of schooners, along with a window seat filled with interesting knickknacks and a pair of ship models. Most of the chambers on the second floor are also quite spacious and are furnished with high, queen-size four-poster beds, and still more Oriental rugs topped by lovely antiques. One of the bedrooms is decorated with a lovely crimson floral wallpaper, and adjoined by a bathroom which is certainly eye-catching as it is painted a tropical lime green. Those who enjoy sunny spaces, may wish to reserve Room 5, a corner room with many windows. It has been furnished with a double bedstead, but one of its most interesting aspects is the mural of a library wall which was painted by the owner's wife, Sierra. The third floor chambers have ceiling fans and sloping eaves. Regardless of the bedroom, guests are certain to appreciate the festive floral wall treatments, coordinated decor, and the eclectic assortment of antiques and period furnishings that make each room unique. All of the bathrooms are private, and a few of them have been carved out of the house's original closets.

Bowser will certainly appreciate the residential neighborhood that surrounds The Bertram Inn. From here, it is an easy walk to the many interesting shops, restaurants, and boutiques in the area. The Boston College campus is within easy driving distance of the inn and provides some wonderful open green space for walking with Bowser. There are also many parks in and around Brookline that require no car to find, but are well worth visiting with your canine cohort. We were pleased to discover the inn, and feel that it provides a nice respite from the normal city environment.

The Charles Hotel

One Bennett at Eliot Street
Cambridge, Massachusetts   02138
(800) 882-1818, (617) 864-1200, Fax (617) 864-5715

Manager: Brian Fitzgerald
Rooms: 252 doubles, 44 suites
Rates: Doubles $195-265 (EP), Suites $375-625 (EP)
Payment: AE, MC, DC, DSC, MC, and VISA
Children: Welcome (cribs, cots, highchairs, and babysitters can be arranged)
Dogs: Welcome with a refundable $100 damage deposit
Open: All year

Harvard Square has always been a hub of activity for Cambridge, while still managing to hold onto its unique community feeling. The Charles Hotel, set just off the square, offers the intimacy of a small hotel, yet has the sophistication that is often best exemplified by many of the larger four-star hotels across the river in Boston. The Charles Hotel is actually a part of a larger complex, that is comprised of a number of distinctive shops and excellent restaurants. Within the hotel, guests will also find two equally intriguing restaurants and a full-service health spa.

The original designers of The Charles Hotel created interesting guest rooms that have withstood the test of time. Down quilts with subdued geometric patterned coverlets adorn the beds. These spaces are brightened by light contemporary wallpapers and pine furnishings. Reproductions of Shaker furnishings are evident from the writing desks to the armoires that conceal both a television and mini-bar. Standard amenities include three telephones and two televisions (one in the bedroom and the other in the bathroom). The good-size bathrooms are outfitted with scales, hair dryers, and a full complement of soaps, shampoos, and lotions. The showers have shaving mirrors mounted in them and thick terry robes are comfortable for either after-bath lounging or to cover guests as they make their way to and from the indoor pool. During our visit, a sampling of Origins therapeutic herbal extracts had been left in the room for us to try. There is also a book delivery service, which can deliver virtually any book directly to the guest rooms. The hotel has five different room configurations. Even the smallest of these is fitted with an intimate sitting area. The larger chambers provide enough space for a breakfast table, and the suites have separate living rooms and wet bars, as well as additional amenities.

The warmth reflected in the guest rooms is also apparent in many of the hotel's public areas. Handmade antique quilts hang on the walls throughout the building alongside original "realist" art. As guests make their way up and down the central staircase, they will certainly notice the collection of quilts covering one huge two-story wall. Upstairs, there are two restaurants and the Regatta Bar. The informal *Bennett Street Cafe* is a terrific place for breakfast and lunch, but it is especially well known for its Sunday brunches, which have earned them a "Best of Boston" award. The *Regatta Bar* (which has also won the "Best of Boston" award five times as being the best jazz bar), on the other hand, is a stylish bar which features local jazz groups, as well as visiting artists such as Herbie Hancock, Stan Getz, Dave Brubeck, and Chick Corea. *Rialto* is the newest addition to the hotel. Under the watchful eye of Michela Larson and award wining Chef Jody Adams, this too will undoubtedly be winning accolades before too long. With the change in cuisine, also came a change in the restaurant's physical appearance. The new Mediterranean theme is reflected in the openness of the dining room, and in its earth tone decor.

After dinner it is always fun to walk through Harvard Square. Many of the bookstores stay open late, and of course there are also a variety of night clubs, theaters, and comedy clubs that offer evening entertainment. Harvard Square is also known for its street-side entertainment that ranges from guitar trios, folk singers, and steel bands to magicians, mimes, and jugglers. For those who choose to stay within the hotel complex, there is the state-of-the-art health club, Le Pli. This is a private three-story spa offering steam rooms, whirlpools, a sauna, and an array of high-tech workout equipment. Special programs include aerobic dancing, as well as a full range of herbal body wraps and body massages. Guests will also discover an indoor swimming pool surrounded by walls of windows and an array of interesting artwork suspended from the ceiling.

If Bowser is anxious to go for a walk, we recommend taking a nice stroll down by the Charles River and then back up along Brattle Street, where there are some lovely historic mansions. Others might want to take Bowser over to Harvard Yard, where there are plenty of grassy areas to investigate. Those who want to wander further afield can hop in the car and head over to Fresh Pond, where there is a reservoir, a jogging/walking path, and a small park. If after all these excursions, Bowser wants to stay at the hotel and rest, guests may leave him with the concierge while they finish up any unfinished business.

The Victorian Inn

P.O. Box 947
24 South Water Street
Edgartown, Massachusetts 02539
(508) 627-4784

Innkeepers: Steven and Karyn Caliri
Rooms: 14 doubles
Rates: $90-190 (B&B)
Payment: MC and VISA
Children: Welcome
Dogs: Welcome with prior approval during the quieter times of the year
Open: All year

Edgartown has long been a favorite destination on Martha's Vineyard, as much for its picturesque harbor setting as for the abundance of interesting shopping and restaurant options. Those who would like to stay right in the center of town, on a street that fronts the harbor, should consider the lovely Victorian Inn. Originally built in 1820, the inn is situated just a block or so off the main street just opposite the infamous Pagoda Tree. The three-story building has white clapboards and black shutters, along with a variety of interesting porches, balconies, and decks.

Once inside, guests will clearly understand where the inn gets its name. This is authentically Victorian, both from an architectural standpoint and in the way it has been decorated. A first floor parlor is probably one of the first chambers guests will enter. The navy blue floral wallpapers are a striking complement to the dark marbled fireplace. The intimate sitting area is framed by tables holding dried flower arrangements, brass lamps, and an assortment of knickknacks. A decanter of sherry is placed on top of the butler's tray table. The dining room is one of the other inviting common areas, found just off the main staircase. A delicate striped floral wallpaper has been used in here, which is accented with dried wreaths and framed prints of noteworthy houses. The handful of tables are surrounded by Windsor chairs. A ceiling fan provides a cooling effect in the summertime, and the fireplace makes the chamber all the more comfortable in the cooler months. On especially warm, sunny mornings guests often enjoy taking their morning meal out to the brick garden terrace. This is one of our favorite places at the inn, as it is surrounded by a tall, white fence and edged with a perennial garden whose flowers inevitably climb up the fence and entwine the arbor. This charming garden setting is enhanced by the large, white umbrella tables. Based on ambiance alone, it is no wonder that the Victorian Inn has won praise from the *Cape Cod Life Magazine* as serving the "best breakfast on Martha's Vineyard."

Guests will be equally pleased with the bedrooms. These vary as much in size and decor as they do in the types of furnishings they offer. One cozy chamber is furnished with a pair of antique milk-painted twin beds covered in colorful country quilts. A basket of dried flowers rests in the windowed alcove that is fitted with shutters. Many of the other chambers are wallpapered in delicate florals and paisleys, reflecting a range of colors from navy to salmon. Off-white wainscotings certainly add to the effect. The combination of sheer curtains at the windows and pale carpets make each of these bedrooms light and airy. Four-poster and canopy beds are placed in many of the chambers, while others have brass or cherry wood bedsteads. As with the common rooms, these chambers are outfitted with brass lamps and sconces, ceiling fans, and dried wreaths and flower arrangements placed on the tables. While one second-floor guest room has an enclosed porch, all of the third floor bedrooms have balconies or decks and the best views of the harbor and Edgartown.

Visitors to Martha's Vineyard will find there are a myriad of diversions to enjoy both in Edgartown and around the island. There are numerous beaches that range from the generally calm waters found at the Bend in the Road to the predominantly surf-like conditions out at South Beach. There are bicycle paths that wend their way around the island and out to the beaches. These are as conducive to bicycling or roller blading as they are to walking or running with Bowser. A walk along North Water Street will lead people out toward lighthouse beach. Heading out a little further down the road, visitors come to a spit of sand that surrounds Eel Pond. This is wonderful place to look for shells, or just watch the sailboats come in and out of the harbor. Take the ferry across the channel to Chappaquidick. From there, it is a short drive to an expansive beach called Wasque, which looks out toward Nantucket. One of the innumerable benefits to vacationing on Martha's Vineyard is that whatever people choose to do on the island, Bowser is a more than welcome participant.

Brandt House Bed and Breakfast

29 Highland Avenue
Greenfield, Massachusetts 01301
(800) 235-3329, (413) 774-3329, Fax (413) 772-2908

Hostess: *Phoebe Compton*
Rooms: *8 guest rooms*
Rates: *$75-110 (B&B)*
Payment: *MC and VISA*
Children: *Not appropriate for very small children*
Dogs: *Well-behaved dogs are welcome with prior approval*
Open: *All year*

The quiet town of Greenfield lies near the banks of the Connecticut River and the main thoroughfare leading from Massachusetts into Vermont. The road that wends past the town center eventually leads to a hill lined with classic antique Victorian homes. Near the crest of this hill, visitors will see a beautifully restored, 16-room Victorian mansion, known as the Brandt House. A winding driveway leads new arrivals past the house's expansive wraparound porch to the rear of the building. It is from this vantage point that the property truly begins to unfold, as guests first see a flagstone patio, set with wicker furniture, that overlooks the terraced lawns, lovely gardens, and a clay tennis court.

We were pleased to discover the Brandt House, and it alone is worth a visit Greenfield. The renovation of the house took some two years and was orchestrated by Phoebe Compton. From the intimate foyer, guests will find their way into the adjacent billiard room, which is dominated by a red felt pool table set on an Oriental rug. A windowed alcove is accented by potted plants, and in the winter months, a fire is crackling in the hearth. Guests will then pass through a pair of pocket doors, across red fir floors covered with dhurrie rugs, and into the living room. This lovely chamber has one of those deep, soft sofas that people want to curl up in and never leave. Huge, formal pine chests and tables have a soft patina, that is even prettier at night with the flickering lights, emanating from the fireplace, dancing across their surfaces. A piano sits off to one side, while the sunlight streaming in from a windowed alcove brings out the detail in the wainscoting and beamed ceiling.

Phoebe can usually be found tending to her other guests or preparing an afternoon treat in her bright, modern kitchen. Another pair of pocket doors leads from the kitchen into a fabulous sunny space, the dining room. A long wall of French doors, along with a pair of windows, allows sunlight to stream across the huge oak table that seats twelve for breakfast comfortably. Guests may dine here family-style, or at a private table set in a living room alcove. On sunny, warm mornings, many head outdoors. The enormous wraparound porch, is outfitted with a lovely mixture of wicker and glass furnishings set amid a pair of rocking chairs, a white wicker bench, and a porch swing suspended from the boxed beams. Another favorite spot to take one's breakfast, or to just relax for that matter, is on the slate terrace overlooking the formal gardens. The breakfasts are a light Continental fare, with homemade granola, freshly baked breads and muffins, and coffee or tea on the abbreviated menu. Weekend guests are usually offered an entrée, as well.

The bedrooms are just as appealing as the mansion's common rooms. These are accessed by way of a central staircase, which leads to doors opening into individually decorated chambers. The lovely color schemes range from crimson and slate gray to a variety of pastel hues. Sunny alcoves are common, but if guests want a fireplace, they should request it in advance. The fluffy feather beds are often covered with beautiful white linen duvet covers, and small Oriental rugs or dhurries have been selected to cover the fir floors. Although the third floor chambers are somewhat smaller, they appear larger and lighter due to the skylights set into the eaves. Even the bathrooms benefit from the extra natural light these roof top windows provide. Vases of dried and fresh flowers accent the handsome array of antique furnishings. This is country elegance at its best, with wicker, pine, and classic English antiques combining for a delightful, albeit eclectic, effect. The little extras, such as bathrobes, remote controlled televisions, and private telephones make guests feel welcomed and comfortable.

While many may find it difficult to leave their luxurious bedrooms, the sun room is another wonderful spot for relaxing. Here, three walls of windows create a virtual greenhouse for all the plants. Attractive blue sofas and matching chairs with ottomans invite guests to put up their feet and either read or watch television. Phoebe has also installed a microwave in here, for those who may want to prepare their own snacks. There are over three acres to investigate with Bowser, as well as good walking paths in the adjacent woods. In the winter months, the local pond freezes for skating and the woods are a cross-country skier's paradise. More structured diversions, such as golf, white-water rafting, or downhill skiing are just a short drive from the B&B. History buffs will undoubtedly want to visit the picturesque village of Deerfield and its perfectly preserved antique homes. Anyone who wants to hike in the local hills should check out Mount Grace, Erving, or Wendell State Forests, all of which are due east of the Brandt House. Wendell State Forest is the largest of these, offering 9,000 plus acres of wilderness to explore with Bowser.

Harbor Walk

6 Freeman Street
Harwich Port, Massachusetts   02646
(508) 432-1675

Hosts: Marilyn and Preston Barry
Rooms: 6 doubles, 1 cottage
Rates: Doubles $45-60 (EP), Cottage $600/week
Payment: Personal checks
Children: Not appropriate for children under the age of two
Dogs: Welcome in the first floor room
Open: April 1 through November 15

Anyone familiar with the Cape knows about Hyannis and Chatham. The former was made famous by the Kennedys and the latter has become newsworthy due to the recent ocean storms that have breached the town's barrier beach and washed away valuable property. Travelers who are looking for a seaside destination that combines the feeling of these two towns, should consider staying in Harwich Port. This unpretentious community lies along the south coast of the cape overlooking Nantucket Sound. Just a short walk from the picturesque Wychmere Harbor area, with its array of shops and fine restaurants, visitors will find the Harbor Walk.

In 1880, Ensign Rogers built this expansive Victorian summer house to seek refuge from the ocean, and at the same time, to stay close to it. Today, the house is set behind a large, sculpted hedge in a quiet, residential neighborhood. Even with the passage of time, it is still resplendent with its wraparound porch, huge eaves, multiple dormers, and seemingly endless additions. In keeping with the nautical theme, a crushed shell driveway leads new arrivals onto the property. As they approach the house, they will be able to more closely inspect the decorative shingling and the detailed corner pieces that frame the tops of the porch pillars. In the summer months, baskets of impatiens hang from the porch.

Although the outside of Harbor Walk appears to ramble, the inside is actually quite intimate. The living room is furnished with an eclectic array of pieces, ranging from antique to the more contemporary. This is a well lived-in home, where guests feel as though they are part of the Barry family. Some even feel free to use the Nordic Track that is conveniently placed near the television in the living room. The breakfast room is one of our favorite spaces in the house. Windows encircle the room, and in front of each one is a pretty wicker planter filled with a profusion of flowers. The burgundy and cream colors in the wallpaper reflect the Colonial period and accentuate the deep blues and reds in the Oriental rug covering the hardwood floor. Sheer tie-back curtains allow the sun to permeate this inviting room. The oval mahogany table always has a fresh arrangement of flowers, and is often set with fine glass and china on French Provincial place mat. Each morning, a Continental breakfast is served, which guests may enjoy at the table, in their room, or out on the porch. There are many wonderful homemade treats; however, the house specialty is Kütchen.

The bedrooms are primarily found on the second floor of the house; however, people traveling with a dog will stay in the Bayberry Room on the first floor because it provides easy access to the outdoors. Guests will notice this room immediately upon entering the house, as its doorway frame is tucked under the diagonal staircase that climbs to the second floor. The Bayberry Room is an ell-shaped chamber, whose centerpiece is a four-poster bed draped with a colorful handmade quilt. The painted hardwood floor is topped by a braided rug. A set of windows lines the corner of the room and overlooks the small yard. The private bathroom has a stall shower. Most of the upstairs bedrooms reflect the same feeling, with four-poster beds that rest on painted hardwood floors. The walls are a mix of pastel colors that have been combined with stenciling to create an inviting seaside atmosphere. These chambers have either private or shared bathrooms.

There are plenty of opportunities for exercising Bowser in Harwich Port. The residential neighborhood lends itself to long walks. Early in the morning is a great time to head for the beach to stroll along the water. In the summer months, sailing, tennis, and golf are the predominant diversions of choice. There is also a 22-mile scenic bicycle path that proves enticing. If Bowser is the energetic sort, he may enjoy walking along with you or following alongside as you bicycle. Some of the more noteworthy people-oriented pleasures include a visit to the weekly auctions, a seasonal craft festival, and the nine-day Cranberry Harvest Festival.

Harbor Village

P.O. Box 635
Greenwood Avenue
Hyannis Port, Massachusetts   02647
(508) 775-7581

Manager: Marijane Mahan
Rooms: 20 one- to four-bedroom cottages
Rates: Summer season $850-1,400 per week (EP, one week minimum),
    Off season $100-150 per night (EP, 3-night minimum)
Payment: Personal checks
Children: Welcome (cribs and highchairs are available)
Dogs: Welcome with prior approval and a $25 fee
Open: May to mid-October

Over the years, Hyannis and Hyannis Port have received an inordinate amount of media attention due as much to their celebrated residents as to their white sand beaches and warm waters. As a result, this once sleepy summer community has become inundated with tourists and retirees. It is still a very popular vacation destination; the trick is in finding a peaceful corner to call your own. The Harbor Village in Hyannis Port offers a welcome solution.

While the Harbor Village cottages are only a few minutes from downtown Hyannis, the 17 acres surrounding this retreat make it seem much more remote. A black iron fence and a pair of cobblestone pillars flank the entrance to the gravel drive leading to the cottage resort. Guests wend their way through groves of scrub pine trees and planters overflowing with flowers, until they arrive at the center of the complex. The cottages, some of which are replicas of noteworthy Cape Cod homes, are located around the perimeter of the circular drive offering views of the grounds and the sparkling Nantucket Sound. Each is privately owned and thus unique in both design, decor, and furnishings.

The cottage exteriors vary from gray, weathered shingles to painted clapboards and shutters. Some of the small-paned windows are decorated with window boxes teaming with flowers. The charming, attractively landscaped yards are fronted by split-rail fences, and the large decks offer views of the tidal cove, the sound, or the woods. A grill is provided for each of the cottages, allowing guests the opportunity to cook out on their private deck. When they do venture back inside, there is a fully-equipped kitchen (some have dishwashers) with either an adjacent dining room or separate eating area. Living rooms have fireplaces, comfortable furnishings, and cable televisions. The decor ranges from country to contemporary, with some that are just plain eclectic. The cottages have from one to four bedrooms. The largest of these is the Red School House, located in the center of the complex. Linens, towels (large beach towels are not offered and guests are advised to bring their own), and blankets are provided, as is daily maid service. Before making a reservation, we recommend deciding which amenities, furnishings, and decor are most suitable. Some people might be more concerned with the cottage's relationship to its neighbors and the water. Each cottage does have a water view, some are just more distant than others.

The Harbor Village offers all guests direct access to the tidal cove which, since our last visit, has unfortunately filled in somewhat due to the number of coastal storms this community has suffered. There is also a private boat house and a sandy beach for guests to use. The Harbor Village is an ideal mini-resort for those who prefer to be off the beaten track, but still close enough to the stores and restaurants. A footpath leads out to Quohog Beach. This should be a favorite walk for Bowser in the early morning and evening. Anyone who wants to take an interesting day trip, can bring Bowser on the ferry that leaves from Hyannis for Martha's Vineyard or Nantucket. While there is a state forest and a state beach within a half-hour drive of Hyannis Port, many visitors prefer to bring their canine companion and investigate the picturesque shorelines, ponds, and lakes in the immediate area.

Walker House

64 Walker Street
Lenox, Massachusetts   01240
(800) 235-3098, (413) 637-1271, Fax (413) 637-2387

Innkeepers: *Peggy and Richard Houdek*
Rooms: *8 doubles*
Rates: *$57-160 (B&B)*
Payment: *Personal checks*
Children: *Not appropriate for children under 12 years of age*
Dogs: *Accepted with prior approval*
Open: *All year*

The Berkshires are a wonderful place to visit any time of year, and in the heart of these scenic hills lies the picturesque town of Lenox. Long known as the summer home for the Boston Symphony Orchestra, the tiny village has always attracted people with an interest in the arts. Over the last century, they have built grand "summer" houses and before that, lovely Federal style houses along the main streets in the town. The Walker House, built in 1804, is one of the oldest buildings in town and one of the few remaining examples of classic American-Federal architecture. The Houdeks have owned the inn for almost 15 years. Although they once were involved in the arts in California (Peggy was an opera singer and editor for an arts magazine and Dick was an art critic and an administrator for an art school), they decided to leave their careers behind and start a new life in the New

England area. They packed up a "truckload of inappropriate furnishings from the Early L.A. Spanish period," and drove to their newly purchased 9,000 square-foot Colonial mansion in the Berkshires. They realized that their eclectic combination of furniture and the traditional backdrop of the house were incompatible, so they quickly switched gears. Two months later the place was more appropriately furnished and painted to reflect its New England heritage. They welcomed their first guests, wondering all along, "Would strangers want to stay? For a weekend? Here?" The answer was, and is, a resounding "Yes!"

Upon entering the foyer, visitor's eyes are drawn to the high, detailed ceilings and the long, graceful staircase. Further down the hall, which is lined with an array of antique doorstops that Peggy has collected over the years, there is a large dining room with a fireplace. This formal space has an added touch of whimsy, as a menagerie of stuffed animals can be found comfortably sitting around the dining room table and on the surrounding armchairs. Bowser will probably be more interested in the resident house cats that can occasionally be seen roaming around the inn. In the morning, all of the stuffed animals relinquish their places to the guests, who are then offered a generous Continental breakfast of juice, fresh fruit, and homemade croissants, biscuits, and muffins. Assorted cereals are also available, as is coffee, tea, and milk. If it is a particularly sunny morning, this repast is served on the veranda, where guests are surrounded by white wicker and potted plants. In the afternoon, guests may meander back into the dining room for formal tea. This is one of our favorite spots at the inn, as the wall of windows dominating the end of the room provides beautiful views of the formal gardens that stand out against the dark green backdrop of pine and cedar trees. A massive sliding wooden door leads from the dining room into the parlor. This spacious forest green chamber contains many treasures, including an old music box, a grand piano, and deep, comfortable sofas facing the large fireplace. People are welcome to enjoy a quiet evening in here, or visit the library for a high tech option. Here, walls of bookshelves merely set the tone for the operas, films, and plays that are shown on the seven-foot television screen.

When guests are ready to retire at night, they will go to sleep in a bedroom named after one of the Houdeks' favorite composers. Some might stay in rooms bearing the names of Beethoven, Mozart, Handel, Chopin, Tchaikovsky or Verdi. One of these chambers is furnished with a canopy bed and beautiful Victorian antiques that the Houdeks have acquired at auction over the years. Another room has a gigantic brass bed facing a working fireplace. A pair of white iron and brass double beds have been selected for the green and white garden room. The bedrooms toward the rear of the house are particularly bright and sunny, whereas the rooms in the front are slightly darker and a little more formal. All of the bathrooms are spacious and private, and some even have claw-footed bathtubs. Special touches abound, such as the split of white wine and two glasses that have been set out on the bureaus.

The Walker House is situated on three and one-half acres of land in the center of Lenox, making it easy to investigate the town center and do a little window shopping with Bowser. The ample grounds give guests and their dogs enough space to stretch their legs. The hills surrounding Lenox provide terrific hiking options, as well. October Mountain State Forest is a short drive from the inn, and contains over 16,000 acres of forests and trails. The Pittsfield State Forest is just up the road and offers an additional 10,000 acres to explore. A bit closer to home, guests will find the Audubon bird sanctuary, located just off of Undermountain Road. Bowser might want to take a nap, while his human companions borrow one of the inn's bicycle and explore the lovely terrain. Options abound at the local lakes, swimming and boating are popular in the summer and ice skating and fishing in the winter. The winter months also draw a good-sized ski crowd, who may choose from a variety of downhill and cross-country ski resorts in the region.

Sherman-Berry House

163 Dartmouth Street
Lowell, Massachusetts   01851-2425
(508) 459-4760 (telephone and fax)

Hostess: Susan Scott
Rooms: 3 doubles
Rates: $50-60 (B&B)
Payment: Personal checks
Children: Welcome but they "sometimes find the home tedious."(cribs, cots, highchairs,
*   and babysitters are available)*
Dogs: Well-behaved dogs are welcome with prior approval and a $10 fee
Open: All year

The Sherman-Berry House was originally built in 1893, which is probably as long as the enormous tree, whose trunk takes up a good portion of the street, has also been standing here. Frederick and Amelia Sherman were some of the first residents to build a home in the then fashionable Tyler Park district. Some 30 years later, in 1938, the Berrys and their five daughters purchased the house and lived there for almost 46 years. Thus, when Susan and David bought the house in 1985, they decided to create a centennial stained glass window, which outlined the heritage of the house. This lovely four-by four-foot window can be found on the first floor landing, and is just a sampling of the other two dozen stained glass windows located throughout the B&B. Some of these are mounted in window frames and others are hung from the ceiling by wires.

There are a number of common rooms guests will enjoy relaxing in during their stay. The cozy parlor has a handsome hardwood floor, with an intricate inlay of light and dark woods found around the perimeter. An antique love seat and delicately carved matching sidechairs are upholstered in deep green velvet. A great old player piano is placed in the corner and is topped with over a hundred rolls of music. A marble bust rests on a pedestal, and a variety of house plants line the window ledges. The adjacent living room is decorated in much the same manner but is furnished with a sofa, a pair of armchairs, and a rocking chair set around the central fireplace. The mantel contains some Americana collectibles, while other memorabilia is framed on the walls.

The guest chambers are all located on the second floor. The Rose Room, named after Rose Sherman, has rose patterned wallpaper and a large, Oriental rug set upon the hardwood floor. Guests have nice views of the garden, reflecting pool, and fountain from the antique white iron and brass bedstead that is covered with a handmade quilt. The second bedroom, called Katie's Chamber, is named after a daughter of the previous owner. It is similar in design to the Rose Room, but is substantially brighter with light streaming in from the windows. It is furnished with a brass trundle bed, antique bureau, and rocking chair. The third room, which is available on occasion, is located just down the hall and is outfitted with a large Victorian Murphy bed.

Each morning guests congregate in the dining room for a deluxe Continental breakfast, which is a complete change from the traditionally defined version. The menu for the morning primarily depends upon Susan's creative frame of mind. Over the years, guests' favorites have leaned toward Belgian waffles, enormous vegetable omelets, and assorted fruit dishes. The surroundings are as interesting as the conversation and food. A large china hutch rests against one wall, decorative plates line the wainscoting, and silver Victorian egg cups are set on the massive sideboard. A wicker baby carriage filled with dolls awaits interested youngsters in the corner, and an assortment of potted plants surround the formal dining room table. Should the weather be particularly favorable, then many enjoy taking this meal on the large front porch.

The surrounding neighborhood has quiet streets that are pleasant for early morning or evening walks. A favorite destination is the nearby Tyler Park. Those wishing to stray a bit further afield may wish to visit either the Lowell National

Historical Park or the Lowell Dracut State Forest. Susan also recommends investigating the New England Quilt Museum, taking the Mill and Canal Tour, or possibly passing by the house in which Bette Davis was born. Other noteworthy options include visiting the picturesque towns of Concord and Lexington, as well as Henry Thoreau's famed Walden Pond.

Danforth House Bed & Breakfast

121 Main Street
Nantucket, Massachusetts   02554
(508) 228-0136

Innkeepers: Lyn Danforth and Peter Arsenault
Rooms: 2 suites
Rates: $100-175(B&B)
Payment: Personal checks
Children: Welcome
Dogs: Welcome
Open: All year

The Danforth House is an antique Colonial home, located slightly off the beaten track, yet right in the heart of Nantucket's historic district. The house has been in the Danforth family since 1940, when Lyn's paternal grandmother purchased it as her summer home. The Danforths enjoyed their summers here, so much so that when the house became part of the family estate, Lyn decided to move here full time and open it as a B&B. Although it is open year-round now, the B&B still maintains its informal summer house atmosphere.

Anyone arriving by ferry can walk ten minutes up Main Street to the Danforth House, or take a cab. We recommend the walk, however, as people will pass by the historic Pacific National Bank, Three Bricks, the Civil War Monument, and a collection of beautifully preserved antique homes. Bowser will certainly enjoy stretching his legs after the long ferry ride from the mainland, and visitors will learn to navigate the cobblestone and brick-lined Nantucket sidewalks. The B&B stands out, if only because of the festive flags flying from its facade. Otherwise, it is the epitome of discretion as there is no sign announcing it as a B&B. After stepping into the small foyer, we were immediately drawn into the first floor living room that is filled with comfortable family antiques. A grandfather clock is placed in one corner of the room, while elegant old-fashioned sofas and tables rest on the well-worn rugs covering the hardwood floors.

Lyn was unfortunately off-island during our visit; however, Peter graciously showed us around the house. He told us that all of the furnishings have been in

Lyn's family for years. As we walked into the charming pink-hued dining room, we found a circular antique table that not only dominated the space, but also appeared as though it had been the site of many family meals over the years. Breakfast is served here each morning, at a "mutually convenient time to all staying in the house." Guests may take this Continental fare in the dining room, or out in the garden. Fresh muffins and Portuguese breads are accompanied by yogurt, seasonal fruits, cereals, and hot tea or coffee.

As we climbed the stairs to the second floor, we couldn't help but feel that we were privy to a small piece of Nantucket history. A hutch placed on the landing contains an assortment of classic books, including many about the island. Guests will find two suites of bedrooms encircling a small common area. Although shared, it feels like a private sitting room, with a television and VCR available for guests' use. The microwave is an added convenience. Directly off this room is our favorite suite. The canopy bed, which still has the original horsehair mattress, originally belonged to Lyn's grandmother. The duvet cover and canopy are created from a crisp blue and white print cotton fabric. At the end of the bed, and off to the side, lies one of the B&B's original working fireplaces. Just off the main bedroom, there is a second smaller bedroom with an antique double bed, various tables and a chest of drawers. As with the rest of the house, the antique furnishings in here are quite attractive and look as though they have been well utilized, and also well cared for, over the years. Just off this suite, there is a small deck that overlooks the backyard and wetlands. Although we visited in the off-season, Peter assured us that the daffodils and other bulbs would soon be in bloom. The second suite is located on the front of the house and is dominated by a huge, carved wooden headboard. There are also two wonderful old bureaus found in this chamber, as well as comfortable armchairs. The hardwood floors are covered with thin Oriental rugs. A small passage leads guests into a twin-bedded room with maple beds covered in colorful comforters.

Bowser will certainly love exploring the yard, while his human companion relaxes in one of the pretty, weathered teak garden chairs or benches. Bowser may enjoy following paths that crisscross through the wetlands; however, we are fairly sure his companion will want to head into town. Nantucket is a very dog friendly place, and we have been told that the dogs are sometimes more infamous than their masters. As people wander the streets, they too will soon feel as though they are part of the fabric that makes this island so interesting. There are hundreds of acres of conservation land to explore with Bowser. One of the perennial favorites is the Great Neck Reservation out by Wauwinet. Closer to town, walkers will find more open unspoiled land out by Cliff Beach, Dionis Beach and Eel Point. There are leash laws on Nantucket; however, dogs have a certain freedom here that is a welcome change from other more restrictive seaside communities.

Wherever one's travels eventually lead during the day, you are certain to enjoy the homecoming at night. During our visit, Peter described this as an informal place, but one which has a wonderful aura and a sense of graciousness. We would have to agree with him; there is no doubt in our minds that guests are fortunate to have Lyn share her home with them.

Jared Coffin House

P.O. Box 1580
29 Broad Street
Nantucket, Massachusetts 02554-1580
(800) 248-2405, (508) 228-2400, Fax (508) 228-8549

Owners: Margaret and Philip Read
Rooms: 8 singles, 52 doubles
Rates: Singles $55-85 (B&B), Doubles $100-200 (B&B)
Payment: AE, DC, DSC, MC, and VISA accepted but prefer payment by personal check
    or cash
Children: Welcome (only eight rooms available)
Dogs: Welcome with prior approval
Open: All year

Jared Coffin, a wealthy ship owner, built one of Nantucket's first three-story mansions in 1845 for his wife. Only a short time after it was completed, she decided that Boston would be a better place to live. The Coffin family sold the mansion and moved to Boston. Just a year later, it barely survived a devastating fire that claimed many of the nearby houses and town buildings. For the next century, the mansion was run as a hotel. Unfortunately, after this era it changed hands a number of times and slowly fell into disrepair. Finally in 1961, the Nantucket Historical Trust purchased the Coffin mansion and completely restored it to its former stature. Today, the Jared Coffin House occupies an enviable location on Broad and Center streets. It is comprised of six buildings; two are attached to the main building and the others, the Daniel Webster House, Harrison Gray House, and Henry Coffin House, are within a block. With the exception of the Daniel Webster House, each is also an antique mansion built in the early- to mid-1800s.

The elegance of this era has been graciously preserved in all of the buildings. The formal public rooms have Oriental rugs and impressive English antiques and reproductions. Guests feel quite at home relaxing in these inviting chambers either reading in front of the fire or perhaps playing a board game. The living room in the main house is actually comprised of two separate chambers that are joined with a wide archway, making them feel like one. The wood floors have been painted with black and white squares to resemble tile. Many of the intrinsic features in these rooms, such as handcarved woodwork, high ceilings, and marble fireplaces, are also found in other parts of the inn.

As one might imagine, the bedrooms are as varied as the buildings they occupy. One guest chamber in particular, which is ideal for those traveling with a dog, can be found in the Harrison Gray House. This room has all the antique features that one would expect with the exception of a loft built into a cathedral ceiling. A mahogany canopy bed rests on an Oriental rug, and two quilt covered twin beds are reached by ascending a wooden ladder to the loft (children love this aspect of the room). A private second entrance leads outside. There is also a pair of inviting common areas in the Harrison Gray House. The parlor is outfitted with a fireplace surrounded by lovely antiques and period furnishings, while the multi-windowed sun porch has comfortable rattan furnishings.

Another one of our favorite bedrooms is on the second floor of the Jared Coffin House. This corner guest room is graced with many high windows. A canopy bed with its hand-embroidered bedspread and matching canopy is the focal point of this chamber. An elegant mahogany Chippendale bureau is placed beside the bed, and a sofa is pushed up against the far window. Finally, for those who are in search of a few modern appointments combined with classic antiques, there is the Daniel Webster House. In many cases, the wide pine floors are covered with area rugs and the walls are papered in subtle floral prints. The canopy beds are either antique or fine reproductions. Built-in alcoves contain a remote control television and a refrigerator. The bathrooms in this building, as in the rest of the accommodations, are well stocked with baskets of French camomile soaps and shampoos.

Dining at the Jared Coffin House is a delightful experience as well. Our favorite place is the dark, cozy Tap Room with its enormous mahogany bar. Unlike the more formal Jareds, the Tap Room is open all year. Patrons may sample from the appetizer menu, which includes an excellent clam chowder, oysters and clams on the half shell, and clams casino. Some choose to try the crabcake sandwich, Welsh rarebit casserole, or French dip sandwich. Others prefer the prime rib, baked stuffed lobster, or the blackened swordfish. Long term guests may also enjoy investigating the array of other fine dining options available around town.

The Jared Coffin House has been an institution on Nantucket for years, and has welcomed guests traveling with a dog for as long as we can remember. Within easy walking distance of the inn, there are a variety of small beaches, quiet lanes, and interesting stores, galleries, and boutiques. The Nantucket State Forest is also a good spot to explore with Bowser. Across the island there are acres of conservation land, and secluded coves that are only accessible by boat.

The Nesbitt Inn

P.O. Box 1019
21 Broad Street
Nantucket, Massachusetts   02554
(508) 228-0156 or 228-2446

Innkeeper: Dolly Nolbit
Rooms: 2 singles, 11 doubles
Rates: Singles $38-45 (B&B), Doubles $55-75 (B&B)
Payment: MC and VISA
Children: Welcome
Dogs: Welcome
Open: All year

Nantucket is a multi-generational home for many of its year round and summer residents. Many of the historic homes have been owned by the same families for decades, although in some cases they have been converted to inns or B&Bs when they became too expensive to maintain privately. This is not the case with The Nesbitt Inn, which was built in 1872 specifically as an inn and more than 120 years later continues to accommodate the island's visitors. It is located toward the top of Broad Street, which is the main venue connecting the ferry dock with town.

The inn was built in a grand Victorian style. Its white exterior is accentuated with elaborately carved cornices and moldings, along with bay windows. In the summer months, a small front porch is dotted with old-fashioned chairs and hanging baskets of impatiens. Once inside, the Victorian touch is immediately evident, leading us to believe that very little has changed here over the years. We were greeted by the two resident house cats who leisurely strolled out of the owner's sitting room. Guests have their own sitting room too, situated just off the front entrance. The decor is strictly Victorian, from the settees and armchairs to the lace curtains covering the windows. The pink and purple blossoms of the African violets set in a sunny front window, nicely complement the colors in this chamber.

A fire is usually blazing in the fireplace on cold afternoons and evenings. A long set of stairs, lined with an Oriental runner, leads to the second and third floor bed chambers.

Because The Nesbitt Inn was built as an inn, the bedrooms are conveniently arranged off a long, wide hallway that runs the length of the building. The quietest of these chambers is situated to the rear of the house, overlooking the enclosed backyard; however, the sunniest and most architecturally interesting chambers are located toward the front. All of the bedroom walls have old-fashioned Victorian floral wallpapers in soft pink, burgundy, and cream colors. The lustrous hardwood floors are covered with area rugs. Many of the furnishings are original to the house. Guests often sleep in brass beds that are covered with simple white spreads or cotton coverlets. The bedrooms on the third floor are the most private, have the highest ceilings and the most architectural appeal. We liked the ones with the arched windows, multiple eaves, and intimate alcoves. Accent pieces consisted of light pine armoires or mirrored bureaus, as well as rocking chairs and marble-topped side tables illuminated by painted lamps. Even though the island enjoys a fairly steady sea breeze, there are ceiling fans to help circulate the air on particularly hot summer days. Many of the bathrooms are shared at the inn; however, guests have the added convenience of sinks placed in their bedrooms. We have to stress that this is an informal establishment, but one that is both reasonably priced (for Nantucket) and extremely clean. Dolly and her husband are also very gracious and have a great respect for their guests' privacy.

On the second floor landing, near the "Captain's Quarters," there is a small area where guests will find an array of information on Nantucket, including the ferry schedules, island transportation, and restaurant menus. Guests are invited to enjoy the Continental breakfast served at the inn, or they may take a leisurely walk and find a variety of the excellent restaurants. The Nesbitt Inn is well situated in the heart of town, so that shopping and sightseeing are easily accomplished with Bowser. As we were talking with some of the locals, they mentioned that during the summer months, they often see dogs asleep at their owner's feet at the many outdoor cafes. Some visitors might be interested in taking a walking tour of the historic district, with maps provided by the Chamber of Commerce. There are also acres of conservation land on the island, one of the more popular spots is Great Point. Visitors and their canine companions will need a four-wheel drive vehicle to get out to the lighthouse; however, the walks out here are both peaceful and quiet.

Bullard Farm Bed and Breakfast

89 Elm Street
North New Salem, Massachusetts   01364
(508) 544-6959

Hostess: Janet Kraft
Rooms: 1 single, 2 doubles, 1 suite, 1 dormitory room
Rates: Single $60 (B&B), Doubles $70 (B&B), Suite $90 (B&B), Dormitory per
*   person $30*
Payment: MC and VISA
Children: "Well-behaved children" over the age of three are welcome
Dogs: Welcome with advance notice provided they are "leashed and with owner at all
*   times" ($20 fee)*
Open: All year

Those who are relatively unfamiliar with the mid-section of northern Massachusetts, will be pleasantly surprised by its beautiful scenery, picturesque lakes, and historic villages. One of these sleepy hamlets is North New Salem, which is located along the northwest shore of Quabbin Reservoir, and just a short distance from the classic New England towns of Amherst, Northfield, and historic Deerfield.

Winding back country roads lead to the charming Bullard Farm Bed & Breakfast. The white Colonial house was built in 1796, and was once used as the town's post office before being purchased by the Bullard family in 1884. Today, visitors will know it when they see the circular driveway that fronts the large red barn and historic house. Janet is the most recent member of the Bullard family to occupy this property, although she has not always lived here. She spent many years in the coastal Massachusetts town of Cohasset, then inherited the family home and decided to move inland.

The front path leads to a screened-in porch surrounded by an array of birdfeeders. Guests enter the house through a 1950s kitchen, and just beyond lies a small breakfast room with paned windows overlooking the 13-acre field. Each morning, a full country breakfast is served in here (or in the dining room), which emphasizes the use of fresh ingredients to create the homebaked muffins, breads, and coffeecakes. As guests make their way through the house, it becomes clear that its antiquity has been well preserved. When Jean moved here in 1990, she found an assortment of antique furnishings in both the attic and basement ranging from trunks, chests, and sidetables to a rope bed, a breakfast table, and an array of copper and pewter collectibles.

One of our favorite places is a sitting room with wide board floors that are covered by a braided rug. An antique shelf clock tops the mantel, along with pewter plates, pitchers, and candle holders. The Colonial stenciled wallpaper and antique furnishings add to the feeling of authenticity in this room. Farther down the hall, guests will find a wonderful old dining room. Wide board floors have been worn down over time, and we could almost imagine residents of the house sitting around the crackling fire 150 years ago, warming themselves and enjoying the views through the paned windows. Today, a large sideboard is filled with glass jars of cereals, teas, snacks, and candies for guests to enjoy during their stay. The study, just down the hall, can be converted into an additional guest room if necessary, but more often than not, house guests can be found in here either watching television or listening to music.

The upstairs guest chambers maintain the same antique appeal as the common rooms. The painted wide board floors (some are almost two feet wide), coupled with period furnishings and antiques make these rooms all the more charming. Unobtrusive wallpapers or neutral color tones enhanced by wallpaper borders, set the decorative motif. The beds are covered with cotton spreads or country quilts. Those who are traveling as a group, may wish to consider the Dormitory Room, which is located on the second floor of the completely refurbished barn. The first floor is usually reserved as a meeting space, and also has a bathroom, kitchenette, and bar. The second floor is an open space, where Janet sets out cots based on the number of guests she expects that night. We stopped by during hunting season, and the B&B was literally filled to the rafters with hunters who were using all of the B&B rooms, as well as all of the cots out in the barn.

Bowser and friends will find plenty to do right on the premises. There are over 300 acres of land, including the woodlands that line the banks of the Swift River. Flocks of wild turkey and groups of deer can be seen during most months of the year. Some visitors like to bring Bowser over to the enormous Quabbin Reservoir, as it has miles of nature trails to investigate. History buffs will thoroughly enjoy learning about the history of the dams, which lined the Swift River in the 19th-century. Several mills operated here, and one of these was owned by the Bullard family. Bowser might also enjoy investigating the banks of the river, and his two legged-companions will probably be intrigued with the remnants of the old dams and sluiceways found along here. Others might want to visit Bear's Den and historic Deerfield, which are both just a short drive away. While there is more than enough open space right at the Bullard Farm, those who would like to go on more extensive hikes will find the Erving, Petersham, and Wendall State Forests are located nearby.

The Essex Street Inn

7 Essex Street
Newburyport, Massachusetts   01950
(508) 465-3148

Manager: Lori Pearson Hay
Rooms: 13 doubles, 3 suites, 2 townhouses, 2 apartment suites
Rates: Doubles $75-85 (EP), Suites $90-125 (EP), Townhouses and
     Apartment Suites $145 (EP)
Payment: AE, DC, MC, and VISA
Children: Welcome
Dogs: Welcome with prior approval
Open: All year

    The Essex Street Inn was built in the late 1880s and is set alongside other buildings in Newburyport that are almost two and three times that age. Located on a quiet one-way street, the inn is less than a block from Newburyport's main shopping area. Upon entering the tan clapboard building, we noticed an unusual pair of matching staircases that were divided by a center wall. We learned later that this was once a duplex, but that most of the dividing walls have been transformed into archways to create a more spacious common room. This chamber is decorated with floral wallpaper and contains a wonderful antique clock and several comfortable couches.

    The inn has accommodations to suit most travelers' needs. With each subsequent renovation, there have also been modern additions to the bedrooms. Just as each bedroom is different, so are the bedsteads, which vary from four-poster and canopy to brass and maple. They might be covered with white cotton spreads, Vermont quilts, or down comforters. The larger bedrooms have comfortable sitting areas, as well as antique bureaus and sea captain's chests. Some of the more interesting bedrooms are located on the third floor, and feature sky lights, set into the beamed ceilings. Each of the suites also varies in size and in decor, as well as appointments. Brick fireplaces warm guests on cool nights and small patios provide a refreshing outlet on warm summer evenings. Other noteworthy suite features are the gourmet kitchens and large whirlpool baths. A two-bedroom apartment suite, offers fireplaces in both the sitting room and bedroom. One final option is the other apartment suite, which has one fireplace, two separate bedrooms and private bathrooms. All of the accommodations offer air conditioning, a telephone, and a color television.

    There are a myriad of things to do in downtown Newburyport with Bowser. It is easy to spend time roaming the quaint side streets, browsing in the numerous shops, or just walking in the park along the waterfront. There are also self-guided walking tours of Newburyport, as well. These run along High Street and focus on houses that were built between the 17th- and 19th-centuries. The Maritime Museum and Chamber of Commerce also provide extensive brochures and detailed maps. Plum Island is well worth a visit, especially in the off-season as the bugs are often quite voracious in the summer months. There are also seven miles of beaches on Plum Island. Bowser might prefer a trip to either the Halibut Point Reservation, where there are tidal pools, or to Pebble Beach where he can romp along the water's edge.

The Morrill Place Inn

209 High Street
Newburyport, Massachusetts   01950
(508) 462-2808

Innkeeper: Rose Ann Hunter
Rooms: 10 doubles
Rates: Doubles $55-90 (B&B)
Payment: Personal checks
Children: Not appropriate for small children
Dogs: Welcome
Open: All year

The Morrill Place Inn is a fine example of a sea captain's mansion, and is one of many that line Newburyport's main thoroughfare. In the 1800s, during the town's shipbuilding heyday, many of the sea captains who lived here made enormous sums of money and spent a portion of their fortunes constructing the magnificent Federal-style homes we still find here today. In 1806 Captain William Hoyt built a 26 room, three-story home. It incorporated many typical Federal features, including balustrades, cornices, and carved mantels, as well as an elegant hanging staircase. Over the years, many of these buildings have fallen into disrepair, but Captain Hoyt would be thankful that Rose Ann Hunter came along, some fifteen years ago, to restore his wonderful old home.

Rose Ann was formerly a host at another Newburyport bed and breakfast; however, when the old Morrill estate came up for sale in 1979, she decided to buy it and put her energies into refurbishing this property. Her dream was to eventually open an inn, but she needed some financial backing to bring the house back to its original elegant condition. She devised a plan that would involve utilizing the talents of those involved in the annual Newburyport Showcase. A dozen or so interior designers were contacted and convinced to donate their services to the Showcase. Each designer was given the responsibility for decorating a room or section of the house in return for the exposure they would receive. As Rose Ann is quick to point out, no expense was spared in the process. For example, thousands of dollars were spent just to make the balloon curtains for the front living room. All of this is history though, and today guests will enjoy the decorative touches and historic ambiance of the inn's 26 rooms.

The bedrooms are all located on the second and third floors of the mansion. Bedsteads run the gamut from antique four-poster and canopy to day beds. One chamber is furnished with both a queen and twin bed set against a series of double-hung windows and surrounded by walls papered in lavender and white latticework. The fireplace adds warmth to this light and airy space. Another chamber has high ceilings, which almost seem to dwarf the large four-poster canopy bed. An added touch is the hand-painted wide board floor, that has been finished to resemble a carpet with its corner turned over. The same attention to detail is in evidence throughout all of the bedrooms, with delicate stenciling on the walls, painted floors, and even a whimsical hand-painted mouse that can be seen dashing into his hole on a radiator cover. Vibrant chintz curtains frame many of the windows; fireplace mantels are set with beautiful hand-painted tiles; and antique clocks are placed amidst the Sheraton-style antiques.

An informal, sunlit sitting room on the second floor awaits those who want to visit or perhaps watch a little television. An enormous mirror, framed in fabric, is set above a grouping of white wicker furniture. On warm summer days, a ceiling fan sends refreshing breezes through the room. For those who prefer to meander about the house, hoping to find their own little nook, there are still the formal parlor, dining room, living room, and fireplaced library to investigate.

A Continental breakfast is served each morning on the lace covered table in the formal dining room. Guests might take a moment to inspect the unusual faux marble finish around the fireplace. This is the art of painting wood to resemble a marble finish. This same technique has also been applied to the walls, where metal combs have been used to etch out designs in the glaze. On warm summer days, many guests are inclined to venture out through the French doors onto the summer porch to enjoy the peaceful morning.

During our visit, Rose Ann was putting the finishing touches on a room that had received substantial water damage due to a radiator leak. The piano had been spared; however, the floors and ceiling needed to be redone. As she was showing us around the inn, her daughter, Kristin, emerged from the rear of the house carrying a replacement rug to put on the newly refinished floor. Rose Ann informed us that in addition to their daily housekeeping duties, she and Kristin also spend a good deal of time shopping for food, as well as picking out new fabrics and furnishings that keep the inn looking fresh. In addition to operating an historic inn, Rose Ann also spends a good deal of time conducting seminars and lectures on the fundamentals of operating a successful inn. Her outside interests always seem to reflect her ultimate goal — which is to please her own guests.

We like Newburyport and the surrounding area because it is very conducive to people who are traveling with a dog. A long walk from the inn will bring visitors to the revitalized downtown. The main street, and side streets, are lined with interesting boutiques, shops, and restaurants. The nearby beaches are also quite lovely, although the water is decidedly on the chilly side for swimming. Just outside Newburyport is Maudslay State Park, which is ideal for hiking in the summer, or cross-country skiing in the winter. The Salisbury State Beach Reservation is another good option. Resting on over 500-acres, visitors can enjoy water activities from its scenic shoreline. Horseback riding, fishing, and bicycling are also popular diversions in this area. Rose Ann has been welcoming guests traveling with dogs for years, and she is also able to offer some additional suggestions for unique outings in and around Newburyport.

The Windsor House

38 Federal Street
Newburyport, Massachusetts 01950
(508) 462-3778; Fax (508) 465-3443

Innkeepers: Judith and John Harris
Rooms: 3 doubles, 3 suites
Rates: Doubles $75-90 (B&B), Suites $115 (B&B)
Payment: AE, DSC, MC, and VISA
Children: Welcome with advance notice (cribs, cots, and babysitters are available)
Dogs: Welcome with prior approval
Open: All year

The Federal-style Windsor House was built by Lieutenant Aaron Pardee in 1786, just in time for his wedding. The final design combined a mansion and a ship's chandlery, and utilized three different styles of architecture. After years of assorted owners, the house was renamed The Windsor House in 1978. This sturdy brick building has withstood New England winters for many years, due in part to its massive 18- to 20-inch thick brick walls. However, once in a great while, a strong "noreaster" can actually blow rain into the house through fissures in the brick. Since our last visit, Judith and John have been hard at work restoring a few portions of the inn, while always being mindful to keep its historic integrity intact.

Two sitting rooms occupy the first floor, both are simply decorated and appropriately furnished with period antiques. A wide stairway leads up to the guest bedrooms. Each chamber on the second floor has very high ceilings and is quite spacious. Wideboard floors are covered with area rugs. In addition to the period furnishings, each chamber is named after its original occupants. The bridal suite is located in one corner of the house, with a queen bed amid a few selected antiques. The nursery, just across the hall, has light pink floral wallpaper and two antique mahogany beds with carved pineapple finials. (It is interesting to note that all the mattresses in the house were specially made to fit the antique beds.) A crib and an assortment of toys rest in the corner alongside a comfortable rocking chair.

The Nanny's bedroom, appropriately enough, is situated next door to the nursery. This is beautifully and simply furnished. The standouts are the high double four-poster bed and Sheraton-style bureau. The top floor contains Aaron's old study, which has a wall of floor-to-ceiling bookshelves. From the double bed, guests can catch a glimpse of the ocean in the distance through the original windows framed with Indian shutters. Of the six bedrooms, three share a bathroom and the others have private baths. The bedroom that is most appropriate for those traveling with their canine companions is called the Merchant's Suite. This enormous first-floor room was formerly used as a provisioning store, a butcher shop, and part of a ship's chandlery for the better part of 50 years. Today, guests will find the 14-foot ceilings literally dwarf the period furnishings which are set around the double and twin bedsteads. What makes this particular chamber especially great for dogs is the separate outside entrance. One of the only reservations Judith has about visiting dogs is that they not bother her pets. Other than that, she finds guests traveling with dogs to be a most delightful addition to the household.

People who frequent B&Bs have learned that the breakfasts often vary greatly in quantity, as well as quality. Judith's culinary creations are not to be missed. Although she has spent a number of years in England, she draws much of her cooking experience from John's Cornish heritage. Breakfast is served in the former chandlery around a large oval wooden table, which fills only a portion of the cavernous sunken kitchen. The setting is truly unique, with exposed brick occupying an entire wall and huge racks of pots and pans hanging from the 14-foot high open-beam ceilings. The full English breakfast usually commences with a cup of specially blended coffee and assorted fresh fruit. Then Judith will inquire about any egg preferences, her specialty being herb scrambled eggs with delicious, spicy homemade sausage placed on the side. Most will undoubtedly appreciate the time and effort Judith puts into her meals and will certainly enjoy the lively conversation around the breakfast table.

The Windsor House is located in an historic section of Newburyport. The streets are quiet and lend themselves to long walks with Bowser. Some people, after spending the day in Newburyport, might want to visit one of the local state forests. Anyone who is interested in a nature walk, can follow the extensive trails and open spaces in nearby Georgetown, Rowley, or Willowdale State Forests.

Hargood House

493 Commercial Street
Provincetown, Massachusetts   02657-2413
(508) 487-9133

Host: Robert Harrison
Rooms: 19 suites
Rates: $77-181 daily (EP), $493-1,200 weekly (EP)
Payment: AE, MC, and VISA
Children: Not appropriate for children under 10 years of age "in season"
Dogs: Welcome with advance notice and prior approval
Open: All year

Most people, when they think of a vacation by the sea, envision the sounds of waves crashing, the smell of saltwater, and cool ocean breezes. The Hargood House takes advantage of its waterside setting by providing unobstructed water views, privacy, and spacious accommodations. Located in the quieter, east end of town, in four buildings dating back to the 1800s, the Hargood House combines old-fashioned grace and modern ingenuity.

From the street, the inn's facade is a classic New England Cape, but as guests walk to the water side they will find walls of floor-to-ceiling windows and sliding glass doors. Expansive decks and more intimate covered patios allow guests to easily extend their living space to the outdoors. Although it is difficult to describe an average suite, we can state unequivocally that almost all of them offer fabulous water views. The interior architectural design varies as well. Some suites provide exposed beam ceilings, and others combine brick and rough-hewn driftwood wallboards, that are reminiscent of an old-fashioned ship's cabin. One chamber is a duplex with a bedroom and private bathroom located on the first level and a living room and kitchen situated upstairs. Rooms 7 and 8 are the perennial favorites because they are located at the end of one building, closest to the water, and have three walls of windows and doors overlooking the sparkling bay. The kitchens are well-stocked with matching china and good quality stemware and flatware. Dishwashers and full-size refrigerators top off the list of welcome modern kitchen amenities. The only four suites that do not offer panoramic water views are located across the street from the main building, in the North House. Most of these are expansive two-bedroom chambers, that offer a few additional amenities which almost compensate for their lack of a water view.

The waves don't normally crash at the Hargood House, but the water does lap against the pilings. A lawn surrounded by gardens overlooks a small sandy beach and the water. Guests seem content to relax on their lawn chair or rest in a hammock for hours, either reading or watching the tide roll in and out of the bay. If the weather changes (as it is apt to do in New England), guests may head inside, stoke their Franklin stove, and either watch the fog roll in or see a spectacular ocean storm unfold. Inclement weather also brings visitors into the town center, which is just a short walk from the Hargood House. Provincetown is rich in art galleries, fine restaurants, and unusual shops. The Pilgrim Monument, several lighthouses that line the point, and the Marine Aquarium are a few of the other in-town diversions. Bowser would certainly enjoy the walk to town; however, there are additional open spaces that should also be considered. For most, Provincetown has more than enough beaches, parks, and sights and attractions to satisfy them for their entire stay. Anyone who does want a change of venue may enjoy a short trip to the Head of the Meadow Beach or Highland Beach in North Truro, Nauset Beach Light in Eastham, and R.C. Nickerson State Park in Orleans.

White Wind Inn

174 Commercial Street
Provincetown, Massachusetts 02657
(508) 487-1526

Manager: Russell Dusablon
Rooms: 2 singles, 10 doubles, 1 apartment
Rates: Singles $25-30 (B&B), Doubles and Apartment $60-115 (B&B)
Payment: AE, MC and VISA
Children: Welcome
Dogs: Welcome with a $50 deposit, refundable at the end of the stay
Open: All year

The quaint, winding one-way streets lend a certain historic charm to Provincetown; however, they can just as easily become quite congested with onslaught of the summer tourists. The White Wind Inn, with its in-town location, allows visitors the luxury of parking their car upon arrival and never using it again. Walking and bicycling are the preferred modes of transportation for exploring the town center and investigating the array of stores, restaurants, and galleries.

Originally built in 1825, this Victorian house was once home to a wealthy shipbuilder. More recently, Sandra Rich purchased the building and began operating it as a guest house. New arrivals usually park along the side of the house, and ascend a short flight of stairs to the wraparound porch. From here, it is easy to watch the activity on the main street below. The interior of the inn is cozy, although a sense of spaciousness is created by the high ceilings in many of the common rooms. Antiques and soft carpeting lends a warmth to others. The two resident dogs are usually on hand to welcome Bowser. A central staircase leads to many of the accommodations. Each bedroom is individually and tastefully decorated. One chamber has a mahogany four-poster bed, covered with a forest green floral spread, that faces a fireplace. Many of the other rooms are a little more streamlined and are furnished with contemporary pieces. The dark gray Berber carpet is quite attractive in one recently updated chamber. The brass bed in here, is complemented by a sofa bed covered in a floral fabric. One of the nicest features in this space is the view of the historic houses and water from both the windowed alcove and private balcony. Most of the bedrooms also have ceiling fans, and all provide a refrigerator, television, and a modern, private bathroom. Those who are in search of accommodations that offer balconies overlooking the water, intimate window seats, and charming sitting areas will find plenty of them to choose from at the White Wind Inn.

Each morning, most like to gather on the front veranda, where a Continental breakfast is served. Here, guests can sip a cup of freshly brewed coffee and slowly wake up in the comfort of their deck chairs. As the air warms, the quiet beach just across the street often tempts guests away from their chairs and down to the water. Of course, there are also the larger Provincetown beaches with their ocean surf to provide exhilarating fishing and swimming opportunities. However, the main draw of this inn is its proximity of the variety of stores, galleries, and restaurants in town. Bowser might enjoy a walk to the top of the hill to find Pilgrim Monument. There are also miles of beaches in and around Provincetown, many of which allow visiting dogs that are kept on leashes.

Hawthorne Hotel

On the Common
18 Washington Square West
Salem, Massachusetts   01970
(800) 729-7829, (508) 744-4080, Fax (508) 745-9842

General Manager: Michael Garvin
Rooms: 83 doubles, 6 suites
Rates: Doubles $92-185 (B&B), Suites $195-295 (B&B)
Payment: AE, CB, DC, DSC, MC, and VISA
Children: Welcome (cribs, cots, highchairs and babysitters are available)
Dogs: Welcome with prior approval, a damage deposit is required
Open: All year

One of the best ways to learn about historic Salem is through reading about and visiting the interesting museums, antique homes, and scenic waterfront. One of the most dramatic events in the town's history took place in 1692, when a fear of witchcraft swept through the area. Before an end could be brought to this mass hysteria, 20 lives had been sacrificed. Soon thereafter, Salem became known for shipbuilding, thus allowing for the growth of the town's port and related industries. After the early 1800s, shipping declined and the town began to rely on the strength of its industry and more recently on the influx of tourism to maintain its economic base. One of the residents, who later immortalized this town through his writings, was Nathaniel Hawthorne. In the 1920s, the citizens of Salem formulated a rather unique public subscription drive to build their first hotel. It was only natural that it be named after one of its more notable benefactors.

Today, this handsome six-story brick hotel overlooks the Salem Common and has sweeping views of the town's historic buildings. Once inside, new arrivals will find a very traditional wood paneled lobby accented with brass fixtures and gilt edged mirrors. Wing chairs, sofas, and coffee tables are interspersed with large potted plants and Oriental carpets. This same feeling is carried through into both Nathaniel's, the intimate dining room, and the more club-like, Tavern on the Green. Classical music is provided by a pianist, who sets the tone Nathaniel's elegantly appointed dining room. Sage green walls and detailed moldings and wainscotings create a tranquil dining atmosphere. The Continental menu provides many traditional choices, such as prime rib, filet mignon, and grilled salmon, along with a special house pasta. One of our our favorite after-dinner choices is Tavern on the Green with its honey colored wood paneling and fireside setting.

After an enjoyable meal, guests often head up to their bedrooms. Although these chambers are decorated and furnished in much the same manner as the common areas, they do vary somewhat in size. Reproduction mahogany-toned furnishings are a stark contrast to the sand-colored walls. Impressionist and nautical prints, as well as brass lamps provide decorative accents. Full length draperies frame views of the distant ocean and surrounding town. Some of the guest chambers offer a connecting bedroom and sitting room with a sofabed. This configuration is often ideal for families or groups of friends. Whichever bedroom combination best suits guests' needs, the comfortable accommodations, central location, and helpful concierge provide the basis for a very relaxing stay in the Salem area.

There is an array of interesting attractions in town, including the Salem Witch Museum, the House of Seven Gables, Pioneer Village, Peabody Museum of Salem, and the Salem Maritime National Historic Site. Bowser will certainly enjoy walks through town; however, there are also terrific excursions to be enjoyed in the neighboring Marblehead, Beverly Farms, and Manchester-by-the-Sea. The town of Gloucester features Ravenswood Park, which is a densely-wooded preserve containing a number of paths that are perfect for long walks. North of Salem, visitors might want to take Bowser to the 700-acre Bradley Palmer State Park in Topsfield or the 2,400-acre Willowdale State Forest in nearby Ipswich. Both offer hiking in the summer and cross-country skiing in the winter months.

The Salem Inn

7 Summer Street
Salem, Massachusetts 01970
(800) 446-2995, (508) 741-0680

Innkeepers: Diane and Richard Pabich
Rooms: 27 doubles, 5 suites
Rates: Doubles $89-150 (B&B), Suites $109-150 (B&B)
Payment: AE, CB, DC, DSC, MC, and VISA
Children: Welcome (cribs, cots, and babysitters are available)
Dogs: Welcome with advance notice and prior approval provided they are not left alone in the rooms ($15 fee)
Open: All year

The Salem Inn is a lovely four-story Federalist style building built by sea captain Nathaniel West in 1834. Mr. West was a man of many accomplishments as he was the first Salemite to circumnavigate the world. The main portion of the inn is actually a combination of three town houses he built for each of his three daughters. Located in the heart of old Salem, and listed on the National Register of Historic Places, the inn is within easy walking distance of Salem's more noteworthy sights. In 1983, Diane and Richard purchased the building, and tastefully decorated the often cavernous chambers with antiques and reproduction furnishings.

The first thing most guests notice about the inn is its nicely landscaped, intimate brick courtyard flanked by iron park benches. This is an ideal spot for breakfast or a relaxing afternoon break from sightseeing. Once inside this old home, guests will find high ceilings coupled with beautifully preserved period wainscotings, hand-carved mantels, intricate cornices, and shuttered windows. A charming living room houses a collection of restored oak furniture that had been gathering dust in the basements and attics of the three houses. When the Pabiches purchased and renovated the homes some twelve years ago, these furnishings were also on the list for restoration. The oak fits in nicely with the creamy white wall treatments and sheer drapes framing the full-length windows. A portrait of Captain West is placed over the fireplace, a portrait that was actually painted by the Pabiches' daughter, Jill.

The inn is divided into sections, one side houses two-room suites that contain kitchenettes. The separate bedroom and living room, with a pullout sofa, makes this an ideal choice for families. Another part of the inn is comprised of queen- and king-bedded rooms, twelve of which have working fireplaces. Those accommodations with the most space and architectural interest are the studio apartments on the fourth floor. Here, eaves and dormer alcoves create charming nooks and crannies, although all of the bedrooms have specially carved moldings that are reminiscent of the Federal period. The decor is very appealing as well, with cream colored walls dotted by botanical prints. A sofa or love seat is often set near a window, along with a graceful oak or pine antique bureau or table. The beds are covered with pretty cotton spreads in either stripes or floral prints. Modern amenities have not been overlooked, and include color televisions, direct dial telephones, coffee makers, clock radios, and air-conditioning. Some of the private bathrooms are even equipped with whirlpool tubs.

Since our last visit, the Pabiches have acquired another building just around the corner from the inn. This expansive Federal is fitted with yellow clapboards and black shutters. The building has been completely restored and while it does not maintain the same historic character as the interior of the main inn, many seem to enjoy the added amenities. Upon entering the house, guests will find an elongated sitting room, which offers a pair of couches set around the central fireplace. During our visit, the Pabiches' daughter, Jill, was in the process of painting a pair of faux marble designs on the walls flanking the front windows. Faux marble is not the only thing Jill knows how to paint, as she has also painted a faux window in Room 113. The guest chambers in this house are decorated in much the same manner as those at the main inn; however, many have four-poster bedsteads and double whirlpools in the modern bathrooms.

Each morning, guests are invited to dine in the charming Courtyard Cafe, which is actually the original site of the three basement kitchens in the original townhouses. The brick walls and stone foundations have been left exposed in here, increasing the sense of antique authenticity. Guests are served fresh fruit, assorted cold cereals, a variety of muffins and pastries, along with herbal teas and freshly brewed coffee. The Courtyard Cafe also has two small dining rooms that are open to the public for lunch and dinner. The nightly fare is traditional and features assorted pastas, native seafood, and tenderloin of beef.

Because of the inn's proximity to town, it would seem natural to put Bowser on a leash and go for a stroll. The inn is located close to the Heritage Trail (a walking tour covering a little over a mile and taking visitors to places like Derby Square), The Burying Point, and the Derby Street Historic District. Those who are enamored with witches will discover dozens of nearby sights and attractions, ranging from the supposed witches' homes to museums such as the Salem Witch House. There are many other towns in close proximity to Salem such as Marblehead to the south and Manchester-by-the-Sea, Gloucester, and Rockport to the north. All have beaches and waterfront areas that are great fun to investigate with Bowser.

Stephen Daniels House

1 Daniels Street
Salem, Massachusetts 01970
(508) 744-5709

Hostess: Catherine B. Gill
Rooms: 2 singles, 4 doubles
Rates: Singles $60 (B&B), Doubles $70-90 (B&B)
Payment: AE, but prefers personal checks
Children: Welcome (cots and highchairs are available)
Dogs: Welcome with prior approval
Open: All year

The Stephen Daniels House was built in 1667 by a sea captain. For ninety years, this simple, four-room home remained relatively unchanged. Then in 1756, Mr. Daniels' great grandson enlarged the house to its current size of 15 rooms. Remarkably, from 1756 until 1931 his descendants resided in this home. Over 20 years ago, it was transformed into a guest house. Today, visitors will find that it still authentically reflects the life of the sea captain, who inhabited it some 328 years ago.

The chocolate-brown clapboarded Stephen Daniels House is centrally located to most of Salem's historic sights. It also offers travelers the hospitality and comfort they would expect to find at a small and very historic New England B&B. Walking inside is like taking a step back in time. Sloping wide pine floors, covered with Oriental rugs, creak as guests wander throughout the house. Years of wear are ingrained in the treads of the rather steep, winding staircases. The enormous brick fireplaces cast shadows on the low, box-beam ceilings and detailed wainscotings. There is a wonderful sense of history in the Stephen Daniels House.

A maze of short hallways leads guests to their bedrooms. The Great Room has a Sheraton field bed covered with a Bates spread. The canopy fabric is also used on both the dust ruffle and drapes framing the windows. Oriental rugs cover the bedroom floor, an antique rocking chair sits off to one side, and a comb-back Windsor armchair occupies another corner. Fresh flowers rest on bedside tables, amid period antiques. Blanket and captain's chests, handmade quilts, muskets, and pewter plates all add to the feeling of antiquity. The Eastern Room, on the other hand, is outfitted with a pair of maple bedsteads, set under a large archway that leads into an eaved alcove. The Rose Room is furnished with a canopy bed and, true to its name, has rose wallpaper accenting the rose-colored wainscoting flanking the fireplace. Each of the chambers also boasts an array of interesting features that include built-in alcoves and recessed bookcases holding an assortment of treasures. The bathrooms are also noteworthy, as they are usually fitted with claw-footed tubs, or in one case, a boxed tub is set near a small fireplace.

The tiny back staircase is fitted with shelves holding a collection of duck decoys. At the base, guests will discover the original kitchen, that still has an enormous walk-in hearth with iron cookware. The breakfast room, where a Continental breakfast is served each morning, is located on the backside of this hearth. Windsor chairs are placed around an antique harvest table, which virtually overshadows the large brick fireplace and corner hutch filled with decorative plates. Guests may also choose to take their breakfast outside on the patio, where they can enjoy the intimate garden and bask in the morning sunshine.

Exploring historic Salem can take the better part of a day. A great way to enjoy the picturesque town center is to meander through the Salem Common, just a few blocks from the inn. Two additional parks worth investigating are the Salem Willows Park overlooking the water and the Forest River Park, where there are two beaches. In addition to investigating the quintessential New England communities of Manchester-by-the-Sea, Marblehead, and Beverly Farms, many visitors also like to take Bowser to the Bradley W. Palmer and Harold Parker State Forests.

Wingscorton Farm Inn

11 Wing Boulevard
East Sandwich, Massachusetts 02537
(508) 888-0534

Innkeepers: Dick Loring and Sheila Weyers
Rooms: 1 double, 2 suites, 1 carriage house
Rates: Double $95 (B&B), Suites $115 (B&B), Carriage House $150 (B&B)
Payment: AE, MC, and VISA
Children: Welcome (cribs and cots are available)
Dogs: "Well-trained" dogs are welcome with a $10 fee, provided they are never left
  unattended
Open: All year

First time visitors to Cape Cod become quickly enamored with its array of beautiful beaches and backroads, relaxed atmosphere, and sense of history. Unfortunately, sometimes one has to look hard to find it when visiting some of the more touristed communities on the Cape. Hyannis and Falmouth draw their fair share of people who come here to shop, grab a ferry for the islands, or take advantage of its many recreational opportunities. There are also the more traditional summer colonies frequented by generations of wealthy Bostonians and New Yorkers, such as Chatham and Osterville.

Anyone willing to try a quieter, and less frequented part of the Cape should visit Sandwich and its environs. True, this is the northern side of the Cape, known for its colder waters, small numbers of tourists, and lack of commercial business. It is located just over the Sagamore Bridge, one of two bridges that connects the Cape with the mainland. Slip onto Route 6A, and follow it to Wingscorton Farm Inn.

This is one of the more authentic inns we have found on the Cape, and it happens to be located in the oldest historic district in the entire country. Originally built in 1758, the farm now rests on seven acres of land dotted with well-manicured lawns, orchards, gardens and mature plantings. The center-chimney Colonial is the centerpiece for the property, trimmed with white clapboards and hunter green shutters. Once inside, guests will begin to understand what makes this place special. It is clear that Sheila and Dick, in the 12 years they have owned the house, have spent an inordinate amount of time ensuring that the restoration of the building and its furnishings is historically accurate. Wide board floors have been painstakingly refinished, along with the detailed moldings and glowing paneled walls

The first common area guests come to is the charming, low-ceilinged keeping room. Hardwood floors are covered with Oriental rugs, while comfortable side chairs and sofas are placed next to a captain's chest and in front of the enormous cooking fireplace. The mantel is painted with a blue milk paint and is topped with an array of pewter plates, cups, and platters. Fresh flower arrangements, authentic collectibles, and an assortment of reproductions combine with antiques to lend an additional air of authenticity to this chamber. An equally cozy library is furnished in a similar manner, with a fireplace surrounded by still more paneled walls. Floor to ceiling bookshelves are overflowing, with just enough space left for the television and an assortment of collectibles. The intimate guest dining room also has an historic ambiance to it, with its low ceilings and wide board floors. A simple drop leaf table is placed in the middle of the room atop a kilm rug. The delicate floral wallpaper is coordinated with the tab curtains framing the windows. In the morning, a hearty farm breakfast is served in here, often made with some of the fruits and produce that are grown on the farm. The meal usually starts with fresh fruit, and homemade breads and muffins. Pancakes or waffles, along with an egg dish, are then accompanied by homefries.

There are several bedrooms to choose from at the Wingscorton Farm Inn. One of these is located just off the front staircase. This is a light and airy chamber due as much to the sheer curtains framing the windows as to the white painted paneling and beamed ceilings. The wide pine floors are covered with a pretty blue rag rug, which picks up the blue accents in the wallpaper. Several pieces of Shaker furniture are placed about the room, with accent pieces including a baby's cradle, sled, and sweater chest. The two upstairs chambers are located on either side of the second floor landing. One bedroom is furnished with a massive four-poster bed that faces a small fireplace set into a wood paneled wall. Braided rugs cover the hardwood floors, a sweater chest rests at the end of the bed, and several duck decoys are placed on top of a maple chest of drawers. The other room is very similar in both decor and furnishings. The four-poster canopy bed is adorned with a country quilt that nicely complements the delicate cranberry tones in the wallpaper. Dark paneled walls surround another tiny brick fireplace, while a cradle, a Shaker chair, and a brass bucket filled with firewood rest off to either side. Several colorful braided rugs cover the wide pine floors. These suites also offer charming sitting rooms, as well as modern bathrooms.

Those who are willing to forgo some of the antique qualities for additional room may be more interested in the spacious Carriage House, located several hundred feet from the inn. Guests will be pleasantly surprised upon entering this beautifully decorated and furnished building. One of the most unusual aspects is the exposed fieldstone foundation that lines the lower half of the interior walls. This, combined with a beamed ceiling, makes the first floor rustic and appealing. The open sitting area is furnished with comfortable couches and side chairs centered on a sweater chest and woodstove. The adjacent kitchen alcove has cherry cabinets surrounding the refrigerator, sink, and stove. A series of small, paned windows, framed with Colonial patterned tab curtains, line the walls. The upstairs loft is accessed by a wooden circular staircase. The beamed cathedral ceilings are brightened by a series of skylights. A queen-size, four-poster bed is flanked by Sheraton-style bedside tables topped with small lamps. Although four people could stay in the Carriage House, two would need to sleep on the downstairs couch bed and walk through the upstairs bedroom to get to the bathroom.

Visitors to the area will undoubtedly enjoy drives along picturesque Route 6A, which wends through a handful of lovely historic towns, as well as by a number of antique stores, interesting shops, and noteworthy attractions. Locally, people might want to visit the Green Briar Nature Center which has a mile long nature trail called the Old Briar Patch Nature Trail. Close by is the Thornton W. Burgess Museum where people can learn more about the famous children's author who is most notable for the *Peter Cottontail* series of books. There is plenty of space to walk with Bowser on the property, or there are the many trails that cut through this part of the Cape. There is also a private beach that is either a one-minute car ride or a five-minute walk from the inn. Here Bowser can romp endlessly or just frolic in the waves.

Ivanhoe Country House

Route 41
254 South Undermountain Road
Sheffield, Massachusetts   01257
(413) 229-2143

Innkeepers: Carole and Dick Maghery
Rooms: 9 doubles
Rates: Doubles: $65-99
Payment: Personal checks
Children: Welcome except on weekends from Memorial Day through Labor Day (cribs
*   and cots are available)*
Dogs: Well-behaved dogs are welcome with a $10 daily fee. They must accompany guests
*   at all times.*
Open: All year

Over the years, people have discovered the Ivanhoe Country House for a variety of reasons. Whether they had a child attending one of the local prep schools, tickets to a summer concert at Tanglewood, or simply needed a Berkshire retreat, this intimate bed and breakfast was the perfect solution. Built in 1780, the expansive house looks a little imposing set behind its rock wall. Once inside though, the interior is quite cozy, with rooms seeming to ramble on forever. Anyone with a penchant for sweets will find a basket full of treats resting on the piano in the foyer. Down each hallway and around almost every corner are hidden alcoves, creaky hardwood floors, distinctive moldings, and interesting collectibles. One of our favorite spaces is the Chestnut Room. This enormous, beamed-ceiling common room is perfect for cold winter days when the fire is crackling and someone is playing the antique grand piano. Others might enjoy selecting a book from the small library or gathering a foursome for a game of cards. Period furnishings rest on the Oriental rugs, and French doors open to the outdoors, making this inviting chamber seem even more expansive.

The guest bedrooms are individually and tastefully decorated in a manner indicative of the Colonial period. Antique beds and period furnishings are a perfect complement to the small floral print wallpapers. Hardwood floors are often covered by braided rugs. The rooms all vary in size and amenities, with some of them being intimate and others quite spacious. The first floor bed chamber, situated around the corner from the main common room, offers a private, screened-in porch. Several of the other bedrooms have working fireplaces — something which we find to be a rarity in most B&Bs. A home of this era should have antiquated bathrooms; however, guests will be pleasantly surprised to find updated bathroom facilities with charming antique features such as claw-footed bathtubs. Families often choose to reserve Sunrise, with its brick fireplace, and Pineview, with its twin finial bedsteads, as they have connecting doors and a kitchenette.

In the morning, a Continental breakfast tray is placed just outside each bedroom door, allowing guests to start the day at a leisurely pace. Hot chocolate, coffee, and a choice of teas are always available, as well as a fresh selection of homemade muffins and breads. The Magherys also thoughtfully provide mini-refrigerators in the hallways, which many frequently use for storing drinks, snacks, and other perishables.

There are plenty of activities to keep guests and their dogs busy during their stay. Some choose to start the day with a refreshing swim in the pool or perhaps a walk on the 25 acres of property surrounding the B&B. The rules about dogs are fairly strict at the Ivanhoe Country House. Dogs must be leashed at all times, walked away from the pool and formal lawns, and never left alone in the rooms. Nevertheless, Carole and Dick are always full of great suggestions for things to do in the area with one's canine cohort.

Mount Race is the easiest option, as it looms behind the B&B, serving as a beautiful backdrop to the house. The Appalachian Trail also runs through the immediate area. Three other places that provide great recreational opportunities for everyone are the East Mountain State Reserve, as well as the Bash Bish Falls State Park which has over 200 acres, and the Mount Everett State Reservation where there are 1,300 acres for hiking, horseback riding, canoeing, or fishing. In the winter, skiers will enjoy the miles of cross-country ski trails available throughout the area. There are also a number of small downhill ski resorts in the immediate area., along with plenty of interesting and picturesque towns to explore, with Stockbridge and Lenox being two of the standouts.

Race Brook Lodge

864 South Undermountain Road
Sheffield, Massachusetts 01257
(800) 645-3677, (413) 229-2916, Fax (413) 229-6629

Host: *Dave Rothstein*
Rooms: *18 doubles*
Rates: *$79-89 (B&B)*
Payment: *AE, MC, and VISA*
Children: *Welcome (cribs and cots are available)*
Dogs: *Welcome in specific rooms with outside entrances*
Open: *All year*

The historic town of Sheffield is located halfway between Stockbridge, Massachusetts and Lakeville, Connecticut. As travelers meander along the backroads leading here, they will begin to lose sense of the surrounding civilization. A huge red barn looming behind a rock wall demarks the entry to the Race Brook Lodge property. The handsome building, which dates back to the 1830s, was purchased by Dave Rothstein in 1991. He wasted no time in putting his architectural talents to work in converting this barn into a lodge, carving out wonderful common areas and guest chambers throughout the historic building.

The informal dirt driveway, lined by a split rail fence, leads guests toward the rear of this expansive lodge. The stairs open onto an informal patio where a handful of tables and chairs are positioned to take advantage of the warmth from the afternoon sun. Inside, the beautifully refurbished living room was our first stop, with its original wide board floors and beamed ceilings providing the backdrop to the eclectic array of furnishings and decorative collectibles. Just beyond the living room is the dining room, where hand-hewn tables are sometimes covered by checkered cloths, or are left uncovered so that guests may enjoy the texture of the worn woods. Oriental rugs mix nicely with Dave's collection of Native American artwork, farm implements, and rustic country collectibles. Guests can enjoy their breakfast buffet in here each morning, where bagels, muffins, hard boiled eggs, fruit, and cereals are laid out next to the juices, freshly ground coffees, and teas. This is also the site of his now famous jazz jam sessions.

Dave formerly owned the Music Inn, just up the road in Stockbridge. From 1969 through 1979, he presented outdoor twilight concerts that incorporated everything from jazz and rock to folk and blues music. He still has a passion for music, and hired an ensemble of musicians to launch the opening of his lodge in 1992. This was such a success, that he decided to offer a regular series of jazz brunches that he schedules for the third Sunday of every month. Guests can enjoy these jam sessions on the patio or in the barn.

If guests are wondering where they will stay in this rambling old place, rest assured there are upstairs bedrooms, first-floor rooms at the front of the building, and six more in a pair of cottages. Each accommodation is distinctive, but maintains a decorative continuity in keeping with the rest of the barn. The Hayloft Suite is one example, where the two high-ceilinged rooms are enhanced by exposed rough hewn beams. Stenciling and original artwork enliven the walls, and tie-back tab curtains soften the small windows. We liked the use of textured fabrics and country quilts on the queen-size beds. The Barn Suite features a large master bedroom, three additional bedrooms, a bunk-bed loft, and three bathrooms. The Summer and Fall Cottages are ideal for those traveling with their canine cohorts, as they not only are set away from the rest of the buildings, but are also nestled along the babbling brook. Their decorative style is similar to the rest of the lodge rooms, and they combine a wonderful array of pottery, quilts, unusually textured fabrics, and country antiques to create a most welcoming environment.

While many will be hard pressed to leave the restful ambiance of the lodge, guests are usually drawn out for a visit to nearby Racebrook Falls. Take Bowser on a half-hour walk up the nearby trail to the summit of the falls. Here there are three separate waterfalls crashing down a 200-foot chasm. This trail also merges with the Appalachian Trail, should hikers be interested in a little additional exercise. Those who want to explore this picturesque region, will find the lovely towns of historic Sheffield, Lenox (home of the Tanglewood summer concerts), and Stockbridge (the site of the new Norman Rockwell museum) all worth investigating. In addition to a handful of cross-country and downhill skiing facilities nearby, there are also a dozen state parks and forests within a half-hour drive of the lodge. One of the larger ones is the Beartown State Forest on over 10,000 acres, where visitors have just about any outdoor recreational activity available to them.

Publick House Historic Resort

P.O. Box 187
On The Common
Sturbridge, Massachusetts 01566-0187
(800) PUBLICK, (508) 347-3313, Fax (508) 347-1246

Innkeeper: *David Cashill Lane*
Rooms: *117 doubles, 13 suites*
Rates: *Doubles $55-89 (EP), Suites $90-130 (EP)*
Payment: *AE, CB, DC, MC, and VISA*
Children: *Welcome (cribs, cots, highchairs, and babysitters are available)*
Dogs: *Welcome in the country lodge with a $5 fee*
Open: *All year*

The Publick House, built in 1771, is located on the picturesque Sturbridge Common. It was owned by Colonel Ebenezer Craft, who offered weary travelers both food and an inviting haven to rest themselves and their horses. Over the years, the surrounding barns, stables, and other outbuildings have been incorporated into a huge, rambling inn. Such care has been taken to preserve its heritage, that the Publick House has been named to the National Register of Historic Places. Across the way, traditional homes form the perimeter to the semi-circular common. This picturesque setting, combined with over 60 acres of land, provides visitors with a good sense of an old-fashioned New England village.

There is a wide variety of accommodations for guests to choose from; however, those traveling with a dog are welcome in only one of them, the country lodge. We normally try to stay away from descriptive reviews of resort motor lodges; however, in this case we have made an exception. Old Sturbridge Village is unique in that it offers all the amenities of a resort, as well as a living piece of New England history. The country lodge is set on a well-landscaped knoll, just a short distance from the Publick House Inn. Six separate buildings contain the 100 lodge rooms. Although a bit on the boxy side, they are attractively decorated with small floral print wallpaper and furnished with traditional Colonial reproductions, giving them a similar flavor to those found in the main inn. Primitive artwork and regional prints fill the walls, while Bates spreads cover the queen-size beds, all of which accentuate the Colonial theme. Although all of the rooms have a small patio, those on the second floor have additional architectural interest because of the cathedral ceilings. One of the primary benefits to staying at the country lodge is that guests are just a stone's throw from the tennis court, swimming pool, shuffleboard, and playground. Bowser will also appreciate the easy access to the grounds.

When guests grow hungry, they will probably head over to the Publick House. There are three expansive dining rooms from which to choose, including The Barn with tables located where the old stalls used to be and the Tap Room with its beamed ceilings and an enormous hearth. Each restaurant offers hearty New England fare, including lobster pie, prime rib, Yankee pot roast, and thick lamb chops. During the holidays, there are even more elaborate themes for the dining rooms. The best of these is the Yule Log Celebration. Waiters and waitresses (sprites and wenches) are dressed in old English garb and serve quite a feast, including lobster, turkey, ham, rounds of beef, venison, tongue, crab, shrimp, and roast suckling pig. Minstrels sing, people dance, and all in all it provides a very memorable day of entertainment. Another dining option, and the best value for families, is Crabapples, located just down the hill from the Country Lodge. Here, guests will find a more casual environment and a menu that will satisfy most palates.

Visitors won't need to search very hard to find entertaining activities, as the Old Sturbridge Village is practically next door to the inn. The village is actually an outdoor museum or, more specifically, an early 19th-century recreation of a New England hamlet. Visitors will enjoy talking to the townspeople, as they are garbed in traditional attire, speak with an authentic dialect, and are well-versed in the traditions of the time. There is also a calendar of the yearly events outlining just what is featured at the village at any given time. These range from maple sugaring, cider making, and sheep shearing to potting, folk dancing, and musket demonstrations. For those who are interested, there is also an array of theme weekends from which to choose. These include Murder Mysteries, a Yule Log celebration, pumpkin growing and decorating, visiting Brimfield (renowned antique auction), and scarecrow festival weekends, to name just a few.

Bowser is not left out of the action either. There is both fishing and canoeing available on the local Quinebaug River. Cross-country skiing is probably the most popular winter activity, and there are trails right on the property. Many also like to pay a visit to the Hamilton Orchards, where they can hike along their nature trail, pick pumpkins and apples in the fall, peaches and plums in the late summer, and raspberries, blueberries, and cherries in the early to mid-summer. Wells State Park in Sturbridge has an additional 1,400 acres, and there is also the tiny Streeter Point Recreation Area. Unfortunately, the Brimfield State Forest is one of the few in Massachusetts that does not allow Bowser as a visitor. There are so many recreational options available to guests and canine companions, both at the Publick House Historic Resort and nearby, that most people will want to make reservations for several nights to fully appreciate the overall experience.

Little Harbor Guest House

20 Stockton Shortcut Road
Wareham, Massachusetts 02571
(508) 295-6329

Host: Dennis Coppola
Rooms: 4 doubles, 1 suite
Rates: Doubles $55-77 (B&B)
Payment: MC and VISA
Children: Welcome
Dogs: Welcome with advance notice and prior approval (must not be left alone)
Open: All year

The Little Harbor Guest House is a rambling, red Cape Cod cottage that was built in the early 1700s. For those who love a quiet country setting, would like to play a little golf, and want to be within walking distance of the beach, this is just the place. This unpretentious guest house, surrounded on all sides by manicured fairways, is located next to the road leading to the Little Harbor Country Club. An important aside, neither the house nor its guests have ever been hit by a stray golf ball.

The expansive cottage is actually nestled on a small knoll, with both a putting green and a swimming pool set off to one side. Upon entering the B&B, most people are drawn to the spacious living room and formal dining room that comprise most of the first floor. A sectional sofa and several side chairs situated around the enormous fireplace provide the framework for the living room. What we found most interesting were the assortment of collectibles, including an old Victrola, as well as a handful of clocks, that were placed around this chamber and throughout the cottage. The adjacent dining room is welcoming, even in the heart of winter, as its coral colored walls lend a degree of warmth to this space. Delicate roses and other flowers have been hand-painted on the fireplace mantel and around the base of the chandelier. Each morning, a Continental breakfast is served in here. This may sound like simple fare, but the homemade pastries, fresh fruits, juices, and coffee or tea, are beautifully presented. To the rear of the dining room, there is a small bar, which is usually an integral ingredient for the evening, as it allows guests to prepare their favorite libations.

The bedrooms are easily accessed by ascending the front staircase, which climbs past an array of photographs that frame a stained glass window. The guest bedrooms are grouped in two sections of the house. The first two chambers, located near the top of the stairs, are decorated in pinks and greens, and are furnished with simple and comfortable pieces. The other two bedrooms are found down a zig-zagging hallway. One of these chambers has a canopy bed with a floral bedspread and coordinated canopy. Pink pencil-thin lines have been painted on the bed posts, complementing the other pink hues found around the fireplace mantel. The last room is often referred to as the Wicker Room, aptly named because it is furnished with an array of white wicker furniture. Although the ceiling is fairly low in here, it is also privy to pleasant views of both the front yard and golf course through the small-paned windows. We also thought the tropical wall treatment was both unusual and fun.

Even though this is a relatively small B&B, guests will find it is not lacking in diversions. There is a good-sized swimming pool and Jacuzzi, which guests may utilize in the summer months. The adjacent putting green is the perfect place to practice before heading over to the golf course. Bowser will certainly enjoy a walk down the road to the beach. The Little Harbor Guest House is situated in a quiet country setting that can be easily explored on foot. Or, visitors may prefer to jump into the car and, within 20 minutes, arrive at the Myles Standish State Forest (over 14,000 acres) or at the Shawme Crowell State Forest (742 acres). The former is inland and heavily forested, while the latter is closer to the ocean and offers some pretty walking trails. Within close proximity to the Little Harbor Guest House are the charming villages of Marion and the many beachside communities lining the shores of Cape Cod. Guests are certain to feel that the B&B is well located to easily access the many other resort destinations in southeastern Massachusetts, yet it is removed from the crowds.

The Victorian

583 Linwood Avenue
Whitinsville, Massachusetts   01588
(508) 234-2500

Innkeeper: *Rick Clarke*
Rooms: *8 doubles*
Rates: *Doubles: $75-100 (B&B)*
Payment: *AE, MC, and VISA*
Children: *Welcome*
Dogs: *Welcome with prior approval*
Open: *All year*

The rose-colored Victorian was built by James Fletcher Whitin in 1871. This 23-room mansion sits atop a knoll, and is surrounded by mature groves of trees, a large pond, a carriage house, and a gate house. The three-story main house not only still has a copper mansard roof line, but, true to its name, is bestowed with many Victorian features. The home remained within the Whitin family for over a century and although the original 250 acres have dwindled to just 50 acres, the intrinsic elegance and beauty of the inn remain very much intact.

As new arrivals step through the etched glass front doors into the inn, they will have a sense of time standing still. The carefully maintained leather wainscotings and polished walnut, cherry, and mahogany woodworking have become more lustrous over the years. Wallpapers are representative of the Victorian period, and are highlighted by crystal and brass sconces, 10-foot high gilt mirrors, and original oil paintings. Everything from the Oriental rugs and marble fireplaces to the antique furnishings and grand piano, create images of another era.

Most of the spacious bedrooms has been named after a particular color scheme or view. Thus, those who ask for the River Room or Pond Room will have views of the water. The one working fireplace is fitted with a Franklin stove and is found in the Armour Room. Heavy wood doors lead into chambers with 12- to 15-foot ceilings, where guests will find wood paneling amid interesting architectural features such as window seats, enormous arched windows, and separate dressing rooms. In one room, a king-size bed is placed among period antiques such as a fainting couch and high boy dresser, while in another, a brass bed is complemented by a Victorian settee. Fresh flowers and potted plants add a festive touch to each of the chambers.

In the morning, a Continental breakfast is served, although more substantial meals can be requested, for a slight additional charge. In many circles, the Victorian is not necessarily known for its overnight accommodations, but for its excellent restaurant. Guests may either dine in the intimate Louis XV parlor with its 14-foot ceilings, piano, gold leaf chandelier, and marble fireplace, or in the large library with its vast collection of books. The latter chamber also contains a fireplace and a matching pair of intimate alcoves, outfitted with just a single table. The ever-changing menu offers selections such as filet mignon, pheasant, rack of lamb, salmon in basil sauce, lobster, or roast duckling. At the end of this lovely meal, many like to take a pleasant walk through the grounds.

Those in search of activities in and around Whitinsville will find Purgatory Chasm in Sutton to be an interesting spot. This half-mile stretch of rock and water is quite spectacular. There are caves to explore, paths to follow, and at the end of the journey, fresh spring water to drink. Also in the area, visitors will discover many ponds and lakes, including Lake Chaubunagungamaug and the Wakefield Pond. Bowser might also enjoy a walk in Walls Reservation or along the trails in either Hopkinton or Ashland State Parks.

Jericho Valley Inn

P.O. Box 239
Route 43
Williamstown, Massachusetts   01267
(800) JERICHO, (413) 458-9511

Owner: Ed Hanify
Rooms: 25 suites and cottages
Rates: Suites $48-228 (B&B), Cottages $108-238 (B&B)
Payment: AE, DC, MC, and VISA
Children: Welcome (cribs, cots, babysitters, and highchairs are available)
Dogs: Welcome in the cottages
Open: All year

Williamstown is a great place, offering visitors far ranging cultural and recreational choices. Aside from attracting parents visiting their children at Williams College, there are others who like its location — close to the Jiminy Peak Ski Resort, Vermont's Green Mountains, and the Berkshire Hills. The Jericho Valley Inn is situated just five miles south of the town center, where it rests on a 350-acre hillside setting. While the inn is a popular three-season destination, its main draw is in the winter, when many of the guests use it as a base for skiing throughout the region.

From rural Route 43, the Jericho Valley Inn resembles a very up-scale motor court, with two good-sized wings connected to the main building. Upon closer examination, guests will see these buildings are fronted by small white picket fences and hedges which imbue it with a sense of charm. A second building, containing only suites, is set unobtrusively over by the swimming pool. Guests traveling with a dog will be most interested in the handful of colorful cottages that are located up a small, paved road that bisects the surrounding woods.

As guests enter the reception area, they will begin to understand what makes the Jericho Valley Inn so unique. The cheerful common room is festive with its polka dot wallpaper, huge comfortable sofas and chairs, and light pine furniture. Flower arrangements and plants, placed in pretty bowls and wicker baskets, further enliven the space. A large fieldstone fireplace takes up an entire wall, making it the focal point for this comfortable area. A variety of maps, restaurant information, and activity ideas can be found in an array of brochures that are displayed alongside the front desk. There is also a small, fireplaced breakfast room, where a variety of breads and muffins, along with beverages, are available each morning for all guests of the inn to enjoy.

As we mentioned, there are several types of accommodations to choose from, all of which have been updated over the last year. The rooms in the main building are nicely decorated chambers with coordinated fabrics covering the queen-size finial beds and framing the windows. Plush wall-to-wall carpeting softens footsteps and provides the basis for the other comfortable furnishings. The private bathrooms are modern and well-equipped with thick towels and soaps. Color cable televisions and direct dial telephones are other welcome conveniences. Those wanting slightly more space should request a suite. The decor is exactly like that of the main inn rooms, but they offer a choice of one-, two-, or three-bedroom configurations. We liked the living rooms which are outfitted with fireplaces, as well as the fully-equipped eat-in kitchens.

Finally, there are the cottages located in a secluded hillside setting. These not only vary in color (red, yellow, green, and white), but also range in size from one to three bedrooms. Ed is justifiably proud of the renovations to all of these accommodations. Over the last year, they have painted and wallpapered each cottage, and have put floral spreads on the beds and coordinated draperies around the windows. The furnishings are all new too, as well as the wall-to-wall carpeting. These units feature living rooms with fireplaces, along with televisions and sofa beds. The kitchens are fully-equipped and good-sized. Each of the cottages also has individual heat and air-conditioning to ensure guests' comfort during their stay. Picnic tables are set invitingly around the grounds, allowing everyone to enjoy the warmth of a summer's day or the picturesque fall foliage.

As we mentioned earlier, Jiminy Peak is the closest downhill skiing to the Jericho Valley Inn. Bowser might be more interested in a trip to the Mount Greylock State Reservation to accompany his human companions on either a cross-country skiing or snowshoeing outing. In nearby Dalton, there is the Waconah Falls State Park, which comprises just over 100 acres. The Honwee Mountain or Drury Mountain State Forests are also easily accessible from the inn and have many hiking trails. Bowser might want to visit Clarksburg State Park, as well. There are over 3,000 acres to explore here, along with places to canoe or kayak. Guests who stay here will find the Hanifys are always happy to answer questions, provide recommendations for area activities and attractions, and make arrangements for any special needs that might arise.

The Williams Inn

On the Green
Williamstown, Massachusetts   01267
(413) 458-9371, Fax (413) 458-2767

General Manager: Carl Faulkner
Rooms: 17 singles, 81 doubles, 2 suites
Rates: Singles $85-115 (EP), Doubles $100-145 (EP), Suites $160-190 (EP)
Payment: AE, DSC, MC, and VISA
Children: Welcome, no charge for children under the age of fourteen when staying with
*   their parents (cribs, cots, and highchairs are available)*
Dogs: Welcome in the first floor bedrooms for a $5 fee
Open: All year

The original Williams Inn was set in the middle of the Williams College campus; however, that building has since been converted into a student dormitory. Today, the newer Williams Inn lies on the edge of campus. From the outside, the inn looks like an expansive motor lodge; however once inside, guests will see that it is more reminiscent of a traditional country inn. The few features that could not be duplicated are the sloping creaky floors, wainscoting, and beamed ceilings. But what guests may forego in historic charm, they gain in modern amenities.

The public areas at the inn have been painted in traditional Williamsburg blues and greens and are furnished with reproduction English antiques and period furnishings. The one exception to this traditional color scheme is found in the dining room. This space has a sense of graciousness about it, despite its bold, crimson walls. The food is good, with dinner entrées that include a chicken breast Dijonaise, tortellini Cajun style, and filet mignon. One of the more popular meals at the inn is Sunday brunch, as much for its varied selections as for the sheer abundance of food served. The adjacent Tavern is the most contemporary of the public rooms, with large windows overlooking the inn's grounds and beyond to the college.

Guest bedrooms have been tastefully decorated in several color schemes. Mauve tones are combined with either pale green or blue wall treatments. Coordinated quilted and fitted chintz coverlets and dust ruffles encase each of the beds. Brass floor and table lamps are placed next to wing chairs and on the bedside tables. The bathrooms have been updated with new fixtures, Corian sinks, and heat lamps. The Williams Inn is a combination of a traditional country inn and a large hotel, providing charming rooms and modern amenities. Those wishing to get some exercise or unwind after a long day will be pleased with the heated indoor swimming pool, Jacuzzi, and individual men's and women's saunas. For those who prefer to just relax after a long day of cross-country or downhill skiing, there is a comfortable sitting room with a blazing fireplace.

One of the inn's best features is its proximity to Williamstown. Bowser will certainly enjoy walks into the charming village, or around the Williams College campus. Sporting events, art festivals, and a terrific summer theater are just a few of the many seasonal events that are offered through the college. In the winter months, guests can take Bowser cross-country skiing on trails that begin near the inn. Downhill skiing is as close as Jiminy Peak, or a bit farther away in neighboring Vermont. State parks are abundant in the area. The largest of these is the Mount Greylock State Reservation with over 12,000 acres of land accessible to Bowser and his hiking, cross-country skiing, or snowmobiling friends. A bit closer to Williamstown, there is the Savoy Mountain State Forest which also provides just about any wilderness recreational opportunity visitors could imagine.

Lane's End Cottage

268 Main Street
Yarmouth Port, Massachusetts   02675
(508) 362-5298

Hostess: Valerie Butler
Rooms: 3 doubles
Rates: $80-95 (B&B)
Payment: Personal checks
Children: Welcome with prior approval
Dogs: Very well-behaved dogs are welcome with prior approval
Open: All year

The charming hamlet of Yarmouth Port is an enchanting destination for those who are interested in investigating some of the Cape's more historic towns set off the beaten path. Lane's End Cottage is a pretty, weathered shingle Cape, fronted by a low, white picket fence and lovely perennial gardens. Guests will find it by looking for a narrow gravel lane, which is situated just across from the tiny town common, and following it down a hill to the cottage. The 290-year-old home was rolled to its current location by oxen in the early 1850s, although guests would never know that today, as it is surrounded by large shade trees and dense woods. Following the path to the front door, new arrivals should take a moment to look at the original bulls-eye glass in the windows over the doorway. Once inside, guests will be greeted by the very affable Valerie, and her elderly Golden Retriever.

To the right of the intimate entry, where a stand is brimming with umbrellas for those who have forgotten to bring their own, is the lovely sitting room. Afternoon sunlight pours in over the sofa and side chairs, which are set invitingly around the front windows. The low table is graced with interesting coffee table books. Included in the collection is a journal, authored by previous guests, that is full of ideas for interesting places to go and things to do in the area. A fireplace further sets the tone for this space, as does the array of American and English antiques set around a lovely old grandfather clock.

Just steps from the sitting room, guests will enter into a dining room. Each morning, a hearty repast of homemade breads, muffins, or popovers, coupled with hot cereals or eggs, is served in here. This meal, weather permitting, can also be taken out to the cobblestone terrace and enjoyed amid the potted plants. Occasionally, deer can be seen foraging in the woods. The authentic country kitchen is where guests are often found, however, chatting with Valerie as she prepares breakfast, or a little delectable that might accompany afternoon tea. We discovered during our visit that even though Lane's End Cottage is nestled off the beaten track, Valerie has had scores of guests since she opened the house as a B&B in 1983. In addition to hosting visitors from the West Coast, she has also had travelers from as far away as Tokyo and Armenia. She informed us that one guest loves the B&B so much she has stayed there over two dozen times!

Each of the guest rooms at the Lane's End Cottage is desirable in its own way. One of these is located just off the formal entry. This sunny corner room is decorated with a floral wallpaper and is accented with a rose trim. The queen bed is incredibly inviting, as it is covered with a featherbed and a down comforter. A fireplace, coupled with the lovely family heirlooms, makes this room truly exceptional. There are additional thoughtful touches as well, such as the telephone that does not ring, but can be used for dialing out. To the rear of this room is an elongated bathroom, which also contains a washer and dryer set behind a pair of closet doors. One of Valerie's off-season projects will be to remove these doors and convert the space into a shower. During their stay, guests are often drawn out of the room, through the glass doors, and onto the wonderful cobblestone patio where the surrounding woodland setting unfolds. In the morning, the birds can be seen flying from tree to tree, and at dusk a family of deer often shyly makes its way toward the house. The other two bedrooms are located upstairs. One has a queen-size bed that is covered with a colorful comforter, and the room is filled with pretty knickknacks. The rather small bathroom is enhanced by a skylight. The other chamber offers a pair of twin beds that are also invitingly draped with feather beds. During our visit, we found a cat sprawled out on one of the beds, basking in the afternoon sun.

We thoroughly enjoyed the Lane's End Cottage for many reasons, most of which involve relaxing and having the sensation of really getting away from it all. Some enjoy basking in the outdoor sun, reclined on the chaise lounges set on the patio. Others prefer to curl up with a good book in front of the fireplace. Bowser will undoubtedly want to explore the woods, or lead his companions on long walks through the village. Beaches, ponds, and parks are also just a short distance from the the B&B. Visitors are not far from the Nickerson State Park, where they may hike, swim, and explore with Bowser. This mid-Cape destination allows visitors to either head into some of the more populated communities, meander along rural route 6A, or just find a deserted beach and enjoy the lovely setting.

The Village Inn

P.O. Box 1, Route 6A
Yarmouth Port, Massachusetts 02675
(508) 362-3182

Innkeepers: Esther and Mac Hickey
Rooms: 10 doubles
Rates: Doubles: $55-75 (B&B)
Payment: MC and VISA
Children: Welcome with advance reservations (cribs, cots, and highchairs are available)
Dogs: Well-behaved dogs are welcome, but may not come into the common areas.
Open: All year

Visitors to the small towns along Cape Cod's King's Road (Route 6A) will be pleased to discover they are still brimming with New England charm and history. This portion of the Cape remains relatively unspoiled, particularly when compared to the more commercial southern side. As visitors drive along 6A, they will see that many of the traditional sea captain's homes have been transformed into quaint country inns or exclusive antique shops. The Village Inn, fitted with white clapboards and green shutters, is one such example. Built in 1795 for a local sea captain, this Colonial home stands in the heart of Yarmouth Port's historic district.

Not much has changed at The Village Inn since we first started writing about it almost ten years ago, and for that we are thankful. Most people enter the

B&B through a side door, which leads into the quaint, country kitchen. This dark wood-paneled chamber is brimming with pots and knickknacks collected from other eras. From here, guests will step up into the original dining room, which today contains a piano. As they walk further into the house, new arrivals will begin to appreciate all that the Hickey's have done to preserve the unique historic features of their wonderful old home. The inviting living room is loaded with books and antiques, as well as decorative plates lining the walls. The front parlor is also charming and just a bit more secluded. In the warmer months, breakfast is served on the enclosed porch, and consists of homemade breads and muffins, fruit, coffee, and juice. Anyone who is in the mood for a truly hearty New England breakfast, can ask Esther to create one of her breakfast specials. She is always more than happy to oblige.

There is one downstairs bedroom at the B&B. This is the Yarmouth Room, with a queen-size bed and a fireplace. Its crimson floors are covered with braided rugs, and the coffee-colored walls are filled with windows framed by sheer curtains. The private bathroom, located just across the hall, is highlighted by a copper bathtub. Esther finds the copper makes the bath water stay warmer much longer than it would in a traditional tub. All of the other bedrooms are located upstairs off the main hall. Old-fashioned floral wallpaper and framed prints line the walls. These are decidedly simple guest chambers, containing maple frame beds draped in calico coverlets and handmade quilts. Brewster is a warm, coral pink guest room, while the light and airy Truro is painted a pastel yellow. Braided rugs cover the wide board floors that are painted a faded avocado green. The country furnishings merely enhance the otherwise undisturbed beauty of the house, where wainscotings, ceiling moldings, tiny fireplaces, and built-in bookshelves are the focal points.

Bowser will undoubtedly want to investigate the acre or so of land at the Village Inn, which is separated from the house by a split-rail fence. First-time visitors to the area often enjoy a leisurely drive down the winding Route 6A, which leads to other charming, historic villages, an array of antique stores (this region is renowned as an antique mecca), and countless picturesque ponds and saltwater beaches. Others prefer exploring the neighboring back country roads by way of foot or bicycle. Those who are interested in golf and tennis need only travel a short distance to find these recreational options.

Vermont

The Inn at High View

RR #1, Box 201A
Andover, Vermont   05143
(802) 875-2724, Fax (802) 875-4021

Innkeepers: Gregory Bohan and Sal Massaro
Rooms: 6 doubles, 2 suites
Rates: Doubles $90-115 (B&B), Suites $125 (B&B)
Payment: MC and VISA
Children: Welcome in the suites (cribs, cots, and babysitters are available)
Dogs: Welcome in the suites
Open: All year except for two weeks in April and November

The Inn at High View is aptly named, as it sits perched on a Vermont hill with spectacular panoramic views of the distant mountains. Andover is an intimate hamlet that lies between other well-traveled towns such as Weston, Chester, and Ludlow. We visited in the fall, when the foliage was at its peak, the air was crisp, and the sky a deep blue. As we left the main road and headed up a steep country lane, we rose above the tree line and saw open fields and a few farms. At the top of one rise, we came upon The Inn at High View.

The house is a typical Vermont farmhouse. It was built in 1789 and, from the exterior, still appears authentically preserved. The traditional metal roof is dotted with brick chimneys and framed by eaves and gables. The property around the inn is surrounded by pine and maple trees and delineated by rock walls and adjacent pastures. A pool, just below the inn, is surrounded by a rock wall, creating a more natural setting. The white gazebo stands in stark contrast against the brilliant orange, gold, and red hillsides below.

Most people enter the inn by way of the screened-in porch. As we stepped through the front door, it was hard for us to imagine that during the 1950s and 1960s the inn was used as a Swedish Ski Club. The thickly carpeted rooms are decorated with a mix of contemporary and country furnishings. Although the inn still has its antique characteristics, there are many modern features, as well. The living room has a light blue, semi-circular sectional sofa placed in front of the fireplace. A coffee table is brimming with a full complement of magazines. In one corner a chess board has been placed upon a charming game table.

The bedrooms are furnished with country pine antiques and reproductions. Most are furnished with either oak or canopy beds covered in down comforters and Vermont quilts. One of the more popular chambers is a queen-size bedroom that lies just behind the reception area. Its corner location allows for plenty of sunshine to permeate all corners of the room, and makes it privy to some of the more spectacular valley views. Anyone traveling with Bowser is welcome to stay in one of the two-room suites. The colors in these reflect what is found in the other guest rooms — a melange of peach and green, or green and pale blue. The beauty of these spaces is that they offer separate outside entrances, making it easier to go on walks with Bowser. One suite contains a bedroom with two double beds and a separate sitting room, while the other has a double bed and small sitting area within each of the two rooms.

In the morning, guests enjoy gathering around the circular Queen Anne table in the cheery red dining room. Some of the best views of the valley can be enjoyed through its paned windows. Greg tells us that the breakfasts are hearty, but not fancy. One of their most popular meals is French toast made with cinnamon raisin bread and topped with raspberries. Waffles and pancakes are often complemented by seasonal fresh fruit. A variety of egg dishes can be made to order and are often enjoyed with homemade biscuits, bacon, or sausage. We thought the idea of "moonstruck eggs" was unusual. Anyone who missed the movie should know that the yolk is removed, the eggs are fried with peppers, and then served with hash browns. Lighter fare is available upon request and can include cereals, yogurt, or fresh fruit. The atmosphere around the breakfast table is always convivial, with guests busy planning their day's adventures.

There are plenty of activities at the inn which Bowser will find engaging. The inn is set on 52 acres that guests can hike on in the summer, and use as an informal cross-country ski area in the winter months. People generally ski along the property until they reach another area which has an additional 15 kilometers of trails. Bowser will enjoy an immense amount of outdoor freedom during the visit. Just south of Andover, there is the Williams River State Forest, where people and their canine companions will encounter still more hiking options. Others may prefer investigating the Okemo or Hapgood State Forests.

Hill Farm Inn

RR 2, Box 2015
Arlington, Vermont 05250
(800) 882-2545, (802) 375-2269

Innkeepers: Regan and John Chichester
Rooms: 11 doubles, 2 suites, 4 cabins
Rates: Doubles $75-110 (B&B), Suites $110 (B&B), Cabins $75-90 (B&B)
Payment: AE, DSC, MC, and VISA
Children: Welcome (cribs, cots, and highchairs are available)
Dogs: Welcome in cabins for $10 daily per pet (May 20 - October 20)
Open: All year

Set on a hill, overlooking the Battenkill and Green Mountains, stands the Hill Farm Inn. The farm dates back to 1775, when 50 acres of land were deeded to the Hill family by King George of England. By 1790, they had built a small guest house, which is still standing on the property today. The main farmhouse, constructed in 1830, was built on a site about a mile from the inn and then hauled by a team of 40 oxen to its present location. Then, in the early 1900s, Mettie Hill began accepting boarders, thereby beginning the Hill family innkeeping tradition. Aside from its role as an inn, the farm was also an active dairy until 1986. Today, the farmland has been preserved with the help of the American Farmland Trust and the Vermont Land Conservancy. What this means to guests is that they are able to still enjoy the rural landscape surrounding the inn.

We have visited the Hill Farm Inn on a number of occasions over the years, but on this trip we noticed a few subtle changes. The rambling white farmhouse appeared fresher with a new coat of paint, as did the screened-in porch, which contained a few pieces of pretty white wicker furniture. The property around the inn also seemed more manicured and its gardens were festive with colorful flowers. As we stepped into the house though, we noticed that the dining room was still painted a lovely shade of pale blue. Regan emerged from the kitchen to greet us, and we soon learned that she and her husband, John, along with their toddler, were the new owners of the Hill Farm Inn.

Even though a few things have changed for the better at the inn, others have thankfully stayed the same. The big country kitchen, although slightly modernized, is still the foundation for the inn. Here, Regan creates the hearty breakfasts guests enjoy each morning. The meal usually begins with the delicious Hill Farm granola and yogurt, along with freshly baked breads. Those who need a bit more sustenance, may be offered a choice of blueberry pancakes, waffles, or French toast drenched in real maple syrup and accompanied by Vermont-cured bacon or ham. The Hill Farm Inn used to serve dinner; however, the Chichesters have found that with the wide variety of excellent restaurants available locally, there really isn't a need for them to do so anymore. The dining room tables are often reserved for an ongoing jig-saw puzzle, or are laden in the afternoon with wonderful baked treats as well as coffee or tea.

Guests may take their refreshments into the adjacent common room. This is a sunny and inviting space, with a large modern sofa and other comfortable chairs set on hardwood floors. The pastel colors in the huge arrangement of wildflowers ties together the many colors in here. Select a magazine from the dozens laid out on the enormous coffee table, and settle down in front of the fire. Others might prefer to play the piano, which is placed against a wall. A staircase leads from the living room to the upstairs bedrooms; however, those traveling with Bowser will be far more comfortable in the cabins located a hundred yards from the main farmhouse.

The white-washed cabins are cozy, although minimally appointed. Guests should not expect an array of antiques, knickknacks, and extra amenities, but they will certainly appreciate the clean and attractively decorated rooms. Country curtains hang at the windows and cotton coverlets adorn the beds. Butternut is the largest cabin and offers two bed chambers located off a central sitting room. A refrigerator is a welcome added convenience. Maple, on the other hand, has one double bedroom and an adjacent sitting room equipped with a day bed. The Willows provides the same configuration as Maple, but has twin beds which can be combined to form a king-size bed. Finally, Mulberry is the smallest of the cabins, but what it lacks in size it makes up for in mountain views. All of the cabins have two additional amenities, private bathrooms and small porches which have terrific views of the surrounding property.

There are acres of property to explore and quiet country roads to walk on. Follow the road down the hill to a storybook New England church and adjacent graveyard. A stroll up the road will certainly offer the best views of the valley below. The Hill Farm Inn has a mile of frontage along the Battenkill River, which is renowned for its fly fishing. Bowser might be more intrigued with forays along its banks. The town of Arlington is close to the inn, and is also adjacent to a portion of the Green Mountain National Forest where visitors will find just about any recreational option available to them and to Bowser. Nature trails in the Shaftsbury State Park, and in both the Arlington and Rupert State Forests, are additional options.

Greenhurst Inn

RD 2, Box 60
Route 107
Bethel, Vermont   05032-9404
(802) 234-9474

Innkeeper: Lyle Wolf
Rooms: 12 doubles, 1 suite
Rates: Doubles $50-95 (B&B), Suite $100 (B&B)
Payment: DSC, MC ,and VISA
Children: Welcome (cribs, cots, and highchairs are available)
Dogs: Welcome with prior approval, but must not be left alone in the room
Open: All year

The idea of Victorian mansions and Vermont don't necessarily coincide; however, in the tiny town of Bethel travelers will be pleased to discover a fine example of Victorian architecture in the Greenhurst Inn. The house was built in 1890 as a private residence for the Harrington family of Philadelphia. They only lived in it a short while, and by 1916 it had been converted into a small country hospital. Finally, in the mid-1930s, the grand Victorian was sold to Kate Green, who decided to open it as an inn. More recently, in 1981, Lyle Wolf purchased the inn, imbued it with his eclectic sense of style, and had it listed on the National Register of Historic Places. From its corner location, it is one of the most prominent landmarks in Bethel.

Upon entering the rambling old home, new arrivals usually need a few moments to become accustomed to the light. Once they do, the high ceilings, detailed woodworking, and original brass fixtures are revealed. To the left and right of the front entry are the intimate parlors, filled with antiques obtained over the years at country auctions or borrowed from Lyle's personal collection. Interspersed with these lovely pieces, guests will also find a vintage Victrola and piano, as well as more modern conveniences such as a television, VCR, and stereo. But the centerpiece for the huge foyer is the grand carved staircase that curves up to the second floor guest rooms. Lining the walls is Lyle's unique collection of framed, 100-year-old advertisements he has taken from the original magazines in which they appeared. Framing, we soon discovered, is only one of Lyle's many hobbies.

As guests ascend the stairs to the upper floor, an array of interesting details continues to unfold. The original second floor bedrooms were designed for the owners of the house and their family, while the back wing was designated for the staff. One bedroom of note is the former doctor's operating room. The doctor relied on natural sunlight to illuminate the room; therefore, this chamber is filled with floor-to-ceiling windows. Other bedrooms have ornate fireplaces, rounded sitting alcoves, or small libraries. Guests will find that each space has been tastefully decorated, offering features such as handmade quilts covering the carved wood or brass and painted iron bedsteads. In addition to the mints on the pillows, there is also a tray on the bureau holding a bottle of Perrier, a corkscrew, and a small envelope bearing the inscription "Never a headache at the Greenhurst." Although many of the baths are shared, this potential inconvenience is compensated for by a thoughtful selection of Gilchrist and Soames bath crystals, French-milled soap, a mending kit, and a spare toothbrush and toothpaste. To the rear of the inn, there are the smaller and cozier chambers, that are also filled with antiques. While these are very charming, they lack some of the Victorian character found in the bedrooms designed for the original family members.

In the morning, a deluxe Continental breakfast is served in the spacious and ornate dining room. Fresh fruits, quick breads, muffins, and an assortment of preserves are always available, as is cold cereal. After breakfast, many people like to plan their day's outing. Some choose to start it off with a game of croquet or tennis on the inn's courts. Those who are interested in traveling a little farther afield will find the Appalachian Trail threading its way through the region. Silver Lake is a great choice for swimming and picnicking, as is the nature trail at Texas Falls. Lyle is also a good resource with ideas on what to do with Bowser, and will certainly know of any secret places that might appeal to both Bowser and friends.

The Hugging Bear Inn

Main Street
RR1, Box 32
Chester, Vermont 05143
(802) 875-2412

Innkeeper: Georgette Thomas
Rooms: 6 doubles
Rates: $55-95 (B&B)
Payment: AE, DSC, MC, and VISA
Children: Welcome (highchairs, cribs, cots and babysitters can be arranged)
Dogs: Well-behaved dogs are accepted in the off-season, not on holidays or July through
October ($10 nightly fee)
Open: All year

Teddy bears have been around almost as long as there have been children to enjoy them. More unusual though is an antique inn where the teddy bears are the focus of attention, and not the historic furnishings or the decor. Twelve years ago, when Georgette Thomas opened her inn, she never could have imagined that the whimsical bears would appeal to her guests as much as they did to her.

The 1850 Italian Colonnade and Queen-Anne style building, where the bears reside, is part of Chester's large historic district. The inn is difficult to miss on a drive down Main Street, as an array of teddy bears peek out the bay windows at passing motorists, seemingly beckoning them to come inside. A teddy bear flag hangs from the porch, and life-size teddy bears sit on white wicker porch chairs or, in the winter months, drive the sleigh (pulled by more bears) in the front yard. There are also teddy bears in their bedrooms, already tucked into the beds, placed on the dressers and window sills, and even sitting on the night lights. Over the years, Georgette has collected bears of all backgrounds and nationalities. There are life-size and miniature bears, doctor bears, dancing bears, puppet bears, soft bears, bristly bears — a bear for every mood, personality, or occasion. The bears used to reside exclusively at the inn, but they quickly outgrew their home. Georgette knew that she had to do something, so she decided to open a shop in the Carriage House for them, filling it with over 4,000 types of teddy bears.

It is difficult not to talk about bears when describing the Hugging Bear Inn, but we will try. There is a distinct Victorian feeling to the inn, with a preponderance of oak on the floors and the walls, lace fabrics covering the windows, and country antiques gracing the rooms. There are a number of common areas in the house, including a fireplaced living room with comfortable sofas and a small study that doubles as a game room. In addition to a television and VCR, Georgette has also stocked the study with a wide variety of board games and toys. In the evening, guests follow the curves of the oak staircase to their bedrooms. Each of these chambers is somewhat different, but all are outfitted with teddy bears. One of the most interesting rooms is located in the turret, where rounded walls surround the antique bed draped with a floral comforter. Another bedroom has a more juvenile motif with two double beds covered in teddy bear comforters. An oak bureau in here is indicative of the sampling of American furnishings guests will find in the other bedrooms as well. This was our fourth visit to the inn, and we found that it was just as charming as when we first discovered it ten years ago.

Breakfast is perhaps one of the more social times at the Hugging Bear Inn, as guests gather around the large table in the dining room for the morning's fare. The hearty meal varies; however, it is always accompanied by a selection of cold cereals and fresh breads, as well as juice, hot chocolate, and coffee. The main dish for the day could include eggs (prepared in a variety of styles), French toast, or the house special, blueberry or apple pancakes. Afterwards, some choose to take Bowser for a walk along the hillside behind the inn, while others prefer to stroll down main street for a little window shopping. Just outside of Chester, there are a few state forests that are worth investigating. The Williams River, W.C. Putnam, and the Grafton State Forests are all just a short drive from the inn and offer fun picnicking and hiking opportunities. In the winter months, the focus turns to cross-country skiing, and skiers can bring Bowser to the state forests just outside Grafton and Chester.

As a final note, it is unfortunate that those traveling with a dog are limited to off-peak periods; however, guests who visit during the winter months are certain to enjoy the quieter times in Chester. The tourists are gone, the main street is relatively uncrowded, and visitors can gain a better sense of what this town might have been like around the turn-of-the-century.

The Inn on the Common

Box 75
Craftsbury Common, Vermont 05827
(800) 521-2233, (802) 586-9619, Fax (802) 586-2249

Innkeepers: Penny and Michael Schmitt
Rooms: 14 doubles, 2 suites
Rates: Doubles $200-270 (MAP), Suites $230-270 (MAP)
Payment: MC and VISA
Children: Welcome (cribs, cots, and babysitters are available)
Dogs: Well-behaved dogs are welcome, advance notice is preferred ($15 fee per pet per visit)
Open: All year

When we first visited The Inn on the Common, we came away with a feeling that we had found one of the more unique inns in all of New England — ten years later, we still feel that way. Here, in the isolated Northeast Kingdom, lies an exquisite, small inn which has obviously been cultivated with great care. The property is as stunning as the inn's rooms, with formal English gardens, manicured hedges bordered by colorful perennials, and breathtaking views of the valley and distant mountains.

The picturesque Craftsbury Common, where the inn is located, is a New England village taken straight from a Norman Rockwell canvas. Each of the antique Federal homes lining the village's main road are painted white, creating a pristine frontispiece to the rolling hills and stands of maple and spruce that surround them. The inn is comprised of three buildings that adhere to the same architectural style of the private homes on the common. The main inn was built in 1795 by the town's founder; the south annex was added later by his son, and the north annex was completed in 1840.

The main inn remains our favorite building, with guest rooms located at the top of a steep, narrow flight of stairs. Guests will still find beautiful handmade Vermont quilts covering the antique four-poster and canopy beds. These quilts usually set the color scheme for the rooms — seafoam green complementing a coral pink or a cornflower blue, or a red and green floral pattern against a stark white background. Elegant country antiques and reproductions complete the elegant country decor. Although there are clock radios in the bedrooms, the absence of telephones, televisions, and other modern amenities is in keeping with the historic ambiance. The private bathrooms are well stocked with Gilchrist and Soames soaps and shampoos, and after the bath guests can wrap themselves in thick terry robes. Those who prefer huge spaces, might reserve the first floor bedroom in the annex across from the main inn. This spacious chamber has been decorated in sage green, with coordinated draperies at the windows and a handmade quilt covering the bed. Pretty glasses have been set out on a tray, perhaps waiting to be filled with wine from the Schmitts' extensive wine cellar. Several of the chambers contain fireplaces or woodstoves, while others have sitting areas and garden views.

There are plenty of inviting common rooms in each of the buildings, all of them containing many intimate nooks and crannies. The formal living room in the main inn is brimming with antiques and beautifully upholstered chintz furniture. The fresh flower arrangements, found throughout the inn, add the finishing touches to each room. Those who have forgotten their reading materials will find that the built-in bookshelves offer an extensive selection. The informal library, just across the hall, is a favorite spot for before and after dinner socializing. Guests often meet here for cocktails before going into the formal dining room for dinner.

As lovely as the bedrooms might be, it is the food that has won praise from restaurant critics and travel writers over the years. No two menus are ever alike, because the chef chooses to prepare only what is fresh and available on any given day. There are always two appetizer selections, which might include a seafood mousse drizzled with a creamy chive sauce, asparagus with hollandaise, or trout á l'orange. Soups range from the chilled nectarine to the carrot cumin. Three entrées are served each evening, with choices of chicken, fish, or meat. The mixed grill of duck and chicken is often brushed with a fresh mint berry glaze. The grilled rabbit is braised in a broth of stock, vegetables, and dark beer and then grilled with a maple syrup glaze. Those who like a traditional tenderloin of beef with bernaise butter or veal marsala served in a rich marsala wine cream reduction, might also discover these dishes on the menu during their stay. Diners can select from an extensive wine list, finding something that will undoubtedly serve as the perfect complement to their meal. During our visit, the desserts included a molasses strawberry layer cake, fresh blackberry mousse, and an orange chocolate butter cake.

After such an elaborate meal, many people like to take a leisurely stroll around the inn's grounds, where they should find plenty of stargazing opportunities in the clear nighttime sky. The Inn on the Common is not the sort of place for a one night stay; it is a vacation destination that allows guests to completely relax amid tranquil surroundings. In the summer months, they are free to linger over a game of English croquet, take a refreshing dip in the swimming pool, or play a game of tennis on the clay court. For those inclement days, the television and extensive video library are available in the inn's annex. This is another wonderful room, with cool slate floors holding the huge, deep sofas that flank the fireplace. Guests are also encouraged to take advantage of the facilities at the Craftsbury Sports Center. This is located on Big Hosmer Lake and offers swimming, sailing, horseback riding, canoeing, fishing, and even sculling. Bowser will delight in the long walks through the village and down the quiet country roads. There are miles of hiking trails in the area, and the staff is happy to direct visitors to those trails that best fit their ability level. In the winter months, the activities switch to snowshoeing, skating, and cross-country skiing.

As we mentioned earlier, we have been writing about the Inn on the Common for years. The Schmitts have always enjoyed welcoming guests traveling with a dog. Penny informed us that she has guests who regularly fly out with their dogs, from as far away as the West Coast, so that the entire family might enjoy a traditional New England country inn experience.

Barrows House

Dorset, Vermont 05251
(800) 639-1620, (802) 867-4455, Fax (802) 867-0132

Innkeepers: Jim and Linda McGinnis
Rooms: 19 doubles, 6 suites, 3 cottages
Rates: Double occupancy $180-240 (MAP)
Payment: AE, DSC, MC, and VISA are accepted, but personal checks and cash are
*   preferred*
Children: Welcome (cribs, cots, and babysitters are available)
Dogs: Welcome in the Birds Nest, Field House, and the Carriage House cottages for a daily
*   fee of $10*
Open: All year

The property on which the Barrows House sits has been a landmark in the scenic town of Dorset since the late 1700s when it belonged to the Dorset Church. The original house was built in the 1800s as a home for the Reverend William Jackson. The home and land were subsequently purchased in 1900 by Experience and Theresa Barrows, who turned it into a boarding house. The Barrows House is named after them. Today, the Barrows House offers a wide variety of accommodations housed in traditional white clapboard and black shuttered buildings, set well back from the road and on 12 acres of land.

We have written about the Barrows House for quite a few years, and have seen a couple owners come and go. It has been through another change of ownership since our last visit. The latest twosome are Jim and Linda McGinnis, who continue the seemingly never-ending process of updating and redecorating the guest rooms. Anyone traveling with a dog will be offered accommodations in one of three cottages. The smallest of these is Birds Nest, which provides guests with a queen bed and a separate sitting room with a daybed. Another good choice is the Field House, which offers another queen-size bedroom and a sitting room with two additional beds. The Carriage House is the final option and is equipped with two floors of living space. Some of the single beds can be combined to form king beds if necessary, and the loft space is equipped with bunk beds for the kids. A sitting room with a day bed provides a little extra sleeping space, should it be needed. All of these cottages also have a scattering of modern conveniences such as a television, refrigerator, and air-conditioning. The cottages are decorated with simple furnishings, old-fashioned pine or maple beds and oak bureaus predominating. Some of the rooms also have sectional sofas and bright wallpapers.

We like the Barrows House because there is plenty of space for Bowser to explore, and there is an abundance of on-site activities. There are two all-weather tennis courts and an outdoor heated swimming pool, as well as croquet, badminton, and basketball. Guests may borrow one of the inn's bicycles for exploring the hilly terrain. Locally, Bowser might want to take his two-legged friends into the Green Mountain National Forest for a hiking expedition. Emerald Lake State Park has lakes and streams for swimming and fishing. Rupert State Forest is slightly off the beaten path, but close to Dorset and worth investigating. Back at the inn, many retreat to the sauna to relax and soothe their aching muscles before dinner.

Those seeking a formal environment might want to eat in the main dining room, while others wanting a more casual feeling will choose the club-like Tavern Room. Obviously, with the change in owners, also came a change in the menu. Appetizers include a chilled basil ravioli with marinated tomatoes and mozzarella, duck and garlic sausage wontons, and an asparagus, cheddar cheese, and Bass Ale soup. The entrées include salmon with a sundried tomato pesto cream topped with sautéed spinach and toasted pine nuts, pork chops with fresh chutney and a sundried cranberry and orange sauce, and the grilled sirloin of beef with a four peppercorn sauce. Specials range from a pan roasted Texas antelope with a lingonberry orange sauce to a hazelnut crusted salmon roulade with shiitake mushrooms, roasted peppers, and goat cheese on sweet red pepper fettucine with a dill beurre blanc.

After dinner it might be fun to explore the acreage around the inn with Bowser. There are only a few doggie rules to be aware of during a stay here. Dogs are not allowed in the swimming pool area, and their owners must clean up after any walks on the grounds. The chamber maids will not clean the rooms unless the dog is gone; therefore, guests are asked to let the office know when they are planning to leave their rooms. Provided guests adhere to these simple guidelines, they should have a thoroughly relaxing stay at the Barrows House.

The Old Cutter Inn

RR1, Box 62
Burke Mountain Access Road
East Burke, Vermont 05832-9707
(802) 626-5152

Innkeepers: Marti and Fritz Walther
Rooms: 10 doubles
Rates: $52-66 (EP), $92-104 (MAP)
Payment: MC and VISA
Children: Welcome
Dogs: Always welcome
Open: All year except April and November

The Old Cutter Inn, originally built in 1845, occupies one of the more unique and scenic locations in this part of Vermont. Located at the end of a steep winding road leading to nearby Burke Mountain, the red-shingled farmhouse has a breathtaking view of the mountains, valleys, and distant lakes. The house, barn, and carriage house were originally built as a working dairy farm. The property was later abandoned, only to be purchased by the owners of Burke Mountain, who transformed it into an inn. In 1977, the Walther family bought the inn and have been steadily making improvements to it ever since. On our most recent visit, a huge renovation to the original farmhouse had just taken place, creating a second dining room, new intimate bar, and sunny common area.

Although the inn boasts a number of accommodations, it is perhaps best known for its excellent food. The original beamed-ceiling dining room is quite elegant and is privy to views of the picturesque hills surrounding Lake Willoughby. The new dining room, while unable to offer the same sort of views, does have windows overlooking Burke Mountain. Ambiance aside, the extensive selection of appetizers and entrées will undoubtedly draw diners' attention away from the vistas toward the dinner menu. While the restaurant has physically changed, the appetizer menu has remained relatively the same, although the number of entrées has increased. Appetizers include baked mushroom toast a' la creme, smoked rainbow trout, country pâté, or escargot. Those who are in the mood for traditional entrées will find rack of lamb and beef Wellington to be delicious choices. The inn specialty of veal medallions sautéed in butter with shallots and white wine and then covered in a fresh mushroom and light cream sauce, is a tradition for many patrons. The duck a' l'orange, veal piccata, and rainbow trout stuffed with crabmeat and mushrooms are other popular selections, as well.

Overnight guests are especially fortunate, because after consuming a delicious gourmet meal, they can walk just a few steps to their bed chambers. The bedroom decor at the main inn is rather simple, with Colonial-style wallpaper and country antique furnishings. Some of these rooms are tucked away in the eaves of the farmhouse; however, guests traveling with a dog will stay in the carriage house rooms, which are more typical of a traditional ski house. Although the carriage house is old, the bedrooms are decorated with contemporary furnishings. One of the exterior doors opens into a small foyer, which has two separate chambers off of it. One of these is a twin-bedded room, with an adjacent sitting room containing a couch and a corner sink. The other room not only has a small sitting area, but also a queen and a twin bed. Guests will be pleased to note that all of these accommodations are pleasant and clean, and some even feature direct access to porches that offer spectacular valley views. The wall-to-wall carpeting, individual thermostats, and private baths are welcome amenities as well. Our favorite space is undoubtedly the apartment suite. This was where the Walthers lived from the time they first bought the inn until they had their second child. Today, guests can enjoy these comfortable rooms. A door leads directly into a small kitchen and eating area, with a table occupying a sunny spot next to a window. Wide pine floors lead back to the living room with its comfortable sofa, chairs, and exposed brick fireplace. A television is an added convenience, as are the sliding glass doors that open to a porch. The two upstairs bedrooms are cozy, and enhanced by the Williamsburg blue trim around the doors and country curtains at the windows.

Visitors are drawn to the Old Cutter Inn because of its proximity to beautiful mountains — an asset in all seasons. Although East Burke tends to be popular with those who enjoy great downhill and cross-country skiing, others prefer the summer months when they can either bicycle along the quiet country roads or walk on the many trails which surround the inn. Bowser can stay busy hiking locally, as Burke Mountain is within the boundaries of Victory State Forest, or drive north along scenic back roads, and spend the day in the Willoughby State Forest. This is adjacent to the spectacular Lake Willoughby, which is truly one of the most beautiful lakes in New England. After exploring the mountainous countryside, a refreshing dip in the swimming pool is always a great way to rejuvenate one's tired muscles. If the weather should turn inclement, our favorite spot is the farmhouse's attractive common room with its vaulted beamed ceilings and bright yellow walls. The green and white checked sofas and oak rocker are usually occupied by other guests who are also drawn to this inviting space.

We have included The Old Cutter Inn in our books for many years, and with good reason. The Walthers just keep improving the inn, the food, and now the physical space. Anyone who is searching for a beautiful mountaintop setting, and a variety of outdoor activities, should definitely consider staying here and exploring the Northeast Kingdom.

Berkson Farms

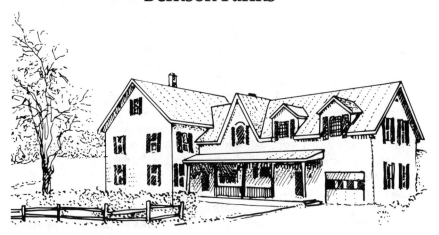

Route 4
Enosburg Falls, Vermont   05450
(802) 933-2522

Owner: *Sidney Berkson*
Rooms: *4 doubles, 1 suite*
Rates: *Doubles and suite $55-65 (B&B)*
Payment: *Personal checks*
Children: *Always welcome (cribs, cots, and highchairs are available)*
Dogs: *Welcome*
Open: *All year*

Northern Vermont, more commonly referred to as the Northeast Kingdom, is a part of New England that remains relatively unchanged. The people who do take the time to follow its backroads are rewarded with the sight of seemingly endless emerald green pastures and rolling hills dotted with storybook farms. Berkson Farms is no exception. Here, guests have the opportunity to become a part of the working dairy farm, complete with cows, sheep, deer, lambs, geese, ducks, rabbits, and chickens. There is enough going on to both entertain and educate children and adults alike. The 600 acres of open land certainly make this an ideal vacation destination for Bowser as well.

Some who come to Berkson Farms want to relax, but just about everyone finds they eventually get involved in the day-to-day business of farming. Guests may choose a different job each day, from collecting eggs, helping to milk the cows, or bringing in the hay. In the spring, many enjoy either collecting the buckets

127

of sap from the maple trees or learning about preparing a garden for planting. Guests and their canine companion will not spend their entire vacation working, however. There are also streams with waterfalls and swimming holes, and mountains dotted with hiking trails, as well as local golf and tennis. In the winter months, Bowser can explore the miles of cross-country ski trails or watch his two-legged friends try to ice skate. Enosburg Falls is not far from Jay Peak, a small resort with great downhill skiing. Visitors can also drive north a short distance to Carmi State Park where they will find Lake Carmi.

After a busy day on the farm, or exploring the nearby area, guests will certainly sleep soundly at night. The bedrooms are located in a two-story wing attached to the original farmhouse. These have been recently renovated, which unfortunately meant stripping away some of their historic character. They are filled with an eclectic assortment of country antiques and modern furnishings and each has beautiful views of the surrounding pastures and hills. The largest of the guest quarters is located at the end of the building, and has a private bath and more than enough room for Bowser to make himself comfortable.

In the morning, well-rested helpers are rewarded for their previous day's efforts with a full country breakfast. The charming dining room is decorated with rose wallpaper and furnished with an old-fashioned mahogany sideboard. Guests gather around a huge circular table to enjoy their meals. The breakfasts are always plentiful, hearty, and home-cooked. In the winter, muffins, hot cereal, and French toast or pancakes are the favorites. Juice and plenty of hot coffee are welcome accompaniments. In the evening, guests are also invited to enjoy the enormous, family-style meals that feature local meats, fresh vegetables, homemade breads and desserts. When guests are not helping with chores or off on adventures, they tend to gather in the living room and library, which exude the same sort of casual, country atmosphere.

Berkson Farms has been around for years, providing a real farm experience for generations of vacationers. The open spaces and relaxed environment truly make it a vacation for guests and their four-legged friends to enjoy together.

Silver Maple Lodge and Cottages

RR1, Box 8
Fairlee, Vermont 05045
(800) 666-1946, (802) 333-4326

Innkeepers: *Sharon and Scott Wright*
Rooms: *8 doubles, 6 cottages*
Rates: *Doubles $48-62 (B&B), Cottages $56-68 (B&B)*
Payment: *AE, DSC, MC, and VISA*
Children: *Welcome*
Dogs: *Welcome in the cottages with advance notice and prior approval*
Open: *All year*

The Silver Maple Lodge and Cottages is a welcome new addition to our book. The property is actually a combination of a 1700s antique inn and attractive 1950s cottages. The house was part of a farmstead until the mid-1920s, when Elmer and Della Batchelder purchased it. They soon converted the house into an inn and it has been used in this capacity ever since then. The Wrights bought it from the Batchelders in 1985 and have been renovating and upgrading all of the rooms and cottages since then. Nothing is overdone at the Silver Maple Lodge, because the Wrights have been careful to make simple yet appropriate changes to the place.

We arrived at night, when the light spilled invitingly out through the many windows lining the wraparound, screened-in porch. Gourds and pumpkins lined the steps leading up to the porch. As we opened the door to the inn, we were pleasantly surprised to see country antiques filling the foyer. The entry opens into the attractive dining room, where darkly stained country antiques stand out against the soft pink walls. Just beyond this chamber is a slightly more contemporary living room. We easily could have spent the evening in here, sitting on the couch, reading a good book, and enjoying the warmth from the fire. A television with VCR are electronic forms of entertainment, but there is also an extensive collection of board games and books that seem even more appealing. An upright piano looks as though it has been well used by guests over the years. Anyone traveling without a dog is welcome to stay at the main inn, where the rooms are filled with country antiques and brass or white iron beds draped with Vermont quilts.

Anyone with Bowser in tow will want to stay in the cottages instead of the inn. These are grouped to one side of the inn, and are surrounded by maple trees, mature plantings, and lawns. From the exterior, the cottages are quite attractive with their white clapboard walls and hunter green trim. The small porches are set with Adirondack chairs. Some of the cottages have been completely refurbished and modernized. One of our favorites is Cottage 18. This is probably the most spacious and well-furnished unit, with more than enough room for the small sitting area and fireplace. The kitchenette gives guests the option of creating their own meals and eating them at the small dining room table. The deep burgundy and green color schemes are found in both the fabrics selected for the furnishings and for the bedspread. Cream-colored tab curtains frame the small paned windows. Cottage 19 is also furnished in a similar fashion and even has a small fireplace that adds to the atmosphere. Its knotty pine walls lend an air of authenticity and character to the place. The remainder of the cottages are more camp-like in decor, with hardwood floors covered in braided rugs, maple beds, and camp-style furnishings. We found all of the cottages to be extremely clean, and well-stocked with linens.

In the morning, all guests are treated to a Continental breakfast laid out buffet-style in the dining room. Sharon offers all the standard breakfast items, along with her many kinds of homemade breads. Afterwards, Bowser might want to take a short stroll on the grounds. The country road that runs by the inn is relatively busy and so it might be best to hop in the car to explore some of the nearby areas. While one might not equate Fairlee with the more upscale Woodstock, it is an appealing destination that is central to many of New Hampshire's and Vermont's resort communities. We liked its simple rural charm and proximity to the highway. Guests should know that the inn backs up against I-91, which can potentially pose a noise problem at times. The Silver Maple Lodge also lies in the Connecticut River Valley, within minutes of the river and of Lake Fairlee and Lake Morey. The Thetford Hill State Park is within a short driving distance of the inn, where visitors will find some nature trails to walk on with Bowser. We enjoyed the short drive across the river to Orland, New Hampshire where many elegant Colonial and Federal homes line the road. Upon returning at the end of the day, guests will find hot chocolate, tea, and freshly baked muffins awaiting them.

The Hayes House

Box 92
Bear Hill Road
Grafton, Vermont 05146
(802) 843-2461

Hostess: *Margery Hayes Heindel*
Rooms: *1 single, 3 doubles*
Rates: *Single $30 (B&B), Doubles $65-75 (B&B)*
Payment: *Personal checks*
Children: *Not appropriate for children under the age of 4*
Dogs: *Welcome with advance notice and prior approval; they cannot stay in the room alone*
Open: *All year except April*

The charming town of Grafton was established over 200 years ago, serving as a busy center for lumbering, sheep ranching, and a number of cottage industries. Unfortunately, the Civil War had a devastating effect on this and many other Vermont communities. It was not until the Windham Foundation was formed in 1963 that the entire Grafton area began a strong resurgence. The foundation in charge of ensuring that the village was well maintained and preserved its historic integrity. Today, the refurbished town center is filled with antique homes that have been beautifully preserved. This is an easy place to walk through, and we encourage guests to leave their car at the Hayes House and explore on foot.

The Hayes House reflects a bit of this history. Built in 1803, it pre-dates its next door neighbor, an antique covered bridge, by some 67 years. Nothing has changed since our last visit, with the exterior still painted a cheery blue, and the interior furnished with an eclectic array of antique and contemporary pieces. A knickknack or country collectible fills every nook, leaving just enough room, of course, for the resident cat and Chesapeake Bay retriever. It is a warm and comfortable place that guests soon think of as their home away from home.

The bedrooms are as cozy as the common rooms, and are outfitted with either twin or double beds covered with simple Bates spreads. The chamber on the first floor is particularly delightful, with its waist-high, finial bed (a giant leap or small stool is a requirement for gaining access to it), fireplace, and private bath. The bathroom is noteworthy for another reason, the whimsical wallpaper printed with newspaper stories makes for interesting reading. The upstairs bedrooms also have their share of country antiques and comfortable furnishings, contributing to the very cozy ambiance. Thoughtful touches include fresh flowers on the bedside table in the spring and summer months, and a bowl of fruit and a plate of tasty homemade cookies to alleviate any "before bed" munchies.

Breakfast is a Continental affair that includes freshly-baked muffins and breads served with homemade jams and preserves. This is complemented by fruit juice, coffee, and tea. Those who like to nibble on snacks during the day, are welcome to store them in the extra refrigerator in the kitchen. In the wintertime, Margery has a steaming pot of homemade soup on the stove that guests may help themselves to after 2 p.m.

Diversions are abundant at the B&B, as well as in and around Grafton. Bookshelves in the house are stocked with a wide variety of selections. Many guests like to read in the bentwood chairs out on the porch, while listening to the melodic sounds emanating from the babbling brook. The sunny living room, with its bright red sofa, is equally inviting on a cold winter's day. Grafton village is a two-minute walk from the Hayes House. Many of the antique homes have been nicely restored, offering interesting sightseeing, and the scenic country roads are a great place to take a leisurely walk. In the wintertime, this area becomes a cross-country skiing mecca. Many enjoy piling on the layers of clothing, putting together a box lunch, and taking Bowser out for a day of skiing. Those who would like to explore the quieter sections of these scenic Vermont woods will find the Grafton State Forest, Okemo State Park, Townshend State Forest, and the massive Green Mountain National Forest all just a short drive from the B&B.

The Tyler Place
on Lake Champlain

Box 73, Route 7
Highgate Springs, Vermont 05460
(802) 868-3301 or 868-4291

Hosts: The Tyler Family
Rooms: 18 inn rooms, 27 cottages, 5 lake-side apartments
Rates: Inn Rooms $105-137 (MAP), Cottages $106-158 (MAP),
*   Apartments $137-158 (MAP)*
Payment: MC and VISA
Children: Always welcome (cribs, cots, highchairs, and babysitters are available), an
*   extensive and supervised children's program is offered*
Dogs: Welcome with prior approval in the cottages
Open: End of May to mid-September

If the thought of summer camp for families sounds appealing, then The Tyler Place is certain to be an ideal vacation spot for adults, kids, and the family dog. The 165-acre resort is located on the shores of Lake Champlain and is entirely self-contained. Youngsters ranging in age from 3 to 18 years will find a myriad of group activities available to them. Children are placed together according to their age bracket (Pre-Midgets, 0-2 years; Junior Midgets, 2-3 years; Senior Midgets, 4-5 years; Juniors, 5 1/2-7 years; Pre-Teens, 8-10 years; Junior Teens 11-13 years; and Senior Teens, 14-16 years), and spend their days under the supervision of high school and college-aged counselors. The midgets have their own house, a gigantic building that has separate areas designated for different age groups and ability levels. There is state of the art play equipment and even a dining room full of child-sized furniture. Life-size cartoon characters have been painted in bright colors on all the walls, creating a very cheery play environment. The outdoor playgrounds are equally tantalizing. For those parents who prefer individualized attention for their children, there is the parent's helper program, as well as babysitters. The Junior/Pre-Teen recreation center is also well-equipped, but with items that appeal to an older crowd.

Each age group has carefully planned activities available to them, so that while the little ones are enjoying a Dinosaur party or lawn games, the older children might be having a treasure hunt or kayaking. The list of programs is certainly the most extensive we have seen. Of course, all of this scheduled and supervised time for the children allows their parents to enjoy their camp experience as well. Choose from tennis, sailboarding, sailing, water-skiing, canoeing or kayaking, bicycling, and golf. Later in the day, families can get together for volleyball, softball, basketball, soccer, or horseshoes. If the day should turn inclement, the main lodge offers Ping-Pong, pool tables, Foosball, and a full exercise room. A new addition, and one the Tylers are justifiably proud of, is the indoor heated swimming pool, a nice complement to the lake-side pool.

Although Bowser will not be able to enjoy supervised "doggy" programs, there are still plenty of ways to include him in this vacation. There are seemingly unlimited walks that dogs can take on the property. It will be tough to keep water-loving canines out of the lake, which is not a problem as long as they are kept away from the main water sport areas. Guests could also paddle or motor in one of the boats borrowed from the resort. The 5,600-acre Missisquoi National Wildlife Refuge is just a short distance from the Tyler Place, and certainly worth investigating. There are hills and flatlands, as well as trails along the shore that are equally interesting to explore with Bowser.

Guests traveling with their canine companion are welcome in any of the cottages. Some of these were built 100 years ago, with the most recent being just 40 years old. They are located within a few minutes' walk from the main inn, tucked into knolls, and set along small rocky outcroppings and inlets along the lake. They are all very different in design and feeling, ranging from rustic to deluxe summer cabins. Some are quaint, white-shingled houses with red shutters, while others are dark brown shingled cottages with screened-in porches. The houses and cottages offer from three to six rooms, and all of them have working fireplaces. Couples may reserve a one bedroom cottage with a kitchenette, while families would undoubtedly prefer the houses with a living room, full-size kitchen, and numerous bedrooms. They are primarily furnished with white wicker, the walls papered in floral patterns, and the hardwood floors covered with neutral area rugs. Waverly and Laura Ashley fabrics do much to enhance the informal atmosphere.

Meals are another area in which The Tyler Place excels. They are impressive, not so much for their gourmet fare, but for the way in which they are planned. Meals are served in the main building, in a very large and attractively decorated dining room. Breakfasts are buffet style, with a Continental fare provided for late arrivals. In the evenings, adults have the option of enjoying a very civilized dinner, bordering on the romantic. This is because pre-school children dine together in a separate room with their own menu, as do the junior and senior children. This allows the parents to linger over their meal, and perhaps visit with some of the other adult guests. Those who choose to can partake in the after-dinner theme nights, such as Monte Carlo or the South Sea islands. Movies, videos, and guitar sing-alongs are some of the other evening activities available, as well.

Some prospective guests may think that all of the scheduled activities and guitar sing-alongs might sound a bit contrived, but, trust us, it isn't. Everyone does exactly what they want to while on vacation here. The Tylers seem to know just what people are looking for in a family vacation. Finally, because they have kept the resort small, and have a large number of repeat guests, the Tyler Place is usually fully booked in July and August. Those who prefer a quieter vacation experience should consider visiting either early or late in the season, when it is not quite so busy.

Cortina Inn

Box HCR-34
Route 4
Killington, Vermont 05751
(800) 451-6108, (802) 773-3331

General Manager: *Theodore Bridges*
Rooms: *91 doubles, 6 suites*
Rates: *Doubles $150-224 (B&B), Suites $200-319 (B&B)*
Payment: *AE, CB, DC, DSC, JCB, MC, and VISA*
Children: *Welcome (cribs, cots, highchairs, and babysitters are available)*
Dogs: *Well-behaved dogs are welcome with prior notice and advance approval in the first
       floor rooms*
Open: *All year*

We like the Cortina Inn and give it high marks, but we should stress that it
is not really an inn, but is rather a full-service hotel. It has all the qualities of an inn,
such as personal service, good food, and individually decorated rooms, but its
three buildings contain two floors that are lined with a total of 97 bedrooms. Most
guests enter the inn through the main entrance, where they will walk past a
fieldstone fireplace and check in at the reception desk. Adjacent to this is the inn's
main common room, whose centerpiece is a sunken, freestanding, black iron
fireplace surrounded by comfortable seating. The barn board walls of this two-
story chamber are lined with an eclectic collection of local art. Just off this room is
a restaurant, small gift shop, and some of the inn's older guest rooms. While some
people might enjoy their proximity to the restaurant and health club, we prefer the
more deluxe accommodations located at the far end of the complex.

As guests walk through the inn to reach these guest chambers, they will come
to a second common area which is very different from the first. Deep, comfortable
sofas are set in front of a fireplace, classical music is playing in the background, and
Queen Anne-style side and armchairs are arranged in small groupings. The
French doors and huge windows make this a very sunny space. The bedrooms just
beyond this chamber are our favorites. Each has been decorated differently;
however, the common element is a profusion of pretty floral fabrics. The color
schemes for the bedrooms range from deep green and maroon to soothing blues
and greens or a combination of light yellow with vibrant accents. Brass or pine
four-poster beds are usually covered in chintz fabrics that coordinate with the
draperies framing a pair of windows. The good quality, English reproduction
furnishings include formal armchairs, writing desks, and armoires. One notable
chamber has a desk built into a wall, lending even greater architectural interest to
the room. Bedside tables are often draped in still more chintz, and are set with
brass lamps and clock radios.

The larger suites offer a fireplace, two-person Jacuzzi, refrigerator, library, wet bar, a color television, and even a separate room with bunk beds. Other chambers include the court-side suites and king fireplace rooms, each featuring a fireplace, king-size bed, and sitting area. We recommend requesting a room overlooking the back of the property as they are more scenic than those which face rural Route 4. Bowser will certainly appreciate being able to walk from the room to the outdoors through the private outside entrances.

Once on the property, there are plenty of things to keep people busy. The inn has built an extensive nature trail and has put together a booklet describing all of the flora and fauna that walkers will see along the way. The grounds surrounding the inn are quite pretty with a stream, a pond, and well-manicured lawns giving it an almost park-like setting. Guests should bring their tennis racquets, as there are eight tennis courts to play on. There is also a mountain biking and hiking center located at the inn. Here, guests can pick up a map, grab Bowser, and head out for hikes or rides. One trail leads to nearby Pico. The Ross Trail, that begins at the inn, meets with the Blue Ridge hiking trail that climbs up through mountains to a nearby waterfall. Those who want an exceptionally long day hike can actually hike from the inn up to the Chittenden Reservoir. At the end of the day, guests will return to the inn and find beverages and snacks awaiting them.

Whetstone Inn

Marlboro, Vermont 05344
(802) 254-2500

135

Vermont

Innkeepers: Jean and Harry Boardman
Rooms: 12 doubles, 2 apartments
Rates: Doubles $55-85 (EP), Apartments $75-90 (EP)
Payment: Personal checks
Children: Welcome, but not appropriate for children under two years of age
Dogs: Welcome with prior approval
Open: All year

The Whetstone Inn lies in the diminutive town of Marlboro, the center of which is comprised of a church, a post office, and the inn. The Colonial home was originally built in 1785 as a tavern for the townspeople and passing stage coach passengers. To this day, the inn and the village remain relatively unchanged.

Although the crimson front door is sure to catch one's attention, most people follow the path to the side door, where they emerge into a closet-sized entry. A very homey and inviting living room is immediately off to one side and is crammed with an eclectic assortment of contemporary couches and chairs, some country antiques, and a piano. The trim is painted a Williamsburg blue and the tab curtains reflect a stenciled Amish design. The shelves in here are literally bursting with books and knickknacks. Collectibles are scattered throughout; gone are the old slots originally used for the town's mail (when the inn served as the post office), to be replaced by a pillar and scroll clock on the mantel.

There is a variety of guest rooms located all through the inn. As guests walk into the main foyer, they are most likely to first notice the "good morning" staircase, whose treads have been painted to resemble a carpeted runner. The upstairs rooms have beamed ceilings and painted wide pine floors and trim, which enhance the inn's antique features. The guest chambers have been painted in various traditional colors, some are gold, others a dark peach, and still others a pale green. The furnishings are mostly informal country antiques, featuring captain's chests, rocking chairs, and old jugs that have been converted into lamps. Antique beds are draped with colorful country quilts. Windows, framed by white lace or brightly patterned curtains, offer views of the pond, white birch groves, and forested hillside. There are a few specific rooms that might appeal to guests traveling with a dog. One of the first floor bedrooms is good sized, has hardwood floors, and is furnished with a pair of twin beds draped in simple blue and white cotton spreads. Another suite of rooms is tucked into the back of the house. We liked this sunny and festive space, with its yellow walls and twin beds covered in crimson floral cotton spreads. An adjacent sitting room is enlivened with its golden walls, and a kitchenette allows guests to prepare snacks or meals. Although some bedrooms contain the original antique fireplaces, they are purely decorative.

After a peaceful night's sleep, guests will be awakened by heavenly smells emanating from the kitchen. The dining room is dominated by an enormous old-fashioned cooking fireplace, which has a dozen or so pewter mugs hanging from its mantel. Sunlight usually streams in over the wooden tables set simply with red runners. The menu varies with the day and the guest. Harry is justifiably proud of his waffles, which he only half-jokingly claims are the best in the country. Those who are in the mood for something else may try the eggs cooked any way or pancakes topped with pure maple syrup. Fresh fruit is a breakfast staple as well, along with tea and freshly ground coffee. On Saturday nights, and some week nights, dinners are served for a very reasonable price. The main course ranges from lamb and chicken to fish and veal. This is accompanied by either a hearty cheddar cheese Senegalese soup or a corn chowder, as well as fresh vegetables and other homemade goodies. Desserts are especially enticing, especially the maple mousse and brandy Alexander pie.

In the summer months, guests or their canine companions might want to take a refreshing dip in the little pond behind the inn. There are also numerous walks that lead down picturesque country roads. The Molly Stark State Park is just a few minutes away and is a great place for hiking. A drive west on scenic Route 9 leads people to the Woodford State Park and a branch of the Long Trail. Cross-country skiing can also be found right on the inn's property. The start of the trail is just to the right of the side door and leads skiers up the forested hillside. The Boardmans own the property to the tree line, and the remainder is owned by Marlboro College. The students have actually cut and maintained the trails through these woods, making for great winter skiing with Bowser.

Red Clover Inn
at Woodward Farm

Box 7450
Woodward Farm Road
Mendon, Vermont 05701
(800) 752-0571, (802) 775-2290, Fax (802) 773-0594

Innkeepers: Sue and Harris Zuckerman
Rooms: 11 doubles, 1 suite
Rates: Doubles $120-200 (MAP), Suite $160-235 (MAP)
Payment: MC and VISA
Children: Welcome, not appropriate for children under 8 years of age
Dogs: Welcome in the carriage house rooms
Open: All year

Just off the thoroughfare between Killington and Rutland, there lies a country road that wends past stands of pine trees and eventually leads to the Red Clover Inn. An antique farmhouse, barn, and carriage house are encircled by white fences, all of which combine to create a wonderful pastoral setting. We arrived at night, but when we woke up the next morning, the surrounding mountains provided a spectacular backdrop. It is easy to envision why, in 1840, General John Woodward decided this would be an idyllic spot to build his summer retreat.

When we last visited the inn, we were intrigued with it, but felt the Carriage House rooms (where Bowser is welcome) needed a little more attention. However, over a year ago the inn was purchased by Sue and Harris Zuckerman, their children, and their dog, Boomer, who focused their collective energies and creativity upon the inn. The metamorphosis is certain to delight both new and returning guests. As guests enter the inn, they probably won't immediately notice any changes. The first floor common rooms are still pretty much the same, with the three intimate dining rooms and a sunny keeping room. As Sue and Harris explain, these spaces were already quite attractive and comfortable, it was the bedrooms that needed some help. They started on the main inn, by painting and re-papering many of the bedrooms, and then placing Vermont-made quilts on top of the antique bedsteads. The quilts are always the decorative centerpiece for the bedrooms, with their deep green and red star configurations or pale blue and pink patchwork designs. Sue has been responsible for coordinating the effect, even to the point of making sure the towels and sheets complement the decorative theme. Their most popular bedroom is the completely renovated Mountain Suite. In addition to the superb mountain views to be enjoyed from its small sitting area as well as from the queen-size bed, the addition of a fireplace and Jacuzzi tub truly sets this room apart from the others.

As lovely as the rooms are in the main inn, the Carriage House rooms are most appropriate for those traveling with a dog, as they have separate outside entrances. This two-story building has a variety of innovative spaces that Sue has either completely restored, or is in the process of refurbishing. Quilts are, once again, the focal points for these charming bed chambers. One of these accommodations has a small sitting room on one level, with a foldout bed, and a steep set of stairs leading to the private loft bedroom. Another room, which is one of the largest, is located on the ground floor and faces the front of the property. Pretty oak spindle beds are covered with red and green star patterned quilts, and even the pillows have matching quilted shams. The festive effect is complemented by accents such as grapevine wreaths and attractive prints. The furnishings are often carefully coordinated with the accent pieces. One of the more notable examples is the red and green suite with its red bureaus coordinated with the red in the quilts. The side chairs are often covered in fabrics that are coordinated with the linens draped over the bedside tables. One of the chambers has a three-foot door leading to a small deck, while another has a small sitting area on one level, and a pretty bed just a step or two down, on another. Sue has painted one of these chambers a pale yellow, while another has floral wallpaper. The bathrooms are outfitted with Red Clover soaps and shampoos, as well as a number of washcloths, towels, and other assorted doodads. Our bathroom, for instance, had a whimsical little rubber duck placed on the side of the tub. We noticed, in the course of our tour, that other bathrooms also had cute little bath creatures as well.

At the end of the day, it is especially pleasant to settle into the relaxed pace at the Red Clover Inn. Most people start their evening in the tiny bar, located just off the keeping room. We could have spent hours here, sipping wine and chatting with Sue, but the wonderful aroma emanating from the kitchen lured us into the dining room. Under candlelight, guests can leisurely peruse the extensive gourmet menu. When the Zuckerman's bought the inn, they also hired a fabulous chef, who successfully turns the fresh, local ingredients into wonderful meals each night. Appetizer selections include the pheasant ravioli with a pesto and tomato coulis, smoked duck breast with an orange cranberry relish, and the house-cured gravlax served with a saffron creme frâiche. It should be noted that the inn smokes all its own meats and fish. The roast tomato garlic soup with pesto, or corn and mussel chowder are two of the more popular soup offerings. The entrée selections are equally innovative, and range from a breast of pheasant with a sauce of mustard and pancetta to a tournedos of venison with a wild mushroom sauce. The dessert tray is always brimming with homemade delicacies, but during our visit, we opted for the baked apple with cinnamon. After dinner, some guests like to walk along the quiet country roads, while others retreat to the warmth of the Keeping Room's fieldstone fireplace. There are magazines to read, games to play, and a variety of comfortable sitting areas. It is here, as well as in the breakfast room, that the Zuckerman's have put out pictures of their family, greatly adding to the personal feeling of the inn.

In the morning, guests rise to a full breakfast. The sunny breakfast room is our favorite place for this meal. Guests are free to take a mug from the hutch and pour themselves a cup of coffee or tea. Harris is the breakfast chef, creating a variety of wonderful treats. We started with fresh fruit, followed by pancakes. Of the three pancakes, one had fresh strawberries, another had bananas, and the last had apples baked into it. These were accompanied by bacon and sausage. On another morning, guests might enjoy the cinnamon raisin French toast or one of Harris' skillet surprises.

There are plenty of ways to work off all of the culinary indulgences. In the summertime, the swimming pool is a favorite gathering spot. Other options include volleyball, badminton, or any of the other assorted lawn games the Zuckermans have hidden away. There are also tennis courts located just across the road, available to those who have brought their racquets. Bowser will be pleased with all of the back roads and trails cutting through the countryside. The Long Trail and Appalachian Mountain Trails intersect just up the mountain near Killington. In Chittenden, there is also an equestrian center, where enthusiasts can either take a lesson or a ride along one of the trails. Also near Chittenden is the Gifford Woods State Park and south of the inn is the Aitken State Forest. Wintertime opens up another group of options, which could include cross-country skiing right on the 13 acres of property or downhill skiing at Pico or Killington.

The Middlebury Inn

Court House Square
Middlebury, Vermont 05753-0798
(800) 842-4666, (802) 388-4961, Fax (802) 388-4563

Innkeepers: Frank and Jane Emanuel
Rooms: 71 doubles, 4 suites
Rates: Doubles $75-144 (EP), Suites $122-160 (EP)
Payment: AE, DC, DSC, MC and VISA
Children: Welcome, (cribs, cots, and highchairs are available, babysitters can be arranged)
Dogs: Welcome in the motel units for a $6 fee
Open: All year

The Middlebury Inn's long history dates back to 1788, when Judge Gamaliel Painter deeded Simeon Dudley the one-acre lot that the inn would eventually be built on. Six years later, Samuel Mattocks, Jr., built a tavern here; however, it burned down in 1816. Then, in 1827, Nathan Wood constructed a "publick" house that was known as the Vermont Hotel. Over the next century, the hotel was refurbished and modified numerous times until the Middlebury Hotel Corporation purchased the property in 1927 and transformed it into the Middlebury Inn. The Emanuels arrived in 1977 and were pleasantly surprised when the Vermont's Division for Historic Preservation provided the matching funds they needed for the inn's restoration.

Guest rooms are located in three different buildings, the Main House, Porter House Mansion, and the more contemporary Motel. Those who are traveling with Bowser are asked to stay in the motel. This was added in the 1960s, lies behind the historic inn, and offers many modern amenities not found in the Main House or Porter House Mansion. The term motel is somewhat of a misnomer in this instance, as these chambers are far nicer than traditional motel rooms. Additionally, the ease of outside access makes these accommodations ideal for dog owners. The rooms are good-sized and their walls are decorated with English country floral wallpapers. Antique reproductions are intermixed with more contemporary furnishings. Bates spreads cover the pairs of double or twin bedsteads and foldout sofas and side chairs create intimate sitting areas. Many people welcome the modern amenities, which include color cable televisions, two telephones, air-conditioning units, and coffee makers. The oversized, modern bathrooms have hair dryers and baskets containing soaps, shampoos, and assorted other bathing necessities.

Of course, all guests of the Middlebury Inn are welcome to use any of the facilities. The most notable of these are the two blue dining dining rooms, one of which offers floor-to-ceiling windows and plenty of sunlight. One of these bright alcoves is a virtual greenhouse of plants, which provide a pretty backdrop to the cloth covered tables. The menu has changed slightly since our last visit, although it still offers fried Cabot cheese dipped in a marinara sauce and the native woodland mushrooms tempura as appetizers. The soups are among the more interesting offerings, with lobster bisque and the chilled strawberry soup topping the list of house specialties. Entrées include the sole paupiettes, the roast Long Island duck, and a venison sautéed with shiitake mushrooms, sun-dried tomatoes, and a madeira wine. The sole filets are stuffed with spinach, lobster, butter, and crumbs, baked, and then drizzled with a mornay sauce. The delicious popovers are a popular side dish.

The Middlebury Inn may not be situated amid sprawling acres of open land, but it is very conveniently located to the center of town and to the picturesque Middlebury College. There are a number of specialty shops, restaurants, and art cooperatives (don't miss the Vermont State Craft Center at Frog Hollow) catering to both college students and visitors. Some people enjoy taking a short walk with Bowser, across the Otter Creek Footbridge for a scenic view of the falls, and then on to the college campus, where there are acres of open land to explore. Just up the road is UVM's Morgan Horse Farm and east of the inn is a portion of the Green Mountain National Forest. Check with the ranger station in Middlebury for weather conditions and hiking maps before heading out on the trails. For wintertime fun, there is plenty of local cross-country skiing, as well as downhill skiing at the Middlebury Snow bowl.

Four Columns Inn

P.O. Box 278
230 West Street
Newfane, Vermont 05345
(800) 787-6633, (802) 365-7713 or 365-4550

Innkeepers: Jacques and Pamela Allembert
Rooms: 12 doubles, 5 suites
Rates: Doubles $100-125 (B&B), $200-250 (MAP),
*   Suites $140-175 (B&B), $240-265 (MAP)*
Payment: AE, MC, and VISA are accepted but personal checks or cash are preferred
Children: Welcome, but they must be very well-mannered
Dogs: Well-behaved dogs are welcome, but they cannot be left alone in the room
Open: All year except a few weeks in April and November

The Four Columns Inn is a gracious white clapboard mansion built in 1830 by General Pardon Kimball for his wife. General Kimball wanted the house to reflect her Southern heritage, consequently, he used architectural features such as massive two-story Greek Revival columns to create this classic building that is now a focal point on the tiny village's common. The hand-hewn beams and moldings that were so laboriously crafted over 150 years ago are merely the accents for today's beautifully decorated guest rooms.

More recently, in 1965, the mansion's original barn was renovated to house the inn's gourmet restaurant, bar, and sitting room, along with some additional guest rooms located on the second floor. In some of the chambers, the original hand-hewn beams have been left exposed, while others feature fireplaces, separate sitting rooms, and large walk-in closets. The informal country and Colonial antiques were individually selected for each of the bedrooms. Some of the standouts are the unique bedsteads, which range from brass to canopy. One bed, of particular interest, is a four-poster, which was hand-carved by a local craftsman. The only modern features are air conditioning and private bathrooms, which are most welcome concessions to the present. On any given night, two fortunate guests are welcome to stay in the cozy cottage that lies alongside the pond. This is perhaps the best place for Bowser as it allows easy access to the property and a great deal of privacy.

Anyone staying at the inn would be remiss if they did not eat here as well. The ambiance alone, is one good reason to venture into the dining room. A raised brick fireplace and soft candlelight illuminate this elegantly appointed space where small tables are draped in French Provençal fabrics with white overlays. Copper pots hang from racks along the wall, while decoys and other American folk art are placed on the shelves. The menu is varied, and changes daily, attracting people from all over the region. Appetizers range from a smoked salmon and horseradish mousse, and a lobster raviolette with sun-dried tomatoes, olive oil, and Parmesan cheese to a pistachio pâté with apricots and cognac and spinach ravioli with pignoli nuts and garlic. During our visit, swordfish with a black olive and caper vinaigrette; a grilled roasted pheasant baked with a ginger raspberry red currant sauce; and the venison chops with artichoke bottoms and Swiss chard, topped the menu. Other selections included a grilled duck breast with berry sauce, salmon with ginger, sesame oil, soy and lemon, and the curried shrimp with basmatti rice, warm greens, and pineapple yogurt salad. After a wonderful meal, the last stop before bed is the tiny, pewter-topped bar.

In the morning, the meal is lighter, but no less interesting. Being a strict vegetarian, the breakfast chef tries to create healthy fare for her guests as well. Often oatmeal with fresh pears and dates, freshly baked muffins, and juice are a few of the more popular selections. If there are only a few people staying at the inn, she will make waffles or pancakes, but don't look for bacon or sausage to accompany them.

When not sampling the fabulous food or sleeping in the cozy bedrooms, most guests are drawn outside to the remarkable property surrounding the inn. As they explore the grounds, they will first come upon a small reflecting pool, some ponds, and finally a swimming pool surrounded by fieldstone walls topped with perennial gardens. At the rear of the property, there is a swiftly flowing stream which people, and Bowser, can cross on a makeshift footbridge that merges into a trail leading up the mountain. This is a perfect environment for Bowser to explore with his human companions. After a long walk, many are content to return to the privacy of the stream side setting, flop into an Adirondack chair or hammock, and watch the birds as they flit around the feeders. Anyone who prefers a lengthier excursion, can visit the local Townshend State Forest and Molly Stark State Park. Hikers will find that their best options remain in the Green Mountain National Forest.

Shore Acres Inn and Restaurant

RR1, Box 3
Route 2
North Hero Island, Vermont   05474
(802) 372-8722

Managers: Susan and Mike Tranby
Rooms: 23 doubles
Rates: $72-98 (EP)
Payment: DSC, MC and VISA
Children: Welcome (cribs, cots, highchairs, and babysitters are available)
Dogs: Welcome with prior approval and a nightly fee of $10 for the first night and $5 for
   every subsequent night. Dogs must be walked behind the inn and not in front of
   the lake-side rooms.
Open: Lake-side units open May 1 to November 1, B&B units open
   November 1 to May 1

As the Shore Acres Inn and Restaurant enters its fifth decade, it is our pleasure
to note that not much has changed over the years and yet so much has improved.
For instance, the same panoramic views of Lake Champlain, Mount Mansfield,
and the Green Mountains can be enjoyed from any of the rooms. A sense of rural
charm is pervasive over the 50 acres of manicured grass and hay fields. Also
remaining relatively unchanged is the half mile of private shoreline that is not only
lovely but also allows easy accessibility to the lake.

Perhaps the most notable change to occur over the years, is in the guest rooms.
There are a variety of accommodations available, ranging from the lake-side
chambers to the bed and breakfast quarters found in a separate cottage on the
property. The B&B rooms have a Scandinavian look to them, created through the
use of contemporary light pine furnishings, white walls, and crisp blue and white
fabrics. Air conditioning, clock radios, and color televisions are welcome additions.
All of the B&B rooms have distant views of the lake from both the windows and
from the semi-private decks.

The most popular rooms are located along the lake, in a long, low building.
From the rear, it resembles a sprawling motel, but step through one of the
breezeways toward the lake, and one gets a very different impression. The
Tranby's have worked hard over the years to renovate the rooms, painting the
natural board walls and trim with fresh, white paint and updating the bathrooms
with white linoleum and pretty cotton shower curtains. Starched curtains frame
the windows, blue and white comforters cover the traditional maple beds, and the
other furnishings are often Scandinavian in design. Small refrigerators are ideal
for storing snacks and drinks. Although the rooms are not terribly spacious, each
has some sort of writing desk nestled into a back corner and chairs or couches

placed next to the picture windows. What the rooms lack in spaciousness is compensated for by their 180-degree views of, and proximity to, the lake.

From their porch, guests can watch the martins as they dart in and out of the three bird houses that have been erected for them. Flowers bloom in the planters placed in front of the bedroom windows, which merely enhance this peaceful setting. It is easy for guests to walk from their room to the expansive lawn. Activity choices are abundant, including shuffleboard, volleyball, along with a children's playground. Most people spend their days on or near the water though, opting to borrow a row, motor, or paddle boat and explore the inlets. Windsurfers are also available, and people may swim from the private beach. Since our last visit, the Tranbys have even added a small, informal golf course. There are acres and acres of land for Bowser to romp on and, of course, an entire lake to cool off in afterwards. The Knight Point State Park and Grand Isle State Parks are just south of Shore Acres, and the site of additional recreational opportunities. Take the ferry from Grand Isle Station to New York State for the day, or stay closer to home and visit the summer home of the Royal Lippizaner horses. Anyone who wants to relax and do nothing at all, will find more than enough excuses to stay at the inn.

In the summer months, the restaurant and reception area are the hub of activity at Shore Acres. The dining room joins the two wings of waterfront guest rooms. Guests usually enjoy breakfast and dinner here, and often elect to take a box lunch with them on their day trips. The evening menu emphasizes hearty homemade meals, accented with vegetables and herbs picked from their garden. Some like to start the meal with the four onion soup, chilled tenderloin with three mustards, or the Shore Acres coconut beer shrimp with an apricot glaze. Entrées include selections such as the apple island chicken in a cider sauce, charbroiled lamb chops with a mint and walnut sauce, or the shrimp with garlic, capers, wine, basil and lemons. Each table in the informal restaurant also has a superb view of the water.

The Shore Acres Inn is a low-key, intimate resort that everyone (including Bowser) is certain to enjoy. Moreover, the Tranbys are great hosts, who go out of their way to accommodate their guests' needs. Perhaps this is the reason for the high return rate among their guests.

Johnny Seesaw's

P.O. Box 68
Route 11
Peru, Vermont 05152
(802) 824-5533

Innkeepers: Nancy and Gary Okun
Rooms: 8 doubles, 4 suites, 4 cottages
Rates: Doubles $70-130 (B&B), Suites $70-150 (B&B), Cottages $80-150 (B&B)
Payment: MC and VISA
Children: Welcome (cribs, cots, highchairs, and babysitters are available)
Dogs: Allowed in the rooms and cottages with separate outside entrances. The lodge has
anextensive, but fair, pet policy.
Open: All year except April, May, and November

One of the many wonderful things about Johnny Seesaw's is that it doesn't change much, and when it does, it only gets better. We think the Okuns define their hostel quite well when they say, "we're not quaint, charming or elegant. We're Seesaw's." It remains, true to its roots, a simple, rustic lodge attracting those who love the outdoors. Built in 1927 by a Russian logger as a dance hall and road house, life at the lodge has certainly calmed down, but has not lost its intrinsic tradition of relaxed, informal hospitality. The central common room, containing multiple sitting areas, a bar, and a dining room, remains our favorite place at Johnny Seesaw's. In fact this room *is* Johnny Seesaw's, and is often where guests go when they are in search of activity. A central copper fireplace surrounded by red leather sofas is the favorite gathering spot for those who enjoy kicking off their boots and warming their toes in front of the fire. Other intimate sitting areas offer equally inviting navy, green, and red patterned wing chairs. The cozy bar is easy to find, just walk a few steps and look for the *Peru Yacht Club* sign set above the old fashioned wood bar. The window seats in here offer panoramic views of the surrounding mountains.

Although the lodge is relatively small, it still offers a wide variety of sleeping arrangements, ranging from cozy doubles to the more expansive suites and practical cottages. Since our last visit, some of these rooms have been updated with the addition of brass beds covered by Waverly floral spreads and topped with a handful of coordinated pillows. The windows are often framed in the same fabrics, but more importantly, offer some pretty valley views. The furnishings tend to be primarily simple country antiques, such as oak bureaus and straight back chairs. One of the suites, which is ideal for anyone traveling with a dog, offers a separate bedroom with a king-size bed and comfortable living room with a sofa, armchairs, and a television. Once again, the addition of slate blue and pink floral fabrics is just the touch that was needed to bring this space to life.

The cottages are fairly utilitarian in nature, but still attractively and comfortably furnished. We saw the converted chicken coop, which we thought would be ideal for skiers. The beds were comfortable, there was a futon to accommodate extra guests, and a fireplace in the living room that would certainly be fully stoked on a cold night. The other three cottages are located behind the chicken coop, and are similar in style, with private baths, two or more bedrooms, and modern amenities that include refrigerators, televisions, and clock radios. Anyone in search of a few more conveniences, space, and privacy, should reserve a cottage. Those traveling with a dog will appreciate the separate outside entrances.

All the room rates include a full breakfast. This can include French toast, eggs made to order, a variety of berry pancakes, and homebaked muffins. Although dinner is no longer automatically included in the fare, it has been rated by some critics as the "best Yankee cuisine in New England." The appetizer menu remains much the same with the lobster tortellini and scallops cooked in a sherry garlic tomato sauce topping the menu. The entrée selection has changed since our last visit. The seafood fettucini served with shrimp, crabmeat, and mushrooms in a light Parmesan cream sauce, prime rib of beef, and pork chops seasoned with maple syrup, are three interesting choices. The lemon walnut chicken, Cornish game hen with a raspberry glaze, and the sautéed veal with a sherry mushroom sauce were also high on our list. After dinner, the small game room is always a popular gathering place. The two video games, television, and more importantly, the pool table, certainly provide enough diversions for most guests. There is even a small dog bed in there for the resident dog. (Bowser is not allowed in the game room, bar, or main lodge.)

A leashed Bowser is welcome, however, to stroll the grounds. During the walk, guests are certain to come across the clay tennis court and a marble-rimmed Olympic-sized swimming pool. Close to the lodge are Bromley and Stratton ski mountains. In the wintertime, the skiing is great; and in the summer, Bromley has a wonderful alpine slide and Stratton plays host to a LPGA golf tournament. The summer and fall months offer opportunities to hike on the Appalachian Trail (which is just behind the lodge), try a little horseback riding, or test one's angling skills on the many lakes and streams nearby. There are also plenty of state forests to explore on cross-country skis or on foot. The Hapgood State Forest is within a five-minute drive of the inn, while the Emerald Lake State Forest is just a little further up the road. The lodge is also in the heart of the Green Mountain National Forest. The net result is that there are virtually unlimited outdoor recreational opportunities available for both Bowser and his two-legged companions.

Over the years, Johnny Seesaw's may have been many things to many people, but today it can truly call itself a "Legend" and get away with it.

Okemo Lantern Lodge

P.O. Box 247
Proctorsville, Vermont 05153
(802) 226-7770

Innkeepers: Pete and Dody Button
Rooms: 11 doubles
Rates: $80 (B&B), $120 (MAP)
Payment: AE, MC, and VISA
Children: Welcome; they must be reasonably well-behaved and parents must be responsible
Dogs: Welcome only with advance notice and prior approval
Open: All year except the months of November, December, and April

If an unpretentious Vermont village, Victorian houses, and a homey atmosphere all sound appealing, then the Okemo Lantern Lodge is just the place to stay. This 1800s Victorian inn is a great retreat during any season. There are nearby downhill skiing trails for winter recreation, great hiking trails and bicycle routes in the summer months, and an abundance of fishing, hunting, and leaf peeping opportunities available in the fall. The Buttons have created a cozy retreat that travelers can use as a base for many of these excursions.

It is not difficult to find the Okemo Lantern Lodge, just look for a bright blue house outlined by a wraparound porch. Even in the fall, the white wicker chairs were still set out with their festive blue cushions. As guests step in from the front porch, they emerge into the inn's foyer. Most people stop for a moment to inspect the antique post office slots, which contain a number of brochures on the region's activities.While there is a distinct Victorian flavor to the inn, it is by no means overdone. The fireplaced living room, set just off the reception area, contains a comfortable red leather chair, oversized sofa, and plenty of books, magazines, and games set out on the sidetables. Anyone who is curious about how to play these games, and others, might enjoy reading the thick reference book on all the games in the world that usually sits out on the coffee table.

A winding oak paneled staircase, just across from the living room, climbs past a very pretty stained glass window to the upstairs bedrooms. As is typical with an antique inn, each bedroom is a little different. Our favorites are located in the front of the house, as the rounded walls and eaves give them a little more character and space. A delicate yellow floral pattern was chosen for both the cheery wallpaper and fabric on the canopy bed in one of the chambers. Several bedrooms have contemporary floral wallpapers, while others, such as the intimate Rose Room, reflect an old fashioned Victorian motif. Antique and wicker furnishings, set alongside interesting collectibles, give each bedroom a unique flavor. Those with a sweet tooth will appreciate the little dishes of candies set out on the sidetables. Some of the bathrooms are shared, although anyone lucky enough to have a private one will find it to be good-sized and well appointed. One of the "coolest" bathrooms, according to our tour guide, is just off the Green Room, with its angular ceilings and skylight. The bed chambers to the rear of the inn are the Rose, Yellow, and Green Rooms. The latter is primarily hunter green which goes well with the carved, dark oak headboards. The Yellow Room, on the other hand, was quite festive with its lighter furnishings, and the cozy Rose Room was simply charming with its rose patterned wallpaper.

In the morning, the aroma of coffee is sure to arouse even the deepest of sleepers. The dining room, like the rest of the house, is intimate and welcoming. The full menu includes blueberry pancakes, French toast, omelettes, as well as side orders such as cob-smoked bacon and homemade coffee cake. At the end of the day, guests will return to find homemade soup and crusty bread, along with some tasty hors d'oeuvres waiting for them. The neat, old-fashioned cookstove is still utilized to warm up many of these delectables. Dinner is a bit more formal, as guests dine by candlelight. The meal is always different. Some nights there might be a hot artichoke dip to start, followed by broccoli soup and a Greek salad. The New York strip steak is served with a red wine sauce, or there could be a hearty beef stew instead. Fresh vegetables, a flavorful rice or potato, and freshly baked breads complete the affair. On the afternoon of our arrival, there was the delicious smell of garlic and of a simmering stew emanating from the kitchen. As we followed the smell to its source, we found Dody laying out brownies for a group of bicyclists who were soon to arrive.

Bowser will be as pleased with the outdoor activities, as his two-legged companions are with the inn. There are plenty of state forests to visit in the area. Just south of the inn is the Proctor-Piper State Forest and to the east is Mount Ascutney and the Ascutney State Park, which encompasses over 1,900 acres. The Wilgus State Park is close to Ascutney, and even though it has only 100 acres, there is an array of nature trails for Bowser to investigate. Visitors can pick up the Long Trail in nearby Wallingford, and follow it as it wends through the Green Mountain National Forest. In the summer months there are also rivers to fish in and swimming holes to cool off in after an energetic day of hiking or bicycling.

Ten Acres Lodge

14 Barrows Road
Stowe, Vermont 05672
(800) 327-7357, (802) 253-7638, Fax (802) 253-4036

Innkeepers: Eric P. Lande
Rooms: 16 doubles, 2 cottages
Rates: Doubles $100-160 (B&B), Cottages $225-275 (B&B)
Payment: AE, DSC, MC and VISA
Children: Welcome (cribs, cots, and highchairs are available)
Dogs: Well-mannered dogs are welcome in the cottages
Open: All year

The Helprins were the longtime owners of the Ten Acres Lodge, but on a recent visit we learned they had sold the inn. The new owner, who also owns the Edson Hill Manor, and staff have continued the long-standing tradition of offering personalized service and tantalizing New England cuisine in an historic setting. We are pleased to say that very little has physically changed with the inn. The main building, which was built as a farmhouse in 1840, is still furnished with country antiques. A fieldstone fireplace is shared by both the living room and cozy library. The latter, which is loaded with a variety of classic books, has a wonderful cushioned window seat that is ideal for some leisurely reading. The small living room has two deep sofas set next to the fireplace, providing a perfect setting for sipping afternoon tea, sampling baked goodies, or just enjoying an after-dinner drink.

Those traveling with a dog are welcome in the cottages. These are a one-minute walk from the inn and accommodate between four and eight people. They are usually reserved by either a family or two to three couples. Each cottage reflects a Vermont country theme, with reproduction antiques, Williamsburg colors, and a cozy decor setting the overall mood. The Red Cottage is the largest with three bedrooms. Wide pine floors are covered with rag rugs and some of the ceilings are natural board. Although the brass or carved wood bed frames are covered by simple white cotton spreads, they are enhanced with big pillows and fluffy down comforters. Oak bureaus and simple sidetables complete the decor. The bedroom walls are papered in either a delicate English country print or with small pink tulips set against a white backdrop. The two bathrooms are not state of the art, but are clean and offer basket of Gilchrist and Soames soaps and shampoos. The living room is especially inviting with its gray and red chintz sofa and matching chair set invitingly in front of the fireplace. A duck decoy rests on the mantel, and a few other knickknacks are placed on tables around the room.

The Gray Cottage has much the same feeling as the Red Cottage, with hardwood floors, braided rugs, and traditional furnishings. It provides a kitchen, where guests may create their own meals, as well as a table set invitingly in front of a paned picture window. A corner fireplace in the living room is surrounded by a rust sofa and two armchairs covered in whimsical fabrics. Two double beds covered in down comforters fill one guest room, which is also illuminated by pottery lamps. The cable television and a telephone are the two additional modern conveniences found in both cottages. There are also suites available in the Hill House, the inn's most contemporary accommodations. These are very attractive, each containing a fireplace and sitting area, as well as reproduction furnishings and antique beds. Air conditioning, telephones, and cable televisions are added features that many people find appealing.

The inn's breakfasts are ample, with a seemingly endless array of selections that are served buffet style. During our visit, quiche, homemade granola, baked ham, and assorted cheeses were just the start. These were followed by a fruit salad loaded with raspberries, along with coffee cake, brioche, and almond croissants. Fresh squeezed orange juice, as well as strong, freshly ground coffee and an assortment of teas were the perfect complements to the meal. While there are many fine restaurants in Stowe, very few can match the overall ambiance and quality found at Ten Acres Lodge. With the new owner came a new chef, who is still preparing many of the long-time favorite menu items and adding some of his own. The appetizer selection includes a roasted eggplant soup, a Vermont rabbit terrine, and the wild mushroom ravioli with a spinach walnut pesto and nutmeg Parmesan cream. While the appetizer menu is quite exotic, the entrée menu proves to be a little more mainstream. Some diners choose the grilled pork loin with a sweet potato gratin, the halibut with shrimp and scallion dumplings and a black bean ginger vinaigrette, or the beef tenderloin with horseradish mashed potatoes, carmelized shallots, and thyme.

There are plenty of things to do on the property. While Bowser is resting, guests might want to swim or play tennis. The swimming pool is tucked between the cottages and the inn, making it a very private retreat. In the summertime, many enjoy the extensive hiking trails that are located just five minutes from the inn. The Underhill State Park is also nearby as well, and provides plenty of land to explore. In the summer months, a tiny road close to the inn leads directly to the Cambridge State Forest, another outdoor paradise for Bowser. In the colder months, cross-country skiing is the activity of choice with Bowser, and the hot tub is a terrific place to rejuvenate afterwards. Guests are also free to use any of the facilities at the Edson Hill Manor as well. This includes horseback riding, the use of their pool, or meals in their restaurant.

Green Mountain Inn

Box 60
Main Street
Stowe, Vermont 05672
(800) 445-6629, (802) 253-7301, Fax (802) 253-5096

Innkeeper: Patty Clark
Rooms: 54 doubles, 4 suites
Rates: Doubles $79-150 (EP),Suites $125-200 (EP)
Payment: AE, MC, and VISA
Children: Welcome (cribs, cots, highchairs, and babysitters are available)
Dogs: "Well-mannered dogs" are welcome
Open: All year

Some people come to Stowe to get away from it all. Others like to be in the center of things, close to the restaurants and stores. The Green Mountain Inn is particularly appropriate for anyone in the latter group. Built in 1833, the inn is listed on the National Register of Historic Places and offers a variety of accommodations and amenities that are usually associated with larger hotels. The main building went through major renovations around its 150th birthday in 1983. By preserving the inn's antique qualities, and adding some modern features, the management created a very appealing overnight destination.

When guests first enter the inn, they will see gleaming hardwood floors leading to a small reception area. From here, an open center staircase climbs to the bedrooms. Just beyond the staircase, there is an inviting common area. A pair of sitting rooms have been painted in traditional Williamsburg colors and furnished with antiques and good quality reproductions. The dark green Chippendale-style sofas, flanking the fireplace, are set on Oriental rugs. There is even a small chess board placed on a leather-topped table.

The guest rooms are located in four different buildings, two of which are historic and two that are more contemporary. We used to prefer the antique rooms, with their creaking and sloping hardwood floors, original wainscotings, and unusually shaped spaces. During our most recent visit, however, we were surprised to see that the newer part of the inn had been greatly improved in both decor and furnishings. These accommodations are terrific for anyone traveling with a dog as they have separate outside entrances.

The barn red exterior is appealing; however, the interiors are even more so. The bedrooms vary in size, but all have been recently redone in a Colonial style with 18th-century furniture crafted specifically for the inn. The canopies on the pencil post beds match the fabrics on the bedspreads. Thick down comforters keep guests warm in the winter months, although each chamber also has individually controlled thermostats, as well. The white walls are stenciled just above the red chair rail. The sidetables are draped and set with brass lamps, clock radios, and telephones. Our bedroom had a wall of built-in drawers and a nook for the television. The bathrooms did not escape the renovation process either. The Corian-style counter tops are set with enameled fixtures. The walls have are papered in a crisp blue and white print, and the showers protected by coordinated shower curtains. There is an assortment of Caswell Massey shampoos, conditioners, bath gels and soaps which enhance anyone's bathing experience. Blow dryers are extra conveniences as well. All of these rooms are centered around the outside swimming pool and are just a 30-second walk to the health club.

Those who are interested in some on-the-premises exercise will want to visit to the fitness center, housed in an old barn to the rear of the property. This is a fully-equipped spa with everything from aerobic classes and steam rooms to racquetball and squash courts. Lifecycles, treadmills, and rowing machines nicely complement anyone's fitness routine. Of course, all of this exercise also helps to work up a healthy appetite.

Two very good restaurants can be found at the Green Mountain Inn. The main dining room, known as Main Street, is the most formal and historic restaurant. The menu varies with the season and during our visit, the Bar Harbor Maine crabcakes, New England corn chowder, and smoked Vermont pheasant ravioli topped the list. Entrées were equally traditional and included a Vermont turkey dinner, Yankee style pot roast, and grilled rack of lamb. The tortgiglioni pasta with lobster and mussels looked terrific.

The Whip Bar & Grill is located downstairs, is much more casual, and is usually packed. From the grill, there are the barbecue beef ribs or smoked chicken quesadilla with all the toppings. Of course, some people like to mix and match, choosing perhaps the oysters on the half shell or Duxbury mussels as an appetizer and then the stuffed sole or pasta primavera as a main course. Desserts are truly delectable, ranging from blueberry-apple crumb pie and a lemon-carrot cake to a concoction called chocolate sin. In the morning, blueberry pancakes, French toast, and omelettes are available. The outdoor patio, accessible through a pair of French doors, is a favorite place to dine in the summer, as it overlooks the pool and a stream.

Bowser will be happy here, there are plenty of walks to take in and around the inn. If visitors like quiet side streets, then they may walk along the backroads that are lined with shops. Main Street is quite busy, but still provides plenty of window shopping opportunities. The Long Trail cuts through this area, for hikers seeking a fun day hike. Mount Mansfield State Forest and the Little River State Park are two additional options just south of town. Stowe is a four-season resort, offering a full complement of recreational pursuits that will delight both Bowser and his human companions. Skiing, snowmobiling, snowshoeing, and skating are some of the winter diversions, while hiking, canoeing, swimming, and fishing are summertime alternatives.

The Mountain Road at Stowe

P.O. Box 8, Route 108
Stowe, Vermont 05672
(800) FOR-MTRD, (802) 253-4566, Fax (802) 253-7397

General Manager: *Bill Mintzer*
Rooms: *24 doubles, 6 condominium suites*
Rates: *Doubles $60-170 (B&B), Condominiums $130-380 (B&B)*
Payment: *AE, CB, DC, DSC, MC, and VISA*
Children: *Welcome (cribs and cots are available)*
Dogs: *Small pets accepted by advance reservation with a $15 fee*
Open: *All year*

There are several places in Stowe that welcome guests traveling with a dog, and we have tried to include a range of types of accommodations that should meet most traveler's needs. Just when we thought we had found them all, we discovered The Mountain Road at Stowe, which is actually a cross between a resort and a luxurious motor lodge. It is located well off the main road leading to Mount Mansfield, and is not only attractively landscaped, but also offers a wide variety of guest accommodations. In the warmer months, the drive leading to the resort is lined with white planters overflowing with flowers, and there are even a few whimsical replicas of cows and other farm animals dotting the lawns.

The Mountain Road has certain characteristics that remind us of a typical motor lodge, but the resemblance is merely superficial. For instance, even though all of the guest rooms have outside entrances, the doors of these have been painted in bright blue or yellow and hanging plants and planters line the walkways. Open the doors, and the very appealing interiors are revealed. This is especially true in the case of the original guest rooms at the main lodge. These were typical motel rooms; however, they have been recently upgraded and are now quite charming. We were pleasantly surprised to find either brass or country pine beds draped in French Provincial fabrics, pastoral watercolors on the walls, and thickly carpeted floors. The furnishings, which range from coffee tables and writing desks to bedside tables, are very attractive pine reproductions reminiscent of the Queen Anne period. A small sofa or armchairs provide extra seating in some of the rooms. The amenities in here are similar to what we find in more luxurious hotels, including a nook containing a dry bar, refrigerator, and a coffee maker. The bathrooms are extremely well appointed as well, with massaging shower heads, an array of toiletries, and blow dryers. The satellite cable televisions, direct dial telephones, and clock radios are welcome additions. This building also houses a few, two-story condominium suites.

The adjacent Club building offers studios and suites that are more spacious and equally well appointed. Each is attractively decorated with Scandinavian-style furnishings and offer all the same amenities as those found in the main lodge.

The primary difference between the lodge and Club rooms is more space, fully-equipped kitchens with microwaves, and perhaps a stereo system in the fireplaced living room or a Jacuzzi in the tiled bathroom. In a typical one-bedroom suite, the bedroom lies near the entrance of the unit. These are carpeted, and usually have two beds that are draped in quilts. The living rooms have a fireplace, comfortable couches, and array of brass knickknacks.

All guests may go over to the main lodge for breakfast, or they may take this meal in their room. The buffet consists of fresh coffee and tea, juices, muffins, bagels, and cereals. We liked the common room, with its beamed and vaulted ceiling and a wall of plate glass that revealed pretty views of Mount Mansfield. We were also drawn to the small seating arrangement in front of this window, although the huge hunter green sofas flanking the fieldstone fireplace were also appealing. This chamber is also a popular place to congregate in the afternoon when guests can be found reading from the collection of magazines, books, and complimentary newspapers while sipping a cup of tea, hot cider, or cocoa.

During a portion of the day, many people stay at The Mountain Road to enjoy all of the activities available at the resort. In the winter months, the AquaCentre is a popular option. This is equipped with an indoor heated pool, a huge Jacuzzi, a sauna, and an exercise room. Upstairs, there is a game room with three or four tabletop games and a variety of soft armchairs. The outdoor pool and hot tub is appealing in the summertime, although Bowser might be more interested in exploring the stream or the woods on the property. The resort lends bicycles for those who are interested in following the Stowe Recreation Path that lies just across the road, or exploring some of the other backcountry roads. Anyone who wants to strap on some snowshoes and try some winter hiking with Bowser, can rent them locally and head up to the Mount Mansfield State Forest. The front desk also has an array of information about other local hiking or cross-country ski trails that start right in Stowe and wend through the hills.

Notch Brook Resort

1229 Notch Brook Road
Stowe, Vermont 05672
(800) 253-4882, (802) 253-4882

General Manager: *Daniel Wesson*
Rooms: *33 doubles, 8 apartments, 25 condominiums*
Rates: *Doubles $72 (B&B), Apartments $135 (B&B), Condominiums $165-250 (B&B)*
Payment: *AE, CB, DC, MC, and VISA*
Children: *Welcome (cribs, cots, and highchairs are available)*
Dogs: *Welcome, dogs must be leashed on the property*
Open: *All year*

The Notch Brook Resort, a four-season condominium complex, is located on a wooded hillside with distant views of Mount Mansfield. Each of the apartments and townhouses is privately owned and rented to the public through the resort management. While some of the decorating touches are personalized, the management is responsible for periodically refurbishing the units. The basic floor plan may include up to three different levels that contain a living room with fireplace, dining area, fully-equipped kitchen, modern bathroom, a deck or terrace, and up to three bedrooms.

Most of the accommodations were built in the mid-1970s, and the exteriors are attractive but fairly utilitarian. The interior architectural lines are clean and simple, accented with the use of brick and lightly stained woods. The good-sized living room is the focal point for the townhouse. In here, guests may bask in the warmth of the fireplace, while enjoying the views of the mountains through the floor-to-ceiling windows. Many of the bi- and tri-level townhouses have window seats, alcoves filled with bookshelves, and couch beds as added conveniences. Each year, the management makes an attempt to update some facet of each unit. During our most recent visit, they were in the process of replacing most of the old Scandinavian furniture in favor of slightly darker yet equally contemporary pieces. The entertainment centers are fronted by glass doors, and contain cable televisions and stereos. They have also put new rust carpeting in many of the units, and replaced some of the worn sofas with new leather or upholstered pieces. On another level, guests will find the dining room, complete with a large oak table and chairs. The adjoining kitchen is fully stocked with more than enough pots, pans, plates, glasses and utensils. They have remembered all of the essentials, including dish towels and garbage bags. Daily maid service helps in making it a vacation for everyone.

One of the best features of this complex are the additional facilities and amenities that guests are encouraged to utilize. Not only are there two tennis courts and saunas, but there is also an outdoor heated swimming pool which is open throughout the year. Along the top of the fence that surrounds the pool are planters filled with yellow marigolds that add a touch of color throughout the warmer months. The hospitality room has a VCR and big screen television where first-run movies are shown each night. The resort's ski room keeps guests' skis properly tuned. The shuttle bus service from the resort to Mount Mansfield, provides skiers with the luxury of not having to navigate a car on the potentially slippery roads. Finally, each morning, a complimentary Continental breakfast is served, providing juice, coffee, bagels, English muffins, and toast.

Notch Brook Resort is located on a large piece of property, which will give Bowser ample opportunities to exercise. Its hillside location is private, and guests can enjoy strenuous walks either up or down the road that runs by the resort. There are even trails in the nearby forests that are worth exploring as well. The Stowe Recreation Path runs from the old section of the village and along the Mountain Road to Mount Mansfield. It is easy to pick it up at any point along the way. South of Stowe hikers will find the Putnam State Forest, while to the north there is the quiet Northeast Kingdom.

Topnotch at Stowe Resort and Spa

P.O. Box 1458
4000 Mountain Road
Stowe, Vermont 05672
(800) 451-8686, (802) 253-8585, Fax (802) 253-9263

General Manager: Lewis M. Kiesler
Rooms: 4 singles, 79 doubles, 7 suites, 15 townhouses
Rates: Singles $168-226 (EP), Doubles $128-236 (EP), Suites $210-544 (EP),
*   Townhouses $430-525 (EP)*
Payment: AE, DSC, MC, and VISA
Children: Welcome (cribs, cots, highchairs, and babysitters are available)
Dogs: Small dogs are welcome in the hotel
Open: All year

Although Topnotch at Stowe is far from being an intimate inn, it is operated like one, with an emphasis on personal service and old-fashioned hospitality. Physically, Topnotch is enormous, but its original designers have divided it up into small sitting areas and hallways that zigzag through the main building. People often gravitate to the fireplaced bar or the greenhouse areas, where a canopy of hanging plants creates a soothing effect. Deep sofas and paneled walls give one room the feeling of a formal study. But the most dramatic space is the central living room. In most rooms like this, the huge fireplace is its centerpiece; however, that is not the case in here, where plate glass windows reveal exceptional views of Mount Mansfield. There is even a telescope, so that guests can gain even better views of the local scenery. It may be difficult to turn away from the views, but when people do they might notice the huge moose head on the fieldstone wall or the bronze statue of a horse placed on a nearby table.

The dining room is located just off the living room and offers an excellent menu. The Maryland lump crabcakes, chilled lobster and shrimp salad, and the maple-cured smoked salmon and scallops are just a few of the appetizer selections. For dinner, guests might enjoy the lobster and shrimp scampi, grilled Canadian salmon, or a ratatouille of eggplant, artichokes, roasted peppers, and oyster mushrooms. The baked stuffed oysters with crabmeat, spinach, and roasted peppers is also appealing, as are the country mixed grill, beef filet, veal noisette, and lamb loin. After a satisfying meal, most people are content to slip off to bed.

Physically, the bedrooms are rather simple in design, although occasionally a darkly stained rough hewn wall or built-in bookshelf adds some architectural interest. However, they have all been beautifully decorated and furnished. Along with a complement of antiques and good quality reproduction furnishings, a hand-tied, Vermont patchwork quilt often covers the bed. The color schemes vary, with perhaps hunter green and burgundy as the backdrop for the coordinated

French Provincial fabrics at the windows and draping the tables. We certainly enjoyed the idea of sitting in front of our picture window, while enjoying breakfast and the Sunday paper along with the garden and mountain views. A fragrant selection of Topnotch soaps, shampoos, and lotions, as well as mouthwash and emery boards, are placed in the modern bathrooms. These have been recently refurbished with fresh wallpapers and marble countertops. Other personal touches include ice (delivered to the room each afternoon), turned-down beds, and fine chocolates placed on the pillow at night. Bottles of Vermont spring water are also welcome additions.

The staff at the Topnotch at Stowe can honestly say they offer a complete resort experience. The tennis complex is a tennis player's dream, with four indoor and ten outdoor courts. For those who would rather swing a club or mallet, there is both a putting green and croquet course. They have upgraded their Spa program over the years and now provide a full complement of aromatherapy, reflexology, and beauty treatments, along with massage and aerobics programs. The Spa is also equipped with a 12-foot whirlpool with cascading hydro-massage waterfalls, along with a 60-foot indoor pool. Swimming is also available in an outdoor heated pool. The pool area, and the buildings, are surrounded by colorful perennial gardens, rock walls, and dense foliage. Bowser can walk on the resort's 120 acres, where he will come across hiking trails that lead into the mountains. The equestrian center is always busy, and in the winter months, the cross-country ski center provides all levels of trails for skiers. Bowser can also come along on a sledding expedition, or follow the six-mile recreational path that wends through scenic forests.

Whitford House

RR 1, Box 1490
Vergennes, Vermont   05491
(800) 746-2704, (802) 758-2704

Hosts: Bruce and Barbara Carson
Rooms: 3 doubles, 3 suites
Rates: Doubles $60-70, Suites $125
Payment: Personal checks
Children: Welcome (a crib is available)
Dogs: Welcome with advance reservations
Open: All year

Once in a while, we stumble upon an inn that is truly remarkable. Late one crisp fall evening, we found just such a place in the Whitford House. It is located in Addison, a tiny dairy town near the southern shores of Lake Champlain. From Middlebury, we traveled along miles of backcountry roads before reaching the welcoming lights of the inn. Barbara and her two friendly beagles immediately came outside to greet us and led us into a spectacular room, where a roaring fire in the two story fieldstone fireplace immediately took away the chill we had been feeling.

While other guests were preparing to go out for dinner, we were settling into the soft rust-colored sofa and blue armchair grouped around the fireplace. As we munched on hors d'oeuvres and sipped tea, we were able to talk with Bruce and Barbara about the inn. The Whitford House was actually built in the 1790s. Along the wall in the front parlor are wonderful black and white photographs that were given to the Carsons shortly after they purchased the house. From these, guests can see the various changes that have taken place to the house over the years. For instance, the plain facade was enhanced with the addition of an elegant front veranda and side porch soon after the house was built. Rock walls were constructed a short time later, and a picture dated 1880 reveals the addition of a back porch. Just like their predecessors, the Carsons have also made some significant changes to the home, always keeping its antiquity in the forefront of their minds.

They actually bought the house a few years ago, after having lived in Laguna Beach, California for 37 years. Aside from refinishing the floors, painting many of the common and bed rooms, and general restoration, they decided to create more space by converting the original barn into an expansive common room. The ceiling rises two stories, and the back wall is lined with windows and French doors. A grand piano fills a small portion of this space, while comfortable sitting areas are set up to take advantage of the incredible views of the fields and distant Adirondacks. From this wonderful chamber, we went up a few stairs to the huge, modern country kitchen. The adjacent library is quite formal and has another fireplace that is usually blazing. Barbara used to be an English teacher, and she has packed the floor-to-ceiling bookshelves with her collection of classics, as well as those she and Bruce have read over the years. Everything is neatly displayed in categories, allowing guests to easily find something that interests them.

The stairway to the bedrooms literally gleams with beautifully restored woods. Random-width wide pine floors are covered with area rugs that do little to dampen the sounds of creaking wood underneath. The four bedrooms lie at the top of the front stairs. Actually, there are three guest bedrooms and the Carsons' suite. When the inn is full, they will often offer their own bedroom and private bathroom to their guests. These fortunate visitors will enjoy the king-size bed that is covered with a down comforter and a mohair throw which is neatly folded at its base. This space essentially a huge loft, where guests look through the walls of windows to the Adirondacks. Guests will also see the lath and plaster which has been purposely left exposed in the eaves.

The other chambers are equally inviting and are furnished with specially selected country antiques. Nothing is overdone, and everything works well together. These three bedrooms are painted either a pale pink, sage green, or pastel yellow. Guests may choose a chamber with twin beds or a double, all of which have soft cotton sheets and down comforters. One bedroom had a full-length mirror that matches the naturally stained, beaded oak headboard. A marble-topped table has a copper pot filled with purple, violet, and white wildflowers. There are always interesting paintings or contemporary lithographs to be found in the bedrooms and common areas. Otherwise, guests will not find a lot of knickknacks cluttering the house; instead there are a few unusual, carved figures from the southwest resting on tables and shelves. Barbara went to school in this part of the country, and so here, amid all this New England history, there are reminders of her past. The only potential drawback to the inn is the absence of private bathrooms; however, the one shared bath is huge, modern and stocked with an array of amenities. There is a claw-footed tub and glassed-in shower, along with lots of jojoba bath gels, oatmeal soaps, and baskets of towels. A blow dryer is an added convenience. During our visit, Bruce and Barbara were converting a carriage house into two additional suites. If these spaces are anything like those in the main house, they should be spectacular. The additional privacy, and ease of access to the outside, will also make them ideal retreats for those traveling with a dog.

In the morning, guests often gather in the library, which has even more expansive views of the surrounding countryside. In here, a tray of coffee, tea, juice, and breads are set out. The morning of our visit, we were treated to waffles with maple syrup, sausage and bacon, as well as fried apples. The day before, Barbara had cooked a Mexican meal with fritattas and fresh fruit. Guests are served in the formal dining room, around a large antique table that gives people an opportunity to visit with one another and exchange ideas for the day's activities. During breakfast, we learned that one fellow down the road was starting an ostrich farm and another was raising emus; however, the majority of the Carsons' neighbors are dairy farmers. Bowser would certainly enjoy walks on the Carsons' 600 acres, or along the dirt roads that wend through the area. Just eight miles away, in the town of Addison, is a recreation area called DAR, with over 95 acres of land. Chimney Point is also close to the inn, and here visitors will find a bridge that connects Vermont to New York State. The Green Mountain National Forest is nearby, and offers virtually unlimited hiking opportunities. Many also enjoy driving north to Shelburne Farms and taking a tour of both the spectacular working farm and the picturesque mansion, situated on a bluff overlooking Lake Champlain.

By special reservation, the Carsons also serve an elaborate dinner created by a chef they bring in just for such occasions. Guests dine by candlelight in the dining room and library, which is usually just the right way to end a perfect day.

Basin Harbor Club

Vergennes, Vermont 05491
(800) 622-4000, (802) 475-2311

Owners: Pennie and Bob Beach
Rooms: 38 doubles, 77 cottages
Rates: Doubles $130-180 (B&B), $218-327(AP), Cottages $262-460 (AP)
Payment: MC, and VISA
Children: Welcome (cribs, cots, highchairs, babysitters, and children's programs are
*   available)*
Dogs: Small, well-trained pets are welcome in the cottages with a $5 daily charge, must
*   be leashed and kept away from the waterfront and pool*
Open: June 15 through October 16

In an era of constant change, it is amazing to think that one family could stay in the same business, in the same place, for almost 110 years. The Beach family, owners of the Basin Harbor Club since 1886, is one such unique breed. Those who benefit most from the Beach's years of experience are the guests of the Basin Harbor Club, most of whom have made the annual trek to the resort for years.

After visiting the Basin Harbor Club several times over the last decade, we now know just what draws people back year after year — a consistently high level of personal service, a formal yet surprisingly unpretentious atmosphere, excellent food, and a virtually unlimited selection of activities. The resort is set on over 700 acres overlooking Lake Champlain, on which guests will find 77 cottages, an 18-hole golf course, 5 tennis courts, an Olympic-size swimming pool, hiking and jogging trails, and a variety of lakefront activities.

Although there are a number of double rooms available in three separate buildings, guests traveling with Bowser will want to stay in the cottages. Each is unique in terms of size, layout, and manner in which they are furnished. Some of these are made of stone that is inset with Palladian windows and decorative eaves, while others are white clapboard with festive red roofs. Each exudes a unique charm, and are in no way rustic. The interior architectural features vary as well, with some of the cottages having vaulted ceilings, modern bathrooms, and walls of French doors. Others are holdovers from the past, with small-paned windows, fieldstone fireplaces, and creaking, sloping floors. The decor varies, although guests will usually find the hardwood floors covered in bright rag rugs, along with traditional sofas and chairs slipcovered in chintz or bright cotton fabrics. The sidetables are often constructed of maple or pine and the chairs caned in natural wicker. The physical configurations also vary, with some cottages providing good-sized living rooms and a couple of bedrooms. Others have this basic layout along with additional amenities such as a wet bar, a refrigerator, and an old-fashioned porch or modern deck. First-time guests should request a map illustrating

161

all the cottages and their locations so that they can more easily choose their accommodations. Those looking for a little more privacy would be apt to choose the cottages on the bluff overlooking the lake, while others might want to be close to the waterfront, golf course, or tennis courts.

The Basin Harbor Club provides guests with just about anything one might want on a vacation. Sports-minded guests have plenty of land and water-based options to choose from during their stay. The harbor area is the hub of activity, where people can rent sailboards, Sunfishes, canoes, outboards, paddleboats, or rowboats. The resort has a 40-foot boat that tours the lake once a day. Bicycles can also be rented, allowing greater flexibility in exploring the area. Lawn games, such as croquet, shuffleboard, badminton, and volleyball, are also quite popular. Golf is a favorite pastime throughout the season. In the peak summer months, from late June through early September, young children may benefit from the supervised Little Champs program (ages 3-7), that takes place at the playground and at different areas on the property. There is also a playhouse stocked with games, books, and toys that is very appealing on rainy days. There are cookouts, supervised swimming programs, arts and crafts, and scavenger hunts which should keep even the most active child quite entertained. The older Harbormates (ages 8-12) have a less structured, but equally entertaining, program with canoe trips, water skiing, and golf and tennis clinics.

There is the distinct possibility that the Beaches offer so many athletic options because most people need to burn off the calories they consume during meals. Breakfast and dinner are served in the elegant Lakeside Main Dining Room, where walls of windows offer scenic lake views. White linen tablecloths, silver, and crystal are placed among elaborately folded napkins. The beautiful fresh flower arrangements truly catch one's eye, whether they are overflowing from an Oriental bowl or in small vases. In keeping with tradition, men are asked to wear jackets and a tie to the evening meal and women are asked to dress appropriately. The menu changes daily, but appetizers during our visit featured a Napoleon of duck or marinated scallops. The entrées varied from a shrimp, lobster, and scallop Newburg and a grilled Mahi Mahi to the Vermont lamb, prime rib, and polenta lasagna. The dessert menu has something to please everyone. A few of the perennial favorites are the espresso mousse in a lace cookie basket with a creme Kahlua sauce, the pecan pound cake á la mode, or the chocolate pots de crème. The wine list has received accolades from the *Wine Spectator* magazine, and scotch drinkers will also be pleased with the extensive list of 10-16 year old single malt scotches that are available. Others prefer to spend their after dinner time in the formal living room where sage green walls create a neutral setting for the mahogany antiques, Queen Anne wing chairs and tailored sofas. When the nights are warm, guests often walk outside to the grassy knoll where the bright red, yellow, and green Adirondack chairs are privy to the panoramic lake views and starry skies.

As one might imagine, the Basin Harbor Club is a paradise for dogs as well. Although it is requested that Bowser be leashed at all times, we are sure he will enjoy exploring the extensive acreage. There are miles of walks along the shore front, wooded trails to follow, and endless swimming opportunities (not in the harbor area, though).The Button Bay State Park offers additional nature walks. The Long Trail is close to the resort, should people want to spend the day in the mountains. Most discover though, that once they arrive at the Basin Harbor Club, they have very little reason to go anywhere else.

Millbrook Inn

Route 17, RFD Box 62
Waitsfield, Vermont 05673
(800) 472-2809, (802) 496-2405

Innkeepers: Joan and Thom Gorman
Rooms: 7 doubles
Rates: $50-80 (B&B)
Payment: AE, DC, MC, and VISA (but prefer cash or checks)
Children: Not appropriate for children under six years of age.
Dogs: Welcome in specific rooms during the summer and fall, cannot bark, and must not
be left alone in room
Open: Closed from April through mid-June

The Millbrook Inn was originally built in the 1850s as part of a dairy farm. This Cape-style farmhouse has been used as an inn, however, since 1948, about the same time that Mad River Glen was founded. It is situated just outside of Waitsfield on the road to Sugarbush and Mad River Glen. It is a cozy, personal place with just seven bedrooms, yet it offers guests the benefit of a gourmet kitchen (and chef) that is usually associated with larger establishments.

When the Gormans bought the inn some fifteen years ago, they made many changes to the place that today are part of the inn's intrinsic charm. Even after all these years, we still like walking into the warming room with its rock floor and antique Glenwood Parlor stove. We always seem to visit during the fall, when the stove is fully stoked and is throwing an enormous amount of heat into this cozy space. Just beyond this chamber is the equally inviting parlor with a fireplace. Hidden on the first floor is a bedroom, which gives guests an indication of what lies upstairs. The Willow Tree Room has delicate willow trees stenciled along the top of the walls. The two antique maple beds have soft comforters on them, while a built-in bookshelf offers extensive reading materials. This is a large bedroom and an ideal choice for those traveling with a dog.

Upstairs, there are additional chambers, each with an individual personality. Most of the rooms already had their own unique nooks and crannies, so the Gormans just needed to furnish and decorate them. There is extensive stenciling in the bedrooms. For instance, in the Henry Perkins Room, which is named for the founder of the inn, there is a double bed draped in a pretty handmade quilt and stenciling reflecting American folk art patterns. There is also the Waterfall Room, with its matching waterfall double bed and dresser, and the Wedding Ring Room, with its double wedding ring quilt that lies on the antique rock maple bed. Another particularly memorable chamber is the Shell Room, so named for the shell-shaped inlaid headboard and matching dresser. Guests will find the stenciling is quite extensive in this part of the house as well, ranging from pineapple motifs and overflowing flower baskets to decorative vines and colorful berries. Somehow, Joan has also found time to make many of the quilts covering the antique beds, some of which have recently been converted from doubles into queens.

Meals are served in the downstairs dining room. After transforming the old dining room into a cozy sitting area, a new addition created space for the gourmet country restaurant. French doors open to a terrace and the garden (from which many of the fresh herbs and vegetables are selected). The tables are covered in floral overlays, which merely enhance the cheerful feeling in here, even in the midst of winter. While breakfasts are excellent, the dinners are even better. What both have in common is the emphasis on fresh, natural ingredients and the Gorman's original recipes. The mussels Millbrook are steamed with fresh herbs, tomatoes, garlic and shallots and are terrific as an appetizer. Homemade pasta dishes are a standard staple. One of these is the garden lasagna that is loaded with eggplant, zucchini, yellow squash, fresh mushrooms, a ricotta-parmesan filling, homemade sauce, and fresh spinach pasta. The hand rolled spinach fettuccine is tossed with a sauce of Cabot cheddar, fresh Parmesan, Vermont mascarpone, and sun-dried tomatoes to create the three cheese fettuccine. A roasted Vermont lamb, pork, or ham is always on the menu, as is the five-peppercorn beef tenderloin. The most inspired choices on the menu continue to be the authentic Indian dishes. Chicken Brahmapuri is a village-style curry served with homemade tomato chutney. Badami Rogan Josh is as exotic as it sounds. Local lamb is simmered in a curried sauce of cardamom, cumin, coriander, coconut, almonds, ginger, yogurt, and tomatoes, emerging as a very spicy and extremely rich entrée.

As hard as they work, the Gormans enjoy this lifestyle, particularly when they compare it to the one they left behind in New York. However, it has not come about without a tremendous amount of effort and ingenuity. Those who reap the benefits, of course, are the guests. The Gormans are also never too busy to offer input on where to go or what to do in the area. Many think of the Mad River Valley and its adjacent ski areas as merely a winter resort; however, the summer and fall are equally enjoyable and provide even more outdoor opportunities to enjoy with Bowser. Of course, hiking is a natural in the mountains (the Long and Catamount Trails are close to the inn), but there is also canoeing along the Mad River and even Windsurfing at Blueberry Lake. Bowser might not be welcome on the golf course or tennis courts, but his two-legged companions should find these to be pleasant diversions. The property around the inn is also quite pretty, with expanses of grass and enormous maple trees. Mo, the resident Springer Spaniel, is usually on hand to accompany Bowser in exploring the grounds.

The Inn at Weathersfield

Route 106 (near Perkinsville)
Weathersfield, Vermont 05151
(800) 477-4828, (802) 263-9217

Innkeepers: Mary Louise and Ron Thorburn
Rooms: 9 doubles, 3 suites
Rates: Doubles $175 (MAP), Suites $205 (MAP)
Payment: AE, DSC, MC, and VISA
Children: Not appropriate for children under eight years of age
Dogs: Very well-behaved dogs are welcome with prior approval and on a case-by-case basis
Open: All year

The Inn at Weathersfield was built by Thomas Prentis in 1795. The original four-room farmhouse was situated on 237 acres of woods and fields. Over the years, the bedrooms and a carriage house (now the dining room) were added to meet each of the subsequent owner's needs. During its 200-year existence, this homestead has been used as a tavern and stagecoach stop, a sanctuary for the slaves hiding along the Underground Railroad, and, more recently, as a summer estate.

The elegant, columned inn lies at the end of a rather long, rock walled drive. Mature trees line the lane and a picturesque pond can be seen in the field. The inn, which has been lovingly refurbished and maintained over the years, has maintained its rich architectural history with the addition of a few more pleasing modern conveniences. Guests should expect a labyrinth of rooms at the Inn at Weathersfield. Some of these open directly into one another through wide arches and others are substantially more private. The dark foyer is enlivened by dried flower arrangements, baskets hanging from the original hand-hewn beamed ceilings, and a crackling fire. The expansive dining room also has beamed ceilings and walls that are offset by intimate windowed alcoves overlooking the perennial gardens. The fieldstone fireplace is surrounded by walls of shelves that are brimming with collectible books. The few areas of open wall space contain remarkable oil paintings of scenic landscapes. It is the combination of little things, like a silver punch bowl resting on a side table, glass vases filled with roses or lovely arrangements of wildflowers, and chintz fabrics framing the windows, that truly set the overall mood in this chamber.

The menu is equally rich with enticing offerings. The appetizer selection includes salmon or trout in a puff pastry, the Vermont quail with pheasant sausage, and a venison paté with a blueberry sauce. A salad and sorbet cleanse the palate before the entrée arrives. On the night we visited, there was a roasted rack of lamb with a mint mustard sauce, a roast duck with mango and Thai fruit, and a poached salmon filet with a dill and cucumber vinaigrette. The beef tenderloin in a filo pastry with shrimp and artichoke stuffing, veal medallions on a fruit compote with black pepper cider sauce, and the seafood sausage with a tomato cream sauce and onion purée are equally appealing. The dessert tray varies with the evening; however, the white chocolate cheesecake with raspberries and creme de cassis or the chocolate truffle cake remain the perennial favorites. Ron is an important part of the dining experience, as he assumes both the role of wine steward and pianist. In addition to the wonderful music, the elegant ambiance and friendly staff combine to make this a very memorable dining experience.

As guests walk further into the inn, they will discover other common rooms and dining areas. One of our favorites is the sunny library, filled with a collection of over 4,000 books. The sloping and creaking wide-pine floors add character to this room, just as they do to the rest of the rooms at the inn. A garden room, with a slate floor, seems to be just the spot to enjoy one of the ample breakfasts or a delightful afternoon tea. The formal living room is tucked just off the foyer, near the front of the inn. The fireplace in here is flanked by paneled walls and the room is filled with a sampling of the Thorbur's exquisite English and American antiques. Some of the more notable examples are the chest of drawers, glowing with a rich patina, along with a formal sofa and sidechairs. Guests will also find a grandmother's clock, old fashioned chess table, decorative quilts, and an array of period pine and mahogany furnishings throughout the inn.

Many of the guest rooms are found by ascending one of the three staircases, with the most interesting being the split staircase just off the dining room. As guests climb the stairs, they will see a variety of Mary Louise's quilts hanging from the wall. Most of the bed chambers are located in the original building; however, a few can also be found in the newer post-and-beam addition. Every piece of furniture, from the canopy and four-poster beds to the bureaus, is antique. The warmth of the handmade quilts is supplemented by electric bottom sheets and fireplaces or woodstoves. Quaint rocking chairs grace the sitting rooms, and private decks are terrific in the quiet morning hours. Bowls of fruits and nuts are left on sidetables, while mints rest on the pillows. The bathrooms are private and unique, some still have the original claw-footed tubs.

Guests will discover that the 21 acres surrounding the inn are just as enticing as the interior of the building. Some enjoy the peacefulness of the gardens, while others prefer the lawn games which include croquet, badminton, volleyball, and horseshoes. Anyone who is interested in a more aerobic workout, can visit the exercise room complete with a Finnish sauna and an array of fitness machines. Seasonal alternatives include sleigh rides, sledding, and both cross-country and downhill skiing in the winter; apple picking, foliage hunting, and golfing in the fall; and walking or bicycling along the picturesque back roads in the summer months. The nearby Wilgus State Park and Ascutney State Park also offer varied seasonal recreational opportunities. At the end of the day, guests return to High Tea and dine on delicate sandwiches and pastries that complement the international teas and coffees. In the summer months, most are happy to take this repast on the back patio, which is shaded by white umbrellas.

The Darling Family Inn

815 Route 100
Weston, Vermont   05161
(802) 824-3223

Innkeepers: Joan and Chapin Darling
Rooms: 5 doubles, 2 cottages
Rates: Doubles $75-95 (B&B), Cottages $85 (EP)
Payment: Personal checks
Children: Welcome in cottages; they must be over 10 years of age to stay in the inn rooms
Dogs: Welcome in the cottages with prior notice
Open: All year except Christmas

The Darling Family Inn was built over 160 years ago and is surrounded by acres of pastures. Today, the only major change is scenic Route 100 running by the inn; however, this does not present a problem as the inn is set well off the road, protected by stands of trees. The inn was built in the Colonial style, with hardwood floors, beams, cozy rooms, and an assortment of English and American country antiques. In the summertime, from their bedroom windows, guests are treated to the sight of extensive perennial gardens that are framed by rock walls. Those traveling with a dog can enjoy the views of the gardens as well, but from two of the intimate housekeeping cottages located on a hillside above the inn.

Tucked into a grassy, rock-studded knoll behind apple trees and bushes, the coffee colored cottages are surrounded by green pastures dotted with grazing cows. The cottages are a great choice for those traveling with a dog because they not only offer privacy, but also more than enough space to spread out. The cottages are decorated with simple, country furnishings. The antiques that fill the inn are noticeably absent here, leaving comfortable sofas and chairs for guests to relax on. A solid maple drop leaf table is placed in front of a window in one cottage, and an oak desk occupies a similar space in the other. Sheer white tie-back or red checked curtains frame the paned windows in these cottages, while colorful Vermont quilts cover the beds. For a small stipend, cottage guests are also invited to eat breakfast at the inn, provided they give the Darlings a little advance notice. We highly recommend these hearty meals, as guests are given a choice of French toast, either blueberry, blackberry, and raspberry pancakes, or eggs served any style. Depending on the choice, the entrée can be served with home fries, ham, bacon, or sausage. Those who simply want a bowl of delicious oatmeal, some toasted English or homemade muffins, or just a rich cup of coffee or chocolate may request that, as well. Should cottage guests wish to sleep in, they may also prepare their own repast in the well-equipped cottage kitchenettes.

We have been writing about The Darling Family Inn for years, and always enjoy our return visits. The property surrounding the inn offers well-manicured grounds, as well as open fields. In the summertime, the swimming pool, tucked just below the inn, is a welcome retreat. A hammock hangs behind the house, which is perfect for relaxing in on a hot summer's day. There is also a lot of open space to explore. One word of caution: there are cows grazing in the area, so guests may want to leash Bowser so they do not frighten each other. Many people take a box lunch and head out for day hikes in the local mountains or fishing at one of the nearby streams. Cross-country skiing is available throughout the area in the wintertime, and one trail begins right at the inn's back door. The quaint town of Weston is nearby, offering a summer theater, a terrific selection of Vermont craft and antique stores, and the famous Weston Priory, home of the singing monks. When it comes time for dinner, the Darlings put out the wine and cheese, along with menus from all the restaurants in the area, so that guests may leisurely peruse their assorted options.

Three Church Street

3 Church Street
Woodstock, Vermont   05091
(802) 457-1925

Innkeeper: *Eleanor C. Paine*
Rooms: *11 doubles*
Rates: *Doubles $70-100 (B&B)*
Payment: *MC and VISA*
Children: *Welcome (cots are available)*
Dogs: *Welcome with prior approval*
Open: *All year except the month of April*

Three Church Street sits beside the village green in the heart of the quintessential New England village of Woodstock. This Federal-style home, built in 1830, was the first bed and breakfast in Woodstock. Visitor's first impressions of Three Church Street are of the stately foyer. Take a moment to look at the bust of Marquis de Lafayette that has occupied a small alcove in the foyer for the last century. The living room is just off the central hall. A long case clock, several cream colored couches, a baby grand piano, and a marble fireplace all create a sense of elegance in this pale yellow chamber. The library, also found on the first floor, is a more comfortable and informal space; this, too, is warmed by a woodstove in the winter. This room houses a television, comfortable sofas and sidechairs, and numerous books and magazines.

The beauty of Three Church Street lies in the fact that it feels more like a family home than a B&B. Mrs. Paine has eight children, and when half of them left home, she decided to turn the extra rooms into guest bedrooms. Once all of her children moved away (some have returned to help run the B&B), the home became a full-fledged B&B. In all the years we have been writing about Three Church Street, nothing has really changed. Many of the bedrooms still reflect the personality of the individual child. Original floral wallpapers adorn many of the walls, and an eclectic assortment of homey furnishings, acquired by the family over the years, fill the rooms. One of the largest of these chambers overlooks the street. It has a canopy bed and a woodstove, as well as enough room for a sofa and separate dressing area. There are antiques and tiny collectibles scattered throughout, completing this very inviting scene.

A complimentary breakfast is served each morning in the dining room, which overlooks the grounds. Chintz-covered tables are set with candles, and glass mugs are waiting to be filled with freshly brewed coffee. Name cards direct guests to the appropriate table. Once settled, they may choose from a number of breakfast items, including hot and cold cereals, French toast, and a variety of berry-filled pancakes. On Sunday, the menu expands to include Eggs Benedict and poached or scrambled eggs. Afterwards, some people choose to visit in the small sitting area off the dining room. White wicker chairs and couches are grouped to allow easy conversation and provide views of the attractive grounds, river, and nearby Mount Tom.

For those who are craving a little exercise, there is a clay tennis court and a swimming pool located on the property. Others prefer more leisurely activities and opt to take a walk with Bowser into town. This takes all of two minutes, although visitors can usually spend an hour or two perusing the numerous shops. Horseback riding is available through the Green Mountain Horse Association in South Woodstock. People who want to include Bowser on a hike will find plenty of trails to explore on Mount Tom, through Billings Park, and along the Appalachian and Long Trails. Anyone searching for additional swimming or boating options can make a short trip to Silver Lake in Barnard. Although Woodstock is the site of the first ski tow, better downhill skiing is found at nearby Suicide Six. The cross-country skiing is terrific as well, although Bowser will not be able to participate if guests are heading to the local cross-country ski center located just down the road.

Kedron Valley Inn

Route 106
South Woodstock, Vermont 05071
(802) 457-1473, Fax (802) 457-4469

Innkeepers: Max and Merrily Comins
Rooms: 25 doubles, 2 suites
Rates: Doubles and suites $114-189 (B&B), $154-229 (MAP)
Payment: AE, DSC, MC, and VISA
Children: Welcome (cribs, cots, highchairs, and babysitters are available)
Dogs: Welcome, but they must be quiet in the guest rooms, leashed on the property, and cannot be on the beach.
Open: All year, except for the month of April

The Kedron Valley Inn has long been, and remains, one of our favorite inns in New England. Perhaps this is because its many charming facets continue to mellow with age, including the beautifully decorated rooms, excellent food, and yes, even the innkeepers. Ten years ago, Max and Merrily Comins knew they wanted to run a country inn, but could not imagine exactly how it would all fall together. Both of them had successful business careers in New York City, which gave them the financial means they needed to buy an inn. After finding and purchasing the 165-year-old Kedron Valley Inn, they refocused their energy toward its complete restoration.

The original Federal-style brick inn is truly the essence of what we imagine a country inn to be. It is nestled into the bend of a country road, with a huge veranda marking the entrance to the front door. As guests step into the high-ceilinged foyer, they could be drawn in a number of directions. If it is a cold winter's evening, the fire in the sitting room hearth usually beckons, as does the handcrafted oak bar. From here, people can peek into the pretty peach and cream colored dining room, where candlelight illuminates the intimate tables and quilts hanging against the walls. The quilts, as it turns out, are an intrinsic part of the Kedron Valley Inn. They fact that they are in every common room and guest room is interesting, but even more remarkable is that they all come from Merrily's private collection. She found many of them years ago in her family's attic, and learned the quilts had been crafted by Merrily's grandmother, great-grandmother, aunts, and cousins. One of the more noteworthy quilts can be found in the sitting room, a 1950s friendship album quilt which was made for Merrily's grandmother, Olive West. Just across from this quilt is another intriguing Greek cross quilt, which is comprised of 57 different fabrics arranged in over 100 patterns. A 100-year-old postage stamp quilt has 3,206 squares of fabric in it. Guests who want the history of the quilt in their bedroom, need only ask, as they each seem to have a unique story associated with them.

Just as each quilt is unique, so is each bedroom. When the Comins first bought the inn, they also inherited the furniture that was there. Many of the antiques that guests see today were "in disguise," when they bought the inn. Some beautiful pine pieces had actually been painted black, but once stripped, the original beauty of the wood and fine craftsmanship became apparent. These pieces, and others, have been surrounded with elegant floral wallpapers, chintz fabrics, and complementing color schemes. With the exception of the lodge rooms, most of the guest rooms in the tavern and inn have either woodstoves or fireplaces. The antique four-poster, canopy, or oak beds are set on braided or hooked rugs covering the wide-board floors. A few of the private baths have old-fashioned, claw-foot tubs, while the remainder offer more modern shower/bath combinations. Gilchrist and Soames shampoos are complemented by the Sappo Hill soaps (personally tested by the innkeepers and judged to be the best).

All guests are treated to a full country breakfast during their stay. This is served in the intimate dining room, where nooks and crannies afford each table an additional sense of privacy. Freshly baked breads and muffins are prepared each morning, and often arrive at the table still warm from the oven. Other breakfast choices include Cajun-style eggs, cheddar or Swiss cheese omelettes, French toast, and blueberry pancakes.

After a day's adventure, guests should find plenty of room for the innovative dinners served at the Kedron Valley Inn. The cuisine could be called "Nouvelle Vermont," because of the emphasis on local Vermont products which are used in most of the dishes. Depending upon the time of year, the light and cool gazpacho or heartier roasted butternut and acorn squash bisque might be found on the menu. Guests can also dine on a wild mushroom gratin in a toasted brioche, a baked camembert en croûte, or the fresh pheasant and venison sausage served over French lentils and roasted garlic. This may be supplemented by salmon stuffed with an herbed seafood mousse and wrapped in a puff pasty; rack of lamb with a Pommary and maple glaze, or the sole poached in champagne and lemon with julienne leeks. The venison chop is stuffed with the inn's fruit chutney and served on a creamy chévre sauce and the chicken is rolled in pistachio nuts and served with a lemon butter.

Aside from the beautiful rooms and an excellent restaurant, there are also plenty of activities available at the inn. Guests are welcome to go horseback riding and on surrey rides, as well as swim in a large spring-fed pond. The latter is fondly known as the *Kedron Valley Beach Club*. Although Bowser is not allowed on the beach, there are plenty of walks to take on the inn's 15 acres. The Comins' golden retriever Blondie, is getting older, but might be convinced to come along on the walk. During our visit, a yellow lab accompanied us everywhere. The Comins have also come up with an extensive list of hikes that can be enjoyed in the area. Luce's Lookout offers spectacular views, as does Mount Tom. Mount Peg is a "peaceful woodland hiking trail" and Ascutney Mountain offers a forest setting and some small waterfalls. In the wintertime, there are sleigh rides and a number of great spots for cross-country skiing (dogs are not allowed at the cross-country ski center, but there are plenty of other spots in the nearby woods to choose from). While Bowser rests, perhaps his companions might want to drive to Woodstock and visit its many shops, galleries, and antique stores that line the two main streets of town.

New Hampshire

Haus Trillium Bed & Breakfast

RR 1, Box 106
Sanborn Road
Ashland, New Hampshire 03217
(603) 968-2180

Hosts: *Susy and Roy Johnk*
Rooms: *3 doubles*
Rates: *$50-65 (B&B)*
Payment: *Personal checks*
Children: *Welcome (cots are available)*
Dogs: *Welcome with advance notice and prior approval*
Open: *All year*

Trillium is a native wildflower that grows in the woodlands of New England, with three delicate white petals and three green sepals. In many ways, the Haus Trillium is reflective of its namesake. Simple, yet beautiful in its simplicity, this bed and breakfast is a special place, set in the hills of New Hampshire's Lake Region.

We visited the Haus Trillium one fall day, and even though the brilliant colors were scattered across the ground, there was still a great deal of inherent natural beauty to be found on the twelve acres. Even without the foliage, the enormous trees kept the 100-year-old farmhouse and barn partially hidden from the quiet country lane. A long drive leads up the hill to the house, an antique structure with several additions created over through the years. Roy had been in the barn, but noticed our arrival and quickly came out to greet us. It became clear during the course of our visit, that he has a real love for puttering in his barn, just as Susy has a penchant for working with clay.

In order to understand a bit about the B&B, it is important to know a little something about the Johnks. Susy is a native of Germany, and Roy is an American. They met in Germany many years ago, and after marrying there, spent the next 15 years living in Susy's homeland. When they moved to the United States, they brought with them a number of family antiques and their, now shared, European background. Two of the most impressive pieces of furniture that made the trip are in the dining room, an enormous and ornately carved dark oak table and leather chairs. Equally noteworthy is the sideboard, which stands eight feet long and seven feet high. This is also a heavy, intricately carved piece, whose effect is lightened slightly by the small, glass doors across the top. These open to reveal a collection of pottery. Adjacent to the dining room is the small breakfast room, which contains a grandfather clock that is of the same period and style as the other two pieces. There are numerous other small European treasures and collectibles placed about the house. We found a few of these in the living room, an inviting space that runs the width of the building. Its walls of windows not only let in a lot of indirect light, but also provide scenic views of the orchards and meadows below. In the afternoon, a fire often warms this room where guests can be found enjoying sherry or tea and some sort of baked goodie.

Just off the living room is the first floor bedroom. This offers a private bath, is bright with color, and is attractively furnished with an assortment of pieces. Our favorite bedrooms are upstairs at the other end of the house. These private spaces are quite romantic, primarily due to their simplicity. The corner room offers a queen bed covered in a white spread and adorned with a huge, puffy European down comforter. A table and two chairs are set invitingly off to one side, while a brick fireplace provides as much warmth as it does atmosphere. Even on a cloudy day, there is an abundance of natural light permeating this chamber. The room next door is equally pleasing. Although it does not have a fireplace, the low ceiling makes it quite cozy. The room's large window overlooks the hillside that slopes along the back of the property. The bed is covered with a pale floral quilt and yet another thick, down comforter. A bureau is set against the white walls, completing the effect. There is an elegance and style in the simplicity of these spaces, giving guests the impression they are staying in a European pensione.

After an restful night's sleep, a full breakfast is awaiting in the morning. Aside from fresh coffee and juices, there are usually options that range from fluffy pancakes and French toast to quiche and a German apple cake. These are accompanied by pastries and muffins that are also homemade. After breakfast, or at some point during their stay, guests are welcome to visit Susy's potting studio in the basement of the house. This is another bright space, with a wall of sliding glass doors that open to the flower gardens and meadows. Susy creates many beautiful things here, and during our visit she was hard at work on angels that she would be selling during the holiday season. Usually their 16-year-old Bichon Frisé, Dolly, is at her side while she works.

We found Susy and Roy's genuine warmth to be a big part of the draw to the Haus Trillium; another is its peaceful country setting. Although it is only a short drive to Ashland, guests have no sense of the town, only of the quiet. Bowser will certainly enjoy walks along the country road that runs in front of the B&B. There is also a hiking trail on the property that is located on the hill behind the house. Further afield are Little Squam Lake, Winona Lake, and Lake Wakewan. Bowser is usually not allowed on the public beaches (in season), but can always explore the shoreline. Waterville Valley and Loon Mountain also provide great hiking opportunities in the summer, and obviously are also quite popular with skiers in the winter months. The Johnks are familiar with a variety of other places in the area that are fun to explore with a dog, just ask, and they will be happy to offer their suggestions.

Watch Hill Bed & Breakfast

P.O. Box 1605
On the Old Meredith Road
Center Harbor, New Hampshire 03226

Innkeeper: Barbara Lauterbach
Rooms: 4 doubles
Rates: $65 (B&B)
Payment: Personal checks
Children: Welcome (over the age of 10 are preferred)
Dogs: Welcome with advance notice
Open: All year

Anyone who wants some insight into the Watch Hill B&B and its owner, need only ask about how the B&B got its name and the rest becomes clear. Barbara moved to this area a few years ago; however, in her previous life she raised champion Bullmastiffs at her Watch Hill Kennel in Cincinnati, Ohio. Although she no longer owns any dogs, it is quite obvious that she still has a love for the breed. There is a striking charcoal drawing in the B&B's brochure of her two original dogs, which is merely a precursor to the rest of the memorabilia and pictures found around her intimate B&B.

We were intrigued with the Watch Hill B&B from the moment we saw it. The blue/gray farmhouse, with its hunter green trim, sits tucked into a hill overlooking Centre Harbor and beyond to Lake Winnipesaukee. This is actually one of the oldest homes in town, built in 1772 by Joseph Senter. Joseph was the brother of the town's founder, Moses Senter. Its current owner, Barbara Lauterbach, also has an interesting background. Barbara, aside from raising Bullmastiffs, has also had years of culinary training at some of the most prestigious schools in the world. She attended the Cordon Bleu in England and Giuliano Bugialli's in Italy, and worked with famed chefs, Julia Child and Jacques Pepin. While she can create just about any type of delicious meal, and often does, her specialty is baking. As a representative for King Arthur Flour, she conducts cooking classes at the New England Culinary Institute in Vermont, but guests of Watch Hill need only spend a night or two here to sample some of her many gourmet foods.

The day we arrived was rather cold and gray; however, once we stepped in off the porch, we were overwhelmed by the cozy atmosphere of the house. We could hear the antique grandfather clock ticking as we explored the two rooms off the tiny foyer. On one side is the living room, decorated in rich browns and filled with a combination of American and European antiques intermixed with some contemporary pieces. To the right is our favorite chamber, the dining room. The walls in here are adorned with hunt prints, and a well-stoked woodstove provides more than enough warmth for diners. The front staircase, lined with a handsome paisley paper, leads to the four bedrooms on the second floor. One cannot help but notice the two framed prints of Barbara's Bullmastiffs. If asked, she will gladly reminisce about her days of raising and training show dogs, but she will just as quickly explain that those days are over. She now owns two cats and a parrot who provide more than enough company. The bedrooms are individually decorated, yet uncluttered. There is a simple country feeling to the rooms, which is accentuated by the eaves of the old farmhouse. Guests share the one bathroom.

Just behind the dining room is a wonderful kitchen, loaded with all sorts of cooking paraphernalia, accoutrements, and gadgets. This equally inviting space is not necessarily open to the guests; however, its comfortable atmosphere would lend itself to long talks over coffee and baked goodies. The kitchen is also worth noting because it is here that breakfast is created. The morning meal is well worth getting up and out of bed for. Barbara often serves a frittata or perhaps pancakes made with farm fresh eggs. She tries to emphasize the use of local products, so her waffles are covered with real maple syrup from New Hampshire, and sausage or bacon is often of the hearty country variety. Of course, there are always fresh breads, both sweet and otherwise, which are instantly gobbled up by the guests.

While there are not many state parks in the region, there are a number of lakes. Of course Lake Winnipesaukee offers various places for renting a boat and exploring the lake with Bowser. Squam Lake is also just a short drive to the north. Many visitors enjoy the trip to Castle in the Cloud, a mountaintop mansion resting on over 5,200 acres. The hiking trails through this area are also very popular, although in the wintertime the cross-country skiers are in evidence as well. Guests are often content to walk up the hill by the inn, which is relatively untraveled and is a good place to stretch one's legs. There are a variety of local trails that Barbara would be happy to recommend to guests and their canine cohorts as well.

Kona Mansion Inn

P.O. Box 458
Jacobs Road
Center Harbor, New Hampshire 03226
(603) 253-4900

Innkeepers: *The Crowley Family*
Rooms: *1 single, 9 doubles, 6 cottages*
Rates: *Single $65 (EP), Doubles $65-140 (EP), Cottages $425-695 (EP) per week*
Payment: *AE, MC, and VISA*
Children: *Welcome (highchairs, cribs, and cots are available)*
Dogs: *Welcome in the cottages and the one inn room with an outside entrance*
Open: *May 15 through October 15*

The Kona Mansion Inn is truly reminiscent of another era, having managed successfully to preserve its connection with the past. But to appreciate the inn's charms, it is important to understand its history. The original Kona Mansion was built by multi-millionaire Herbert Dumaresq, who made his fortune rising through the ranks of the Jordan Marsh Company. Upon retiring in the 1890s, he purchased 2,000 acres of lake-front property on Lake Winnipesaukee and built an opulent mansion. This never was, nor has it ever been, a typical lake house. It is a mock Tudor creation, built of native fieldstone and topped with red tiled roofs. The effect is something akin to a German country estate, and is certainly a startling exception to the understated lake houses that line Lake Winnipesaukee's shores. After building and living in the mansion, Mr. Dumaresq was forced to sell it during the Great Depression. Since that time, the mansion and the property have barely managed to survive the many years of neglect under bank ownership. It was not until the Crowleys purchased it in 1971 that it began to experience a bit of a renaissance.

Today, as visitors leave the main road that wends around Lake Winnipesaukee, they will travel along back roads for a few miles before emerging at the entrance to the Kona Mansion. The green fairways of the par-three golf course are the first sight guests have of the property; however, that is merely a prelude to the dramatic impression the mansion itself makes on first time guests. While the outside might look cavernous, a few steps inside and guests have the distinct feeling of having arrived in a European hostel.

The thick fieldstone walls and low ceilings help to create this sense of intimacy. The first floor has a few public rooms, most of which are dedicated to dining. Choosing our favorite spot here is not easy because each room is so very distinctive — topping our list is one very small room with a fieldstone fireplace and another expansive glassed-in veranda that is privy to lake views. The food here is of the solid New England variety, focusing on roast beef, veal, and chicken, accompanied by fresh vegetables, homemade breads, and desserts. Some menu items of note include the Maine lobster, clam chowder, and native steamed clams. Before sitting down to dinner, many enjoy relaxing in the sitting room with its huge, rounded window seat cushioned with burgundy and green velvet cushions.

Anyone traveling with a canine cohort is welcome to stay in either the one room at the inn with a private outside entrance, or in the unpretentious cottages located down by the lake. The former is room nine and was created from part of the original fieldstone veranda. It boasts a king-size bed, a private bathroom, a television, air-conditioning, and nice views of the golf course from the room's sitting area. The cottages, on the other hand, are easy to spot, as they are painted a mustard color with brown trim. The four long, low buildings are almost identical. They are somewhat hidden behind a row of pine trees, which inhibit any chance for a clear water view. If they sound like simple accommodations, they are; however, they are also affordable, clean, and offer their own unique charm. Cottage One, for instance, is the tiniest with a double-bedded room and private bathroom, along with a kitchenette and small eating area. The other three cottages have two bedrooms each, private bathrooms, a kitchenette, and a separate living area. Televisions are the most modern of the amenities. The otherwise natural board walls, the narrow pine floors, and the cotton calico curtains framing the windows further accentuate the simple cottage motif.

This is an ideal place for those who literally want to relax and do nothing other than enjoy the charms of a lake-side vacation. Lake Winnipesaukee is literally a 30-second walk across a dirt lane to the inn's beach. A turn-of-the-century fieldstone boathouse also rests off to the side. When we visited the resort, it was a rather quiet time of year and the only things that could be coaxed into the sparkling lake waters were a few dozen ducks and Bowser. We could only imagine what it would be like during the warm summer months when people could sit back on the sandy beach, splash around in the warm water, and perhaps navigate their boats or sailboards across the lake. We recommend that in order for guests to truly enjoy their stay here, that they rent or bring a boat or canoe. This gives them access to all the coves lining Lake Winnipesaukee, New Hampshire's largest lake.

The Kona Mansion is an all-inclusive resort, with tennis courts, a par-3, nine-hole golf course, and assorted lawn games. Bowser will undoubtedly enjoy the open spaces here, as the inn lies on over 125 acres. The Kona Wildlife Preserve is also adjacent to the property and boasts 15 miles of hiking trails. Regardless of whether guests and their canine cohorts decide to stay on the premises or explore the picturesque countryside, the Kona Mansion offers them a chance to enjoy simple lake-side accommodations amid a truly unique estate setting.

The Corner House Inn

Box 204, Routes 133 and 109
Center Sandwich, New Hampshire   03227
(603) 284-6219

Innkeepers: *Jane and Don Brown*
Rooms: *3 doubles*
Rates: *$80 (B&B)*
Payment: *AE, MC, and VISA*
Children: *Well-behaved children are welcome (highchairs are available)*
Dogs: *Accepted with prior approval*
Open: *All year except for a few weeks in April and November*

The Corner House Inn lies, appropriately enough, on a corner of two rural routes that intersect the picturesque village of Center Sandwich. The town has long been a magnet for anyone in search of antiques or unusual handcrafted items. Interestingly, this tiny village has one of the largest populations of artists in the entire state, with their wares displayed in the many craft shops, antique stores, and art galleries nearby. The intimate inn is the centerpiece for the village, and is known for serving excellent meals in an historic setting. The Corner House was built by David Hodgdon in 1849, and more importantly, has been in continuous operation for almost 150 years.

Bordered by an antique shop and a museum, the white clapboard inn is easily recognizable with its festive overflowing planters and original stone hitching posts that frame the brick courtyard. The black iron benches are just the place to sit in the summer months while waiting for a table at the popular restaurant. In the cooler months, the parlor is equally as enticing, with its brick fireplace warming all corners of this intimate room. Here, an overstuffed blue and white checked sofa and fanciful armchair with animals cavorting across its back, create a welcoming environment. A small wooden game table is tucked into a sunny alcove, beckoning even those who don't normally think of themselves as games people. In keeping with the area's tradition for handmade crafts, there are an assortment of items scattered about the room that guests may purchase. Thick and colorful locally made trapper's blankets filled one hutch; while a basket of buttermilk soaps wrapped in cloth was placed on a nearby table. Above the doors, visitors will notice decorative hand-painted boards of classic New England scenes, paintings that are reminiscent of those by Norman Rockwell.

Just off the parlor are four separate dining rooms, with high ceilings, wainscotings, and random width hardwood floors. Depending upon the time of day, the mood can be quite different. During the breakfast and lunch hours, the rooms are bright with sunlight streaming in through the many windows. In the evening, the atmosphere is more subdued with tablecloths and candlelight softening the rooms. The one constant in the restaurant is the food, which is always exceptional. Overnight guests are treated to a hearty, full breakfast each morning. This repast could include everything from overstuffed omelets and Eggs Benedict to strawberry pancakes with locally made maple syrup. Lunch and dinner are open to the public, and we recommend that anyone traveling during the busy season make a reservation as the restaurant is usually packed. The appetizer offerings are so good, it is easy to make a lunch or light dinner out of them. Maine crab cakes and the traditional Corner House crepes are difficult to resist; however, the "famous" lobster and mushroom bisque is truly a standout and surely deserves every accolade it has ever received. Entrées are also quite inspired, with the pesto chicken, brandied peach duckling, and shellfish fettuccini (lobster, shrimp, crab, and sea scallops sautéed in a sherry sauce) being just a few of the more noteworthy. The Browns are also justifiably proud of their "award-winning" Oscars, which are variations on the traditional fare. They start with chicken and veal, or a combination of both, and surround them with lobster, broccoli and a bernaise sauce. The Browns' sense of humor somehow makes its way into the menu. For instance, they don't just describe the roast prime rib of beef, they give it personality by describing the two choices of cuts as the "save room for dessert" cut or the "I don't eat dessert anyway" cut.

After a filling meal, those lucky enough to have overnight reservations can head upstairs to bed. A narrow staircase, just off one of the dining rooms, leads to

Victorian inspired guest rooms with their traditional delicate patterned wallpapers. Brass or antique beds are adorned with white Bates spreads or handmade quilts. Peering out from the overstuffed pillows is a little handmade teddy bear. Queen Anne mirrors nicely complement the white wicker and country antiques that fill the rooms. The many potted plants thrive in the sunlight filtering past the white lace curtains.

After a restful sleep, most guests are anxious to explore this rural part of New Hampshire. Even though Center Sandwich was once listed as the sixth largest town in the state (in the mid-1800s), today it could certainly qualify as one of the smaller towns in New Hampshire. The rural surroundings make it a great base for exploring the mountains and rivers that comprise much of this region. Bowser will certainly enjoy the short walk around town. Within minutes of the inn is a series of tiny ponds, which include Dinsmore Pond, Red Hill Pond and Bearcamp Pond. All of these are connected by rivers which provide great trout fishing opportunities. Drive a few minutes to Barville Pond which is connected by a stream to Squam Lake. Launch a canoe here and paddle into the northern section of Squam where a labyrinth of coves await to be explored. The Squam Mountains are just to the north of the inn and provide hiking trails of varying degrees of difficulty. In the winter months, the emphasis turns to downhill and cross-country skiing. The seasons are almost incidental here, as people look for excuses any time of year to dine and stay overnight at The Corner House Inn.

Chesterfield Inn

P.O. Box 155
Route 9
Chesterfield, New Hampshire 03443
(800) 365-5515, (603) 256-3211, Fax (603) 256-6131

Innkeepers: *Judy and Phil Hueber*
Rooms: *11 doubles, 2 suites*
Rates: *Doubles $113-160 (B&B), $190-230 (MAP),*
Suites $153-168 (B&B), $245 (MAP)
Payment: *AE, DSC, DC, MC, and VISA*
Children: *Welcome, under six years of age are free and over six years are*
$15 per night (highchairs, cribs, cots, and babysitters are available)
Dogs: *Welcome, with advance notice and approval of the innkeepers*
Open: *All year except Christmas Eve and Christmas Day*

We are always excited when we discover a particularly outstanding inn — one which mixes beautiful rooms, excellent food, and great architecture. The combination is surprisingly difficult to achieve, but Judy and Phil Hueber have succeeded on all levels. They bought the Chesterfield Inn in 1987, two years after it had undergone an extensive renovation that transformed it from a group of ramshackle farm buildings into an architectural showpiece. Although the Huebers were not responsible for these initial changes, it can be safely said that today the inn is truly their creation.

The original farmhouse, once the centerpiece for the property, is now a minor portion of the inn, but has been connected to the original barn with breezeways and gables. A full two-stories of windows on the front of the building overlook the stone terraces, perennial gardens, and pond. Planters overflow with flowers in the summer, shaded by some enormous trees which also shield the property from the main road. Stepping into the inn, most new arrivals are overwhelmed by the vaulted ceilings. Just beyond the reception area, there is a new formal living room, as well as the dining rooms that have also been recently expanded. The walls of windows in the living room cast natural light over the sofas and attractive reproduction Chippendale and Queen-Anne wing chairs and tables. Deep rose and hunter green color schemes predominate.

There are many qualities which define the Chesterfield Inn and set it apart from other country inns. One of them is the chef, Carl Warner, who has consistently impressed the critics and, more importantly, his patrons, with his innovative menus. The restaurant started as a small room that diners could reach by way of the kitchen. With the recent renovation, those days are gone, although the kitchen is still open and guests can watch Carl create some of his tantalizing dishes. During our recent visit, the autumn menu was in place. First course selections included the blue corn crab cakes with a remoulade sauce, a thinly sliced breast of duck with a mango salsa, and the butternut squash ravioli with Parmesan cheese. The entrées were equally varied. The braised venison with a cranberry apricot chutney, pan fried red snapper with a warm tomato relish, and the cassoulet made with duck, sausage, garlic, and white beans were equally intriguing. Anyone who partakes in a meal here soon understands that it is the simplicity of ingredients and presentation of the dishes that makes them so exquisite.

After a wonderful evening, overnight guests will return to their beautifully furnished and appointed rooms. These are located in the various wings and outbuildings. Open the door to Room 14 and guests will enter a corner chamber predominated by a king-size bed covered with a blue and white star quilt. Off to the side is a secretary containing a book of information on the inn and the surrounding area. A round table is the centerpiece for the small sitting area, while a television is placed unobtrusively off to the side. Another bedroom offers a wall of enormous paned windows overlooking the fieldstone terrace. This room's two double beds are covered with colorful hand-tied quilts. One of the suites is comprised of two enormous rooms, including a comfortable living room and an adjacent bedroom with a king-size bed. Many of the guest rooms have exposed darkened rough-hewn board walls that were taken from the 200-year-old barn, while others gain their antique feeling from the beamed and vaulted ceilings. Each bedroom has been individually decorated, with an emphasis on Waverly floral fabrics covering the walls and often stitched into bedspreads. Garlands of flowers are stenciled on some of the white walls, while others are painted in coordinated pastel color schemes. Each bedroom has a distinct personality, along with a strong sense of country elegance. Although the inn does have an antique ambiance to it, the bathrooms are all modern and are appointed with baskets of Gilchrist & Soames toiletries and thick coordinated towels. There are nine bedrooms in the main building, and three more in the small outbuildings. These are equally sophisticated accommodations, but offer the benefits of private garden patios. They are also nestled into the hillside and framed by small stands of aspen and dogwood trees. The rolling hill behind the inn is covered with grass, and is an ideal spot for guests to walk with Bowser.

In addition to inn's property, there are also the fields just across the quiet road that are ideal for walks with a dog. There is also a small residential area, with little traffic, where walkers could head for a short outing. A hop in the car will bring travelers to Pisgah State Park, a 13,500-acre park with hiking trails for all levels. This is also a terrific place in the winter months, as cross-country skiers can create their own trails through the pristine forests. Just north of the inn, guests will discover the Chesterfield Gorge Natural Area, where footpaths have been cut along the gorge to allow visitors access to this dramatic reserve. Finally, Spofford Lake is just a short drive from the inn and provides visitors with access to both the water and an adjacent golf course.

Bowser will feel right at home here when he discovers that he is not the most unique guest who has stayed with the Huebers. They have had all sorts of pet guests over the years, including a cat, hen, and rooster who accompanied an author who was on tour.

Rockhouse Mountain Farm

P.O. Box 60
Eaton Center, New Hampshire 03832
(603) 447-2880

Innkeepers: *The Edge Family*
Rooms: *15 doubles, 3 bunk rooms*
Rates: *Doubles and bunk rooms $50-58, Children 1-5 years old $26, 6-11 years old*
$32, 12 years of age and older $38, All rates are per person, per day (MAP)
Payment: *Personal checks*
Children: *Welcome*
Dogs: *Accepted with advance notice and prior approval. The Edges are cautious about*
which dogs they permit because they have a wide assortment of "feathered
friends" and farm animals living on the property.
Open: *June 15 through October 31*

The Rockhouse Mountain Farm rests on a home site that is over a century old and has been in operation as an inn since 1946. Two generations of the Edge family have dedicated themselves to quality innkeeping and have, as a result, created a relaxed environment that generations of families return to year after year. Tucked into the side of Rockhouse Mountain, the traditional New England farmhouse is surrounded by 450 acres of fields and woods. Guests in this remote part of New Hampshire will discover wildlife thriving in an unspoiled and picturesque setting. The farm, on the other hand, has a more domesticated form of wildlife in the form of horses, cows, pigs, chickens, peacocks, Moscovey ducks, and pheasants.

The Edges' secret to success lies in their focus on simplicity rather than providing an array of modern amenities and elaborate furnishings. They feel this type of atmosphere best fits with the lifestyle here, slow-paced yet with an abundance of informal activities to keep guests occupied. The vast acreage, water-oriented options on nearby Crystal Lake, and farm chores provide plenty of diversions for guests of all ages. Children will not only enjoy the sailing, fishing, and informal canoe trips down the Saco River, but also the hay rides and cookouts at Crystal Lake. Back at the farm, there is a pond where children are welcome to feed the fish, or they may go over to the barn to visit the animals. If the weather turns inclement, there is even a small recreation room for the kids. Parents are welcome to take part in their children's activities or spend time doing their own thing, whether it be horseback riding, tennis, or even golf. Some of the special activities that many returning guests look forward to are the Saturday night steak roast on the back lawn, the chicken barbecue at the old maple sugar house, and the Swift River cookout and swim. Bowser, who must be leashed on the property, will certainly enjoy the long walks on the old logging road which leads to an ancient Indian cave. In addition to Crystal Lake, there are also a number of small ponds in the area that are terrific on a hot summer's day. Hiking trails are abundant throughout the region, although there are no designated state parks close to the farm. Those who want to venture into the White Mountain National Forest will find it a short drive from the farm. Here, hikers can climb Mount Chocorua and Mount Paugus or visit the Rocky Gorge Scenic Area. Along the Kancamagus Highway, travelers can stop to see the Lower Falls, or further up the road there is a trail head to Sabbaday Falls.

After a full day, the clean and comfortably furnished guest rooms are indeed an inviting place to relax upon one's return. Older children often opt to sleep together in one of the bunk rooms (girls and boys), giving their parents a bit more privacy in the cottages. The simple furnishings, plain spreads on the beds, and old-fashioned bathrooms are reminiscent of another era. After settling down for the night, the only sounds guests are likely to hear are the owls calling to each other and the breezes rustling the branches of the trees.

A full country breakfast is served each morning in the farmhouse. In keeping with the restful nature of the place, this repast is a very casual affair, with guests coming and going as they please. However, the aroma of fresh blueberry pancakes has been known to draw even "non-breakfast eaters" out of a deep sleep. The dinners are a bit more formal, with generous quantities of homemade meat and chicken dishes, breads, fresh garden vegetables, and pies rounding out the menu. The honey is fresh from the farm's beehives, and the raspberries and asparagus come from the gardens. Adults and children eat in separate dining rooms, allowing each to dine at his or her own pace. Afterwards, many choose to settle in before a fire or inspect the collection of antiques, many of which were brought over from Wales by the Edge family. The Edges also have a fine collection of paintings — some of which are registered with the Tate Gallery in London.

We have been writing about the Rockhouse Mountain Farm for years, and know that anyone who is allowed to bring their dog with them is fortunate. We especially like to include the farm in our book because the Edges are very hospitable and friendly and they create a terrific environment for a relaxing vacation.

The Inn of Exeter

90 Front Street
Exeter, New Hampshire   03833-0508
(800) 782-8444, (603) 772-5901

Innkeeper: John H. Hodgins
Rooms: 48 doubles, 1 suite
Rates: Doubles $80-90 (EP), Suite $150-170 (EP)
Payment: AE, CD, DC, DSC, ENR, MC, and VISA
Children: Welcome (cribs, cots, and highchairs are available)
Dogs: Welcome; but cannot be left alone in the room if the dog is a "barker"
Open: All year

The Inn of Exeter was made possible by a generous gift from Mrs. William Boyce Thompson and her daughter, who gave the inn to Phillips Exeter Academy to accommodate visiting families and "young ladies who came to visit Academy students." The brick, Georgian-style inn was built in 1932. Architecturally, the inn has remained much the same; however, over the years it has been tastefully updated to include some more modern amenities.

A few of the original rock hitching posts still flank the walk leading to the front door. There is a sense of elegance about the inn that visitors immediately feel upon entering the foyer. The public rooms are quite sumptuous and filled with period and reproduction antiques. The centerpiece in one common room is a three-pedestal table surrounded by eight Chippendale-style chairs. This is accented by an antique secretary, sidetables topped with brass lamps, and leather chairs placed near two marble fireplaces.

The guest rooms vary in size and decor, but all are filled with reproductions and antique furnishings which include maple and four-poster beds covered in Bates spreads. In some rooms, old-fashioned writing desks contain the authentic inkwells. The colors in the striped or floral wallpapers and sheer draperies are fairly neutral, as is the complementing trim. Each chamber has modern conveniences such as individual climate controls, color televisions, telephones, and tiled bathrooms. A fruit basket is also placed in each of the bedrooms. Guests will be pleased with the wide variety of room configurations, as well as the fact that some of these chambers adjoin. Since our last visit, a few of the larger chambers have been divided to accommodate additional guests.

Exeter has a variety of eating establishments, catering to all types of tastes; however, guests should also consider The Inn at Exeter for at least one of their evening meals. The ambiance in the dining room is matched only by the fine cuisine. Appetizers include smoked salmon with a cucumber tartine, scallops and shrimp alfredo, and a baked brie and spinach surrounded by filo. Veal sautéed with morels, key lime juice, and cream; venison roasted with Port wine and wild mushrooms; and scallops, shrimp, and lobster sautéed with garlic and served over fettucine are just three of the many excellent entrée choices. The inn also has a fine wine list for their patrons' perusal.

The courteous service, elegant decor, and comfortable guest rooms are just a few reasons travelers may want to think about staying at The Inn of Exeter. Bowser will certainly enjoy strolling over to the grounds of Phillips Exeter Academy. After walking the property, Bowser may want to rest while his two-legged friends take advantage of their sports' facilities. Squash and tennis, as well as swimming are just a few of the options avavailable to guests of the inn. Although the inn is located inland, a short drive will bring people to the scenic seaport towns of Portsmouth and Newburyport. Those in the mood to hike with Bowser can drive an even shorter distance to either the Bear Brook or Pawtuckaway State Parks, where they will find plenty of hiking trails. The town still maintains a quiet New England charm that can be thoroughly enjoyed by walking through the lovely residential neighborhoods filled with stately historic homes.

The Inn at Crotched Mountain

marilyn S. Pratt '74

Mountain Road
Francestown, New Hampshire 03043
(603) 588-6840

Innkeepers: John and Rose Perry
Rooms: 13 doubles
Rates: 60-70 (B&B), $120-140 (MAP)
Payment: Personal checks
Children: Welcome (cots, highchairs, and babysitters are available)
Dogs: Welcome with a $5 nightly fee. Dogs are not to be left alone in the room unless
they are crated.
Open: All year except April and October

The Inn at Crotched Mountain is in an ideal location, set on the north side of Crotched Mountain and privy to beautiful views of the Piscataquog Valley. Originally built in 1822, the farmhouse had a secret tunnel connecting its cellar and the Boston Post Road. Slaves were hidden here during their journey north along the Underground Railroad. In the 1920s, the farm entered a new era, gaining fame for its prize-winning sheep, championship horses, and Angora goats. After a devastating fire in the mid-1930s, the farm was completely rebuilt. For a short time it was used as a part of the Crotched Mountain ski resort, then it was sold to the Perrys in the mid-1970s.

Today, the ivy-covered brick inn maintains its tradition of offering travelers a comfortable place to stay coupled with exceptional hospitality. As visitors meander through the house, they will find a number of inviting common rooms. The living room is one of our favorite spots, a cheery place with twin fireplaces, period furnishings, and bold floral prints covering the sofas and matching side chairs. An antique sewing machine table has been converted into a side table and a harvest table usually holds, among other things, a vase of fresh flowers. Oriental rugs cover the gray painted hardwood floors. Those who want a little more privacy will enjoy the intimate sitting room. The beamed cathedral ceilings overlook the Perrys' interesting collection of antique carpentry tools, along with a deer's head that has been mounted on the wall.

The guest rooms at the inn are simply appointed with country furnishings. They are not long on frills, but do provide clean and comfortable surroundings that are certain to please most vacationers. Many of the chambers offer private entrances, allowing easy access for dogs, and all seem to have terrific views of the mountains. If a private bathroom is important, then we recommend guests request one when making a reservation as some of the rooms have shared baths. Of course, the luxury of a fireplace makes a few of the guest chambers highly desirable.

The informal dining room is enhanced by a brick fireplace that is always well-stoked in cold weather. Rose and John, whose backgrounds are in hotel and restaurant management, are quite adept at creating delicious meals. While weekday guests are on the B&B plan, weekend visitors have both breakfast and dinner included in their room rate. Breakfasts can range from hearty to a more Continental variety. Skiers usually like to bulk up for the day and often opt for the eggs or French toast topped with pure maple syrup, which are accompanied by homefries and either bacon or sausage.

For dinner, there are a number of courses and options. The tantalizing appetizers might include smoked mussels or the lemon-pepper chicken wings. Entrées range from the roast loin of pork and maple orange-soy pork chops, to the filet mignon with a bernaise sauce. The menu has not changed much since our last visit, which leads us to believe that guests are quite content with the varied fare. In the summer months, Rose likes to use the herbs and vegetables from her garden to add a little extra freshness and zest to each entrée.

Even though the winter months provide good downhill and cross-country skiing possibilities, summer is an equally appealing time to visit, and one that is much quieter. The inn has two clay tennis courts and a 60-foot swimming pool on the premises. There is plenty of property around the inn to explore, as well as quiet country roads. Cross-country ski trails begin from the inn, and guests can also snowshoe across miles of pristine back country or ice skate on one of the many ponds.

Excellent hiking can be found on Crotched Mountain, and great fishing in the nearby rivers or on Powder Mill Pond. Neighboring Greenfield State Park is unfortunately off limits to Bowser; however, a bit further south the Miller State Park does allow leashed canine friends.

Lovett's Inn
by Lafayette Brook

Route 18
Franconia, New Hampshire   03580
(800) 356-3802, (603) 823-7761

Innkeepers: JoAnna and Lee Wogulis
Rooms: 30 doubles, 7 cottages
Rates: Doubles $100-140 (MAP), Cottages $120-150 (MAP)
Payment: AE, MC, and VISA
Children: Welcome
Dogs: Welcome in the cottages with advance notice and prior approval
Open: All year

Lovett's Inn by Lafayette Brook has been a fixture in these parts for years, although when we visited, the new owners had only been on board for five weeks. Those five weeks were during the peak foliage season, and they were very busy learning the ropes and juggling their house full of guests. With all of these demands being placed on them, they were gracious and surprisingly calm, leaving us to believe that subsequent guests will certainly be in for a great experience.

The main inn was built in 1784, and is listed on the National Register of Historic Places. Step through the antique door and guests are immediately drawn into the inviting common rooms. To the right, there is a small reception area and sitting room, brightened by crimson walls, with a few well chosen antiques, chairs, and side tables. Just beyond this room is the fireplaced dining room, where tables are covered with linens and set with fine china. When we arrived, guests were enjoying a quiet and romantic meal lit by candlelight. With the change in ownership came a change in chefs. Although the new menu was still being developed, the seasonal menu offered that night contained trout, New York strip steak, and veal, all of which were accompanied by wonderful sauces and a full complement of fresh vegetables. After dinner cocktails are offered at both the marble bar or in the sitting room. While JoAnna and Lee were busy tending to their guests, we were free to wander around a bit.

As we walked past the front door, it swung open, leading JoAnna to comment that the ghost of Lovett's was playing games again. The very inviting sitting room was being warmed by a fire. The previous owners are responsible for the wonderful wallpapers and rich colors found throughout the inn. A burgundy paisley print wallpaper fits in beautifully with the rough hewn beamed ceilings. The evening candlelight cast a soft glow over the antique furnishings as well. Just beyond the sitting room is a step down into a garden room with walls of windows.

The bright colors lent a sense of summertime to this space, even though the cool days of fall were upon us. There were plenty of books to choose from, as well as some games, although many people feel just as comfortable relaxing and taking in the expansive views of the property.

Included in the view are the cottages. These are rather unique for New Hampshire, having been built of cinder blocks and then painted white. From the outside they appear quite modern and stark in design. Upon entering them, we were pleasantly surprised by the attractive, homey decor. The plate glass windows, framed by tie-back curtains, offer scenic views of the grounds and surrounding mountains. The decor is strictly Colonial, with Bates spreads covering the king-size beds and down comforters resting at their bases. A maple bureau, and a small table and chair often complete the furnishings. In the cooler months, the old-fashioned radiators do a good job warming the rooms; however, guests also enjoy snuggling up to the fireplaces, which can be found in most of the cottages. The modern amenities, such as private baths and cable television are welcome additions.

The Wogulis' eleven-year old Cocker Spaniel, Princess, accompanied us on a tour of the grounds. The main inn lies to the front of the property, while the cottages are laid out in a semi-circle behind it. A heated swimming pool and whirlpool are major draws in the summer months, along with a small pond. Guests are free to walk the property with their leashed dog, or explore the woods behind the inn. Although Franconia Notch State Park is not terribly conducive to dogs, Crawford Notch State Park is slightly more canine friendly. By following Route 3 from Franconia, visitors will quickly arrive at the state park. A section of the Appalachian Trail lies just outside of Franconia, and great hiking is available this region; hikers with dogs must keep in mind, however, that the White Mountain National Forest, which comprises the majority of the wilderness area, welcomes dogs on all of their hiking trails, provided they are leashed at all times.

The Horse and Hound Inn

205 Wells Road
Franconia, New Hampshire 03580
(603) 823-5501

Innkeepers: *Jim Cantlon and Bill Steele*
Rooms: *8 doubles, 2 suites*
Rates: *Doubles $55-65 (B&B), Suites $115 (B&B)*
Payment: *AE, DC, DSC, MC, and VISA*
Children: *Welcome*
Dogs: *Welcome with advance notice and a $10 fee*
Open: *All year except April*

If The Horse and Hound Inn conjures up images of the English countryside, it is meant to. Although the original farmhouse reflects its New "English" heritage having been built in 1830, 150 years later an English gentlemen bought the place, expanded it, and tried to run it as a British country inn. Unfortunately, this endeavor failed, as did several more recent attempts by other innkeepers. The two current owners are Jim Cantlon and Bill Steele. Together they have turned this mountain hideaway into a full service inn and ski lodge, providing excellent food, a friendly bar, and comfortable guest rooms.

The inn is situated just outside Franconia, on the way to Cannon Mountain. Its location, on the edge of the White Mountain National Forest and Franconia Notch State Park, makes it a terrific destination for those vacationers and canine companions who enjoy the outdoors. To reach the inn, guests turn off the main road from Franconia, onto a dirt road which leads to the inn. From the outside, it is easy to distinguish the original farmhouse from the long, two story addition that houses the dining room and most of the guest bedrooms. Jim was on hand to greet us that night, a personable man who obviously has a lot of enthusiasm for innkeeping. Not too surprisingly, he also has quite a passion for skiing, and even though it was only October, he was more than ready to hit the slopes.

The first impression visitors have of the inn is of the inviting living room. This is filled with an eclectic assortment of furnishings and comfortable sofas. The sitting areas in this expansive space lend themselves to private conversations or quiet reading. Full length, tie back floral draperies do much to enhance the room, as well as the assortment of knickknacks culled from Jim and Bill's private collections. Those who choose to relax in front of the fire will notice the book on teddy bears set out on the coffee table. The teddy bear theme is evident throughout the inn and especially in the bar, where patrons are greeted by a confluence of bears perched high in the alcoves around the room. This is perhaps our favorite place in the inn, with darkly stained, paneled walls and a stunning old-fashioned bar. Jim tells us that during ski season this convivial place is usually packed with skiers regaling one another with the day's best ski stories.

Many guests have such a nice time talking in the bar, that they end up spending their entire evening at the inn, enjoying dinner in The Hunt Room. This rather elegant space, also reminiscent of Great Britain, is distinguished by the dark-hued paneled walls and the soft light emanating from the candles. A fire in the brick hearth casts a warm glow across the cloth covered tables set with china. Bill is in charge of the kitchen, turning out innovative meals that reflect the season. A sampling of items on the fall menu included mushrooms stuffed with seafood, shrimp Alfredo, and a baked French onion soup. The hearty Continental offerings that diners could choose from ranged from roast duckling and broiled lamb chops with mint jelly to the filet mignon finished with mushrooms and artichoke hearts or a sauce Chausser. Lighter fare includes the pasta primavera and the stir-fried beef, shrimp, or smoked chicken. A full breakfast, served in the same room, includes the latest egg or pancake dish of the day, accompanied by freshly baked breads and muffins, juice, and coffee or tea.

Upstairs, guests will stumble across a few more of their hosts' collectibles. Some might notice the antique table in the upstairs hallway, or perhaps a small needlepoint cushioned chair. The bedrooms are available in a variety of configurations in both the original farmhouse or the newer addition. We found, that regardless of the room, the doors to the chambers are their most striking feature. These are, in most cases, the original doors from the 1800s that have developed a rich patina over time. Open them to reveal the individually furnished bedrooms. Some offer ample amounts of sunlight, while others provide enough space for an entire family. Several are decorated in pale greens, and others have a robin's egg blue color scheme. A few country antiques are intermixed with other more contemporary furnishings. The eclectic combination of colors and furnishings are attractive and somehow meld together quite nicely.

While the inn is comfortable, the access guests have to the out-of-doors is even more enticing. The Horse and the Hound is located in a fairly secluded spot, making it easy to walk Bowser. Just off the back of the inn, there is a patio and lawn where many guests tend to congregate in the warmer months. The local Franconia Notch State Park is worth exploring, although dogs are only allowed in the dog walk areas. Summertime lends itself to bicycling and horseback riding, golf and tennis, or summer theater. Of course Bowser cannot participate in all of these events, but his owners will certainly enjoy the options. A short drive in the car will lead travelers to Coppermine Brook and on to Bridal Veil Falls. While the Franconia Notch State Park is fairly limited in permitting visitors access with their dogs, the White Mountain National Park allows hikers to explore their many trails. In the winter months, guests can head out right from the inn for a little cross-country skiing or they may drive a few minutes to Cannon Mountain for excellent downhill skiing.

The Hanover Inn

P.O. Box 151, On The Green
Hanover, New Hampshire 03775
(800) 443-7024, (603) 643-4300, Fax (603) 646-3744

Manager: *Matthew Marshall*
Rooms: *98 doubles, 6 suites*
Rates: *Doubles $186-196 (EP), Suites $239 (EP)*
Payment: *AE, DC, MC, and VISA*
Children: *Welcome (cribs are available at no charge), children under 12 years of age are free of charge when sharing a room with their parents*
Dogs: *Welcome*
Open: *All year*

The Hanover Inn is owned by, and located just across the street from, Dartmouth College. The inn was founded in 1780 by General Ebenezer Brewster, and was then known as the Dartmouth Hotel. Unfortunately, it burned in 1887 but was rebuilt two years later and Dartmouth College ultimately took ownership in 1901. An east and west wing were added more recently, greatly increasing the size of the building. Even though there are over 100 guest rooms, the interior still retains a strong sense of charm and tradition that is in keeping with its Ivy League background.

During our last visit, the hotel was in the final stages of its long renovation, but upon our recent return, we were pleased to see that all the work had been completed. The hallways leading to the guest rooms have traditional duck and hunt prints lining the walls. Our favorite chambers continue to be the corner suites as they offer the most space and light. The fourth floor rooms are almost as appealing, however, as they are set in the eaves and extremely private. The overall decor in most of the accommodations is distinctly Colonial, with floral wallpapers accented by wainscoting and fine quality mahogany reproductions. Finial bedsteads are covered with white woven spreads and eiderdown comforters are neatly folded at their bases. Chippendale-style chairs are placed in front of two-drawer writing tables and floral patterned wing chairs are illuminated by standing brass lamps. Subtle rose, green, and blue color schemes highlight many of the rooms, while others are bathed in the traditional Dartmouth green and autumnal colors. The televisions are concealed in the armoires and those needing computer services can tie directly into Dartmouth's impressive system through a little high-tech wizardry. The tiled bathrooms are equipped with blow dryers, as well as a nice complement of Gilchrist and Soames aloe vera bath seeds, soaps, shampoos, and lotions. After a bath, guests can don their Sea Island cotton bath robes and perhaps ponder a visit to the Hayward Lounge for traditional afternoon tea.

The Hayward Lounge is an inviting room, bathed in pale hues of yellow and rose. The camelback sofas, Queen Anne armchairs, and mahogany end tables create intimate sitting areas and lend it an additional air of formality. Light streams in from the multitude of floor-to-ceiling paned windows. Later in the day, guests will want to dine at the Daniel Webster Room, where the seasonally changing menu specializes in traditional New England fare. A sampling of some recent selections included braised escargot with wild mushrooms and polenta, roasted oysters with tomato and fine herbs, and a charred lobster with roasted corn and sundried tomatoes. Entrées are equally varied, with dishes ranging from maple roasted duck with cranberries and port, and roast rack of lamb with marjoram pesto, to chestnut crusted loin of Old Moses Farm venison and sweet potato spaetzle and beef tenderloin with grilled portabello mushrooms, roast garlic, and cabernet. In the warmer summer months, The Terrace is a favorite gathering spot for drinks and a sampling of the inn's lighter fare. The informal Ivy Grill has a contemporary look to it, and serves hamburgers, salads, and chicken dishes.

The Hanover Inn's ties with Dartmouth College are of great benefit to inn guests. For instance, the college's athletic facilities, which include a heated indoor swimming, squash, and racquetball, are just a short walk from the inn. The Hood Museum has ever changing exhibits that always attract interest, and the Hopkins Center for the Performing Arts is the focal point for plays, films, and concerts during the year. Shopping is literally steps from the main desk, with the exclusive Simon Pearce glass studio located right in the building. Bowser should have a great time exploring the grounds of Dartmouth College, which lie just across the street from the inn. There are literally acres of grass and paths which are perfect for stretching one's legs. Down the hill, walkers will find the Connecticut River which is as scenic as it is ideal for boating and fishing. There are also a number of local hiking trails, which hikers can explore with Bowser, and the inn can provide detailed guide maps. In the wintertime, the activities shift to cross-country and downhill skiing, both of which are located close to the inn.

Riverside Inn

Route 16A
Intervale, New Hampshire   03845
(603) 356-9060

Innkeepers: Anne and Geoffrey Cotter
Rooms: 7 doubles
Rates: $44-85 (B&B)
Payment: AE, DSC, MC, and VISA
Children: Welcome
Dogs: Welcome with prior approval
Open: All year

When Geoff and Anne acquired his family's summer home in 1983, they put their restaurant careers on hold and dedicated themselves to renovating this historic building. What they created was a little jewel, where every nook and cranny is filled with their family's heirlooms. Since that time, they have been able to do the two things they love most: run an intimate inn and create superb meals for a small number of guests. They have, in fact, developed such a special place that many guests reserve rooms for weeks at a time, using the inn as a home away from home, while enjoying the picturesque White Mountains region.

As with many old-fashioned summer homes, the interior was comprised of a catacomb of bedrooms that were originally constructed to accommodate the owners, their house guests, and the staff. In keeping with the history of the house, Geoff and Anne have named each chamber after original family members. The third-floor bedrooms were formerly the maid's and chauffeur's quarters. Now their simple board walls give these eaved-rooms character, while brightly painted yellow or red bed frames provide wonderful accents of color. Most of the guest rooms on the second floor are substantially larger and a bit more formal, with pretty fabrics on the antique brass or carved wood beds. Anne and Geoffrey have an eclectic and attractive collection of antiques, ranging from English pieces to a variety of Victorian furnishings. The corner rooms are very appealing because of the beautiful sunlight coming in through their many windows. For those seeking a bit of privacy, there is a combination of three rooms tucked off to the rear of the house, with their own separate rear entrance. A radio and a fan are just two of the many thoughtful amenities provided, along with some less conspicuous items such as mints set on the bedside table. If a private bathroom is important, then we suggest requesting one when making reservations.

This is an inn where guests settle in quickly and easily. Even during the peak season, there are only 16 people in residence, which allows Geoff and Anne to make the small inn experience all the more personal. Guests are comfortable selecting a book from the built-in shelves that line the front staircase, and relaxing in the intimate living room before the fireplace. There is even a small television here, just in case someone needs to stay in touch with the rest of the world. Most opt to settle in among the Victorian antiques and visit, although everyone is eventually drawn to the glassed-in porch. This section of the inn is wonderfully informal, with the brightly painted (and well-stocked) bar, plants, and ample amounts of sunlight creating a festive environment. Small stools, set by the windows, face out toward the shaded yard and river just beyond. The dining room is located next to the sun porch and, by contrast, is quite elegant with its deep rose-hued walls.

For breakfast, Anne creates bountiful waffle, pancake, or egg dishes that are quickly consumed. Fresh corned beef and eggs can frequently be found on the menu, along with English toast (a variation of French toast made with English muffins). During our visit, the aroma of fresh bread baking in the oven was drawing most guests into the kitchen. On Friday and Saturday nights, the inn opens its doors to the public for dinner, a meal that should definitely not be missed. The fare is always changing and quite innovative. One recent dinner menu included Genoa rollups as an appetizer, with either free range chicken, salmon with dill sauce, or pork with a cranberry rum sauce as the main course. For dessert there was the famous booze pie and a pear-cranberry crisp. All the dishes are created with the freshest ingredients, including vegetables from the summer garden.

Bowser should be delighted with the Riverside Inn. Especially since the property surrounding the inn is ideal for a good romp. The Saco River that flows by the inn is equally appealing to water dogs, and there is even a great swimming hole and beach just downstream. In the afternoon, a hammock often beckons humans, while Bowser relaxes in the shade of the surrounding trees. The nearby mountains are ideal for hiking as well, with trails located within walking distance of the inn. Intervale is actually a quiet community, particularly in comparison to the neighboring town of North Conway, which has a vast array of discount shopping options. We prefer to stay close to the Riverside Inn, where the quiet streets and back roads can be ideal for leisurely walks. In the winter months the downhill skiing is convenient at Black Mountain, Mt. Cranmore, and Attitash. The Mt. Washington Ski Touring Center is also just a few minutes drive from the inn, although Bowser may wish to stay home for this outing.

Whitney's Inn

P.O. Box W
Route 16B
Jackson, New Hampshire   03846
(800) 677-5737, (603) 383-8916

Owners: Barb and Bob Bowman
Innkeeper: Kevin Martin
Rooms: 18 doubles, 9 suites, 2 cottages
Rates: Doubles $90-150 (MAP), Cottages $135-156 (B&B), Children's rates $18-30
Payment: AE, DSC, MC, and VISA
Children: Welcome (cribs, cots, highchairs, babysitters, and children's menu are available)
Dogs: Welcome in the cottages for a $25 fee
Open: All year

For 57 years, Whitneys' Inn has been a family vacation tradition. For most of that time, the people that kept this tradition alive were Bill and Betty Whitney and family. However, in 1992, there was a change in ownership when Barb and Bob Bowman bought the inn. The Bowmans, who also own the Inn at Jackson, the Folger Hotel and Cottages on Nantucket in Massachusetts, and the Henry Farm Inn in Chester, Vermont, wanted to preserve the special feeling of Whitneys' Inn while, at the same time, making some improvements. Kevin Martin has remained as manager of the inn.

Physically, the inn has a lot going for it. The main building dates back to 1842, offering an antique ambiance mixed with some modern amenities. Wide board floors lead past the front desk and sitting areas to the dining room. Guests pass by the formal living room with a brick fireplace, comfortable sofas and armchairs, and tables. There is usually an ongoing puzzle set up in here for people to work on during their leisure time. Downstairs there is a recreation room which is ideal for children, with table tennis, lots of board games, and a television equipped with a VCR. Those who are looking for activity ideas can consult the enormous three ring binder at the front desk which lists, in sections divided by age, all the games and puzzles the inn has on hand.

Any returning guests know that the dining room has always been one of the inn's main draws. When the Bowmans took over, they hired chef Rob McCarthy whose new menu has received accolades from magazines such as *Bon Apetit*. The breakfast standouts are the homemade corned beef hash, French toast, omelettes, and pancakes. However, it is the dinner menu that is most noteworthy. Appetizers include the sundried tomato ravioli covered in an herb cream sauce, trout smoked on applewood, and artichoke hearts sauteed in garlic, roasted red peppers, and wine. The entrées range from grilled orange sesame chicken and pan seared scallops tossed with pesto, sundried tomatoes, toasted pine nuts and broccoli, to

London broil in a citrus honey marinade and the roast duckling with a cranberry-orange glaze. On Wednesday night (in the summer), there is a lobster bake, complete with clam chowder, barbecued chicken, corn on the cob, and salads. They also offer a children's version which substitutes hamburgers and hot dogs for lobster. Every night during the inn's peak periods, there is a supervised children's table where kids eat early as a group and then head off for games and fun. Their parents are left to enjoy a leisurely candlelight meal. Although Bowser does not enjoy quite the same privileges, he will certainly be happy with the accommodations and grounds.

Guests traveling with a dog are welcome in the two cottages that are just a minute's walk from the main inn. Although these storybook cottages have different names, Juniper and Spruce, they are otherwise identical, including their Williamsburg blue exteriors. Small slate patios are appointed with outdoor furniture and firewood is neatly stacked near the front door. Window boxes overflow with flowers during the summer months, making the cottages especially inviting. Each offers a living room and two bedrooms, along with a kitchenette. The living room has comfortable sofas and chairs, as well as a television. The two focal points for the room are the fireplace and the mountain views through the plate glass windows. The furnishings are very attractive modern pieces, which combine nicely with a smattering of country antiques lit by pottery lamps. The bedrooms have a combination of double and twin beds. Each of these is draped with an attractive calico quilt in subtle maroons and deep blue tones. Paned windows are framed by cotton curtains. In addition to being extremely private, the cottages also allow easy access to the outdoors.

A walk up the hill gives people spectacular panoramic views of the entire Presidential Mountain range. The fourteen acres of land are also well worth exploring, including the ski trails which provide terrific hiking opportunities in the summer months. Tennis, shuffleboard, volleyball, and assorted lawn games are all popular diversions as well. In the basement of the main inn, there are usually extra badminton and tennis racquets, along with wiffle balls and bats. The spring-fed pond is a natural draw for many people (and Bowser) who enjoy the small sandy beach. There is even a little shaded area, where picnickers can enjoy lunch. Just down the road, Jackson Falls is an inviting river of cascades and pools that are perfect for swimming in on a hot summer's day.

In the winter months, guests will find it an easy walk to the lifts in the morning, and a quick ski to the cottage for lunch, and then again at the end of the day. While the downhill skiing is terrific, the extensive network of cross-country ski trails are even more popular. After a day of skiing, there is ice skating on the lighted rink (skates are available to borrow although it is recommended that people bring their own) and sledding (which might even be appealing to Bowser who can romp alongside the sled or tag along for the ride). After a long day of outdoor activities, there are two popular places at the inn for early evening libations. The Greenery Lounge is an intimate spot with an old-fashioned bar, plenty of hanging plants, and lots of windows. The Shovel Handle Barn is appropriately enough located in a huge barn adjacent to the inn, and offers apres-ski festivities such as live entertainment on the weekends.

It would seem that Whitney's Inn offers it all, including "extras that aren't extras"; however, what makes it particularly appealing to us is that they manage to do it all without losing their sense of intimacy and personalization. Perhaps this is why, after so many years, that guests continue to make a vacation here an annual tradition.

The Dana Place Inn

P.O. Box L
Pinkham Notch
Jackson, New Hampshire 03846
(800) 537-9276, (603) 383-6822

Innkeepers: *Harris and Mary Lou Levine*
Rooms: *35 doubles*
Rates: *Doubles $85-125 (B&B), $125-185 (MAP)*
Payment: *AE, CB, DC, DSC, MC and VISA*
Children: *Welcome (cribs, cots, highchairs, and children's menus are available)*
Dogs: *Welcome with prior approval in certain rooms with outside entrances, but are not permitted in the inn's common areas*
Open: *All year*

In New England, many inns are actually converted antique homes that have interesting histories. The Dana Place Inn is not unusual in this regard. It was named after Mr. and Mrs. Otwin Dana, the original owners of the property, who received it as a wedding present in the mid-1870s. After farming the land for 15 years, they decided to go into the innkeeping business. Their hostel, then known as Ferncliff Cottage, was merely the beginning of a long-standing innkeeping tradition that Harris and Mary Lou Levine keep alive today.

We have visited the Dana Place many times over the years, and happily, much about the inn remains the same. The first floor of the original white farmhouse is a restaurant, and most of the accommodations are set in the second-floor eaves. Over the years, additions have been made to the inn by various owners which have created a labyrinth of passages leading to the guest rooms. The largest of these chambers lie to the rear of the inn and overlook the gardens, river, and mountainside. Some of the bedrooms are simply furnished with country antiques, while others have more contemporary reproductions, but none are overdone with clutter or fluff. Guests will enjoy items such as good reading lamps, writing desks, and soft carpeting that serve to enhance these otherwise ordinary rooms. French or sliding glass doors allow guests and their canine companions easy access to the 300 acres of woods, orchards, and gardens that surround the inn.

What makes the Dana Place Inn particularly appealing is the plethora of activities and the generally relaxed nature of the staff and the other guests. In the winter, many like to cross-country ski from the inn along the Ellis River to Jackson. Here, they may have lunch and catch a shuttle back up the hill. Since the inn is located at the base of Mt. Washington, it is also easy to get to Wildcat for downhill skiing or to the Appalachian Mountain Club base camp, where many set off for their own cross-country treks. The famous Tuckerman's Ravine is also nearby, for those who like the idea of climbing to the top of a mountain and then skiing down. Summer visitors might wish to borrow a racquet and balls and play tennis on either the hard or clay courts, and then go for a refreshing dip in one of the local swimming holes. The front desk also has maps of the favorite bicycling routes, as well as local hiking and walking trails.

Working up an appetite rarely seems to be a problem for most guests. Breakfast and dinner are served in one of the four intimate dining rooms that overlook the mountains and gardens. There are usually a variety of options available for breakfast. Some of the favorites include the buttermilk pancakes with blueberries, Eggs Benedict, French toast, and crepes. Children usually opt for the Disney toast made with thick sliced Texas toast that is dipped in brown sugar and cinnamon.

The dinner menu is more extensive and is usually included in the fare. Many people enjoy their drinks and appetizers in the small pub before gravitating into one of the more intimate, candlelit dining rooms. Our favorite one has a fireplace and just seven tables. The menu changes seasonally, but some of the more interesting choices for appetizers are the lobster alfredo, escargots, and the smoked seafood plate. This may be followed by salmon with a light dill sauce, a petite filet topped with asparagus, lobster, and hollandaise, and the brandied apple chicken. Although we skipped dessert, most of the guests were raving about the chocolate sin cake and the apple crisp.

Finally, for those who want to relax after dinner, there is a cozy library with several sofas and overstuffed chairs placed invitingly around the enormous fireplace. This is a favorite spot for reading, meeting other guests, and watching the evening movie (although most are so busy visiting, they have little time to watch television). As guests meander deeper into the inn, they will come across another cozy sitting room, where a variety of board games are stacked on the many bookshelves. Just beyond this chamber is the popular indoor swimming pool and Jacuzzi.

We have to say that as much as we like The Dana Place Inn, it is not for those looking for a perfectly appointed country inn filled with priceless antiques and luxurious amenities. It offers, instead, comfortable rooms, good food, and a super location for just about any outdoor activity one might imagine. They are also very accommodating to those traveling with a dog, allowing for both dog and human companion to completely relax.

Ellis River House

P.O. Box 656
Route 16
Jackson, New Hampshire 03846
(800) 233-8309, (603) 383-9339

Innkeepers: Barry and Barbara Lubao
Rooms: 14 doubles, 3 suites, 1 cottage
Rates: Doubles $69-229 (B&B), Suites $99-229 (B&B), Cottage $89-159 (EP)
Payment: AE, DC, MC, and VISA
Children: Welcome, children 12 years of age and under are free of charge when sharing room with parents (cribs, cots, highchairs, and babysitters are available)
Dogs: Welcome in the cottage for $10 per night. They are not allowed on the furniture or bedding.
Open: All year

The village of Jackson has always been very appealing, although we could never find an inn here that welcomed guests traveling with a dog. The Ellis River House, while not located in the heart of the village, is within easy walking distance of the covered bridge marking the entrance to town. The inn is actually situated at the end of a dirt lane, just off Route 16, that leads to a small complex of buildings lining the edge of the Ellis River.

When the Lubaos purchased the property ten years ago, on it was the original Colonial farmhouse dating back to 1893. Even though it evoked a certain country charm, the building did lack certain amenities that modern travelers expect — namely, private bathrooms. Just recently, the Lubaos completed a huge addition, which does not detract from the inn's authentic features but instead adds the conveniences of oversized rooms, central air-conditioning, fireplaces, and private bathrooms (some with whirlpool tubs). These bedrooms have been appointed with country antiques and good quality Colonial reproductions.

Equally as appealing is the tiny cottage tucked into the riverbank, which is perfect for those traveling with a dog. It looks like a miniature version of the main inn; however, it offers plenty of privacy, as well as an array of amenities. A fence with small hearts cut into the top of it frames the entrance to the enclosed patio and cottage. The first floor room has just enough space for the oak trundle bed and hutch containing a cable television, refrigerator, and an assortment of games. A separate nook holds a small table and microwave. The Lubaos have purposely kept this chamber light by using natural board ceilings and walls. A spiral staircase leads to the upstairs bedroom. An inviting bedstead, covered in a striking floral comforter with a black background, has been placed under the semi-circular window. The most noteworthy of the rather simple furnishings is the country pine chest with a goose painted on it. The bathroom is quite modern, and is stocked with a supply of soaps and shampoos. With all of the cooking apparatus, including an outdoor barbecue, guests can certainly create many of their own meals in the cottage. However, we suggest that they let Barry cook breakfast for them over at the inn.

An inviting common room, warmed by a fireplace and decorated with all sorts of country collectibles and crafts, is always humming with activity in the morning. A few more steps bring guests into one of the two dining rooms. The hardwood floors in here are covered by Oriental rugs and a grandfather clock ticks in the corner. A woodstove keeps one intimate dining room warm in the winter months, supplemented by the sunlight streaming in through the multitude of windows. In the evening, the mood is softened by the candlelight emanating from the tables and music coming from the piano. Although the ambiance differs according to the hour of the day, the meals are always satisfying. Breakfast is outstanding, with Barry's breads topping the list of favorite foods. Of the different homemade breads available, his beer bread is unique and his cinnamon bread is unbeatable. There are also specialty omelettes, often made from eggs gathered from the inn's chickens. Bacon, sausage, and many other delectables are also found on the menu.

The evening meal is an entirely different dining experience, with a fixed price menu and a number of intriguing choices. The entrées change according to the season and what is fresh, and during our visit the choices were excellent. Selections included the pasta and fresh pesto, rainbow trout with almonds, and a New York sirloin steak with sautéed mushroom caps. These were accompanied by a potato, vegetable, and of course, Chef Barry's homemade breads. After a hearty meal and a day of skiing or hiking, guests are often tempted into the hot tub, which is found in the atrium overlooking the river. Others might prefer a trip to the pub, a wonderfully informal place that oozes authentic English charm. Two black leather club chairs are pulled up to one window, with other tables and chairs scattered about the room. The fireplace adds to the ambiance, warming those who are sampling from the wide array of beers and extensive wine cellar. A pool table and dart board are available for those interested in stirring up a bit of indoor activity.

Outside diversions are also plentiful at the inn. In the summer months, the heated pool is very popular. Others prefer to visit the pony grazing in the fenced-in pasture. Other activities include volleyball, croquet, or horseshoes on the flat terraced area next to the river. Bowser will certainly enjoy exploring the property and the banks of the river. A number of waterfalls are found in the region. The Glen Ellis Falls are just a 10-minute walk from the inn, while Arethusa Falls can be found in Crawford Notch. Others enjoy taking a three-hour hike along Bemis Brook. The Appalachian Mountain Club maintains trails in the White Mountain National Forest that are also worth investigating. Try Lowe's Bald Spot, North Doublehead or the most difficult climb of all, the one up to Mount Washington. While Bowser cannot participate in the downhill skiing adventures, he can certainly help blaze a cross-country ski trail in the winter months.

Isaac E. Merrill House Inn

P.O. Box 8
Kearsarge, New Hampshire 03847
(800) 328-9041, (603) 356-9041

Innkeeper: Richard D. Levine
Rooms: 22 doubles, 1 suite
Rates: Doubles $59-135 (B&B), Suite $120-135 (B&B)
Payment: AE, MC, DSC, and VISA
Children: Welcome (cribs, cots, and highchairs are available)
Dogs: Welcome
Open: All year

For 220 years, the Isaac E. Merrill House Inn has graced the quiet village of Kearsarge, and it has survived time, additions, and a series of owners with little apparent harm to the facade. Today, this rambling old building, with its huge eaves and small windowed gables, is a bright standout in the sleepy village situated just above the bustling North Conway. The inn is easy to find, with its yellow shingles and hunter green trim. A series of wide stairs, also painted a deep green, lead to a wraparound porch. We visited in the fall, when pumpkins were set out in a festive fashion, and flowers still bloomed from the window boxes.

The inn's well-preserved sense of antiquity disappears inside, reflecting instead the more modern touches of its 20th-century owners. Interestingly, the inn has been operational for 150 years. It started as a rooming house and was run by a local farmer, Isaac E. Merrill, who earned extra money by housing and feeding some of the local artists. By 1888, the Russell family had purchased the farmhouse and adjacent land, turning Mr. Merrill's rooming house into the Russell Cottages. After many, many years of Russell family ownership, the inn went through a quick succession of owners and finally fell on hard times in the 1980s. It was ultimately abandoned and then lay vacant for two years, quietly awaiting someone to purchase it. When Richard and his father, who owns the Dana Place Inn, learned the old place was being sold at auction they thought it would not only be a great bargain, but also a terrific restoration project. They bought the place, "lock, stock, and barrel", which as Richard informed us, was primarily piles of dust.

The dust is long gone, the rooms have been spruced up, and the walls have been painted in varying pastel colors or simple white. Guests will notice that even with all of the work that has been done on the house, many of the authentic moldings, hardwood floors, and other architectural features they might expect to find are missing. This gives the upstairs bedrooms what many consider to be a "ski house" ambiance. The bedroom walls are painted out white, brass beds are covered with floral comforters, and chintz curtains frame the windows. Bureaus are hand-painted with flowers in some of the chambers. The bathrooms, while clean and modern, are strictly utilitarian. The third floor landing has a wonderful sunny sitting area, complete with a small bookshelf tucked into one of the eaves. Six bedrooms open up into this area, making it perfect for groups of friends who can reserve the entire floor.

The Isaac E. Merrill House, also in typical ski house tradition, serves an excellent full country breakfast. The sophisticated breakfast room is probably the most modern part of the inn, with its pink walls, assorted Scandinavian-style tables, and small sitting area. The latter is composed of two oversized yellow and pink floral sofas that flank the fireplace. On cold mornings, the fire is roaring and guests are either scanning the menu or enjoying their hearty meal. The menu includes French toast dipped in a cinnamon-nutmeg egg batter, buttermilk pancakes covered with blueberries, and grilled homemade waffles topped with fresh apples and sprinkled with cinnamon sugar. The Eggs Benedict are excellent, as are the specialty omelettes. Those with substantial appetites can choose from homefries, bacon, sausage, or ham. Dinner can be enjoyed at the Dana Place Inn or at any of the other excellent restaurants found in nearby Conway and Jackson.

To the rear of the inn, there is a comfortable common room that is outfitted with a large screen television. In the afternoon, coffee and tea, as well as other beverages and baked goods are set out to snack on. We liked the Isaac E. Merrill House, as much for its young owner's enthusiasm, as for the casual nature of the place. Guests who stay here are welcome to drive ten minutes up the road and use all of the amenities offered by the Dana Place Inn, including their indoor swimming pool and Jacuzzi, tennis courts, and 300 acres of land. Bowser would undoubtedly enjoy exploring the woods opposite the inn, where he will also discover the Kearsarge Brook. Just up the hill, a mile or so, hikers will reach the summit of Mount Surprise, where they are privy to views of the Saco Valley and Mount Washington. Even closer to the inn is Sunset Hill, with Russell's Observatory and more scenic views. In the winter months, many people choose to downhill and/or cross-country ski at Mount Cranmore, Loon Mountain, or Wildcat.

Thayer's Inn

136 Main Street
Littleton, New Hampshire 03561
(800) 634-8179, (603) 444-6469

Innkeepers: Don and Carolyn Lambert
Rooms: 28 doubles, 6 suites
Rates: Doubles $32.95-49.95 (EP), Suites $69.90 (EP)
Payment: AE, CB, DSC, DC, MC and VISA
Children: Welcome (cribs, cots, and highchairs are available)
Dogs: Welcome with prior approval
Open: All year

Most people are familiar with the charms of an old-fashioned city hotel, with its array of authentic architectural details and a strong sense of tradition, all of which are innate and virtually impossible to replicate. Move all of that to a rural New Hampshire town and the overall effect is much more intimate, yet just as appealing. This is what guests will find when they visit the Thayer's Inn, which has been around since 1850. Its was originally known as Thayer's White Mountain Hotel and its owner was Henry L. Thayer, a successful merchant who also had dreams of becoming a famous hotelier. Aside from building a modern hotel, (modern by his standards) he was also determined to provide a high level of service normally associated with a luxury property.

He maintained a full staff in order to keep the Franklin stoves stoked, fresh water flowing, and the candles lit. At night, before his guests retired, the beds were turned down and heated stones placed between the sheets. This was the day of stagecoaches, and Henry purchased a number of them to shuttle guests between the railroad station and his hotel. The high level of personalized service and the fondness of the returning guests toward Henry was such that by the end of the 1800s, the Thayer's White Mountain Hotel became more simply known as Thayer's Inn. Henry Thayer ran the inn until the late 1800s. John Eames bought the property in 1927 and added a second and third floor, along with modern plumbing. Today, the Lamberts are the resident innkeepers, operating under a family trust that was established by Eames in the mid-1900s.

Many things may have changed over the years, but Thayer's Inn still retains much of the charm and appeal from Henry Thayer's time. It still lies in the heart of Littleton, a town that once provided refuge to those traveling along the Underground Railroad. Today, it lures travellers who want to experience the beauty of the White Mountains instead. Anyone who wants to share some of the history and traditions established by Henry Thayer, will thoroughly enjoy their stay at the Thayer's Inn. Three-story high pillars mark the front of the inn, along with a second floor balcony and a turret topping the third floor. As guests walk through the entry, they will be transported back in time. It is easy to imagine esteemed visitors such as President Franklin Pierce, Nelson Rockefeller, Richard Nixon, and Governor Sherman Adams (Assistant to President Eisenhower), walking these same halls. Much of the moldings and trim work are hand-carved, and an assortment of historic pictures line the halls. In keeping with its heritage, the overall feeling is still very Victorian. Toward the rear of the building, visitors check-in at a small reception area and then head upstairs to one of the simply furnished bedrooms.

As guests ascend the stairs, they might keep in mind that the Ford Foundation tried to purchase the staircase (and the facade) years ago and to incorporate them into its Inn at Dearborn. Thankfully, the owners decided not to sell, and these features remain intact. Each floor has unusually wide hallways lined with antiques. Victorian light fixtures illuminate the patterned carpeting that covers the sloping floors. The bedrooms are not too different from what guests would have found in the 1800s, and there is even a replica of an original bedroom preserved on the third floor for all to examine. The guest chambers are furnished with either well-worn country antique furnishings or an eclectic mix of old and new pieces. Room 1 overlooks the street, and has a burgundy and hunter green color scheme, which is also reflected in the patterned carpet. The bed is backed by an intricately carved wooden headboard, and there is even a small sitting area with swivel chairs. As most of the plumbing has been retrofitted to the building, the bathrooms are all unusual. This one has been crafted out of an old closet, with just enough room for a toilet and a shower. A pedestal sink, holding a basket of soaps, is set unobtrusively in a corner of the room. Down the hall is Room 10, which is perhaps the most requested guest chamber at the inn. Aside from being located toward the rear of the building, it also has a steeply sloping floor that many people find very appealing. The high, pressed tin ceiling fits in well with the walls that have been papered in a tiny blue and rose Victorian print paper. The twin beds are covered in chenille spreads and Queen-Anne armchairs are placed in a corner. Guests will find that just as each bedroom is decorated differently, they are also substantially different in size. Some can accommodate a family, while others are ideal for one person. Where they don't differ is in simplicity of character and added amenities. Telephone and cable color television are standard offerings, and most have private bathrooms. Paddle fans move the still air on hot summer days. During their stay, most people enjoy climbing up to the turret, where they have terrific unobstructed views of the town and mountains around them.

Thayer's Inn is a good choice for anyone who wants to sample a taste of the past. There are shops to explore and many excellent restaurants within walking distance of the inn. Thayer's Inn also has a restaurant, with reasonable prices and good food. Littleton lies on the Vermont/New Hampshire border, giving travelers an opportunity to easily explore portions of both states. Probably the easiest area to investigate is the Moore Reservoir, just north of Littleton along the Connecticut River. This huge hydro-electric project rests on over 3,000 acres, which visitors may walk around provided Bowser is on a leash. Littleton is also easily accessible to the White Mountain National Forest, where hikers can choose from an array of day hikes (information and current weather conditions are available at the ranger station near the Pierce Bridge). From this spot, it is easy to gain access to the Zealand Campground, Sugarloaf Campground, and the many branches off the Appalachian Trail.

Loch Lyme Lodge & Cottages

RFD 278, Route 10
Lyme, New Hampshire   03768
(800) 423-2141, (603) 795-2141

Lodgekeepers: Paul and Judy Barker
Rooms: 4 doubles, 24 cottages
Rates: Doubles $48-82 (B&B) or $110 (MAP), Cottages $350-650 weekly (meals are
    additional)
Payment: Personal checks
Children: Welcome (cribs, cots, highchairs, and babysitters are available)
Dogs: Well-behaved dogs are allowed in the cottages only, with advance notice and
    prior approval. They must have appropriate vaccinations.
Open: All year except Thanksgiving and Christmas

A casual, relaxed, and inexpensive family vacation is not always easy to find — especially one where Bowser can have as much fun as the rest of the family members. The Loch Lyme Lodge is one such spot, providing a rustic atmosphere that everyone can enjoy. Close to Dartmouth College, hiking, fishing, and some of the prettiest lakes in New Hampshire, the cottages offer a myriad of choices for the active family or groups of friends who want to also bring their canine companion.

One word of caution, do not expect to find modern conveniences such as telephones, air conditioning, and color television. As Judy explains, Loch Lyme offers a "rustic country setting and an atmosphere that reminds one of a summer camp for families." The bulk of the 125 acres is comprised of forests and open fields dotted by dark brown shingled cottages with red trim overlooking Post Pond.

Each of the cottages has well-worn hardwood floors, a living room with a fireplace (wood is supplied), a private bathroom, a kitchen or kitchenette, a porch, and 1-4 separate bedrooms. The cottages are kept very clean and are well stocked with linens and fresh towels. Those that are situated closer to the lake are very popular and are often booked well in advance.

Meals at the lodge are also reflective of the casual mood here, concentrating on New England cuisine that emphasizes the use of local meats and fresh vegetables from the lodge's garden. The three entrée selections change nightly, and always seem to provide a little something for everyone. Breakfast is served every day between 8:00 and 9:00 a.m.; however, the Barkers recognize that not everyone likes to jump out of bed early when on vacation, so they also offer the breakfast bar. Here, guests can leisurely choose from a buffet of toast, cereal, and fruit, as well as coffee and tea. Lunch is even more informal, with the summer lunch bar providing sandwiches and salads, along with ice cream cones, for enjoying down at the beach.

One of the best features about the Loch Lyme Lodge and Cottages is that there are virtually endless numbers of ways to enjoy the day. The lake is a two-minute walk from most of the cottages where guests will find a grassy beach. Adirondack chairs are set out on shore and a deep water float beckons those who might wish to swim and/or sunbathe (Bowser is not allowed at the beach area, but can swim in other parts of the lake). Canoes, kayaks, and boats, along with a Windsurfer, will transport people across the lake to even more secluded areas. Badminton, croquet, and volleyball are just a few of the land-based sports available, as well as tennis on one of the two clay courts. Since our last visit, they have consolidated the Little Tikes toys, and now have a small playground in a clearing behind the cottages, where the children can climb to their heart's content. The fields in front of the cottages are often the site of less structured activities, as there are always plenty of rocks for scaling and grassy areas for throwing a ball or frisbee. Adjacent to the lodge are hiking trails that Bowser will love exploring and plenty of places that are ideal for a picnic and afternoon nap. The Appalachian Mountain Trail runs by the village of Lyme, providing hikers with a challenging day hike. For those in search of far more leisurely pursuits, there is a small lending library at the lodge that provides great vacation reading material.

The Loch Lyme Lodge and Cottages are truly unpretentious and a great bargain. People often book their reservations a year in advance for the summer months. Visitors will discover this is a place that draws multi-generations of guests, all of whom look forward to the family-oriented environment, cozy cottages, and lazy days spent down by the lake.

Peep-Willow Farm

RFD 51, Bixby Street
Marlborough, New Hampshire 03455
(603) 876-3807

Hostess: Noel Aderer
Rooms: 3 doubles
Rates: $30-50 (B&B)
Payment: Personal checks
Children: Welcome (babysitting can be arranged)
*Dogs: Welcome with prior approval; they must be kept leashed and cannot disturb farm
       animals ($5 fee)*
Open: All year

Sometimes, when travelers venture off the beaten track, they can find some truly unique B&Bs. The Peep-Willow Farm is one such treasure. Set atop a Marlborough hill, the 20-acre thoroughbred horse farm and fairly new, Colonial-style house have lovely views of the surrounding countryside. This unpretentious home offers guests simple yet comfortable accommodations. Moreover, anyone who has an interest in horses will find the Peep-Willow Farm to be particularly appropriate because it also serves as a training ground for Olympic caliber horses.

Noel is a fascinating woman who has led a rich, widely diversified life. After graduating from college, she postponed a career and decided to work her way around the world. During this sojourn, she was a teacher to Chinese students in North Borneo, assisted in the construction of a kibbutz in Israel, trained polo ponies for the Maharajah of Jaipur, was a Peace Corps volunteer, and tutored two children in a Volkswagon bus as it traveled from western Europe to India. When she finally returned to her native Connecticut, she quickly jumped into the political arena. Deeply concerned about the region's environmental and transportation problems, she mounted a bid for the state senate. Unfortunately, the opposing party had a four-to-one majority that even Noel could not overcome.

More recently, Noel arrived at the idea of opening a B&B. She started the Peep-Willow Farm B&B (named after her first two horses), which she operates while she trains thoroughbred horses for Olympic competitions. Her beautiful and powerful horses are taught to compete in a very challenging three-part event that combines dressage, cross-country jumping, and stadium jumping. Each morning, she rises at around 6 a.m. to tend to her horses. Guests are welcome to assist with the morning chores or to just watch her during her morning workout; however, visitors are not permitted to ride the horses.

Back at the house, morning risers will be treated to a full breakfast of eggs, toast, and bacon or perhaps a vegetarian offering, as Noel is quite willing to adapt the menu according to her guests' individual needs. This repast is served in the kitchen with its family-style breakfast table. The adjacent sitting room is quiet, cozy, and is heated in the winter months by a woodstove. The only first floor bedroom and bathroom are located down the hall from this chamber. Again, the bedroom amenities and decor are most simple, just about what one would expect to find in an unpretentious farmhouse setting. The two upstairs bedrooms are similarly decorated, and offer a little more privacy than the first floor room.

There is plenty for guests and their canine cohorts to do on and around the farm. Many enjoy paying a visit to the friendly horses and farm animals, or exploring the picturesque towns nearby. The country roads are especially lovely for long walks during the fall foliage season. In the winter, Bowser will undoubtedly enjoy some cross-country skiing in one of the local state parks. The farm is also set at the foot of Mount Monadnock, the most climbed mountain in the entire United States. Others may want to visit the Rhododendron, Pisgah, or Otter Brook State Parks that are all just a short drive from Marlborough.

The Ram in the Thicket

24 Maple Street
Milford, New Hampshire   03055
(603) 654-6440

Innkeepers: Andrew and Priscilla Tempelman
Rooms: 9 singles, 9 doubles, 2 suites
Rates: Singles $50-60 (B&B), Doubles $60-75 (B&B), Suites $135 (B&B)
Payment: AE
Children: Welcome (cribs and cots are available)
Dogs: Welcome with prior approval, provided they are kept quiet ($10 fee)
Open: All year

The Ram in the Thicket derives its name from the biblical story of Isaac and Abraham. As the passage describes, Abraham discovered "a ram caught in a thicket," which had been sent by the lord to replace his son, Isaac, who had just died. Andrew and Priscilla felt that leaving their home in the Midwest and fulfilling their life long dream of owning an inn in New England had a similar meaning. Thus, when they finally purchased the Victorian home in 1977, they thought it only too appropriate to name it after this passage.

The inn is set on top of a hill amidst a natural abundance of greenery. Cobblestones line the gravel paths that are bordered by flower gardens. Only after extensive renovations to the old mansion and the conversion of the old music room and library into four charming dining rooms, did the new innkeepers open their doors to the public. The common rooms, intimate bar, and dining rooms are all on the first floor. Sheraton-style antiques are quite at home in these pleasant surroundings.

The guest chambers are more informal and can be found on the second and third floors. The bedroom walls are either covered in floral papers or painted in soft pastel tones and highlighted with stenciling. One room boasts of a four-poster bed, while others have canopy or white iron and brass bedsteads. The built-in features, such as the fireplaces, floor-to-ceiling bookshelves, and decorative wainscotings are particularly appealing. Handmade quilts, white wicker mirrors, and colorful cushioned rocking chairs add a freshness to many of these chambers. One third floor room has a cozy windowed alcove with comfortable futons, which young children often find irresistible. Most of the guest chambers share bathrooms containing claw-footed tubs; one room, however, does have a large shower whose floor is covered by wooden slats.

Each of the dining rooms is individually decorated. One of our favorites has a handcrafted fireplace, blue tablecloths that complement the balloon curtains, and an Oriental rug covering the hardwood floors. The inn is primarily known for its excellent cuisine and international flair. Patrons may wish to start their meal by selecting one of the many appetizers. These might include mussels marinated in white wine, onions, and tomatoes, or a Mexican specialty of pureed black beans with jalapeno peppers and cumin accompanied by corn chips. Entrée choices on a given evening run the gamut from salmon with a raspberry shallot butter sauce to chicken curry made with Asian pears, apples, and the inn's own, freshly ground curry powder. The veal ragout, simmered for hours with carrots, celery, onions, and whole beans, is also quite delicious, as is the rack of lamb served with a mustard hollandaise sauce. If the weather allows, many enjoy dining on the screened-in porch while the sun sets over the hills. In the morning, guests are invited into the smaller breakfast room for a hearty Continental breakfast. This cheery room is decorated in an informal style, featuring decorative plates hanging over both the fireplace and a large sideboard, which is laden with cereals, croissants, breads, muffins, fresh fruit, and juices.

Guests often enjoy visiting the sheep and horses or taking a dip in the swimming pool. For those who play soccer, the Tempelman's dog is an especially interested participant, even if Bowser is not. The hiking and bicycling around the mountain lakes are other great activities, as is the array of downhill and cross-country skiing options. Silver Lake, Miller, and Greenfield State Parks are also just a short distance from the inn, for those who prefer a little hiking.

The 1785 Inn

P.O. Box 1785
Route 16
North Conway, New Hampshire 03860
(800) 421-1785, (603) 356-9025, Fax: (603) 356-6081

Innkeepers: *Becky and Charlie Mallar*
Rooms: *16 doubles, 1 suite*
Rates: *Doubles $49-109 (B&B), Suite $99-129 (B&B)*
Payment: *AE, CB, DC, DSC, MC, and VISA*
Children: *Welcome*
Dogs: *Welcome in the off season with prior approval and a nightly fee of $10*
Open: *All year*

The 1785 Inn lies in the heart of the scenic Mount Washington Valley. The house was built by Captain Elijah Dinsmore on a parcel of land that New Hampshire had given him for distinguished service in The Rangers. Ten years later, he realized that this area had growth potential and secured a license to open a "publik house." By the time the tenth New Hampshire turnpike opened in 1803, the inn needed to be expanded. The most logical way was to raise the roof and add a second floor. Although a three-story wing has been added since that time, the inn has retained much of its original character, with exposed hand-hewn beams and a center chimney which links the 200-year-old fireplaces.

Even though the inn is set just off North Conway's rather busy Route 16, the traffic noise is not really a disturbance to guests. Most people are more likely to remember the overflowing window boxes, large flower gardens, and wine cask planters outside the inn. Once inside, a sense of calm prevails, whether in the authentic wood-paneled pub, the cozy living room, or the intimate study. The latter is tucked away behind the main staircase, and offers guests a selection of books, television, VCR, and an extensive video library.

Most of the bedrooms are located upstairs along a meandering hallway that joins the antique section of the inn to the newer three-story wing. Each of the accommodations has a unique charm, with brass, four-poster, and antique beds predominating. These are accented by white wicker tables and chairs interspersed with some country antiques. Old fashioned rose wallpaper in one room contrasts with more contemporary papers in another. Some baths are shared, and others are private, but each is stocked with hand-milled soaps and shampoos. Aside from these guest rooms, the Mallars have also created a more contemporary space off the back of the inn which can accommodate four adults and several children. The living room and eating area, along with outside deck, make this conducive to longer stays. What many guests find they enjoy most about these accommodations are the unsurpassed views of the valley and mountains. These vistas are complemented by another, even more noteworthy aspect — a fabulous restaurant.

In the morning, a full breakfast is offered consisting of items such as French toast, waffles, pancakes, fried or baked eggs, and omelettes, coupled with homemade breads and muffins. We had a hard time selecting which dining room was our favorite — the one located on the glassed-in porch with panoramic views of Mount Washington, or the beamed-ceiling dining room with its own fireplace. We decided breakfast is best enjoyed on the porch, but dinner should be taken in front of the crackling fire. The variety of menu items is quite remarkable for such a small restaurant. Appetizer selections include smoked salmon raviolis with a gruyere cheese sauce, shiitake mushroom caps stuffed with veal and Camembert cheese, and blackened scallops served with a ginger-pineapple salsa. It is rare that we have difficulty selecting an entrée, but at the 1785 Inn everything sounds equally delicious. The sherried rabbit with mushrooms and tomatoes, raspberry duckling, and veal topped with sautéed sundried tomatoes, shiitake mushrooms, and basil might satisfy some, leaving others to ponder such choices as the grilled shrimp on a roasted red pepper puree or the petite filets of beef with a green peppercorn sauce and wild mushrooms. The desserts are also award-winning, as is the extensive wine cellar.

After a satisfying meal, stretching one's legs is almost imperative. There are six acres surrounding the inn, making it easy to walk Bowser there or on some of the adjacent nature trails. There is also a small play area to keep the children amused, as well as a swimming pool. Pinkham Notch is within a short drive of North Conway and has hiking trails and access to the Crystal Cascades and Glen Ellis Falls. Drive south to the Kancamangas Highway, where stops can be made to view and explore around the Champney Falls, the Lower Falls, and Rocky Gorge.

Twin Lake Village

RR1, Box 680
21 Twin Lake Villa Road
New London, New Hampshire   03257
(603) 526-6460

Host: Richard Kidder
Rooms: 1 single, 17 doubles, 5 suites, 17 cottages
Rates: $325-600 per person, per week (AP)
Payment: Personal checks
Children: Welcome (cribs, cots, highchairs, and babysitters are available)
Dogs: Welcome in the cottages with prior approval
Open: Last week of June through the first week of September

Families are always in search of the ultimate vacation. This often means a resort with individual cottages for privacy and all the meals and recreational diversions included in one price so that *every* member can enjoy their vacation. The Twin Lake Village meets all these criteria, and more, by providing affordable, unpretentious lodging and a multitude of activities for all ages. Located in the Dartmouth-Lake Sunapee Region, on over 200 acres of sloping lawns and wooded hills, the assorted houses and cottages scattered over the property have lovely views of Little Lake Sunapee. The Kidder family has owned and operated Twin Lake Village since 1896, which gives them a great deal of insight into the qualities people are looking for in a lake-side vacation.

Travelers will find the main lodge at Twin Lake Village at the top of a private road that wends along the lake. This is a wonderful old building that is reminiscent of a huge expanded farmhouse, including the enormous wraparound porch which fronts the entire length of the first floor. The porch is one of our favorite places at the inn, as it is festooned with colorful rocking chairs and tables that are privy to expansive views of the property. Just down the hill, past rock walls and perennial gardens, guests will encounter the facilities for many of the inn's activities. These include the tennis courts, a putting green, a shuffleboard court, a badminton net, and a baseball diamond. From the edge of one knoll, there is a great view of the nine-hole golf course and the tall pine trees lining the lake. The sandy beach is a delightful place for children to play (unfortunately the beach and boathouse are off-limits to Bowser), while everyone can jump in one of the rowboats, canoes, paddleboats, sailboats, or kayaks, and venture out onto the water.

A supervised Children's Playhouse for two- to five-year olds is open from 9 a.m. to 12 p.m. each day. This gives parents enough time to play golf, hit tennis balls, spend some time with Bowser, or just enjoy a little break in the action before picking their children up for lunch. There are also a plethora of planned activities, ranging from children's dances, bingo, and bridge to picnics, hiking, and boating events.

Anyone staying at the resort is encouraged to enjoy all three meals at the main hotel. These meals are served family-style and focus on simple foods that everyone is certain to enjoy. Breakfast includes all the usual juices, cereals, and hot beverages, along with griddle cakes topped by pure maple syrup and homemade sweet rolls and muffins. Lunch is equally straightforward, and changes daily, along with the rest of the meals. Many guests opt for the box lunches, allowing for greater flexibility in planning their day's activities. Dinner, although by no means formal, is the one time that gentlemen are encouraged to wear sport coats. This multi-course meal is certain to provide a little something for everyone. A sampling of one summer menu included the roast leg of lamb with pan gravy and mint jelly, broiled sirloin steak, and baked salmon with a yogurt-dill sauce. Choices of mashed or boiled potatoes and fresh cauliflower or cooked cut green beans were a few of the available side dishes. As always, the dessert menu is quite extensive and includes coconut oatmeal cookies, butterscotch brownies, and pineapple upside-down cake.

The cottages are the best choice for those traveling with a dog, providing easy access to the outdoors and an exceptional amount of privacy. The cottage sizes vary, and have between two to eight bedrooms. Some of the hillside ones have been winterized, while those located down by the water have not. All of these Victorian-style, shingled cottages were built in the late 1920s and early 1930s, although most have been updated several times since then. The bedrooms often contain a pair of twin beds set amid dark green rattan rockers and other modest but attractive antique furnishings. The knotty pine or dark wood walls are a contrast to the sheer white curtains at the windows and the throw rugs covering the hardwood floors. Wraparound porches offer wonderful places to congregate, as do the cozy living rooms complete with fireplaces. Most of the larger cottages have full kitchens, while some of the smaller ones are equipped with just a hot plate and a refrigerator.

Bowser will certainly find plenty of open spaces to explore on the premises. Most rarely feel a need to leave the resort as it offers so much in the way of canine and human activities. However, those who do venture off site will find plenty of things to do in the nearby area. To the south are the Winslow and Rollins State Parks where there are plenty of hiking trails in the summer and cross-country skiing opportunities in the winter (the resort does have a winterized housekeeping cottage available during the off-season). There are also a number of small ponds nearby, just ask at the front desk to find out which ones are best for those looking for an adventure with their canine cohort.

Lake Shore Farm

Jenness Pond Road
Northwood, New Hampshire 03261
(603) 942-5921

Hosts: Ellis and Eloise Ring
Rooms: 32 doubles
Rates: $50-60 daily per person (AP), $285-300 weekly per person (AP)
Payment: MC and VISA
Children: Welcome (cribs, cots, and babysitters are available)
Dogs: Welcome
Open: May through October

Anyone who has visited the Lake Shore Farm knows it primarily as a low-key family resort — an ideal spot for the budget-minded traveler who is looking for plenty of outdoor diversions, good home-cooking, and a carefree setting. Since 1926, this rambling farmhouse on Jenness Pond has provided an informal, activity-oriented environment, where guests of all ages (as well as Bowser) will find something to keep them thoroughly entertained and amused.

Lake Shore Farm is characterized by its expansive grounds and rambling farmhouse, with its assorted annexes and additions. Those who try to check-in at a front desk will search in vain, as the heart of the farm's operation is in the kitchen. Eloise keeps all of her reservation paperwork on a desk in the back of this room, which allows her to oversee meals while attending to the business of the day. If, for some reason, the Rings are not immediately available, there always seems to be a helpful staff member passing by who will show new arrivals to their rooms.

The accommodations are located throughout the rambling farmhouse. The bed chambers are usually quite spacious, and are simply furnished with maple beds covered by bold floral spreads or patchwork quilts. The well-worn furniture has obviously seen many guests in its day, but seems to fit in nicely with the country farmhouse feeling. The windows, framed by sheer curtains, provide views of the pond or the sprawling grounds. The overall atmosphere is homey, inviting, and very comfortable. Families, or groups of friends, often like to reserve adjoining rooms which usually offer a double and a twin bed configuration. Guests will soon discover, however, that the essence of any vacation here is the time spent outdoors enjoying the abundance of activities offered at the Lake Shore Farm and in the immediate area.

Anyone, or any dog, who is in the mood to climb, can explore neighboring Catamount Mountain or ask about the hiking in the local Blue Hills Mountain Range. Hikers will also enjoy the trails available at either the Bear Brook or Pawtuckaway State Parks. The kitchen staff will pack a box lunch for anyone who decides to leave for the day. We suspect though, that most will be more than happy to stay on the premises. Bowser will certainly want to meander about the grounds and explore all its hidden nooks and crannies, including the duck pond and the adjacent woods. Some people decide to borrow a rowboat or canoe and test their angling skills on Jenness Pond instead. Bowser can relax under a shade tree while his human companions play tennis, pick blueberries, or try their hand at a little pitch and putt. There is also baseball, basketball, volleyball, and badminton. Red wooden lawn chairs are scattered around the property for those who want to put up their feet for awhile and perhaps read a book. If the weather becomes less than favorable, there is an indoor game room, where Ping-Pong, pool, and an assortment of board games are available. Others enjoy snuggling up in front of the fire which is usually blazing in the downstairs fireplace.

The meals at Lake Shore Farm are all served family-style. The various small dining rooms are a bit rustic and contain tables of varying sizes covered with checkered tablecloths. A freshly baked loaf of bread and pitchers of either juice, water, or milk are placed within convenient reach of everyone at the table. The industrial-size kitchen allows the production of delicious home-cooked foods, satisfying even the heartiest appetites. Each week there is also a cookout, followed by a dance or some other activity geared for "children of all ages, six to ninety-six."

The Glen

First Connecticut Lake
Pittsburg, New Hampshire 03592
(800) 445-GLEN, (603) 538-6500, Winter: (508) 475-0559

Hostess: *Betty Falton*
Rooms: *8 doubles, 10 cottages*
Rates: *Doubles $65-70.50 per person (AP), Cottages $75-80 per person (AP)*
Payment: *Personal checks*
Children: *Welcome (highchairs and cribs are available)*
Dogs: *Welcome in the cottages, but not in the lodge*
Open: *May 15 - October 15*

To some people, Pittsburgh is notable because it is the northernmost town in New Hampshire, while others are more impressed with its unusual history. Until the early 1840s, the town was actually part of an independent state known as the Indian Stream Republic. While the United States and Canada spent years sorting out their border problems, the people who lived here decided to take control of the situation and created a government. They operated under their own laws and with their own military for years until an agreement was finally established between the two countries. There is still a strong sense of independence among the 900 or so inhabitants of Pittsburgh and its environs.

What is most compelling about the region is its natural beauty and the fact that it is still largely uninhabited, except for some private fishing and hunting camps. Travelers who really want to get away from it all will be intrigued with The Glen. This 95-year-old lodge was originally a private estate, but for years hunters and fishermen have been using it as a base for their outdoor recreational pursuits. The lodge is located in a clearing that opens to reveal the shoreline of the First Connecticut Lake, the largest in a chain of lakes that begins at the Canadian border. The complex consists of the rustic main lodge and a series of outbuildings, which are either log cabins or more contemporary cottages.

The lodge is the centerpiece for this small community. It is easy to understand why guests like to spend their evenings here, in front of the massive brick fireplace that rises two stories through the beamed, cathedral ceiling. This place is typical of the old-fashioned hunting lodges that are so common throughout the north country of New England. The natural wood paneled walls are festooned with mounted deer heads, while a stuffed bobcat sits perched on the mantel above the fireplace. Wooden camp chairs, lined with comfortable cushions, form a semi-circle around the fireplace. Soft light is cast by an antique wagon wheel chandelier rimmed with lights. An eclectic assortment of country antiques fill in the decorative gaps. Just off the living room, through a pair of French door, is an informal dining room. Here, the lighter knotty pine walls and small brick fireplace provide the backdrop for the fish that have been mounted on the walls and the forests that can be seen through the windows. Small tables are placed about the room, although the meals are all served in a family-style manner. The fare is not gourmet, but it is fresh, homecooked, and hearty. Breakfast is always substantial, while lunch is a bit lighter and often consists of soup, sandwiches, and a dessert. Dinner is certainly the most elaborate meal of the day, commencing with soup and a salad bar, and followed by a meat or fish dish, a potato, vegetable, and a rich homemade dessert.

While Bowser is not allowed to stay in any of the lodge rooms, he is welcome in the cottages. These are found tucked into the woods or along the lake front. Once again, comfort and cleanliness are the watchwords here. Twin or double beds are found in all of the units, each with one or more bedrooms. The living rooms are decorated with old-fashioned sofas and chairs and informal camp furnishings. From the cottage decks, guests are treated to the exquisite colors of the morning sunrise and the afterglow of the evening sunset.

What most come here to do though, is fish, and they rarely leave disappointed. The staff at The Glen can prearrange for fishing and hunting licenses so that upon arrival, guests can begin their fishing vacation without delay. While the small game hunting season is relatively short, October 1 through October 15, the fishing season starts April 1 and runs through October. The lakes are stocked with trout and landlocked salmon, and the rivers are teaming with rainbow and brown trout. Guests may rent one of the boats that are tied to the lodge's dock, or moored on some of the outlying lakes, bogs, and ponds. Anyone who wants assistance in locating the perfect fishing hole, or in determining where to go to catch a specific fish, might consider hiring a guide to help them get the lay of the land. The Glen also serves as a good base for those who would like to go on an overnight camping and fishing expedition to some of the more secluded rivers and streams in the region.

Fishing does not have to be one's primary purpose for vacationing at The Glen. Birders, or anyone with a love for the outdoors, will find an abundance of wildlife to appreciate, study, or photograph. The white birch, maple, and beech trees provide a lacy canopy to the darker backdrop of spruce and firs. Within these woods, people will find gray jays, mourning warblers, thrushes, and white-throated sparrows. Across the lake, loons can be heard calling to one another. Bowser will delight in the miles of back roads, trails, and woods to explore. This truly is the last frontier for people and their dogs seeking the freedom to explore just about anywhere their feet will take them. While there are over 180 acres of land surrounding The Glen, the 1,700-acre Lake Francis State Park is also a short drive from the lodge and provides additional outdoor hiking and recreational opportunities.

We have to stress that a vacation at The Glen is decidedly a simple one, but it is a place where guests and their canine companions can enjoy the unspoiled bounties of nature and leave the details of their day-to-day routine to the staff at the lodge.

Northway House

RFD 1,
Route 3 North
Plymouth, New Hampshire 03264
(603) 536-2838

Hosts: *Micheline and Norman McWilliams*
Rooms: *3 doubles*
Rates: *$30-45 (B&B)*
Payment: *Personal checks*
Children: *Children are welcome*
Dogs: *Welcome with prior approval*
Open: *All year*

Since the mid-1700s, this part of New Hampshire has attracted those with a love of the outdoors. In many ways, little has changed since that time. This is due, in part, to the protected White Mountains which the National Forest Service preserves from development and abuse. Plymouth lies just at the southern edge of the forest, next to the scenic Pemigewasset River which cuts a path through the valley. Plymouth is a bustling community though, its once rural feeling having been replaced in many areas by development. The Northway House, located along rural Route 3 on the outskirts of Plymouth, is a wonderful little B&B that has continued to thrive as more businesses have popped up around it. The quaint little Colonial is quite charming from the exterior, with its white clapboards and black shutters. It is somewhat protected from the road by a grove of spruce and white birch trees and in the warmer months, bird feeders are buzzing with hummingbird activity.

The Northway House has three good-sized guest rooms, each of which is homey and inviting. Traditional papers brighten the walls and area rugs cover the original hardwood floors. The double and single beds (roll-away beds are available) are adorned with white Bates spreads or comforters and white cotton curtains frame the paned windows. The furnishings are simple, with old-fashioned maple bureaus and straight back chairs filling these intimate spaces. Our favorite bedroom is on the front of the house, with a pair of twin beds and ample space to relax. A pretty mahogany secretary rests in one corner of the room. The one shared bathroom is located at the top of the stairs. It is painted a cheery yellow and offers a combination shower/bath complete with nice thick cotton towels.

As pleasant as the accommodations are, we were most enamored with the Northway House because of its friendly hosts. The McWilliams have a gift of being able to make their guests feel instantly comfortable, as if they were long time friends coming for a visit. Most will feel very much at ease settling down with a good book in the living room in front of the warm fire. Others like to take a quiet moment to visit with their affable hosts. Newcomers will learn that many of the McWilliams' guests have been coming here for years, having discovered the B&B when they were visiting their children during parent's weekend at the local boarding schools and college.

Even though the winter weekends can be busy, the summer months draw even more people to the area. During these warm months, guests will discover a vegetable garden and a flower-lined rock wall bordering a good-sized backyard lined by a white split-rail fence. Each morning, weather permitting, guests are invited to take their hearty English breakfast out to the patio. On more inclement days, the dining room and cozy kitchen area serve as backup dining rooms. Norman is very proud of his wife's breakfasts, particularly her Eggs Benedict and stuffed crepes.

After a delightful repast, most are ready to venture out for the day. Plymouth's central location, on the border of the White Mountains and Lakes Region, allows visitors a wide variety of outdoor options. Squam Lake and Lake Winnipesaukee are within a short driving distance of the B&B; however, Franconia Notch is equally close. We doubt that Bowser will care, as long as there are plenty of ways to stretch his legs. After visiting the caves, some might want to check out the waterfalls at the Sculptured Rocks which are located down a gravel road west of Groton and northwest of Newfound Lake. Those who enjoy downhill skiing will find Loon, Cannon, and Waterville Valley easily accessible.

Philbrook Farm Inn

881 North Road
Shelburne, New Hampshire 03581
(603) 466-3831, (603) 466-3428

Innkeepers: *Nancy Philbrook and Constance Leger*
Rooms: *1 single, 18 doubles, 7 cottages*
Rates: *Single $75-90 (MAP), Doubles $105-135 (MAP), Cottages $500 per week (EP)*
Payment: *Personal checks*
Children:*Well-behaved children are welcome (cribs, cots, and highchairs are available)*
Dogs: *Welcome in the cottages*
Open: *May 1 to October 31 and December 26 to March 31*

In 1853, Susannah and Harvey Philbrook purchased a 19-year old farm in a secluded and scenic part of northern New Hampshire. Ahead of their time, they thought vacationers would also be attracted to this unspoiled region and so they began to ready the property for guests. After renovating some of the outbuildings and constructing an addition, the Philbrook Farm Inn opened in 1861. Sometime during the 1890s, the inn passed into the hands of Augustus and Alice Philbrook, Augustus being the youngest son of Susannah and Harvey. Unfortunately, his wife died soon after having their children, leaving Augustus to run the inn with his Aunt Fannie. Augustus' youngest son Lawrence, and his wife Helen, carried on the innkeeping tradition, and were responsible for constructing the seven cottages. Of their three daughters, Nancy and Connie are still here today, as fourth generation innkeepers, assisted by Ann and Larry Levine, who are Connie's children.

It is unusual for us to give readers the entire history an inn's ownership; however, in this case it is the tapestry of one family which provides the Philbrook Farm Inn with its unique character. Visitors usually feel an immediate connection to the many generations of Philbrooks and Legers. For many, the inn has become a tradition in their own families, with guests often booking the cottages and inn rooms a year in advance, so that they may continue to enjoy their hosts' gracious hospitality and the inn's refreshing simplicity.

After leaving scenic Route 2, new arrivals wend along back country roads for a few minutes before rounding a corner and coming upon the gracious old inn. This huge, white shingled and green shuttered farmhouse has four separate wings with verandas, a glassed-in porch, and a multitude of dormer windows set in the third floor eaves. In the summertime, vibrant perennials overflow from beds which run the entire length of the building. Chairs placed about the expansive lawn offer some of the best unobstructed views of the Carter-Moriah and Presidential mountain ranges. Those visiting in the off-season, can take in these same views from the the warmth of the glassed-in porch.

We have visited the Philbrook Farm Inn many times over the years and are always warmly greeted. On one occasion, during the off-season, we found Nancy braiding rugs and on another, she was busy helping Connie bake bread for the guests. The smell of baked goods is only one of the endearing aspects about the inn, another is the cozy and inviting rooms where guests can make themselves feel right at home. The original living room of the house has shelves packed with books, paintings adorning the walls, and even an award-winning photograph. A small fireplace warms guests as they converse with one another or with one of their hosts. Well-worn hardwood floors lead from this room into either the sunny library, with its comfortable antique furnishings, or to the cavernous living room. The latter was the original dining room for the inn; however, it is now filled with small card tables, a piano, and an abundance of puzzles and games. This is a quiet place where guests can visit, read, or perhaps play a little bridge. Slightly more energetic offerings, such as Ping-pong and billiards, are available in another section of the house.

Upstairs, on the second and third floors, guests will find a variety of traditionally furnished bedrooms; however, those traveling with Bowser will be staying in the cottages. These storybook houses were built by Augustus Philbrook at the turn of the century. Nancy laughingly claims that he was probably the founder of the time-share concept, as he built them for specific families who would come up for the entire summer. In order to ensure they would be well-utilized, he asked the families to sign a 99-year lease in which they would agree to rent the cottages each summer or else find someone else who would. Although most guests do not have the luxury of spending two months in New Hampshire, they do book the cottages for a week at a time — 99-year leases are optional! Several of these buildings are located next to the inn, alongside a brook. Others are set into the hillside, and provide additional privacy and expansive views of the valley below. The cottages vary not only in size, but also in the number of bedrooms and bathrooms. The four housekeeping cottages offer kitchens and living rooms, and anywhere from three to five bedrooms, making them perfect for a family or a number of couples who want to vacation together.

Couples who want the privacy of a cottage, but who don't require a multitude of bedrooms, can stay in either The Shack or The Casino. The first is a quaint log cabin with a queen-size bed and romantic fireplace, while the latter offers a similar configuration, but comes with both screened and open porches. The decor in all the cottages is simple, with hand-braided throw rugs covering the hardwood floors and walls that are either brightly painted or papered in cheerful old-fashioned floral prints. The comfortable furnishings include overstuffed couches and both wicker and bentwood rocking chairs, set around the fireplaces or woodstoves. Guests are certain to enjoy the mix of country antiques and traditional reproductions. We found the cottages to be delightful, and are only sorry they aren't winterized so they could be enjoyed all year.

Even though most of the cottages have kitchens, everyone is invited to dine at the main house. The dining room is quite spacious, with wood-paneled walls and a number of pine tables surrounded by Windsor chairs. One entree is offered each night. Lamb, pork, or beef roasts are the specialties of the inn, as well as roast chicken and baked haddock. These are complemented by freshly picked vegetables from the garden. Even the desserts and pastries are made fresh daily. The inn does not have a bar; however, guests are welcome to bring their own libations.

One of the many appealing things about the Philbrook Farm Inn are the number of activities available on the property that should appeal to Bowser (and an energetic companion). There are over 1,000 acres of trails that are owned and maintained by the inn, some of which connect with the Appalachian Trail. An outdoor pool is perfect for humans, but Bowser might be more interested in taking a dip in a mountain pool or stream. Quiet country roads are ideal for after-dinner walks, while open fields and lawns allow for an impromptu game of catch with Bowser. Badminton, shuffleboard, and horseshoes, are also welcome human diversions.

Those who do decide to stay at the Philbrook Farm Inn will not only enjoy the wonderfully diverse yet simple surroundings, but also experience the hospitality of their hosts, who truly treat their guests as though they were an extension of their own family. The feeling of the family about their inn can best be summed up in a quote that appears at the bottom of their letterhead, "Located in the beautiful Androscoggin Valley under the shadow of the White Mountains, where the welcome mat really says 'Welcome' and the latch-string is always out for those seeking peace, quiet, and contentment in a world turned upside down."

The Hiltop Inn

Main Street (Route 117)
Sugar Hill, New Hampshire 03585
(800) 770-5695, (603) 823-5695

Innkeepers: Meri and Mike Hern
Rooms: 6 doubles, 1 suite
Rates: Doubles $70-100 (B&B), $150-170 (MAP), Suite $100-120 (B&B), $180 (MAP)
Payment: DSC, MC, and VISA
Children: Welcome (cribs are available - $5 per night)
Dogs: Welcome for a $10 per night fee. The Herns have a dog and cat, so guests' dogs must
*   be well-behaved and friendly around other animals.*
Open: All year

The picturesque village of Sugar Hill has preserved a sense of timelessness in a way which sets it apart from many New England towns. Despite its location in the heart of the White Mountains just minutes from terrific downhill skiing and incredible hiking, it has somehow managed to ward off any hint of commercialism. This community has held onto its rural heritage, preserving its historic private homes, assorted country inns, pristine white church, and storybook country store. Travelers approaching the inn will climb a steep, narrow road before emerging on Sugar Hill. The views anywhere in town are spectacular, but perhaps the finest of these can be enjoyed from The Hilltop Inn. Since 1895, almost without exception, the sprawling homestead has been a guest house. Its most recent incarnation has been with the Herns, who for the last ten years have replumbed, rewired, and restored this Victorian house, turning it into one of our favorite inns. What attracts us, and others, to the inn is the warmth, humor, and easy-going nature of Mike and Meri.

While we have always liked it here, we found it even more captivating during our most recent visit. As with a fine wine, the inn has developed a complexity over the years giving it a character both mellow and comforting. The familiar things, like the antique button door handles (rather than twisting the handle, one just pushes the button in the middle of the knob to open the door), English flannel sheets on the antique beds, and the wonderful food are all endearing. The intimate dining room still offers breathtaking views from its many windows and has many newly added, yet subtle, amenities as well. A silver tea service is set out on the sideboard in the dining room, with Mike's vast cork collection resting in a huge clay pot on the floor next to it. The centerpiece of the front parlor is a brass daybed adorned with a pink and green antique patchwork quilt, a multitude of pillows, and a number of whimsical patchwork animals who have taken up residence here. A collection of family pictures fills the tables, Victorian lace curtains frame the windows, and, the newest addition, a red enameled Vermont Castings stove, warms the room. Meri said that with the addition of the stove, guests spend even more time in the parlor reading, visiting, and occasionally dipping into the vast video library for a good movie.

A curved staircase leads from the parlor to the upstairs bedrooms. At the top, a stained glass window casts a multitude of colors over the creaky hardwood floors. A push of the button on the door handle, allows guests to enter each charming bedroom. Each chamber has a distinct personality. One has blue floral wallpaper serving as a backdrop for the brass and white iron bed brimming with pillows and covered with a quilt. The sunny front room is one of our favorites, with pretty hillside views and another brass and iron double bed adorned with a quilt. For those requiring a little extra space and privacy, there is the spacious suite at the end of the hall. Here, the burgundy and hunter green color scheme blends with the mahogany stained wood walls to create an attractive space. Guests walk into a small sitting area with a sofa, and then step down into a huge bedroom dominated by a king-size bed covered in a patchwork quilt. A basket of towels is set amid the Victorian antiques. As with all the other bedrooms, it is the attention to detail that makes these accommodations so unique. In one room, a mirrored antique bureau has delicate ribbons tied to it, and sprays of dried eucalyptus and roses are found above the lace covered windows. Glasses and mints are placed on a small dish. Light might emanate from the lamp shades decorated with dried flowers or from candlelight. Paddle fans turn overhead, providing a gentle breeze on still summer days. Over the years, Mike has renovated all of the bathrooms and even added a few more, giving each room a private bath stocked with plenty of thick towels, glycerin soaps, and shampoos.

In the morning, hot coffee is set out in the breakfast room for early risers (very early risers are given instructions on how to make it themselves). As guests go for refills, they will notice a handwritten note outlining the weather forecast, allowing them to plan their day's activities over breakfast. At a reasonable hour, a full breakfast is served which features a number of excellent choices. During our visit, guests could choose from the apple-cinnamon French toast with pure maple or berry syrup along with bacon, bagels, and fresh fruit. Other offerings include a souffle or eggs and smoked salmon. During the peak foliage season, guests are treated to dinner as well. The menu is constantly changing, but a sample might include the Hilltop paella with chicken, shrimp and homemade sausage, a filet of salmon garnished with shrimp, asparagus, and hollandaise, or the veal baked with lobster, artichoke hearts, and tarragon cream. A full complement of wine, beer, and other spirits serves to enhance the meal. Mike and Meri have been catering for years, and anyone who has sampled their dinners will testify to their culinary expertise.

Among all the inns we review, the Hilltop Inn is one of the most conducive for guests traveling with a dog. The Herns have even gone so far as to put a helpful information sheet in the room (with a biscuit of course), so that Bowser's companions can make the most of the visit from a dog's point of view. The little tidbits of advice range from "You may walk your dog pretty much anywhere along Rte 117 or in our fields. The neighbors all love animals," to "Please let us know if your dog may have people scraps or dog treats (remember they're on vacation too), as we have been known to spoil them!" There are plenty of open spaces to explore in the immediate area, as well as numerous hiking trails that run through the White Mountains National Park. Franconia State Park also has dog walking areas and plenty of hiking trails. In the winter months, Bowser is welcome to go on a cross-country ski tour along the many trails that are adjacent to the inn. But best of all, Bowser is certain to feel right at home with people as gracious and hospitable as Meri and Mike Hern.

Dexter's Inn and Tennis Club

P.O. Box 703
Stagecoach Road
Sunapee, New Hampshire 03782
(800) 232-5571, (603) 763-5571

Innkeepers: *Holly and Michael Durfor*
Rooms: *17 doubles, 1 cottage*
Rates: *Doubles $130-170 (MAP), Holly Cottage $375 (EP), Children are an additional $35 per day when sharing room with their parents*
Payment: *Cash or personal checks are preferred, however DSC, MC and VISA accepted.*
Children: *Welcome (cribs - $5 daily, cots, highchairs and babysitters are available)*
Dogs: *Welcome in the annex or Holly Cottage for $10 per night. "Pet policy: Dogs are not allowed in any of the public rooms, main house, terrace, or pool area. They are to be leashed at all times. We would appreciate it if their constitutionals were taken in the meadows below the parking area."*
Open: *May - October*

Dexter's Inn is located atop a 1,400-foot New Hampshire hill with incredible views of the distant mountains and surrounding lakes. The main house was built in 1803 by Adam Reddington, who was well known for the wooden bowls he carved to hold ships' compasses. Although he was a fine craftsman, the house fell into disrepair over the course of that century, so that when Samuel Crowther, a famous economist and financial adviser to Herbert Hoover, purchased it in 1930 it had much work that needed to be done. Crowther completely refurbished the home, giving equal attention to the grounds, resurrecting the stone walls, gardens, and overgrown lawns. In 1948, Dexter and Genelle Richards purchased the property and started the innkeeping tradition that continues to this day. Since 1969, the inn has thrived under the watchful eyes of the Simpson family. Holly Simpson-Durfor and her husband Michael are the current innkeepers and have been running Dexter's Inn since 1987.

A narrow road leads from Sunapee up a steep hill to the yellow clapboard and black-shuttered inn. A tiny parking area with stone walls is convenient for unloading the car and checking in. The interior of the main inn rambles along in typical farmhouse fashion. There is an appealing formal living room which has been furnished with pale blue and coral chintz-covered sofas and chairs. A fireplace warms this inviting space, with its floor-to-ceiling bookshelves well-stocked with reading material and collectibles. Double French doors lead outside to the screened-in porch where guests can take in the valley views. Connecting the dining room with the living room is a long, wide passage lined with windows that overlook the patio and terraced grounds. Skylights make this a particularly sunny place where people often relax on the red velvet Victorian furnishings. The shelves that line the passage hold a variety of bird and hornet nests, along with a complement of Dexter's Inn mugs, shirts, and other paraphernalia that are for sale.

The dining room is fairly informal (no jackets are required but guests are asked to dress appropriately) and offers excellent cuisine. Prime seating is found at the tables located in front of, and close to, the bay window with its spectacular 180 degree views of the valley and mountains. Nicely prepared and presented entrée selections include a seafood pasta, red snapper, pork tenderloin, chicken picatta, and prime rib, as well as nightly specials. The main course is always enhanced by homemade soups, breads, and desserts. After dinner, many people retire to the informal library and game room found at the back of the house. Here, a fieldstone fireplace is well-stoked on cool nights. A bright green sofa adds a spot of color to the naturally paneled wooden walls in this room. Tables are set up for those who might want to play cards or a board game, while a television in an adjacent chamber, offers additional entertainment.

Bowser and friends are welcome in the annex, which is actually a converted horse barn. Rough-hewn beams and wallboards have been left exposed, revealing sections of the original barn. The Norman Arluck Room (an informal recreation area) appears to have been the old tack room. This cavernous chamber is large enough to easily hold bumper pool, Foosball, and Ping-pong tables, a television, and an eclectic collection of wall hangings. The latter runs the gamut from a mounted deer's head to snowshoes and wagon wheels. The bedrooms are located on the ground level of the original barn, in the wing, or Up The Hill (on the second floor). Each room is simply decorated and comfortably furnished. Traditional Bates spreads rest on twin or queen beds, and walls are papered with a variety of floral prints. One chamber is especially appropriate for guests with a dog, as it has a second private entrance which opens onto a small patio encircled by a rock wall, with an even larger yard just beyond it. In the morning, when juice and coffee are brought to the room, guests can enjoy it on their patio or by a sunny window.

The grounds keepers are kept very busy at Dexter's Inn. The flower beds are brilliant with color, the sprawling lawns are beautifully groomed, and the stone walls are covered with ivy. Mature shade trees surrounding the inn's patio provide a respite from the summer sun. Just beyond the patio, are the three tennis courts and large pool surrounded by hedges. Several hammocks are well-placed for relaxation and privacy. The tennis house doubles as the center for lawn games (croquet, horseshoes, volleyball, and shuffleboard), and even contains a few wooden tennis rackets. During the height of the summer, guests can enjoy the full tennis program with a pro setting up matches, as well as offering junior clinics, private lessons, and a 'stroke of the day' clinic. Some of the more interesting residents at the inn are the Scottish Highland cattle, who do their part to keep the grass and brush trimmed in the surrounding fields.

There are activities galore for dogs and their energetic owners. The inn is located on an unpaved country road that does not get a lot of traffic. Take Bowser over to visit the Durfor's pets — Scottish Highland cattle who answer to the names Alvin, Annie, and Carolyn. There are plenty of open spaces for entertaining Bowser right on the premises. Farther afield, there are also excellent hiking trails in any of the nearby state parks. Mount Sunapee State Park offers hiking, although dogs are not allowed during their annual Arts and Crafts Festival. Mount Kearsarge is another great spot for hiking, containing both the Rollins and Winslow State Parks.

The Tamworth Inn

P.O. Box 189
Main Street
Tamworth, New Hampshire   03886
(800) 642-7352, (800) NH 2-RELAX, (603) 323-7721

Innkeepers: *Phil and Kathy Bender*
Rooms: *11 doubles, 4 suites*
Rates: *Doubles $110-130 (MAP), $85-105 (B&B),*
         Suites $130-160 (MAP), $105-130 (B&B)
Payment: *MC and VISA*
Children: *Well-behaved children are welcome, and "must be under parental supervision*
         at all times." (Highchairs, cribs, cots, and babysitters are available)
Dogs: *Welcome with advance notice and prior approval, must be leashed in the inn and*
         not left unattended in the room. A $5 daily fee is charged.
Open: *May 1 to November 1 and November 15 to March 31*

The Tamworth Inn is unique for several reasons. The first being that it was actually built as an inn in 1833. Most of New England's historic inns were originally private homes, but The Tamworth Inn has always been, and most likely always will be, a country inn. As a result, some of the quirky architectural modifications most buildings undergo in their conversion to inns are noticeably absent here. Just as The Tamworth Inn has remained relatively unchanged for over 160 years, so has the mountain village of Tamworth. White-washed buildings, a general store, and a pristine New England church are beautifully preserved. Across from the inn is a small park and open fields, while just behind it is the scenic Swift River and several acres of manicured lawns.

Although the three-story Victorian inn, complete with a mansard roof and tower, is large and rambling from the exterior, the interior has plenty of charming nooks, crannies, and alcoves. The first floor consists of several dining rooms, a library, a sitting room, and an English pub. While the inn obviously offers lovely accommodations, most remember the wonderful cuisine. The dining rooms are located in three different areas, with the glassed-in porch and its unobstructed views serving as the most popular choice during the summer months. In the winter, the favorite dining room offers the romantic combination of firelight and candlelight. The menu changes seasonally with appetizers ranging from hardwood smoked trout served with a cranberry horseradish sauce, to a provolone, pesto, and garlic cream terrine. A tenderloin of beef and the roast duckling are drizzled with the chef's special sauce and, the roast pork tenderloin is topped with an apple cider sauce and accompanied by an apple walnut cornbread stuffing. Save a bit of room for the house specialty, a profiterole for two, or the chocolate walnut pie that is topped with ice cream and hot fudge.

While some might feel energized after a filling meal, most guests are content to retire to the intimate sitting room, where they can play chess, converse, or read in front of the fire. As with much of the inn, this space is filled with a variety of formal American antiques and good quality reproductions. Braided rugs, complementing the Williamsburg blue walls, are scattered along the hardwood floors. Down the hall, guests will discover a separate library offering shelves of books, a television, and VCR. One of our favorite places though, is the traditional English pub that lies to the rear of the inn. Here, dark wood walls are festooned with the Benders' sled collection, and tiny multicolored Christmas lights create a festive environment all year.

Upstairs there are a variety of bedrooms where guests will feel comfortable. They have all been decorated differently, utilizing attractive country antiques that the Benders have collected over the years. One of the more popular chambers is the pink room, which reminded us of a young child's bedroom with its pale pink and white striped paper, antique baby clothes, and other children's paraphernalia. The one thing about this chamber that is not childlike is the king-size bed, which is made up of two antique brass beds pushed together. Another room has a high antique bed with a pretty Vermont quilt draped over it. At the top of the stairs, on the second floor, is a spacious bedroom done in a rich burgundy with another handmade quilt on the bed. All of the bedrooms are quite intimate and are filled with a multitude of treasures. After a good night's rest, guests meander downstairs to a tantalizing full breakfast. On Sunday, the champagne brunch is always a hit with dishes such as Eggs Benedict, Belgian waffles, and a variety of crepes topping the menu.

Although The Tamworth Inn is located in a quiet country village, this does not mean that it lacks for cultural diversions. In the summer, visitors can get tickets to an evening performance at Barnstormers, which has been offering fine summer stock for the last 64 years (also making it the oldest summer theater in the country). During the day, people will find plenty of things to do in the area. Some choose to explore the Big Pines Nature Preserve has ample walking trails and access to the Swift River. The hiking is also quite good along the trails in the White Lake State Park. A few minutes north of Tamworth is the Hemenway State Forest which provides scenic walking trails. There are also a number of small lakes in the area, including Lake Chocorua, Silver Lake, and Hill Pond. At the end of a busy summer's day, the inn's swimming pool is available for a cool dip, or guests may relax in the hammock down by the river. A gazebo also provides the perfect spot for sipping lemonade and sampling freshly baked goodies. In the winter months, the focus obviously shifts to skiing. Downhill slopes are close to the inn; however, anyone traveling with Bowser might opt for a day of cross-country skiing or even snowshoeing on some of the AMC trails.

Regardless of the season, guests always receive a warm welcome from their hosts. Usually waiting to greet incoming guests are the inn's house cat and dog who concur with the Benders when they say, "accommodations for your pet can be made at the Inn if your pets are as nice as you are."

The Spalding Inn

Mountain View Road
Whitefield, New Hampshire 03598
(800) 368-VIEW, (603) 837-2572, Fax (603) 837-3062

Owners: *Diane Edwards Cockrell and Michael Flinder*
Rooms: *36 doubles, 4 suites, 6 cottages*
Rates: *Doubles and suites $99-109 (B&B), $147-175 (MAP), 1-4 Bedroom cottages*
   $395-770 per week (EP)
Payment: *MC and VISA*
Children: *Welcome (cribs, cots, highchairs, and babysitters are available)*
Dogs: *Welcome in the cottages with advance notification and prior approval*
Open: *Mid-June to Mid-October*

Those who are familiar with The Spalding Inn might still consider it to be a part of another era, primarily catering to an older clientele. This might have been true in the past, but times are changing and so is the inn. The Spalding family owned and operated the inn for over 60 years and developed, during that time, quite a reputation for their gracious hospitality and abundance of activities. But as so often happens with many great old summer resorts, it became difficult for them to continue to maintain their traditions and the overall quality of the inn. During our last visit, in the early 1990s, the former hosts were in the midst of updating the inn to make it attractive to a wider clientele. Soon thereafter, The Spalding Inn was sold to Diane and Michael who have not only managed to maintain the time-honored traditions, but also have started to add some pizazz to the grounds, the facilities, and the restaurant. Returning guests might not immediately notice these changes, but Diane, her daughter April, and Michael are beginning to make their mark.

The resort rests on 200 spectacular acres, which is a combination of wetlands, mountain views, and manicured grounds. The lawns and gardens surrounding the main building, carriage house, and assorted cottages are meticulously maintained. During our most recent visit, the perennial gardens were being put to bed for the winter by the resident horticulturist, Esther Pott. She was busy removing old plants and adding new ones. Esther told us that when she arrived, the once beautiful perennial gardens were severely overgrown, and that she has spent the last two years bringing them back to their original stature. Even in the fall, we could tell that with the return of spring, the gardens would once again be exquisite.

The dark brown, shingled inn still provides a wonderful backdrop for the gardens and the circular drive. With its expansive porch, awnings, and gables, it resembles some of the great country summer houses. Many new arrivals enjoy relaxing on the glassed-in porch, located just off the foyer. This is a casual space, where children and adults can play board games, read books, or settle into a game of chess. This is also where we first began to notice some of the changes at the inn, most notably a whimsical stuffed bunny that was jauntily tucked into a chair.

Just beyond the porch, there is an intimate reception area and an attractive common room. Traditional sofas and hunter green and red patterned wing chairs flank a large fieldstone fireplace. Built-in shelves, trimmed with bulls-eye molding, hold a variety of books. This is one of our favorite common areas at the inn, as much for the family pictures which dot the tables as for the inviting nature of the room. Heading further into the inn, guests will discover the elegant living room and card room. The pale pink and green color schemes are as appealing on the walls as they are in the fabrics covering the sofas and wing chairs. The rich patina of the English antiques and grand piano resting on Oriental rugs, complete the effect. White box-beamed ceilings supported by pillars separate the sitting areas from one another, allowing guests to enjoy their afternoon tea collectively or to have a quiet visit in private. We have always been fond of the equally formal card room situated just beyond the living room. This bright green and white garden room offers plenty of card tables, as well as a small television for guests to watch.

We know that Diane and Michael have been busy sprucing up the guest rooms, in fact they even mention in their newsletter that they are willing to barter work for room nights with anyone willing to do carpentry, painting, stenciling, and even wallpapering. Regardless of who is actually doing the work, their sophisticated and charming sense of style and color is already quite evident in the guest rooms in both the Main Inn and Carriage House. Guests traveling with a dog are welcome in the cottages, that lie on the other side of the tiny dirt road.

These accommodations have not been touched in years, but still manage to retain their 1950s charm. Guests can request a cottage with one to four bedrooms. The resort is perfectly set up to handle families or groups of friends, as many of the rooms connect with a central living room and some even offer functional kitchenettes. Some bedrooms have relatively contemporary wallpapers, while a few are painted white, and still others are decorated with old-fashioned floral papers. White Bates or chenille spreads cover the maple beds. In the living rooms, comfortable sofas, deep armchairs, and Windsor chairs are placed around the fieldstone fireplaces. One living room was furnished with just the basics, and another had a tiny child's wooden chair and table as well as a huge kitchen table covered with a red and white gingham tablecloth. The one word that comes to mind when describing the furnishings is sturdy, although there are some country antiques mixed in as well. We found the overall decor quite appealing, however, in an old-fashioned sort of way. The tiled bathrooms were well stocked with Saks Fifth Avenue soaps, body gels, and shampoos. Sliding doors open to small patios or screened-in porches.

Very few guests come here to spend their days in their rooms though, because most are drawn to the abundance of athletic diversions and spectacular natural beauty of the grounds. There are four clay tennis courts (complete with a resident pro), a heated swimming pool, and one of the finest lawn bowling facilities in New England. Many people are also attracted to the golf, with a nine-hole, par-3 golf course and 18-hole putting green right on the premises. There are also four golf courses in the vicinity of the inn. In the fall, upland game shooting still attracts a large number of vacationers. Michael has even worked out an agreement with the Alderbrook Sportsman Club allowing his guests to receive skeet and trap shooting instruction. Bowser will stay quite busy as there is plenty of property to explore and an assortment of walking trails that have been subtly cut through some of the more overgrown portions of the property. Guests often comment on the magnificent views of the surrounding mountains when out on these expeditions. They are also apt to come across one of the three resident Brittany spaniels that Diane owns.

There are plenty of ways to work up a healthy appetite here, and a fabulous restaurant to assuage one's hunger pangs. The dining room is very attractive, with hunter green carpeting, tables covered with yellow and green chintz fabrics, white overlays, and sparkling glasses and china. In the evening, the soft candlelight sets the mood for the constantly changing menu. Aside from the homemade soups and salads prepared from locally grown greens (often picked from the herb garden just off the Carriage House), there are also a variety of delectable entrées. The traditional favorites, such as the Long Island duck with Bombay sauce, seafood newburg, and veal marsala, are interspersed with Japanese sesame chicken, pasta primavera, and vegetarian raviolis. Dessert and coffee mark the end to a wonderful meal, while in the distance the setting sun casts soft colors over New Hampshire's Presidential Range.

Perhaps the one phrase that most appropriately summarizes the new attitude and energy at the Spalding Inn is the framed quote found just inside the entrance to the inn: "Here on this quiet hill beneath the sky, let all your cares slip noiselessly away. Here, drink of magic that shall lift you high and cleanse your spirit of the earth's dismay."

Stepping Stones Bed & Breakfast

RFD 1, Box 208
Bennington Battle Trail
Wilton Center, New Hampshire 03086
(603) 654-9048

Hostess: *D. Ann Carlsmith*
Rooms: *3 doubles*
Rates: *$45-50*
Payment: *Personal checks*
Children: *Welcome (crib and/or futon is $10 per night)*
Dogs: *Welcome if they are under control and stay out of the gardens*
Open: *All year*

The historic rural village of Wilton Center lies at the end of a winding road lined with mature trees, ribbons of stone walls, and beautiful 200-year-old houses. At the crest of a hill is the village center which is comprised of a Unitarian Church, a handful of lovely homes, Andy's Summer Playhouse (a children's theater), and a rambling auction barn. Just as the road begins a turn to the right, travelers will spot a small sign for the Bennington Battle Trail and the Stepping Stones Bed & Breakfast.

The B&B is surrounded by tiered perennial gardens and dense woods. A stone walkway leads to the summer porch decorated with dried wreaths that Ann makes. Constanza (named after Mozart's wife), Ann's friendly dog, is usually around and anxious to play with guests and their canine cohorts. Most enter the house by way of the breakfast room and kitchen. This is our favorite chamber and, as Ann informed us, everyone else's as well. Huge skylights and a wall of windows lighten the kitchen, while hanging plants and vases of fresh flowers add touches of color to the contemporary country decor. In the wintertime, a wood stove supplements the heat created by the passive solar windows.

Although Ann's passion is gardening (she studied at Radcliffe and obtained a landscape design certificate in 1985), guests will also notice reminders of her other love, weaving, scattered around the house. She has been weaving all of her adult life, and produces beautiful throw rugs along with shawls and blankets. Ann spends the quiet winter months weaving and waiting for the first signs of spring when she can begin tending to her gardens and welcoming new and returning guests.

The guest chambers are easily accessed by way of a rather steep back staircase, or from the more gracious front stairs. The latter has decorative woven blankets draped over the banister. The three upstairs bed chambers are decorated in cheery yellows and greens. Each is filled with unusual, yet traditional, pieces of furniture. A tiny, wooden crib is tucked into one corner of the only room with a double bed. The walls in another space are adorned with attractive framed prints of plants and herbs, reflective of Ann's botanical interests. The beds are covered with down comforters and handwoven rugs grace the floors. The queen-bedded room has a private bath and a chair that unfolds into a single futon bed, ideal for small children. All the bedrooms have lovely views of the surrounding woods and gardens, although Ann creates her own indoor gardens by leaving fresh bouquets of flowers in all the chambers. A modern bathroom is found at the end of the hallway.

The morning meal is always "complimentary, filling, and bountiful, " and is served in the sunny breakfast room. It includes everything from overstuffed omelettes and Belgian waffles with black raspberry syrup to cheese strata and French toast with real maple syrup. Copious amounts of fresh fruit round out this repast. A lighter breakfast of fresh fruit, juice, and coffee cake is also offered. Some enjoy taking this meal, or at least their coffee and tea, out to either the back deck or terrace, both of which offer great views of the grounds. Ann's gardens literally wend around her antique settler's house. They are informal and lush, filled with all sorts of treasures that any horticulturist would find intriguing. But to even the most casual observer, this is a magical place that is ideal for quiet contemplation.

Although Bowser is not allowed to explore the gardens, there are still plenty of interesting adventures to be found in Wilton Center. One walk will lead to a local waterfall, while another to a hiking trail. The center of Wilton is very quiet, tucked up on a hill and well off any main road. The Miller State Park offers some recreational facilities and welcomes visitors with dogs. Temple Mountain is also a good choice for summer hiking, and an even better choice for wintertime cross-country skiing. We have found though, that even with all of the nearby recreational opportunities, most guests are just as happy to stay close to the peaceful Stepping Stones B&B.

Maine

Green Hill Farm

RR1, Box 328
Ashville, Maine   04607
(207) 422-3273

Hosts: Nuna and Ted Cass
Rooms: 2 doubles
Rates: $40-45 (B&B)
Payment: Personal checks
Children: Those "under crawling age and over 7 are welcome" as the house is not
*   child-proofed*
Dogs: "Obedient dogs welcome" with prior approval provided they are leashed out of doors
Open: March 15 - October 15 primarily, other times of year with advance reservations

Anyone who has traveled Maine's scenic coastal highways and byways will surely appreciate the pastoral seaside setting of Ashville. This rural hamlet is located between Mount Desert Island and Acadia National Park, overlooking Frenchman's Bay. Travelers turn off Route 1 and onto a country road to reach the charming Green Hill Farm. The bed and breakfast rests on 35 acres, but immediately surrounding the Colonial house are lovely perennial gardens and rock walls. Although most people are anxious to get inside, Bowser might want to spend a few moments visiting with the resident animals. A loveable Angora rabbit is usually resting in its hutch next to the garage. One recent visitor thought it so adorable that she assumed it was a stuffed animal, that had been placed in the hutch for effect. She was quite startled a few days later when she noticed it moving around! Another small pen houses a few sheep. After investigating the animal menagerie, most new arrivals head off to find the affable Nuna.

The homestead at Green Hill Farm was built in 1818 by, appropriately enough, Green Hill. In the same year that he built his house, he also married Louisa Taft. They made this their home and had children. Their children had children who, in turn, continued to farm the land and hold onto the property until they sold it to the Casses in 1985. While the old pastures are mostly overgrown with hardhack, alder, and tamarack, the house has been thoughtfully restored and beautifully maintained, retaining most of its historic integrity. As they worked on the house, the Casses discovered that someone had converted the former center chimney Colonial in 1865, putting in parlor stoves instead.

As is the case with many New England homes, a sidedoor leads into a "mud" room which opens into a country kitchen. Although there is a cozy and inviting sitting room just off this space, we spent most of our time in the kitchen chatting with Nuna. Once we tore ourselves away from the lively conversation, we were able to explore the rest of the house. A hallway leads to the front door, and a small foyer where we saw a pretty grandfather clock set in the corner. Ascending the central staircase, we couldn't help but notice how the use of pastel colors and vibrant dhurrie rugs seemingly brought additional light into the house. The original, hardwood floors are still intact, and country collectibles fill virtually every nook and cranny. There are two upstairs bedrooms. One has a queen bed adorned with a colorful comforter, while the other chamber offers a pair of twin beds. These bedrooms have been decorated in keeping with the style found in the rest of the house. While the rooms are good-sized and bright, the ceilings are just 6'6", giving some of the taller guests reason to duck occasionally. We, however, especially like the cozy, intimate feeling created by the low ceilings and dormers.

Guests can depend on a terrific breakfast to start the day. They may create their own meal, or choose between pancakes, eggs, and waffles. These are always accompanied by fresh fruit, homemade muffins and breads, juice, and coffee or tea. Well-fortified for a morning of exploring, many guests head off to Acadia National Park. There, they can enjoy scenic vistas, terrific hiking opportunities, and even a little sailing, canoeing, or kayaking. This is a beautiful and unspoiled part of the Maine coast. From Ashville it is an easy drive onto the Schoodic Peninsula, where travelers will want to follow the Shore Road, which is lined on one side by the rocky shore and on the other by dense forests. Winter Harbor is a good spot to stop for lunch and let Bowser walk while his companions windowshop in this intimate seaside village. The Schoodic section of Acadia National Park is found near Winter Harbor, where visitors may drive along a road that takes them out and around Schoodic Peninsula. There are many breathtaking vistas and great hikes all through the park. Just ask the rangers for advice on where to go and what to do when visiting. There is also a handful of classic lighthouses that can be found in this area.

The Driftwood Inn

Washington Avenue
Bailey Island, Maine 04003
(207) 833-5461

Innkeepers: Barbara and Charles Conrad
Rooms: 8 singles, 16 doubles, 5 housekeeping cottages
Rates: Singles $45-50 (EP), Doubles $60-70 (EP), Cottages $385-475 per week (EP)
Payment: Personal checks
Children: Welcome (cribs and cots are available)
Dogs: Welcome with advance notice in the housekeeping cottages
Open: Mid-May to mid-October

Those who have never heard of Bailey Island will be pleasantly surprised to find that even though it is easily accessible, it remains somewhat exclusive and relatively uninhabited because of its size — only one and a quarter square miles. We always enjoy driving down the winding coastal road and across the small bridges to the inn. Guests know they have arrived when they see a small cluster of weathered-shingle homes, a tiny library, and an antique store housed in an old carriage barn. From here, a narrow dirt road rounds a large rambling hedge of beach roses and lilacs to the end, where The Driftwood Inn is situated. Set upon a rocky shoreline, overlooking a picturesque inlet, the inn is a classic example of a Maine summer-cottage community.

The Driftwood Inn, which has been in continuous operation for over 80 years, is comprised of four gray-shingled, Cape-style houses perched over the ocean on a rocky outcropping, as well as several small cottages. The rooms housed in the main inn have natural wood walls and lightly stained hardwood floors. The maple or iron headboards frame beds covered in plain cotton spreads. The rather Spartan decor is enhanced by an eclectic combination of maple bureaus, painted wicker furnishings, and straight-back chairs.

Those traveling with dogs are welcome in the five housekeeping cottages. While these are decidedly more rustic than the inn rooms, they are furnished in a similar fashion. They are located next to a sandy beach, which is just a "stone's throw" from the main inn. Whether guests choose the log cabin, Hillcrest, or one of the other cottages, they are certain to appreciate the fact that they are clean and inexpensive. Moreover, the cottages offer a little more privacy than the rooms at the inn, and are also equipped with cooking facilities. The red cottage is furnished with a pair of twin beds and a king-size bed. There is also a small kitchen area which is divided from the sitting room by a half wall, allowing guests to converse with the chef. An adjacent cottage appears to be more recently renovated and maintains a similar overall design. In this case, the double- and twin-bedded rooms are located on one side of the building, while the kitchen and sitting room with a television, are situated just inside the entrance.

For those who do not want to prepare their own meals, the restaurant also offers meals for a modest additional fee. As with many of the other buildings, the dining room has unfinished wood walls, hardwood floors, wood tables and chairs, and good water views from just about every table. The entrée menu always includes fresh fish, as well as daily specials of roast pork, pot roast, lamb, or chicken. These are always accompanied by salad, soup, rolls, and dessert. While it is by no means gourmet (and does not pretend to be), the food is quite good and hearty enough to satisfy most appetites.

Organized activities are limited at the inn; however, there is a salt water swimming pool set into the rocks, as well as good fishing and swimming in the cove. The picturesque roads around the island lead to many other scenic coves and inlets, where there are more fishing outlets (the Bailey Island Fishing Tournament is held every August) and some wonderfully secluded picnic spots. Visitors can also walk along the quiet country roads with Bowser and not worry about traffic. Should you get the urge to go off island, Bowdoin College in nearby Brunswick is just 15 minutes away and not only has a beautiful campus to investigate, but also some lovely historic homes lining the streets.

Phenix Inn

20 West Market Square
Bangor, Maine   04401
(800) 533-INNS, (207) 947-3850

Manager: Kimberly M. Haven
Rooms: 35 doubles, 2 suites
Rates: Doubles $53-73 (B&B), Suites $75-80 (B&B)
Payment: AE, DC, DSC, MC, and VISA
Children: Welcome (cribs and cots are available)
Dogs: Welcome
Open: All year

The city of Bangor, situated at the head of the Penobscot River, is known in fishing circles for its salmon and was, at one point, the lumber capital of the world. Although the lumber industry in this area has declined, the Penobscot River is still known as one of the finest salmon fishing rivers in the Northeast. In fact, the first salmon caught from the river each year is dubbed "The Presidential Salmon," and is presented to the President of the United States. Today, visitors will discover that, even though much of Bangor was ravaged by fire in 1911, the city has been nicely rebuilt and offers a rich and varied history.

The Phenix Inn is housed in an historic four-story building situated on West Market Square, in the heart of downtown Bangor. The building which houses the inn was originally designed by one of Portland's leading architects, Francis H. Fassett. Unfortunately, its original grandeur was compromised through years of relative neglect and disrepair. The last occupant, a music store, sold the building to the Phenix Management, who completely refurbished the National Historic Landmark and opened it as an inn.

The cozy lobby is most welcoming, with a warmth created through a combination of stained woodwork and forest green walls. The mahogany antiques fit in well with the comfortable leather chairs and sofas. Guests are usually comfortable lingering here for a bit, before they take the elevator to their bedrooms.

These chambers vary in size from the small singles that are perfect for the traveling business person to more spacious queen-size rooms. The floral wallpapers are a nice complement to the mixture of antiques and good quality reproductions. Mahogany and canopy beds are covered with Bates spreads, with writing desks and color televisions set unobtrusively off to the side. The corner rooms are some of the most popular at the Phenix Inn, as guests can relax in the leather wing chairs, which are well situated to benefit from the warm morning sun that pours through the windows. We found the wall-mounted faux marble sinks fit in well with the historic surroundings. The spacious modern bathrooms have large showers and sinks with brass fixtures.

In the morning, guests of the inn are invited to breakfast in a small dining room, which has been simply furnished with attractive butcher block tables. This is a standard Continental fare with juice, muffins, bagels, and coffee or tea. Within walking or a short driving distance of the hotel are movie theaters, bowling alleys, ice skating, swimming, and tennis. The Phenix Inn is often used as an interim destination for those heading deeper into Maine. It serves as a good overnight stop before driving east to the coast and the seemingly countless national and state parks, such as Acadia National Park, Baxter State Park, and Camden Hill State Park. Many also use it as a half-way point to driving up to the Moosehead Lake Region, one of the Northeast's last untouched wilderness areas.

Bar Harbor Inn

P.O. Box 7
Newport Drive
Bar Harbor, Maine   04609
(800) 248-3351, (207) 288-3351

Innkeeper: *David J. Witham*
Rooms: *153 doubles*
Rates: *$59-245 (EP)*
Payment: *AE, CB, DC, DSC, MC, and VISA*
Children: *Welcome (cribs, cots, highchairs, and babysitters are available)*
Dogs: *Welcome in specific rooms in the summer and most other rooms in the*
       off-season for a $15 fee.
Open: *All year*

The picturesque coast of Maine, coupled with the majestic setting of the Acadia National Park, creates the magnificent backdrop for the classic coastal town of Bar Harbor. This lovely region, set on the sparkling waters of Frenchman's Bay, first became popular in the mid-1800s, as artisans painted lovely landscapes of the surrounding waters, mountains, meadows, and forests. Those who viewed these paintings were drawn to this unspoiled region for a first-hand perspective. It was was not too long before there were boats and trains transporting visitors from New York and Philadelphia to this remote peninsula.

By the 1880s, large hotels and expansive "summer cottages" were built to accommodate the influx of wealthy vacationers. At about that time, a club emerged called the Oasis. Some of the most affluent and influential families in America, such as the Vanderbilts, Pulitzers, and Morgans, spent their summers relaxing in the privacy of this weathered-shingle building. This was the beginning of the Bar Harbor Inn. Unfortunately, much of Bar Harbor burned in 1947 during a devastating fire. After this catastrophe, a group of townspeople formed the Bar Harbor Hotel Corporation, which took over the old club and not only refurbished it, but also added several other buildings to entice travelers back to the area.

Today, visitors have few reminders of the 1947 fire and instead see a revitalized Bar Harbor Inn nestled upon seven acres overlooking Frenchman's Bay. The inn is actually comprised of several expansive buildings. The main inn, complete with its restaurant, and the Oceanfront Lodge, lines the edge of property that faces the water. The newly refurbished Newport Building lies on another portion of the acreage and is adjacent to Grant Park.

The white pillars of the porte-cochère marks the entrance to the expansive reception area, which is appealingly decorated in light green with rose accents. An assortment of couches and chairs are set around the fireplace in the sitting area. As we walked deeper into the hotel, we came across the Reading Room Restaurant, which overlooks both the bay and the Porcupine Islands through an enormous curved wall of windows. Natural lights pours in through these windows, which enliven the cream-colored walls and the light blue accents. The menu is long on hearty, New England fare and seafood specialties. The best place to enjoy the hotel's Downeast lobster bakes is on the large terrace. Here, the festive white and yellow striped umbrella tables overlook the lawn and flower gardens. Patrons are often cooled by refreshing breezes from the bay. There always seems to be a parade of beautiful sailing and power vessels making their way past the inn, but for a real treat, guests may take a closer look at the Natalie Todd tied right to the hotel's private pier. She is the largest three-masted schooner in all of Maine.

The guest bedrooms are located in three separate buildings; however, those traveling with a dog are only permitted to stay in the rooms on the ground floor of the Newport Building. Travelers who have visited the inn recently will remember this as a motel. However, last spring, the newly refurbished building was opened and is now decorated in keeping with the rest of the inn. Physically, the only two noticeable differences between these chambers and the other inn rooms are that they are two feet smaller and do not offer unobstructed ocean views. There are four-poster or canopy beds in many of the accommodations. These are set amid Queen Anne-style reproductions which include writing desks, comfortable armchairs and sofas. Earth tone carpeting is the neutral basis for the bright floral wallpapers or pastel color treatments. Framed nautical prints are interspersed with others offering botanical themes or glimpses of the local landscapes. Baskets containing both fresh and dried flower arrangements are nice touches. Guests will appreciate the bathrooms which are good-sized, clean, and modern.

Bowser will truly enjoy walking the grounds, as they offer plenty of grassy areas which are beautifully manicured and shaded by huge trees. There is also a full-size heated swimming pool and a Jacuzzi conveniently accessed by all of the guest rooms. The charming town center is just a block from the inn, and offers an array of shops, art galleries, and restaurants. There are also plenty of local parks within easy walking distance of the hotel. But one of the main attractions, particularly for those traveling with a dog, is a visit to Acadia National Park. Some choose to watch the sunrise from the summit of the 1,500-foot Cadillac Mountain. There are more than 100 miles of hiking trails and even more recreational areas that are perfect for casual walks, bicycling, or wintertime cross-country skiing. This is a paradise for anyone who enjoys the outdoors, and one could easily spend a week walking and or driving along this magnificent peninsula. Other local towns worth visiting are Southwest and Northeast Harbors. The Bass Harbor Head Lighthouse is also quite popular, as are the handful of picturesque islands set just off the coast that are accessible by ferry.

Fairhaven Inn

RR2, Box 85
North Bath Road
Bath, Maine 04530
(207) 443-4391

Innkeepers: Sallie and George Pollard
Rooms: 1 single, 6 doubles, 1 suite
Rates: Single $50-60 (B&B), Doubles and the Suite $60-80 (B&B)
Payment: AE, MC, and VISA
Children: Welcome, provided their "behavior does not interfere with guest's
*   relaxation" (cribs, cots, and highchairs are available)*
Dogs: Welcome with advance notice and cannot be left alone in the room
Open: All year

The Fairhaven Inn was was originally constructed by Pembleton Edgecomb in 1790. His bachelor's home had been a log cabin, but with his upcoming marriage he felt his new wife deserved more luxurious accommodations. Thus, he built a new home for her and their subsequent children. For the next 125 years, the Edgecomb family and their relatives lived in this large house. Subsequent owners have added several rooms, purchased the surrounding acreage, and ultimately renovated the entire estate. The current owners discovered the inn quite by accident. They were visiting their daughter in nearby Freeport, stayed at the inn, found out it was for sale, and decided to buy it. Since our last visit, the Pollards have honed their innkeeping skills even further and seem very comfortable in the roles as hosts.

The Fairhaven Inn is situated a few miles out of downtown Bath on a country road that is lined by pastures dotted with grazing horses. Eventually, travelers come to a cedar-shingled, antique Colonial that is nestled into the side of a hill, overlooking beautiful meadows and the picturesque Kennebec River. A flagstone pathway meanders past a half-dozen birdfeeders to the front door. As guests step into the house, they are immediately aware of the inn's antiquity, which is reflected in the low ceilings and pumpkin-pine wide board floors. Soft music can often be heard emanating from the inviting sitting room. This cozy chamber is also filled with an assortment of board games along with books and magazines. Opposite the sitting room is one of two intimate dining rooms.

Since it was not yet mealtime, we decided to look over the bedrooms instead. As we ascended the central staircase, it was clear that, although the house had not been changed architecturally, the Pollards had refurbished and redecorated the bedrooms and common areas. Each of the bedrooms is individually furnished with an assortment of antiques and period pieces, country collectibles, and dried wreaths and flowers. The use of Colonial colors, coupled with a lovely collection of antique quilts, further enhances the feeling of another era. Each of the bedrooms has nice views of either the meadows or wooded hillside. The overall atmosphere here is quite relaxing and the furnishings very comfortable. While all of the bedrooms are very charming, number seven is our favorite. This spacious room contains a king-size bed and provides particularly pleasant views of the valley and lake. Perhaps the combination of a picturesque setting, the inn's antiquity, and the Pollards' affable nature is the primary reason why so many visitors return year after year.

Each morning, guests are invited to enjoy a delicious meal in one of the two sunny dining rooms. Sallie is a great cook, and creates elaborate blintzes and crepes, as well as homemade muffins, fresh fruit, and hot and cold cereals. After a hearty repast, those who are so inclined can set out to explore some of the inn's 26 acres, while others might prefer to relax and read the morning paper in the spacious tavern, complete with a woodstove. In the warmer months, Bowser might want to investigate the miles of hiking trails close to the inn or perhaps come along on a wintertime cross-country skiing outing. Golf, at the nearby Bath Country Club, is another warm weather option. Visitors have a myriad of reasons for visiting Bath and southern Maine. Many come for the shopping in the galleries, crafts shops, or outlet stores. Others opt to explore the craggy coastline, paddle a canoe down one of the many nearby rivers, or go for an impromptu blueberry-picking expedition. Reid State Park is also close to the inn, and rests on over 700 acres of recreational lands.

At the end of a busy day, many of the guests return to watch the beautiful sunsets from the tavern or patio. Anyone who cannot find their way back to the inn, might encounter one of the locals, who have been known to escort lost guests right to the front door of the inn. Once guests arrive, Sallie and George's natural friendliness takes over, making everyone who visits feel very much at home.

The Inn at Bath

969 Washington Street
Bath, Maine 04530
(207) 443-4294

Innkeeper: Nick Bayard
Rooms: 6 doubles, 1 suite
Rates: Doubles $75-95 (B&B), Suite $130 (B&B)
Payment: AE, DSC, MC, and VISA
Children: Welcome (cribs, cots, and babysitters are available)
Dogs: Small dogs are welcome with advance notice and prior approval, but "must remain in guest room" and cannot wander around the public areas
Open: All year

For over 200 hundred years, the coastal city of Bath has been an impressive ship building center. Situated along the Kennebec River, Bath Iron works has launched over 4,000 vessels ranging from destroyers and battleships to steamships and patrol frigates. During its heyday, many large mansions and Captain's homes were built in what is now known as the historic district. One of these historic homes is now The Inn at Bath. It is located on Washington Street, and is just a short walk to the city park, with its lovely kiosk and fountain.

Located on a corner, the 1810 Greek Revival home looks well-kept with its crisp white clapboards and black shutters. Guests pull into the short driveway located off to the side of the house, where they will find the door that leads into the inn. Feeling like one of the family, guests emerge into the pantry and modern kitchen. From here, new arrivals are usually given a short tour of the house on the way to their bedrooms.

The lovely dining room is one of our favorite places in the house. It is off-white and furnished with an antique mahogany dining room table and equally elegant sideboard. There is no clutter in here, leaving guests free to appreciate the oil painting of a sailing ship. A crystal chandelier and sconces provide subtle lighting, although there always seems to be plenty of natural light streaming past the sheer draperies and into the room. Each morning, guests are invited to partake in a full, complimentary breakfast. This might start with grapefruit or melon and be followed by juice and coffee or tea. The house specialty is a banana French toast or the homemade granola. English muffins or other breads accompany each meal.

Guests usually like to spend their evening in one of the identical parlors. These are wonderful rooms to relax in, as they both offer fireplaces, although only one of them works. Once again, the white walls are a neutral backdrop for the beautiful antiques and chintz covered sofas and chairs. An archway separating them makes these rooms feel more as if they were really one expansive chamber. Guests might also notice a small office, which Nick eventually hopes to turn into a small, secondary dining room.

The bedrooms are located at the top of the main staircase or off the kitchen. These are all attractively decorated chambers, each holding a special appeal. The romantic Lavender Room has an antique four-poster bed placed across from a bay of windows, which is fronted by a comfortable sofa. The Green Room has an antique double bed which faces a fireplace. Another noteworthy guest chamber is the River Room. Formerly part of an old stable, this renovated hay loft has hand-hewn beamed ceilings along with a working fireplace. The sofa is set in an alcove and built-in bookshelves line the walls. The expansive South Room has a great king-size bed, a fireplace, and a sofa set invitingly in front of three windows. This chamber can connect to the Pocket Room, which forms an impromptu suite that is perfect for families.

The two first floor rooms are identical and feature private outside entrances that make it easy for guests to walk Bowser. These are the most recently renovated chambers as well. During our visit, Nick was still waiting for a Williamsburg company to ship the recreated moldings to him. They were three months late; however, we are certain that by now they have finally arrived and been put into place. These two chambers, named East and Garden Rooms, have special intrinsic features such as beamed ceilings, built-in daybeds, wide pine floors, and corner fireplaces with muskets hanging over their mantels. Designer fabrics cover the antiques and period furnishings, and the beds are draped with white spreads. Guests may request private color televisions and telephones. On hot summer days, the air-conditioning is a welcome amenity. Each bedroom also has a modern private bathroom, outfitted with thick towels and bath accoutrements.

We like walking around Bath with Bowser. This is a big town, but a pretty one that has a rich heritage. Visitors might also want to take Bowser on a day hike along Morse Mountain's coastal trails. They could visit Merrymeeting Bay and Swan Island, home to migrating birds. Popham Beach and Reid State Parks are also close by and provide a variety of options that Bowser should find appealing. Popham Beach State Park is located at the end of one of these peninsulas, where visitors can walk with their leashed canine companion or investigate the local Fort Popham State Historic Site, with its granite and brick fort.

The Hiram Alden Inn

19 Church Street
Belfast, Maine 04915
(207) 338-2151

Innkeepers: *Jim and Jackie Lovejoy*
Inn Helpers: *Jennifer, Jon, and Jeffrey*
Rooms: *1 single, 7 doubles*
Rates: *Single $30 (B&B), Doubles $45-50 (B&B)*
Payment: *Personal checks*
Children: *Welcome (cribs and babysitters are available)*
Dogs: *Welcome only with prior approval*
Open: *All year*

The Hiram Alden Inn was built for Hiram O. Alden in 1840. Mr. Alden was primarily an attorney, but during his career he also found the time to be a banker, postmaster, and was the co-founder/president of Maine Telegraph. His Greek Revival home stands, seemingly unchanged, on a quiet street in a residential neighborhood. Since the 1800s, there have been several renovations to the house, with attention paid to preserving its historic and architectural heritage. Thus, when guests walk through the house they will find the ornate pressed tin ceilings, handcarved moldings, marble fireplace mantels, and original fixtures are very much intact. The Lovejoys have owned the house for quite some time, and Jackie, or one of their children, is always on hand to greet new arrivals.

We entered the bed and breakfast by way of a side door. Wending our way through the house, we passed through the dining room and through a rounded archway (complete with a curved pocket door), and into the foyer, which is dominated by a circular, handcarved cherry wood staircase. The adjacent living room is a large, inviting chamber with comfortable furnishings surrounding the fireplace and antique piano.

The guest rooms are located throughout the house. Each of them has been nicknamed by Jackie. The old "sewing room" is a single-bedded chamber which is ideal for a child and is located just off the "master bedroom." The latter is one of our favorite spaces; it is nicely decorated and features a fireplace with blue and white tiles set into the mantel. The "front room" offers a single- and queen-size brass bed, both of which face another antique fireplace. Most of the chambers seem light and spacious, due to the large windows and high ceilings. Beds are covered with Bates or crochet spreads, and many of the walls are decorated with dried flower wreaths. Most of the bedrooms do share a bathroom, although they also offer the convenience of marble pedestal sinks placed in the corners of each chamber.

Anyone who rises early, will find coffee or tea awaiting them. They may want to enjoy this in the living room or take their cup out to the porch and relax in one of the rocking chairs. A full country breakfast is served a short time later in the formal dining room. This charming space is accented by lavender print wallpaper and dominated by a large oval table covered with a lace tablecloth. A pair of French doors lead into an old-fashioned butler's pantry. Jackie's breakfasts always vary, but guests can often choose between blueberry-nut pancakes, a variety of egg dishes, and French toast. These entrées could be accompanied by sausage or bacon, homemade breads or muffins, fresh fruit, and juice.

During the day, there are plenty of trips guests can take from the inn. To the north are the tiny Moose Point and Fort Point State Parks, both of which abut the water and offer scenic picnic settings. To the south, visitors will find Warren Island State Park, that can be reached via ferry boat from Lincolnville. Acadia National Park is a longer drive, but well worth it as there are thousands of acres for people to explore with Bowser. There is also a wonderful town park that is just a short drive from the inn. People-oriented diversions include a water slide, petting zoo, and a host of summertime activities and festivals in the Belfast area.

Belfast Bay Meadows Inn

90 Northport Avenue
Belfast, Maine 04915
(800) 335-2377, (207) 338-5715 (telephone and fax)

Innkeepers: John and Patty Lebowitz
Rooms: 11 doubles, 1 apartment
Rates: Doubles $70-125 (B&B), Apartment $125 (B&B)
Payment: MC and VISA
Children: Welcome (cots are available for $5)
Dogs: "Clean, housebroken, groomed" dogs are welcome for $15 in the annex and the
apartment
Open: All year

We have been writing about the Belfast Bay Meadows Inn for years; however, we have known it as the Penobscot Meadows Inn. In 1993, Patty and John Lebowitz bought the inn, moved their family from Oregon, and have spent the last year making changes to the old place. They have taken their time refurbishing the 4,000-square foot, turn-of-the-century "Downeastern cottage" so that it would be exactly as they envisioned it. This also involved creating an industrial kitchen that would meet their anticipated needs. When we visited, they were just putting the finishing touches on a $150,000 renovation to the adjacent barn, where there is a small meeting space and some additional bedrooms.

The inn is located just off the main road leading into Belfast. Visitors turn onto a gravel driveway and immediately face the gray-shingled, sprawling Gambrel Cape and separate barn. An intimate foyer leads to a charming, fireplaced living room, and an inviting enclosed porch just beyond it. The Lebowitzes have filled the inn with their eclectic assortment of antiques and collectibles from Abida Antiques (their other business that is also housed on the property). These are placed on the Oriental carpets that cover the hardwood floors in here, and throughout the rest of the house.

Another pleasant spot is the wood paneled dining room just opposite the staircase. Each morning a hearty Continental meal is prepared by Patty, who enjoys treating guests to a true taste of Maine by making scrambled eggs with lobster and sweet peppers. She accompanies this with fresh fruit, homemade muffins, juices, and gourmet coffee. Although we liked the dining room, it is even more fun to have breakfast on the expansive back deck at one of the umbrella tables. The distant bay views are often just as appealing as the meal. After breakfast, you might take Bowser for a stroll down the cleared path to the water's edge. There is a small rocky beach there that is a nice place to sit for awhile.

One of the biggest changes the Lebowitzes have made to the B&B was to add private bathrooms to the upstairs bedrooms. Returning guests will notice that the stark white or pastel walls are still a good backdrop for the colorful quilts and wall hangings. This simplicity succeeds in drawing one's eye away from the decorations to the array of antique furnishings. One room has an antique bed with a carved pine headboard and matching bureau. A pretty antique quilt lies at the foot of the bed. Rag rugs or area carpets cover the lustrous hardwood floors. Another room has a queen-size bed with a child's daybed nestled into a sunny window alcove. Most of the bedrooms have meadow or forest views, while two of the guest chambers have distant water views.

Traveling dogs are now allowed in the three bedrooms in either the apartment or converted barn. The studio apartment is available on a nightly or weekly basis. It is located toward the rear of the inn on the ground floor, has a separate entrance, a kitchenette, a bathroom, and a queen-size bed. During our visit, Patty and John were busy completely redoing this chamber. We were told that the furnishings out here would replicate those found in the main building, making us feel very comfortable in recommending them. The barn was also in the process of being remodeled at the time of our visit. Some of the rooms had just been plastered and they expected the entire project to be completed and ready in the spring of 1995.

There are plenty of ways that Bowser can get a little exercise during a stay at the Belfast Bay Meadows Inn. Those who feel energetic can walk to the good-sized town park, as well as explore downtown Belfast. For a more extensive hike, there are also the Moose Point, Fort Knox, and Lake George State Parks within a short drive of the inn. Other nearby options include the half-hour ferry ride to Isleboro (one of Maine's exclusive summer colonies), and the drive south along Route 1 to the classic coastal town of Camden.

Wonderview Cottages

RFD 1, Box 89, Route 1
Belfast, Maine 04915
(207) 338-1455

Owners: Herb and Nancy Foster
Rooms: 20 cottages
Rates: $390-700 per week (EP)
Payment: DSC, MC, and VISA
Children: Welcome (cribs are available)
Dogs: Welcome with advance notice and prior approval ($25 returnable deposit required)
Open: April 1st to late October

Travelers have long found the coast of Maine to be an alluring destination. With every turn of the road, there is another rocky outcropping offering panoramic views of the water or dense stands of pines. Anyone who is interested in an extended vacation to an unspoiled part of Maine, away from the hustle bustle of the touristed towns, we recommend the Wonderview Cottages. Located just three miles east of Belfast and some 60 miles to the west of Bar Harbor, this intimate cottage community has a commanding view of the water from its gently sloping hillside location.

The main house is set just off Route 1. Leading from the house, a dirt road gradually declines toward the water's edge which is dotted with cottages and edged by a circular driveway. The cottages are spaced a good distance from one another and give guests a sense of privacy. The most popular of these (numbers 12 - 19) are just a "stone's throw" from the water and provide unobstructed views of the passing lobster boats and sailboats. Whether next to a shade tree or along the water, each of the cottages faces the shoreline and is privy to southern exposures and refreshing breezes emanating from the bay. A couple of the cottages have a rustic log cabin exterior, but the majority of them are either shingled or clapboarded with green or yellow shutters.

The screened-in porches are furnished with comfortable lounge chairs. Once inside, the overall atmosphere remains light and airy as the walls have been painted in pale colors or have been covered with subtle floral papers. The simple, yet comfortable furnishings, coupled with a few framed pieces of art, enhance the otherwise Spartan surroundings. The sitting and/or living rooms are equipped with both a television and fully-stocked kitchenette. Woodstoves or fireplaces warm these rooms on cool, foggy nights. The bedrooms are equally cozy and are often furnished with maple bedsteads and bureaus. While the cottages' ambiance is appealing, most visitors are inclined to spend the bulk of their vacation out-of-doors. Many look forward to quiet afternoons reading on the porch, a casual lunch at the picnic tables, or relaxing on one of the comfortable chairs placed about the lawn.

Families might be more apt to choose from one of the many lawn games that are spread out under the large shade trees. These diversions include horseshoes, croquet, and volleyball, although the youngest members of the family will likely be drawn to the sandbox, jungle gym, and rope swing. Bowser will undoubtedly be ecstatic roaming on the ten acres of land and along the hundred yards or so of waterfront. Just beyond the confines of the property, there are a myriad of recreational options as well. There are seemingly endless coves which are great for exploring by boat, along with deep sea fishing and whale watching excursions. A day trip to Warren Island provides wonderful picnicking opportunities and 70 acres of land to explore. One of the more popular people pleasures is a trip to a local lobster pound, where diners may pick out their own lobster, have it cooked, and enjoy a delicious meal by the water. Those traveling with their canine cohort may wish to bring him along on a blueberry picking expedition, or to visit one of the numerous county fairs and festivals held in the region. Finally, nearby parks like Camden Hills, Moose Point, and Swan Lake are also excellent choices for outdoor adventures with your four-legged friend.

The Bethel Inn and Country Club

P.O. Box 49
On the Bethel Common
Bethel, Maine 04217
(800) 654-0125, (207) 824-2175, Fax (207) 824-2233

Owner: Richard Rasor
Rooms: 45 doubles, 8 suites, 35 townhouses
Rates: Doubles $140 (MAP), Suites $300 (MAP), Townhouses $210-340 (EP)
Payment: AE, DC, DSC, MC and VISA
Children: Welcome (cribs, cots, highchairs, and babysitters are available), No charge for
children under 12 who are staying with parents.
Dogs: Well-behaved dogs are accepted with advance notice. They are not allowed in public
rooms where food is served
Open: All year except November through mid-December

The Bethel Inn and Country Club has been in existence since 1913, and is the very essence of what one might expect from a classic resort located near the mountains of Maine. The five Colonial-style buildings are set around the Bethel Common and are surrounded by over 200 acres of adjacent land.

Scattered over the acreage are a multitude of accommodations, located in both the rambling yellow clapboarded main inn and the outbuildings. Fireplaces are found in some of the spacious bedrooms with fabulous mountain views, and also in the suites with cozy living rooms. The simple, decorative theme for the chambers is primarily Colonial, with furnishings consisting of Windsor chairs, skirted armchairs, and some antique bureaus and tables. The maple beds are often covered with hand-tied Vermont quilts or white Bates spreads, and in the winter months, down comforters rest at the base. With five antique buildings containing all of the inn rooms, it is easy to understand why no two are exactly alike. Some contain high ceilings and wainscoting, while others might have pressed tin ceilings and fieldstone fireplaces. All provide the modern conveniences, such as televisions, telephones, and clock radios. Some of the private tiled baths even have the original cast iron bathtubs or separate sink spigots for the hot and cold running water, and all provide Lord & Mayfair soaps and shampoos.

Anyone who wants the benefit of modern amenities and is willing to give up the charm of the main inn, may wish to consider the townhouses. These overlook the golf course and are perfect for families or groups of friends traveling together. They are also more isolated, and offer separate outside entrances, which Bowser will appreciate. Guests may choose from a variety of bedroom and bath configurations, allowing even greater flexibility. Standard features in each of these units are a dining room and living room with a fireplace, as well as a fully-stocked kitchen. The Colonial theme still predominates; however, the units are furnished with reproductions rather than antiques.

All guests are encouraged to take full advantage of the amenities and facilities at the main inn — and they do. The expansive columned lobby is especially appealing, with its oversized wing chairs and comfortable sofas. There always seems to be some sort of snack set out for guests to indulge in, perhaps a bowl of ripe apples, crackers and cheese, or cookies and cider. In the morning, newspapers are available here and some even flick on the old-fashioned television set to listen to the morning news. Many enjoy curling up in front of the crackling fireplace, especially on a cold winter's day. Just down the hall, there is a wonderful old library with a wall of windows that look out past the screened-in porch to the mountains beyond. Meals are served in a number of places at The Bethel Inn. The most stunning chamber is the formal dining room, where tables are set with handcrafted china, silver, and glassware. The menu consists of sixteen entrées and changes seasonally. Guests can expect to find staples such as Yankee pot roast, roast prime rib, Maine lobster, and roasted rack of lamb. Some choose to start their meal with the crab, shrimp, and scallop timbali, or the sautéed trio of wild mushrooms in a fresh cracked peppercorn cheese demi glaze. There are also dining opportunities downstairs in the Mill Brook Tavern, where rough hewn beams and walls, coupled with a pool table and big screen television, create just the right pub environment.

Dining options aside, there is a plethora of activities to choose from at the resort. In the summer months, an 18-hole golf course and excellent golf school are popular options, as is the year-round recreation center, and tennis courts. Guests who prefer to be near the water may use the Sunfish, canoes, and sandy beach at the lake. The indoor/outdoor heated swimming pool is appealing in any season and of course, shuffleboard, horseshoes, and other lawn games are available in the summertime. There is also great hiking and mountain biking nearby. Should the weather turn inclement, many indoor games are offered in addition to the complete Nautilus facilities, hot tubs, and saunas in the recreation center. In the winter months, the emphasis obviously changes to cross-country and downhill skiing, ice skating, and even sleigh rides. Some of the best downhill skiing in Maine is just 10 minutes from the inn at the ever-expanding Sunday River.

Bowser will certainly not lack for activities either. There are a number of country walks around the inn. One particularly good one is in the Hastings/Wild River area of the White Mountain National Forest. Here, explorers will find a suspension bridge and the remains of a turn-of-the-century lumbering town. This is one of those regions where there are still plenty of wild, undeveloped forests which are easy and fun to explore. It is an ideal place to bring a dog, particularly one that enjoys the outdoors. Therefore, whether Bowser likes leisurely lopes through town or a long distance cross-country ski venture, he is certain to have his pick of activities at The Bethel Inn.

The Chapman Inn

P.O. Box 206
On the Bethel Common
Bethel, Maine 04217
(207) 824-2657

Innkeepers: Sandra and George Wight
Rooms: 6 doubles, 3 suites, 1 dormitory
Rates: Doubles $55-85 (B&B), Suites $55-95 (B&B)
Payment: AE, MC, and VISA
Children: Welcome (cribs, cots, highchairs, and babysitting can be arranged)
Dogs: Welcome with advance notice and prior approval
Open: All year

The Chapman Inn, one of Bethel's oldest structures, was built in 1865 by a sea captain. While the exterior still retains much of its historic Federal style, many of the previous owners altered the interior to meet their needs. The name of the inn comes from one of the many owners, William Rogers Chapman who was a composer and conductor in the late 1800s and early 1900s. He also played a critical role in founding and running one of Maine's premier music festivals and the Rubenstein Club. Over the years, the building has served as a boarding house, country store, and tavern. Fortunately, the Zinchuks (the owners) have managed to recapture much of the coziness and charm during their tenure at the inn, although many of the original historic architectural features were lost before they arrived.

What we have always found most appealing about The Chapman Inn is the casual ski-house atmosphere, pleasant common rooms, and friendly innkeepers. As with most ski-oriented inns, the bedrooms are strictly utilitarian, providing clean and comfortable surroundings at a reasonable price. An apartment on the first floor is particularly appropriate for guests traveling with a dog. A sitting room with an informal Victorian style sofa and chairs, is nicely decorated with a small print wallpaper. Just beyond this chamber is a huge bedroom, containing a double and a pair of twin beds. A kitchen offers the option of preparing one's own lunches and dinners. Other bedrooms are decorated in a similar fashion, with handmade country quilts covering the beds, and assorted knickknacks placed on shelves and in alcoves. Some of the bathrooms are shared, and a few are private.

Most people spend the majority of their time in the common rooms. The front sitting room is one of our favorites, with a navy blue corduroy sofa and matching sidechairs placed on the wide pine floors. This sunny space is usually warmed by a woodstove, and there is even a large screen television for everyone's viewing pleasure. Just off the sitting room there is an expansive dining room, where skiers and hikers like to load up on complex carbohydrates before heading out for the day. This hearty meal varies, although guests can always count on homemade granola, freshly baked breads, and baskets of fruit. The main course features such dishes as omelettes, Belgian waffles, and pancakes, accompanied by bacon or sausage. This is an "all-you-can-eat repast", which many eagerly look forward to each morning. The inn used to serve dinner; however, the innkeepers now prefer to recommend one of the local restaurants. Most of these are within walking distance of the inn, which makes for a pleasant evening outing.

Bethel is a very quiet town by nature, without a lot of night life. Luckily, most find enough to do right at the inn, as there is a game room with a pool table, darts, and cable television. For those who prefer to soothe their aching muscles, we suggest taking advantage of the two private saunas. In the summertime, guests have access to Songo Pond and the inn's private beach. Here, many like to bring a picnic lunch and relax on the beach, saving the afternoon for some swimming, canoeing, or sailboarding (bring your own board). There is always the Grafton Notch State Park and Evans Notch areas, offering picturesque waterfalls and hiking trails, as well as excellent cross-country and downhill skiing in the wintertime. Other hiking trips that people enjoy are in the West Kennebago Mountain area, just a short distance from the inn. The Chapman Inn is located on the Bethel Common, which in the winter months is transformed into an ice skating rink. While Bowser can participate in just about any of the previously mentioned activities, he might want to just sit and watch while his two-legged friends take to the ice!

The Green Shutters Inn and Cottages

P.O. Box 543
Bay Street
Boothbay Harbor, Maine 04538
(800) 272-1028; (207) 633-2646

Innkeepers: Kay and Clayton Pinkham
Rooms: 1 single, 6 doubles, 7 cottages
Rates: $39-49 per person (MAP)
Payment: AE, MC, and VISA
Children: Welcome (cribs, cots and highchairs are available)
Dogs: Welcome in the cottages
Open: May 15 through September 30

Boothbay Harbor, a favorite tourist destination, is located near the end of a peninsula along the southern Maine coast. Unfortunately, because of its waterside location many of the accommodation selections are rather expensive, and the amenities offered do not always keep pace with the rising prices. The Green Shutters Inn and Cottages is one of the few remaining inn and cottage complexes that is reasonably priced and attractively furnished.

Located at the end of a meandering dirt lane, the inn and cottages are set on the edge of a quiet wooded area with distant views of Linekin Bay. The cottage community was started in 1915 and has not changed much over the years, a fact that both first-time and returning guests appreciate. The main inn is comprised of the office and a good-sized dining room with exposed timbers, lace curtains framing the windows, and a dozen tables covered in bright red and white checked cloth. The Modified American Plan at the Green Shutters Inn is a real bargain, offering an assortment of specialty meats and locally caught New England seafoods. These hearty dishes are complemented by homemade breads, pies, cakes, and pastries. Those who happen to stay through the weekend will thoroughly enjoy the generous Sunday night buffet.

Guests traveling with a dog may stay in the rather rustic, weathered-shingle cottages. These vary, not only in size and decor, but also in the amenities and the views offered. The cottages can house anywhere from two to eight people. Garden and Spruce cottages are the smallest with only one bedroom. Others, such as Bayberry, Stepping Stone, and Terrace are housekeeping units that include living rooms, fireplaces, and fully-equipped kitchenettes. Timber frame or knotty pine board walls add to the informality of some units, while simple country prints enhance others. The beds are covered with cotton spreads and sheer curtains frame the windows. Wicker and pine furnishings are placed on either wall-to-wall carpeting or braided rugs. The most popular cottages have distant water views and are often reserved well in advance.

This is the essence of a cottage community, with a big lodge that has a protected wraparound porch offering bay views. Adirondack chairs are scattered about the green lawns, as well as on the rock patios in front of several cottages. The town is just a ten-minute walk from the inn, while the beach is just a three-minute stroll down a winding path. Guests frequently comment on the fact that they feel so removed from the hustle and bustle of the town center, yet are within easy reach of restaurants and shops.

Some visitors choose to spend the bulk of their vacation at the complex, while others might use it as a base for exploring this part of Maine. Outings could include a visit to the Railway Museum, a day-long deep sea fishing expedition, or possibly a Sunset Cruise. While there are more than enough walking opportunities right in town, those who are in search of a more natural setting, may wish to visit Reid State Park, Pemaquid Point, or Popham Beach. A ferry will also bring interested travelers to Monhegan Island, which is a naturalist's and artist's mecca.

Oakland House

RR1, Box 400
Herrick's Road
Brooksville, Maine 04617
(800) 359-RELAX, (207) 359-8521

Innkeepers: *Sylvia and Jim Littlefield*
Rooms: *5 singles, 12 doubles, 16 cottages*
Rates: *Singles and Doubles $40-110 (MAP), Cottages $200-1,050 (MAP)*
Payment: *Personal checks*
Children: *Welcome in most rooms and cottages (cots are available)*
Dogs: *Welcome; but are limited to certain cottages and must be leashed at all times*
Open: *May to November 1*

In the late 1800s, Herrick's Landing was best known as a passenger drop-off point for the Eastern Steamship Line. The landing was also used by the Herricks to load ice and granite cobblestones to be shipped to other ports; however, it was not too long before they decided to offer overnight accommodations as well. The existing farmhouse, dating back to 1776, was expanded by Jim's great-grandfather and subsequently opened as the Oakland House on July 4, 1889. Since then, the various cottages and the spacious ten-room Shore Oaks building have been added to the original homestead. Guests will quickly discover that while a few things have changed over the years, a certain continuity has been created by the descendents of the Herrick family, who still own and operate the resort. In fact, just last summer they celebrated their 105th year of operation.

Today, those who are looking for a simple, family-oriented vacation are drawn to this rustic Maine resort. Based on their return rate of 75%, it is easy to understand why the Oakland House has become such a tradition with many families. The present owners, the Littlefields, have done their best to create and maintain a sense of privacy for their guests. This feeling extends to the cottages, which are often surrounded by groves of trees that serve as natural barriers. Some of these cottages are tucked into the woods and others are nestled along the water's edge. They vary greatly in appearance, from the very rustic cabins with fieldstone fireplaces and exposed beams to more recently refurbished cottages with picture windows and sliding glass doors. They are all decorated in a similar style with simple comfortable furnishings. Sofas and armchairs often have that well-worn look, and plain cotton spreads cover the maple bedsteads. Most of the cottages are also equipped with private bathrooms, living rooms with a fireplace, and fully-equipped mini kitchens.

While the interior spaces are very inviting, most will find themselves spending a good deal of their time on either the screened-in porches or open decks. Returning guests definitely have their preferences for particular accommodations (and often book them for the following year as they are departing), therefore newcomers should reserve early and specify the amenities, decor, and location they prefer. For instance, Hideaway, with four bedrooms, two bathrooms, a living room with a fireplace, and a porch is located on the edge of a field, and is well-suited for families. The two bedroom Grindstone offers the ultimate in privacy, while Brown Jug has views of Eggemoggin Reach and Little Deer Isle. Those with a penchant for expansive water views will probably be intrigued with the converted Boat House, where large picture windows reveal a panoramic view of the bay as the sounds of lapping waves can be heard from under the living room floor boards. Large groups can always reserve Shore Oaks, a rambling gabled lake house with a wraparound porch and an exposed fieldstone foundation. This was built in 1907 and also happens to be located right on the shoreline. It offers ten guest bedrooms, along with a living room, reading room, and a dining room that serves breakfast exclusively to Shore Oaks' guests. From the wraparound porch, bedecked with wicker rocking chairs, the views of the Eggemoggin Reach and the Camden Hills are unsurpassed.

Sitting and enjoying the views are not the only pastimes at The Oakland House, although they are a terrific way to unwind at the end of a busy day. There are both fresh and saltwater swimming areas, sailing, fishing, and rowing options. Badminton, tetherball, and volleyball, as well as golf at the Blue Hill Country Club are a few of the other diversions. Walking and hiking trails crisscross the property, while the rocky coastline and expansive grounds give dogs and children endless open space to explore. The inn will also arrange deep sea fishing and sailing charters for their guests. Finally, the other neighboring coastal communities, including Blue Hill, Deer Isle, and Stonington are the epitome of the idealized Maine fishing villages. Of course, a longer day trip could bring you to Acadia National Park or the Holbrook Island Sanctuary, where you may hike and explore the rocky terrain.

After an energetic day, guests will appreciate the ample amounts of food served at the Oakland House. The casual atmosphere in each of the three dining rooms is sure to make everyone feel right at home. A hearty breakfast is served from 8 to 9:30 a.m. and features freshly made doughnuts, muffins, hot cereals, eggs, pancakes, and French toast (New England codfish balls are an occasional specialty). Two main dishes are offered each day for lunch, as well as salad, rolls, a beverage, and dessert. Guests can also request that a box lunch be prepared to bring along on an extended hike or fishing trip. Each night, the entrée choices include a meat, chicken, and fish dish. Crab, lobster, and sole might be offered, as well as turkey, chicken, and roast beef. For many people, their most memorable experience is the weekly lobster bake held down on the beach, or indoors if the weather is less than favorable. Lastly, because of the family atmosphere, the inn's hosts do not serve alcohol, nor do they permit it in the dining rooms.

We have written about the Oakland House for a decade, and must say that it continues to get better with each passing year, although little of the physical appearance seems to have really changed. The easy going atmosphere, simple accommodations with wonderful vistas, and an array of unstructured diversions are what make this resort so unique. The Littlefields and their staff have done a wonderful job of keeping the overall feeling intact and in maintaining the kind of low-key environment that makes guests feel right at home.

Blue Harbor House
A Village Inn

67 Elm Street
Camden, Maine 04843
(800) 248-3196, (207) 236-3196, Fax (207) 236-6523

Hosts: Jody Schmoll and Dennis Hayden
Rooms: 7 doubles, 2 suites
Rates: Doubles $85-125 (B&B)
Payment: AE, DSC, MC, and VISA
Children: Welcome in the Carriage House Suites (cribs, highchairs, and babysitters are available)
Dogs: Welcome in the Carriage House Suites with advance notice and prior approval
Open: All year

The Blue Harbor House is a light blue, clapboarded Cape located just a short walk from Camden's picturesque harbor and downtown area. The home was constructed by James Richards, Camden's first settler, in 1768 on a homesite granted to him by the King of England. He was given this special privilege as he was the first person to fulfill all the conditions of being a settler. Today, this nicely restored and completely redecorated inn offers guests a pleasant mix of traditional architecture and authentic furnishings coupled with many of the modern amenities appreciated by travelers.

Guests' first impressions of the inn are usually of the cozy common room, where they will most likely encounter the two resident black labs, Bally and Jenny. A pair of wing chairs and a sofa set around a central table are the focal points for this room. Dried flower wreaths, stenciling, wrought iron standing lamps, and country collectibles provide decorative accents. A milk-painted hutch stands off to one side and a bureau, topped with a basket filled with shells, rests off against a side wall. A pair of French doors open to the expansive glassed-in porch, which provides panoramic views of the distant hills. Here, guests will also find a television, as well as a wide array of board games and books that line the end wall. On cold, wet, or foggy days (not too uncommon for coastal Maine), guests can always wait out the inclement weather while watching one of the movies from the inn's extensive videotape library. Each morning, a delicious breakfast is also served here. Guests may choose from the day's menu or ask Dennis to prepare something special for them. Most are just as happy to make their selection from one of the ever-changing house specialties, which could include shirred eggs, a cheese souffle, blueberry pancakes, or baked apples.

The bedrooms are located on either side of the common room and toward the rear of the inn. They are individually furnished with four-poster, canopy, or brass beds covered by handmade quilts. Braided throw rugs cover the fir floors. The informal country charm is enhanced by the stenciled designs on the pastel walls, coupled with dried wreaths, pottery lamps, and an assortment of country collectibles and folk art. The good-sized, private bathrooms offer modern hotel conveniences, but each has a unique design that is typical of a country inn. Anyone seeking a little more privacy, may wish to consider Rooms B, B1, or C. These are located toward the back of the main inn and are accessed through separate outside entrances. The B and B1 chambers can be connected and feature a queen-bedded master suite, a second bedroom with a pair of twin-size beds, and two private bathrooms (one with a whirlpool tub). Room C is an ideal configuration for guests who are traveling with a dog. The sitting area and adjacent kitchenette provide cooking and living space, which is separate from the spacious bedroom. The large four-poster canopy bed is adorned with a colorful handmade quilt. A pine chest is set attractively at the end of it, and area rugs cover the hardwood floors. As with the rest of the inn, pastel colors set the tone for this space. Bathers will be happy to find there is a luxurious whirlpool tub in the bathroom.

We thoroughly enjoyed the Blue Harbor House for many reasons. While the charming accommodations, delicious breakfasts, and affable hosts were all integral components, we also found its proximity to the downtown area was a luxury, as well. From the inn, it is an easy walk or bicycle ride (bicycles can be borrowed at the inn) down to Camden's shops, restaurants, and harbor area. Bowser might also be interested in venturing further afield. The Camden Hills State Park has miles of hiking trails, or there is always the steep trail up Mount

Battie. Anyone who wants to enjoy the magnificent views but really isn't in the mood to trek up to the top can always drive up for a $2.00 fee. Another rugged hike brings adventurers to the top of Maiden Cliffs, which overlooks Lake Megunticook. A somewhat less strenuous but no less popular adventure is to meander out to the historic lighthouses that line the shore. During the colder months, there is great cross-country and downhill skiing at the Camden Snow Bowl.

Although Jody and Dennis are California transplants, they have made it a point to learn everything they can about Camden's history, lore, and attractions. To this end, they are a wealth of information and are always eager to guide visitors to some of the more notable and less frequented sights and attractions. It is because of these insights, along with their warmth and congenial natures, that the Haydens have been able to transform the Blue Harbor House into a wonderful inn that enjoys a tremendous repeat business.

Hartstone Inn

41 Elm Street
Camden, Maine 04843
(207) 236-4259

Innkeepers: Sunny and Peter Simmons
Rooms: 8 doubles
Rates: $55-125 (B&B)
Payment: AE, DSC, MC, and VISA
Children: Welcome in the suites
Dogs: Welcome with advance notice and prior approval in the suites
Open: All year

Camden, Maine has long been a popular destination for seafarers and historians alike, all of whom are drawn to this classic Maine coastal community. Although the number of tourists continues to increase each year, Camden manages to hold onto its historic integrity by preserving its wonderful old summer "cottages," and limiting the town's commercial development. Visitors will still discover a great assortment of interesting shops, galleries, and restaurants in town, along with magnificent views of the harbor and its moored yachts. Fortunately, the Hartstone Inn is ideally located in the center of Camden and its harbor, which is a convenience in the summer months when finding a parking place can prove a bit unnerving.

The Hartstone Inn was built as a private home in 1835 by Joseph C. Stetson, and has only changed hands three times over the years. The last family kept the house for three generations, eventually selling it to the Simmons in 1985. During their tenure, the Simmons have been hard at work updating the Victorian building and, more importantly, restoring the historic features that had lost some of their luster over the years. Today, guests who enter the cozy foyer will find a comfortable parlor off to their left. The warmth of the crimson patterned wallpaper is brightened by the sunlight streaming in through the bay windows. An inviting sitting area borders the fireplace and beckons travelers to relax, while their hosts take care of the check-in procedure. If new arrivals venture further into the inn, they will find a small common room, that is furnished with forest green accents, walls of bookshelves, an assortment of board games, and a television.

The bedrooms are scattered throughout the house and in the adjacent carriage house. Those inside the main inn have hardwood floors and their walls are decorated in rich mauve, hunter green, or burgundy tones. The many original built-in features are complemented with wing chairs or rocking chairs set around four-poster beds covered with colorful quilts. The overall effect is quite crisp and clean, giving guests an indication of what they will find in the two suites located in another part of the house. To the right of the house, visitors will come to a small cobblestone courtyard, highlighted by a charming fountain and garden. While some may be concerned that they are on a less than favorable side of the building, this is not the case. Not only is the courtyard a delightful spot, but the rooms here are also tucked away from the rather noisy main street leading into town, ensuring that guests are not disturbed by the traffic.

The suites in the modified barn-like structure have been decorated with a somewhat more contemporary flair. These chambers are quite large, with open loft areas making them appear all the more cavernous. Pastel color treatments and light pine trim, coupled with skylights, further enhance the light and airy effect. Hardwood floors are partially covered with dark gray Berber carpets, with floral draperies adding a touch of color. The main floor in each of the suites is comprised of an open space that combines a kitchen and dining area with a sitting room. The latter is furnished with wing chairs, a fold-out couch, and a television. Up the stairs, a queen- or king-size bed is set under the skylighted eaves. Each morning, guests may choose whether or not they wish to take their breakfast in bed or in the main dining room. The former is a Continental affair, while the latter is a multi-course repast that can consist of anything from souffles to blueberry pancakes.

With a full day ahead, many choose to start early and take a stroll down to the village, where there is an abundance of great shops and galleries to browse through. Those who are so inclined, can meander up the road to a more residential neighborhood and view some terrific examples of Downeast architecture. There is also a small park next to the harbor that offers a wonderful vantage point for viewing the passing boats, both large and small. Those who are interested, can reserve time for a Windjammer cruise which will take them past the islands that protect the harbor. Landlubbers, on the other hand, should not miss the opportunity to visit the Camden Hills State Park, where the 5,000 plus acres of land should offer enough space to keep everyone entertained (dogs must be leashed at all times). In the winter months, visitors will find this to be a good spot for a little cross-country skiing as well.

The Manor

Box 276
Battle Avenue
Castine, Maine 04421
(207) 326-4861

Innkeepers: Paul and Sara Brouillard
Rooms: 12 doubles, 1 cottage
Rates: Doubles $65-135 (EP), Cottage: $750 per week (EP)
Payment: MC, DC, and VISA
Children: Welcome (cribs, cots, and highchairs are available)
Dogs: "Well behaved" dogs are welcome with prior approval, cannot be left unattended
in the rooms, and must be leashed inside the inn
Open: Mid-May through October

One would think that after visiting The Manor several times over the last ten years that we would have become immune to its grand scale; however, that is not the case. Five acres of sprawling lawns do not lessen the impressive effect of this large, dark brown shingled "summer cottage" that is reminiscent of another era. Originally built for Commodore Fuller of the New York Yacht Club, this stately home has been run by the Brouillards for years as a wonderful inn, of which the Commodore would certainly be proud.

Ascending the tree-lined driveway, new arrivals pass under an enormous portico linking the main building to another half its size. In the summertime, guests can be found on the raised enclosed porch, which offers sweeping views of the sloping lawn and distant waters. Massive stone stairs lead up into a dramatic, high-ceilinged foyer. Off to the side is the spacious living room, which is rich in colors and textures. The Oriental rugs are topped by comfortable sofas and walls are papered in a rich, navy blue paper. The grand Victorian furnishings couldn't be more appropriate in a home of this size. The detailed moldings and other built-in features are almost overwhelmed by the large fieldstone fireplace. An intimate, windowed alcove looks particularly inviting, as it is surrounded by comfortable sofas and a television placed unobtrusively in the corner.

Beyond the living room, new arrivals will find a long mahogany bar with a green marble top. An array of whimsical pâper maché figures, ranging from seals and walruses to frogs and lobsters, has been placed up in the eaves around the bar and grand piano. Overnight guests, as well as local residents, like to stop in for afternoon hors d'oeuvres and refreshing libations. During the slower and cooler months of the year, many locals even remain for the hearty dinner entrées prepared by the chef. Returning guests will find that the menu has a new tropical twist to it. The restaurant still serves the standard fare, but has also added some exotic selections. Appetizers range from the chicken satay and Vietnamese spring rolls to the raw bar items such as the Spinney Creek oysters, Pemaquid oysters, and mahogany littleneck clams. The entrée selections will entice just about any palate, with grilled venison steaks, Portuguese mussels steamed in white wine, garlic, sweet peppers, and linguica sausage, and a grilled lamb loin served with a minted fruit chutney topping the menu. But whatever dish one does order, the three intimate dining rooms will only enhance the dining experience. One cozy chamber has of a handful of tables set around a fireplace, which is surrounded by a wall of bookshelves and framed Audoban prints. Another, substantially larger beamed-ceiling room, also has a fireplace and an interesting collection of plates lining the walls.

The staircase to the guest bedrooms is wide enough for three or four people to walk abreast comfortably. Antiques line the hallways as well as fill many of the bedrooms. The cavernous guest quarters are as spacious as the public rooms on the first floor. Fifteen-foot ceilings tower above walls papered in a variety of prints. One room has deep red floral paper and an equally unique, antique carved wood headboard. Another bedroom, with views of the water, is twice the size of most formal living rooms. It is furnished with a king-size bed backed by a brass headboard, along with a twin bed and various Victorian pieces. Other chambers feature large window seats, sideporches, and fireplaces. All of the guest rooms have been decorated and furnished with great flair, but not to excess. There is also a guest cottage on the grounds, which could be more aptly referred to as a small house. The decor and furnishings here are similar to those found in the main inn.

The Manor, aside from offering unique accommodations, is a popular destination because of its lovely grounds and variety of activities available nearby. Warm days lend themselves to croquet, tennis or golf, while inclement weather brings guests inside for Ping-pong or billiards in the wood paneled billiards room. Bowser might want to tag along for a bicycle ride or a take a walk in the woods behind the inn. Castine's lighthouse is also a nice jaunt down the road from the inn, although a longer excursion will bring walkers into the town center. After a day of activity, guests return to the comfortable informality of this old-fashioned summer retreat set amid a picturesque Maine coastal community.

The Holiday House

Box 215
Perkins Street
Castine, Maine 04421
(207) 326-4335 or 326-4861

Hosts: Sara and Paul Brouillard
Rooms: 9 doubles, 1 cottage
Rates: Doubles $95-135 (B&B)
Payment: MC and VISA
Children: Welcome
Dogs: "Well behaved dogs" are welcome with prior approval and must be kept on a
  leash in the public rooms and on the property.
Open: Mid-May through the November 1st

In 1604, Samuel de Champlain discovered the area that today is know as Castine. During the next two centuries, this thriving trading region would also be the site of many fierce battles between a handful of countries. Life in Castine certainly has calmed down considerably since those days; however, its interesting heritage and simple lifestyle continue to attract visitors. In addition to its charming waterfront, the town has a host of nicely restored Georgian and Federalist homes and historic stone churches dotting its picturesque rolling hills.

The Holiday House is an Edwardian mansion that was built in 1893 as an elegant "summer cottage." Situated on the shores of Castine Harbor, just a short walk from the town center, the expansive house not only has spacious rooms, but also exceptional water views. Sara and Paul, who already own and operate The Manor (located just a short distance away), bought this terrific piece of property about five years ago. Even though it needed an inordinate amount of work, involving both the grounds and the physical structure, the Brouillards decided they could tackle the restoration. Today, Sara confesses that despite the enormity of the project, she has enjoyed the ongoing process. The guests, in turn, love to see the old home being brought back to its former grandeur.

Upon entering the foyer, guests will first encounter an enormous living room off to the right. Its original features, such as an intimate semi-circular alcove, ornate fireplace, and lustrous hardwood floors are almost secondary to the impressive views. The Brouillards have created several sitting areas that combine comfortable furnishings and lovely antiques set upon Oriental carpets. Just off the living room is a good sized dining room, that also shares the beautiful water views. Although this is a lovely spot for meals, many prefer taking their breakfast on the massive wraparound porch.

The grand nature of the building also carries through into the guest rooms, which are located upstairs. Each is nicely, yet simply decorated with an array of furnishings that range from impressive antiques to smaller captain's trunks and wicker pieces. The worn Oriental rugs covering the floors and the floral draperies at the windows, accented by the dried flower arrangements and seaside or nautical collectibles, greatly add to the charm of these chambers. As with the living and dining rooms, one of the most desirable aspects of these spaces are their lovely water views, which can be enjoyed through the multitude of windows in both the bedrooms and the private bathrooms. One of our favorites is a third floor corner room, which is not only furnished with a king-size bed, but also offers a bow window that provides one of the most dramatic views in the house. As an added note, Sara and Paul are continually adding more furniture and updating the decor; be forewarned, however, a few chambers are still a bit on the Spartan side.

While The Holiday House doesn't pretend to offer an elaborate restaurant or exquisite accommodations, the atmosphere is convivial and inviting. It is also within walking distance of just about everything a visitor might want to do while staying in Castine. The waterfront village is literally two blocks from the inn. The State of Maine's Maritime Academy's training vessel is open for guided tours when it is in port. The Wilson Museum is also a favorite stop, as it displays European and African pre-historic and local Native American items. Bowser might have a little more fun walking along the quiet backstreets and gently rolling hills surrounding Castine. The area is still quite rural, with the exception of the village, and offers lots of pristine shoreline to walk along and woods to explore. Anyone who loves the water will want to bring a canoe and explore the quiet inlets, or perhaps hire a boat for the day and sail amid these picturesque waters. In the evening, everyone enjoys coming home to the spacious bedrooms, lovely common areas, and relaxing atmosphere of the Holiday House.

Farmstead Bed and Breakfast

379 Goodwin Road
Eliot, Maine 03903
(207) 748-3145 or 439-5033

Hosts: John and Meg Lippincott
Rooms: 5 doubles
Rates: $54-60
Payment: MC and VISA
Children: Welcome (cribs, cots, highchairs, and babysitters are available)
Dogs: Welcome with advance notice and prior approval
Open: All year

Those familiar with outlet shopping and the state of Maine know that the first town off the Interstate that offers outlets and discount stores is Kittery. Anyone who stops here will be treated to some bargains, but they will probably miss the essence of this otherwise rural area. In order to capture the flavor of the region, visitors can travel just a few minutes northwest to the small town of Eliot. Eliot was actually a part of Kittery until 1810, around the same time that Maine was also known as Massachusetts. Today, visitors will find that, aside from a few shops and restaurants, a handful of churches, and a state park, Eliot is mostly agricultural, predominated by white-washed farm fences and outbuildings and rolling hills covered with dense stands of trees.

As travelers head away from the coast toward Eliot, they will quickly leave the more urban areas of Kittery and Portsmouth for the pastoral setting of the country. The Farmstead Bed and Breakfast, with its white clapboard edifice and adjacent red barn, fits right into its rural surroundings. The original home was built in 1704 by Caleb Emery; however, it was modified in the late 1800s when a two-story post and beam addition was built onto the homestead. As with many old farmhouses, a series of one-story additions and the building of its huge barn greatly increased its original dimensions. The barn is now gaily bedecked with lobster pots and buoys.

A side door leads into the kitchen, where new arrivals will be warmly greeted by one of their hosts. Anyone interested in learning more about the history of the house, including a recent discovery of a pair of hand-stitched shoes from the 1700s, will likely hear a little about it during the tour of the B&B. One of the first chambers guests pass through is a cozy sitting room complete with a television set and VCR. Further into the house, past the central staircase, there is a chamber containing a brass bedstead covered in a patchwork quilt. Lace curtains frame the windows and burnt-red carpeting softens one's footsteps. The Rose Room, on the other hand, is furnished with a double bed covered by a Bates spread. The green carpeting complements the floral wallpaper in here, and additional amenities include a small kitchenette and tiny deck leading to the backyard. The original master bedroom for the house has been named the Jade Room. It is quite spacious and is furnished with both a twin and a queen-size bed, along with a sofa. Pretty views of the front yard can be enjoyed through the windows. The Jade Room also has the distinction of containing the only private bathroom that has a tub in the house. Guests like the B&B as much for the informal homey decor, as for the thoughtful amenities like the microwave oven and mini-refrigerator found in each of the bedrooms.

Every morning, a full country breakfast is served in the sunny dining room, which overlooks the backyard through a wall of windows. As guests enter, they will pass a small blackboard indicating the morning's meal choices. These options could include egg dishes or delicate pancakes accompanied by thick bacon and sausage. Breads are homemade and the juice and coffee are fresh. Each table has been topped with a room nameplate, making it easy for guests to see where they should be sitting. A spinning wheel set off in the corner merely adds to the country atmosphere. After a hearty repast, some decide to venture onto the enclosed porch, where they will find both a number of games to play and a morning newspaper to read.

Bowser will probably be a little anxious to stretch his legs. The rural country roads are ideal for morning walks. There is also plenty of room for Bowser to run on the extensive acreage that surrounds the B&B. People will find that Portsmouth is a dog-friendly town with scenic cobblestone streets to investigate, a few parks, and an array of excellent restaurants and stores. But as many discover, they are equally content to stay right at The Farmstead and enjoy the low key atmosphere and pastoral surroundings.

The Isaac Randall House

5 Independence Drive
Freeport, Maine   04032
(800) 865-9295, (207) 865-9295

Innkeepers: *Glynrose and Jim Friedlander*
Rooms: *8 doubles*
Rates: *Doubles $70-105 (B&B)*
Payment: *MC and VISA*
Children: *Welcome in certain guest rooms. Young children must be supervised by*
parents at all times (crib, cot, highchair, and babysitters are available)
Dogs: *Welcome in specific rooms, provided they are not left alone in the room*
Open: *All year with a few brief breaks in the winter*

This 1823 Federal-style farmhouse was originally given as a wedding present to Isaac Randall and his wife, Betsy Cummings. Mr. Randall, a direct descendent of Myles Standish and Priscilla Mullins, was an affluent farmer with over 60 acres of land. During the five decades they lived in this house, the Randalls raised eight children. In the years since then, the farmhouse has been used as a way station for the Underground Railroad, a dairy farm, a tourist court, and as an apartment house. Today, visitors will discover a charming inn that is comprised of a nicely restored farmhouse and a large barn, which was formerly used as a dance hall in the 1930s. A winding brick path leads to the side entrance. Once inside, the hallway opens into an enormous country kitchen. This space also doubles as a breakfast room with beamed ceilings that are festooned with an array of hanging copper pots.

This inviting room is basically the heart of the house, with bedrooms located up the stairs, around the corner, and down the side hallway. Each chamber has been painted in pastel blues, roses, and lavenders. The cheery decor is enhanced by an abundance of quaint handmade quilts, many of which are for sale. A good room choice for those traveling with a dog is the Pine Room, which is located on the first floor and has its own private entrance. The decor and furnishings in this chamber are completely different from the other more traditional guest bedrooms. A Southwest theme predominates, as the crisp white walls contrast with the natural wood trim and exposed beams. The bed and throw pillows are covered in a rust-colored French Provincial print. The spacious bathroom features a great old copper bathtub. The Friedlanders, who would eventually like to move to New Mexico, are particularly pleased with the atmosphere they were able to create in this bedroom. Another one of the more unusual chambers has a king-size wicker bed set under the exposed eaves of a steeply sloping roof. Rough-hewn beams, walls, and floors add even more character to this chamber. Handmade quilts, brass accents, and both dried and fresh flower arrangements complete the decorative touches in this and many of the other bedrooms.

Anyone with a hearty appetite will look forward to the delicious morning meal, as well as the friendly conversation that accompanies it. This substantial repast features eggs, Maine blueberry pancakes, French toast, or strata, which are complemented by lemon bread, fresh fruit, and homemade granola. For those who prefer to sleep in, a Continental meal awaits them in the second floor kitchenette, or they may create their own meals there. The adjacent parlor has an Oriental rug covering the hardwood floor and colorful country quilts provide festive accents. A television rests near an antique chest, and a chess table and a wide assortment of board games are available for guests' enjoyment.

Outside diversions are plentiful throughout the area, as well as in the immediate vicinity. There is ample room for dogs and children to play on the inn's five acres and around the spring-fed pond nestled back in the woods. Just behind the house, youngsters will find both a new jungle gym and a full-size train car for their amusement. Bowser will probably opt for a visit to the nearby Wolf Neck Woods State Park, which offers a number of hiking and nature trails. Just west of Freeport is Bradbury Mountain where visitors will find a variety of short day hikes. Although Freeport has become an outlet oasis over the years, it is still possible to travel along the backroads that wend along the shoreline and discover quiet lobster huts, offering freshly caught lobster with all the trappings. Returning at the end of the day, guests are always greeted with baked goodies and a refreshing libation. After many years of entertaining travelers, the Friedlanders seem to have an unerring ability to help guests thoroughly relax and enjoy their time away.

The Crocker House Country Inn

Hancock Point, Maine 04640
(207) 422-6806, Fax (207) 422-3105

Innkeeper: Richard Malaby
Rooms: 10 doubles
Rates: Doubles $65-95 (B&B)
Payment: AE, DSC, MC, and VISA
Children: "Truly well-mannered children are welcome."
Dogs: Welcome in the guest rooms with hardwood floors
Open: May 1 to Thanksgiving

The Crocker House Country Inn lies at the end of the small but picturesque Hancock Point. Originally built in 1884 by a man named John Crocker, the inn has been a landmark since the days when Hancock was both a busy ship building town and a stop for the Bar Harbor Ferry. Crocker sold the house in 1906 and it was bought by the Baroness Olga Lanoff, who was married to a wealthy tea merchant and had become quite famous for her therapeutic tea called Bol Yerba. Her love and dedication to the inn kept it afloat well after Hancock Point's heyday. When the Baroness died, so did the inn. The new owners could not replicate Baroness Lanoff's flamboyant style, nor attract nearly the number of guests she was able to while at the helm.

It wasn't until 1980 that Richard Malaby became involved. He learned about the Crocker House when his brother discovered that it was for sale in the newspaper. Richard was living in Washington D.C. at the time, but after several visits, he became enamored with the community and the inn. He recognized the tremendous amount of work involved in restoring the inn, but felt he could resurrect some of the magic that made it such a success in the early 1900s. Until 1986, most of his emphasis was placed upon the restaurant business; then Richard decided to overhaul the guest rooms and add private bathrooms. With each passing year, the inn grows more and more comfortable in its role as host to diners and overnight travelers alike. One of Richard's more recent changes has been the conversion of the old screened-in porch to accommodate even more dinner patrons.

The decor in the charming bedrooms varies, but guests can often see the wide pine floors around the perimeter of the braided and area rugs. Some guest chambers have delicate English country wallpapers and others are accented with decorative stenciling. Tab curtains and exposed wood beams further accentuate the simple country elegance of the rooms. White wicker chairs and comfortable rockers are placed to take advantage of a nice view or a quaint alcove. Potpourri in decorative jars and vases of dried flowers further add a personal touch. The brass or maple finial beds are usually covered with country quilts or white Bates spreads. The existing bathrooms have not only been nicely updated with showers or restored claw-footed tubs, but also have baskets of fragrant soaps and shampoos.

Every time we visit, we look forward to our delicious breakfast. Over the years, we have sampled such dishes as overstuffed omelets, brandied French toast, Belgian waffles, crab-meat quiches, and huevos rancheros. The fresh brewed coffee is always great, and the assortment of teas are always fresh (perhaps in honor of the Baroness). The evening meal is equally delightful, with everything from the presentation to the service being first rate. Appetizers vary from a paté mousse truffle to oysters Rockefeller. The dinner entrées include poached salmon, local gray sole meuniere, lamb Crocker, and broiled swordfish. The homemade pastries, cakes, and rich mousses have weakened many a strong will.

After the evening meal, guests often head into the common room, where dark red wicker furniture and a built-in bench beckon sated diners. The dried flowers and wreaths are just the right complement to the botanical prints. A collection of antique tools and a pair of cameras add interest to the room, as well. The woodstove always seems well stoked, and occasionally someone will be playing the piano. More often than not, guests are simply content to listen to the relaxing music from the stereo. When the windows are open on warm summer nights, the distant sounds of buoys ringing can be heard in the harbor.

Activities at the inn vary, depending on the season. Richard has added to his lawn games and now has horseshoes, along with croquet. There are some tennis courts just down the road. A leisurely walk around the picturesque point brings strollers past the octagonal library and the second smallest post office in the United States. The inn also has bicycles on hand that guests may use for more distant excursions. Many also like to spend the day on some of the other peninsulas, such as Schoodic Point or in Acadia National Park on the Mount

Desert Island. Visitors can also charter a boat to take them over to Bar Harbor. Of course, at the end of a busy day, guests always enjoy returning to inn, where they can head out to the converted barn and thoroughly relax in the therapeutic hot tub.

Hiram Blake Camp

P.O. Box 59
Harborside, Maine   04642
(207) 326-4951

Manager: Deborah V. Ludlow
Rooms: 15 Cottages
Rates: $85-135 (MAP), $400-700 weekly (MAP)
Payment: Personal checks
Children: Welcome (cribs, cots, and highchairs are available)
Dogs: Welcome, provided they are leashed
Open: Memorial Day through Columbus Day Weekend

Those vacationers who have visited the Camden, Castine, and Blue Hill areas along the coast of Maine, already know about the picturesque islands and coves that can be found on the outlying Penobscot Bay. Some like the bustling tourist destinations, while others prefer to visit a more tranquil section of the state. Travelers with simple tastes and a need for a quiet rural setting will want to investigate the Hiram Blake Camp.

It is located on over 100 forested acres at the end of a peninsula. The camp was founded in 1916 by Captain Hiram Blake and his wife, Iantha. Since that time, many of their family and their extended family, have worked at the camp. Everyone, from the founders' children to their great-grandchildren, have played a part in its success and continue to do so. Today, Lucy Blake Venno, the daughter of Captain Blake, still resides here. Mrs. Venno's granddaughter Deborah and her husband manage most of the day-to-day operations. Deborah's mother, Sandy, is often found tending to the expansive flower and vegetable gardens which supply all of the vegetables for the meals and beautiful flowers for the arrangements. Sandy's husband and son are both lobstermen and, with advance notice, will catch enough lobster so that guests can enjoy it every evening. The family-style meals at the Hiram Blake Camp are hearty all-you-can-eat affairs. Dinner entrées range from fresh seafood, baked ham, and roast beef, to pork, lamb, and turkey dishes. These are accompanied by soup, salad, homemade bread, dessert, and a drink. Breakfast is also offered in the dining room, and includes a variety of egg dishes or blueberry pancakes coupled with bacon, homemade pastries, fruit, and doughnuts.

We found the Hiram Blake Camp to be very low key. The rustic, weathered-shingle cottages and outbuildings are set just a short distance from the shoreline. Once guests arrive, they rarely feel compelled to leave the complex, but rather stay put and enjoy the abundance of natural beauty. The quiet cove is lined with pristine meadows, dense woods, and a rocky shoreline with a pebbly beach. Guests and their canine cohorts can enjoy exploring the property, as well as walking along the extensive trails that cut through both the camp's grounds and the adjacent state park. There is also a handful of good-sized, beamy rowboats that can easily accommodate a small family and Bowser, too. These are great for exploring the coves, islands, and surrounding waters, and best of all they can also be outfitted with sails should the wind pick up a bit. Back on shore, children might enjoy the small playground, or they may head inside the lodge to take advantage of the board games and Ping-pong in the recreation room. There is also a library of books to select from, and many people add to it each season with their own reading that they leave behind at the end of their stay. A vacation at the Hiram Blake Camp is based on simplicity and spontaneity, where guests will never feel as though they have to follow an array of programmed activities.

The weathered-shingle cottages add to the charm of the camp; they are set next to the water's edge, or a hundred or so feet away from it. The cottages range in size from one room to three bedrooms and a living room. Most of the cottages have a pair of bedrooms. Families with several children, or those traveling with friends, may be interested in reserving a portion or all of the Oak Lodge. This cottage is actually a pair of duplexes with each side accommodating six guests. Each is clean and comfortably outfitted with worn pine and rattan furnishings set on top of braided rugs and pine floors. The bedrooms are equipped with either twin or double beds covered in plain spreads. The kitchens are well stocked, as are the cupboards with linens. The bathrooms are very clean and are generally equipped with stall showers. We especially liked the living rooms with their fieldstone fireplaces or woodburning stoves. Painted or naturally stained wood walls are fitted with windows framed in sheer curtains. Finally, there is an array of prints and Downeast collectibles that enhances the feeling of these accommodations. The interiors seem almost inconsequential, however, when, after a long day enjoying the picturesque scenery and the many camp diversions, you just recline on the porch and watch the starry night unfold.

Senter Bed and Breakfast

P.O. Box 149
South Harpswell, Maine   04079
(207) 833-2874

Host: Alfred M. Senter
Rooms: 3 doubles
Rates: $60-70 (B&B)
Payment: Personal checks
Children: Welcome (cots are available)
Dogs: Welcome; but owners are responsible for any damage
Open: All year

Travelers will discover that the rural village of South Harpswell is only a short distance from Brunswick, Maine but seemingly hundreds of miles from civilization. A country road leads to this picturesque point, with its wonderful, panoramic views of the ocean, and its access to these sparkling waters. Alfred Senter is the hospitable host of this inviting bed and breakfast located at the end of one of the private lanes.

When we arrived, we found Alfred tending to his rose garden, where he has well over 50 bushes. He is an avid horticulturist and is always willing to share his knowledge (and possibly a cutting or two) with interested guests. Two good-sized greenhouses are filled with unique varieties of plants and flowers, which he nurtures during the winter months and eventually transplants to his flower beds in the spring, labeling each of the assorted varieties. During the summer months, fresh flowers from the gardens are placed both in the guest rooms and in the common areas.

Dove gray, wood-paneled walls line the hallway which leads into the dining room. In here, and in the adjacent living room, there are overwhelmingly wonderful views of the water and of Bailey Island through the numerous picture windows. The living room is also, not surprisingly, a favorite gathering place, with its woodstove, array of ship models, and comfortable furniture that invite people to relax. Of the three bed chambers available, two face the ocean and the other looks out onto the aromatic rose garden. One cozy bedroom has paneled walls that are stained a light gray. A duvet-covered down comforter adorns a bed that is perfectly positioned to take advantage of the ocean views. Another room has twin beds outfitted with Bates spreads, simple furnishings, and built-in bookshelves. The third chamber is also decorated in a similar homey fashion. Since our last visit, Alfred has been quite busy converting the once shared bathrooms into private bathrooms. He has also re-carpeted the rooms and common areas, and has provided a fresh coat of paint on the wallboards, which accent the fine floral wallpaper.

Alfred is a wonderful host who truly enjoys people. It also turns out that he is a delightful raconteur, entertaining people for hours with his stories. A full breakfast is served in either the light and airy dining room or on the side porch, where a woodvine has entwined itself on the overhead trellis. Those who want an egg and toast, can have it, or if pancakes are more suitable, then Alfred will serve those up as well. A lighter breakfast of juice, fresh breads, and muffins is also available. Afterwards, many enjoy following the grassy path to the long staircase that descends down to the water. Alfred has even thoughtfully built a little bench seat at the halfway point, for guests to rest on and enjoy the views. Bowser will surely love the endless opportunities for exploring along the shoreline. There are also other nearby beaches and a small park to investigate with your canine cohort, as well. The village of South Harpswell is primarily a sleepy summer community. The streets are quiet and the cottages are quaint, making it an ideal area for peaceful walks.

For those who are enamored with the thought of spending longer periods of time along this portion of the Maine coast, Alfred also has a two-bedroom cottage over on Bailey Island. In addition to offering even better vistas of the craggy coast, the cottage is also privy to the melodic sounds of the crashing waves. Anyone who is just passing through, though, will be more than content with the personalized and homey ambiance found at the Senter B&B.

Cabot Cove Cottages

P.O. Box 1082
South Maine Street
Kennebunkport, Maine   04046-1082
(800) 962-5424, (207) 967-5424

Manager: Joseph Dipaolo
Rooms: 15 cottages
Rates: Daily $60-135 (EP), Weekly $375-875 (EP)
Payment: MC and VISA
Children: Welcome (cribs are available)
Dogs: Well-behaved pets are welcome, provided they are leashed (a $25 deposit is required)
Open: Mid-May to Mid-October

Cabot Cove Cottages are cozy, white shingled, one- and two-bedroom accommodations situated on a picturesque tidal cove. The cottages are set around a semi-circular driveway amid cedar, walnut, tulip, and apple trees. The two acres of grounds are nicely landscaped and very well maintained. The simply furnished cottages are ideal for those who want an unpretentious cottage setting, and a base for exploring both Kennebunkport and all of southern Maine.

The pine-paneled cottages have fully-equipped kitchenettes, private baths, and small living rooms. The accommodations are not overly spacious, but they are very clean, tastefully decorated, and most even have views of the water. White wicker and rattan furniture are complemented by attractive periwinkle blue and yellow floral curtains. Bates spreads cover simple maple bedsteads, while extra fold-out single beds are hidden inconspicuously in pine chests. Brass lamps provide additional light for reading or game playing on quiet evenings. Each cottage is also furnished with color cable televisions, as well as linens and towels.

Families traveling with a dog will enjoy this intimate and secluded setting, just as their children will undoubtedly like the swing set/jungle gym, as well as playing badminton and croquet. Several picnic tables have also been placed around the central green for guests' use; these make an ideal spot for an informal evening barbecue. Guests may also borrow one of the dories and explore the harbor and its many picturesque inlets. The tidal inlet is quite warm (for Maine waters) and there are a few private floats that guests may swim out to and sunbathe on. Be forewarned though, the water is very shallow at times, and diving off the floats can be dangerous.

Set just off a quiet lane, the Cabot Cove Cottages offer a great deal of privacy, yet they are also within walking distance of the ocean and Kennebunkport's downtown area. In addition to the shops in town, there are a number of interesting lanes and streets to meander along in the surrounding neighborhood. One popular route begins at the cottages, takes visitors and their canine companions over the hill past The Colony Hotel, and along the rocky coast. Kennebunkport is rich in history, ranging from impressive Colonial homes to beautiful waterfront properties. For those who are interested in investigating other areas, we suggest visiting nearby Portland, an intimate city that has undergone quite a revival. The city's waterfront, assorted parks, and old town section are excellent areas for walking, browsing, or shopping.

The Captain Jefferds Inn

Box 691
Pearl Street
Kennebunkport, Maine   04046
(207) 967-2311

Innkeeper: Warren Fitzsimmons
Rooms: 12 doubles, 3 suites (can also be rented by the month or the season)
Rates: Doubles $85-135 (B&B), Suites $145-165 (B&B)
Payment: MC and VISA
Children: Most appropriate for those over 12 years of age
Dogs: Well-behaved dogs are welcome with prior approval
Open: April through October and holiday weekends in the off season

Detailed moldings, high ceilings, and intricate woodwork are luxuries few people can afford to build into their homes today. This makes it particularly fun to visit the old sea captains' homes, where no expense was spared and the finish work was exquisite. The Captain Jefferds Inn, a 191-year-old Federal mansion originally owned by a merchant sea captain, is an outstanding reminder of this era in home building. In 1981, Warren Fitzsimmons carefully refurbished and restored the home. He took the remainder of the inventory from his New York antique business and used it to furnish much of the inn. Also on display is an extensive collection of folk art, Staffordshire china, and Majolica. The impressive furnishings, fabrics, and antiques coupled with bright decorative color schemes create a unique ambiance that entices most guests back year after year.

Each bedroom is individually decorated. Laura Ashley wallpaper and matching bed linens add a touch of the English countryside to one chamber.

Another is more formal with rose accents and coordinated chintz fabrics framing the windows and forming the bedskirt for the canopy bed. Tables are usually draped with fabrics as well and set with lamps crafted from Oriental vases. Simple country pine antiques and wicker furnishings are interspersed with more formal English antiques, giving other chambers an eclectic yet appealing look to them. Some have massive four-poster beds, while others provide brass bedsteads set alongside bent twig furnishings. All of the bathrooms are private, and most still have porcelain baths and sinks complete with the original fixtures.

Those who require more space and privacy, should inquire about the expansive suites located in the inn's separate 18th-century carriage house. They are not decorated on the same grand scale as the rooms in the main inn, but in more of a cottage-style, which is in keeping with the beamed ceilings and darkly stained hardwood floors that predominate. Warren has amassed an extensive folk art collection over the years, which he prominently displays in these one-, two-, and three-bedroom accommodations. The bent wood chairs and tailored sofas are intermixed with attractive bowls, lamps, and accent pieces. The full kitchens, good sized living rooms, and modern bathrooms make these ideal chambers for anyone planning a longer stay with Bowser.

Every morning, guests are summoned to either the first or second breakfast seating by the tinkling of a bell. This delicious repast ranges from Eggs Benedict and frittatas to blueberry crêpes and New England "flannel" (a combination of corned beef hash and a poached egg). During the warmer months breakfast is served on the east terrace, which is festooned with large white umbrellas and wrought iron patio furniture.

Even on a sunny day, we are drawn to the elegant pastel yellow living room. The bright chintz-covered sofas are surrounded by exquisite English antiques that rest on dhurrie rugs. The Steinway grand piano is backed by a virtual gallery of paintings that covers one of the walls. The sun splashed solarium is also a popular gathering spot, where rattan furnishings are interspersed with white armchairs and still more antiques. The brick patio, overlooking the intimate backyard, is yet another inviting place and is also the site for afternoon tea. After tea, guests frequently can be found walking the grounds and exploring the perennial gardens. It would be more appropriate to take Bowser down the block and let him romp in the small park.

The inn is situated just around the corner from the charming center of Kennebunkport. Many visitors enjoy taking a walk to town or off in the other direction towards the ocean. For those who are in search of a nice sandy beach, we recommend a visit to Parson's Beach. This is a good spot for an afternoon of sunning, swimming, and picnicking. Others may be more inclined to travel farther afield and spend the day investigating nearby Portland or Portsmouth, both of which are thriving cities that offer a myriad of shops, cafes, and parks, as well as interesting historic homes. Bowser will want to accompany his companions on all of these outings, as there are always green spaces to explore, scenic coves to investigate, and picturesque points of interest to check out.

The Colony

Box 511
Ocean Avenue and King's Highway
Kennebunkport, Maine 04046
(800) 552-2363, (207) 967-3331, Fax (207) 967-8738

General Manager: *Carol M. Thomas*
Rooms: *139 doubles*
Rates: *$165-305 (AP)*
Payment: *AE, MC, and VISA*
Children: *12 years of age and over are welcome*
Dogs: *Welcome for a $20 daily fee ("EP")*
Open: *Mid-May to mid-October*

The Colony was built in 1914, but has been a fixture in Kennebunkport ever since the Boughton Family took over operations in 1948. Set on a knoll overlooking the ocean, this massive old hotel combines a casual summer atmosphere with the elegance only a few classic hotels in New England still possess. It continues to be the accommodation of choice for generations of families, including those who travel with their dogs.

The resort is actually composed of the main hotel, the Galland House, and the motor inn (located across the street). We always enjoy strolling into the main building, as it reminds us of a more gracious era when people had the time and the money to spend an entire summer here. The reception area is a cavernous chamber with high ceilings and large windows overlooking the veranda, terraced gardens, and glistening ocean in the distance. There are dozens of intimate sitting areas, where guests may enjoy these views or merely visit with one another. Down a main hall, there are also several public rooms. The most modern of these is a formal viewing room with a large screen television, while the remainder include a traditional card room, game room, and library.

Visitors to The Colony will have the sense that time has basically stood still for the grand hotel, and much of the old world charm is not only reflected in the common areas but also in the guest rooms. The high ceilings create a sense of spaciousness that is not usually found in rooms of this size. The guest chambers in the main hotel are decidedly the most desirable, as many have terrific water views and exude an old Maine charm. Each is traditionally decorated with Bates bedspreads covering maple bedsteads, antique dressing tables topped with mirrors, and brass bedside table lamps with parchment paper lamp shades. Area rugs cover the red fir floors, pastel colors have been selected for the wall treatments, and lace curtains frame the windowed alcoves. The essence of another era also presents itself in the crystal wall sconces and old-fashioned floral fabrics. The tiled bathrooms, complete with the original porcelain fixtures, are either private or connect with an adjacent chamber.

There are many recreational activities available at The Colony. A heated saltwater swimming pool is set on a bluff above the ocean. From its deck, guests not only enjoy wonderful sunbathing opportunities but also panoramic views of the coast. For those who want to try swimming in the brisk ocean waters, there is a nice sandy beach that is just down the road from the hotel. A putting green is also situated on the premises, which gives golfers an opportunity to practice a little before they hit the links at the Arundel Golf Club. Even the most active will be drawn to the many intimate seating areas set about the grounds. One of the more popular vantage points is from the enormous wraparound veranda, with its hunter green wicker chairs and chaises. The Colony hosts a wide range of social events, including bridge parties, contests, dances, guest lecturers, and nightly entertainment.

Rates are based on the American Plan, which includes breakfast, lunch, and dinner. The first two meals of the day are rather relaxed; however, at night guests are asked to wear more formal attire. Our favorite tables in the elegant dining room are situated at the end of the enclosed porch, next to windows, and offer unobstructed views of the ocean and grounds. The terrific vistas, coupled with the delicious meal, provide for an unforgettable dining experience. The ever-changing menu includes such selections as steamed lobster with drawn butter, pan seared sea scallops with a Creole sauce, or the filet of tenderloin in a port wine and shallot sauce. A full complement of vegetables and a fresh garden salad accompany the main dish. A variety of desserts, including raspberry strudel, lemon pudding, Black Forest cake, and the chocolate Mississippi mud complete the meal.

Guests and their canine companions will find nice walks in just about every direction. Steps from the hotel lead to a path that skirts the shoreline for a mile or so. Travel by foot in another direction and visitors will eventually end up in the town center. Here, are art galleries, a few restaurants, and an array of interesting shops and boutiques. Ferry Beach, located just north of Kennebunkport, also offers wonderful vistas, white sandy beaches, and fun nature trails wending through the forest. Another favorite walk is found in nearby Ogunquit, where a wonderful mile-long footpath (Marginal Way) follows the spectacular coastline. Afterwards, some spend time exploring this renowned artists' colony.

The Seaside

P.O. Box 631
Gooch's Beach
Kennebunkport, Maine   04046-0631
(207) 967-4461 or 967-4282

Hosts: Sandra and Michael Severance
Rooms: 26 doubles, 10 cottages
Rates: Doubles $95-160 (EP), Cottages $535-1,095 weekly (EP)
Payment: AE, MC, and VISA
Children: Welcome (cribs, cots, highchairs, and babysitters are available)
Dogs: Welcome in the cottages with advance reservation
Open: May 1 to October 31

Kennebunkport is a lovely and charming seaside community, which should be included in any visitor's tour of Maine's coast. With a myriad of quaint bed and breakfasts, inns, and elegant hotels to choose from, only a handful can claim to have their own private beach, expansive grounds, and bargain rates. Anyone searching for an inn that offers weekly and monthly rentals along with a casual cottage atmosphere, will view The Seaside as an ideal solution.

The Seaside Inn was originally built in 1756; however, the motor lodge and cottages are more recent additions. While the motor lodge and inn do not permit dogs in their guest rooms, the spacious cottages are very appropriate for people traveling with a canine companion. They also happen to be our favorite accommodations. The cottages are perfectly suited for a family or group of friends, who are looking for a self-sufficient vacation experience without all the frills and usual associated costs of a country resort. Surprisingly enough, Sandra informed us on our most recent visit, many of the expansive cottages are rented by just one or two people whose primary interest is just being able to bring their dog along.

These cottages are scattered on 20 acres of sprawling land that abuts over 3,000 feet of sandy beaches. All of them have great views of either the ocean or a tidal river. Each is furnished a bit differently in a traditional Maine style. Single beds with maple headboards and white Bates spreads are the norm for most of the cozy bedrooms. Those who need cots and cribs can rent them for an additional charge. Some cottages offer single-level living, and others have bedrooms upstairs and a living room and kitchen down. One cottage has a circular staircase leading up to the bedrooms. Another two-bedroom cottage has a large living room with naturally stained knotty pine walls framing a huge picture window with a terrific southern exposure. Most offer good-sized living rooms that have comfortable couches, 18th-century reproductions, and rattan chairs adorned with brightly covered cushions. The kitchens are well equipped with pots and pans, dishes, and flatware. A color television is also supplied, just in case guests run out of things to do or encounter a rainy day or two.

Guests are sure to find that there is more than enough space for playing with Bowser on both the grounds and along the beach. After sunbathing and taking a refreshing swim, some enjoy riding their bicycle with Bowser running alongside. A short loop leads cyclists along the shoreline, while a longer ride (or walk) will bring visitors into town, where there is a variety of shops, restaurants, and activities. Of course, there is always the inn's playground, shuffleboard, and croquet course to entertain guests, as well.

The Green Heron Inn

P.O. Box 2578
Ocean Avenue
Kennebunkport, Maine   04046
(207) 967-3315

Innkeepers: Charles and Elizabeth Reid
Rooms: 10 doubles, 1 cottage
Rates: Doubles $65-90 (B&B), Cottage $95-120 (B&B)
Payment: Personal checks
Children: Welcome (cribs are available)
Dogs: Welcome with advance approval in certain rooms
Open: All year except for certain days during the off-season

Kennebunkport is one of Maine's quintessential coastal summer communities, although it has grown steadily over the years and has had to deal with the problems that come with expansion and preservation. The streets are lined with beautifully maintained, classic Federal and Colonial homes. When visitors drive over a small drawbridge and into the village center, they know they have arrived in an especially traditional corner of New England. After finding a parking space, visitors can walk to any number of interesting shops, bookstores, restaurants, and yes, even an old fashioned five and dime.

From here, visitors can drive out to Walker Point, the summer home of President George Bush. As they meander along the water's edge, they will pass marinas on one side and wonderful antique homes on the other. Just before the road reaches the ocean, lies the Green Heron Inn perched next to a saltwater creek. Not only does it have an unusual setting, but is also within walking distance of both the beach and Dock Square.

This classic and expansive bungalow looks festive in the summer months with overflowing window boxes and striped awnings. A short flight of stairs brings guests to a small porch and beyond to an even smaller reception area. After checking in, most like to explore the small inn. Surprisingly, there are a number of common rooms within this bungalow. The elongated dining room has tranquil views of the water through a wall of windows. This is also the site of a delicious breakfast, offered to both guests and the general public. It has gained the reputation as being one of the best breakfasts in the area, with people filling the dining room early on weekends and staying for most of the morning. The fare ranges from Mexican eggs and Eggs Benedict to blueberry pancakes and vegetable frittatas. Some of the daily specials are herbed popovers with buttered eggs, peach melba French toast, and apple and chicken sausage gravy on a buttermilk biscuit. Guests who prefer a lighter breakfast might choose to combine the homemade granola with a strawberry-banana breakfast drink or a peach raspberry yogurt smoothie. When the fog rolls in, guests are often drawn to the cozy fireplaced living room. In here they will find an array of magazines and books, along with some board games. There is also a television, for those who are so inclined.

With all of the breakfast activity on the first floor, it is nice to know that the bedrooms are tucked away on the second. These were renovated a few years ago and are nicely furnished. The decor is crisp, with bright quilts on the beds and framed prints of the area's landscapes. Modern conveniences include television and air conditioning. The best rooms for those who are traveling with a dog are in the adjacent cottage. The recently renovated two-story cottage has rockers placed on the front porch. Once inside, guests will notice similar colors (mauve with green accents) and furniture styles as are utilized in the main inn. The two bedrooms, one with a queen bed and the other with two twins, make this a terrific accommodation for a family or two couples. The addition of a kitchenette, allows guests to create meals for themselves with ease.

There is a great deal to do in the area, and most guests are up early so they may take advantage of the day. We like the walk from the inn out to the beach, and along the rocky shore. A long walk will lead guests past Walker Point and beyond until they finally leave the coast and head inland back towards town or the inn. There are also all sorts of side streets that take walkers past the rambling old summer houses perched on the hill overlooking the ocean. Visitors can also play tennis on the public courts and golf at some of the area's courses.

The Herbert

P.O. Box 67
Main Street
Kingfield, Maine   04947
(800) THE-HERB, (207) 265-2000

Owner: Bud Dick
Rooms: 17 doubles, 3 suites
Rates: Doubles $56 -100 (EP), Suites $110-140 (EP)
Payment: AE, MC, and VISA
Children: Welcome
Dogs: Welcome, but they are not to be left alone in the room
Open: All year

Herbert Wing, a man with political aspirations for the governorship of Maine, constructed The Herbert in 1918. He wanted to create an opulent building, using only the finest materials, in an effort to impress the region's most influential people. Today, guests are usually quite surprised to see a building of this stature in this otherwise rural part of Maine.

Kingfield is primarily known for its proximity to Sugarloaf Mountain and thus attracts its fair share of skiers during the winter months. Many of them find they don't need or want to pay for, mountainside lodging. They gravitate instead to the more charming, albeit eclectic, Herbert. The hotel has a reputation for good hearty meals, quaint guest rooms, and a friendly staff. Bud Dick, and his three assorted labs, run the show and we have to say that they, along with the hotel, develop more and more character with the passing years. When we last talked with Bud, he would occasionally refer to The Herbert as the "woofy palace," due to its ever increasing popularity among the canine set. During our visit, he had eight dogs in residence; however, his record is fourteen. Does he mind? "No," he says. "I've never had a dog set fire to a mattress."

The bedrooms have remained relatively unchanged since we first started to write about The Herbert. Old-fashioned brass sconces and headboards remain polished, and the walls are still papered in a variety of traditional prints. Original pieces of furniture have been restored to further recreate an authentic atmosphere. Most of the bathrooms have Jacuzzi spas, which are a blessing to aching bones after a long day of skiing or other form of outdoor recreation. Some bathrooms are even equipped with old-fashioned telephones. These date back to 1918, or the "Wing" era, when the Western Electric Company wired the hotel for telephones. At the time, The Herbert was renowned as the only hotel north of Boston where guests could receive a call at their dining room table. Another interesting anecdote involves the only bathroom with exposed pipes. Evidently, when the plumbing was being worked on, somebody crossed a pipe and the toilet now flushes with hot water. Quirkiness aside, guests will appreciate such thoughtful touches as the bottles of spring water placed upon the dressers and lollipops set on the pillows.

Descending the circular staircase on the way to dinner, many take a moment to inspect the old-fashioned telephone booths, another example of the classic telephone system. The dining room, with its reproduction Hunter ceiling fans and French crystal shades, has been nicely restored to further rekindle the ambiance of a bygone era. The food, though, is contemporary and innovative, as is the extensive wine list. Appetizer selections include smoked duckling with a muffuletta and dill cream sauce, roasted mushrooms with pine nuts and a red chile stuffing, and tiny quiches filled with shiitaki mushrooms, spinach and sweet peppers. Entrées from the sea have made their way to interior Maine, and include a hearty bouillabaisse, and scallops baked with vermouth, garlic butter, and Parmesan cheese. The sole is stuffed with crab meat, mushrooms, and herbed breading and served with a saffron sauce. Filet mignon, venison chasseur, and prime rib are just a few of the heartier offerings. The desserts are also quite delicious, and range from Black Forest crêpes and peach melba with a raspberry sauce to their mainstay, cordial parfaits made with either Kahlua, Amaretto, or Irish Cream liqueurs. After dinner, some enjoy retiring to the living room for an after-dinner drink in front of the fire. The oak woodwork in this room is particularly lustrous. This is due to a very expensive process called "fuming," where wood is placed in an airtight room and exposed to ammonia vapors until the appropriate color is achieved. It is rarely done any more, due to its prohibitive cost.

For those who desire more a more energetic after-dinner diversion, the Healthworks Spa is outfitted with an array of equipment. There is also a masseuse, hot tub, and steam room. During the day, there are plenty of outdoor activities to enjoy with Bowser. There are several swimming holes and little-known fishing spots that Bud, as well as resident labs Stanley, Steamer, and F.E., are happy to recommend. Golfers will enjoy hitting the links at Sugarloaf Mountain. Hikers will undoubtedly be anxious to venture out along the Appalachian Trail. Fall foliage peepers will thoroughly enjoy the magnificent colors on the seven, 4,000-foot peaks which surround Kingfield. During the winter months, there is also excellent alpine and cross-country skiing, as well as snowshoeing, throughout this picturesque part of Maine.

Enchanted Nights Bed and Breakfast

29 Wentworth Street
Kittery, Maine   03904-1720
(207) 439-1489

Hosts: Nancy Bogenberger and Peter Lamandia
Rooms: 5 doubles, 1 suite
Rates: Doubles and Suite $35-135 (B&B)
Payment: AE, DSC, MC, and VISA
Children: Well-behaved children are welcome (cribs are available)
Dogs: "Furry friends welcome" with prior approval, provided they are not left alone in
the room
Open: All year

Kittery, one of Maine's oldest towns, is also renowned for housing many of this region's outlet stores. Founded in 1623, it was a bustling shipbuilding center for many years, and eventually became the site of the first United States shipyard. Today, Kittery is centrally located for those who want to explore coastal sections of northern Massachusetts, eastern New Hampshire, and southern Maine. One of the more interesting overnight accommodations here is the Enchanted Nights Bed and Breakfast.

This charming 1890s gothic, Princess Anne-style Victorian has withstood the test of time with little compromise. Dramatic, sharply peaked eaves mark the various rooflines, although the focal point is the three-story turret. Two porches, one wraparound and the other an enclosed circular one, are appealing as well. In keeping with the architectural design of the house, Nancy has decorated it with Victorian reproductions, antiques, and an eclectic array of furnishings. Even the walls are papered in patterns that are reflective of the era.

Our first impressions of the interior were of the pressed tin ceilings and ornately carved fireplace mantel in the dining room. These intrinsic features are enhanced by a china hutch, and a pair of glass tables surrounded by wicker chairs. Balloon shades attractively frame the paned windows. A woodstove is usually stoked in the mornings, so that guests are certain to stay warm while dining on their breakfast treats. Some choose the Continental breakfast, which includes homemade pastries, fresh fruit, and a nut salad. Others prefer a heartier repast, and order one of Nancy's full breakfasts. This could include a mushroom and cheese omelette, French toast, or an assortment of pancakes. Afterwards, guests might want to walk through the French doors to the porch that has comfortable furnishings and potted plants. This is a lovely spot to relax and read the paper, while sipping a fresh cup of gourmet coffee.

There are a variety of guest rooms at the B&B. One of the more popular is located on the front side of the house. Guests enter it through an arch draped with a pair of sheer curtains. Once inside this cozy chamber, it is easy to understand its appeal. It is located in the turret, with the ceiling rising to the top of the peak. A windowed alcove looks inviting, while a canopied double bed and a settee covered with an embroidered coverlet nicely complement one another. The floral wallpaper and antique furnishings have diffused light cast over them by the room's stained glass window. Just down the hall, guests will come upon the Floral Room, which derives its name from its period floral wallpaper. Nancy has furnished this room with an ornately carved bed, a marble-topped dresser, and a lovely sidetable. Sheer curtains also frame these windows and area rugs cover the hardwood floors. Another favorite chamber is The Suite, with cathedral ceilings and a large Palladian window. A high queen-size feather bed is set just across the room from a whirlpool bathtub for two. A touch of modernity which most appreciate is the color cable television that can be found in each of the bedrooms. Although the B&B abounds with Victorian character, it is also surprisingly homey and unpretentious.

Recently, Nancy and Peter acquired an adjacent building, which they are completely restoring. During our visit, they had completed two bedrooms and were on their way to refurbishing the rest. They felt this project would take almost three years to complete. In the interim, some of the bedrooms will be open to guests who will not only enjoy their spaciousness and modern amenities, but also the private bathrooms equipped with Jacuzzis.

Bowser will not only enjoy taking walks along Kittery's side streets, but also exploring the neighboring communities of Ogunquit, Wells, and Kennebunkport. An artists' community by reputation, Ogunquit has a terrific cliff walk that wends along the ocean. Kennebunkport and Wells, on the other hand, offer differing perspectives of Maine's coastal communities. For those who are searching for a more natural setting, we suggest a visit to Gerrish Island. Here, visitors will discover the 92-acre Fort Foster Park, which has a beach, picnic sites, a fishing pier, and even a baseball field.

The Trailing Yew

Lobster Cove Road
Monhegan Island, Maine   04852
(207) 596-0440

Innkeeper: *Mrs. Josephine Davis Day*
Rooms: *35 doubles*
Rates: *$50 per person (MAP)*
Payment: *Personal checks*
Children: *Welcome; under 10 years of age are charged $15-30 per night*
Dogs: *Well-behaved dogs are welcome (Monhegan Island has a strict leash law)*
Open: *Mid-May to mid-October*

Monhegan Island, established as a colony by English explorers around 1600, is located approximately ten miles off the Maine coastline. This small, rustic, and rocky island retains much of the same charm that it did over 100 years ago. To this day, the island does not permit off-island automobiles on it, and telephones and electricity (supplied by solar power) are relatively new additions. This sort of lifestyle is not for everyone; however, for those who are intrigued with solitude, deep pine forests, marsh lands, and crashing waves, the island and its inn prove to be an idyllic combination.

The Trailing Yew is a haven for artists and naturalists, offering clean and simple accommodations. Located on a hill above Monhegan Harbor, the inn has a terrific view of the ocean. In addition to the main house, there are four out-buildings. Each of the guest rooms is equipped with an oil lamp for light, a bed, a bureau, and hot and cold running water. Josephine, who has been running the inn since 1926, supplies linens and blankets, but reminds guests to bring flashlights, as well as sleeping bags in the spring and fall. The accommodations are not heated, and thus a sleeping bag or extra blanket does come in handy on the cooler nights.

There is plenty to do on the island. One option is a visit to Cathedral Woods, that is highlighted by its 160-foot cliffs, known as White Head and Black Head. Another outing could include the wildlife sanctuary on the island where as many as 200 species of birds live during the summer months. There are also many hiking trails that traverse the island. Care should be taken on some of these as they can be narrow and rocky in spots.

After a day of exploring the island, people have usually built up a good appetite and a penchant for conversation with the other guests. Even though Josephine is in her mid-90s, she still prepares most of the breakfasts and dinners. The hearty meals are served in the main house and are presented family-style at long tables. There is a selection of fresh fish and usually one meat dish. Breakfast and dinner are included in the price, and lunch is available at an extra charge. Visitors will also discover, after a few days on the island, that they have a greater appreciation for the benefits of a simple and unjaded island lifestyle. As Josephine puts it when she is asked about things to do, there is "the whole island.... there is nothing man-made, only what God made." First-time guests will find the charm and simplicity of Monhegan Island to be quite addictive, which explains why many have been making the sojourn, by ferry boat, to The Trailing Yew for years.

Andrews Lodging Bed and Breakfast

417 Auburn Street
Route 26
Portland, Maine 04103
(207) 797-9157, Fax (207) 797-9040

Hosts: *Elizabeth and Douglas Andrews*
Rooms: *5 doubles, 1 suite*
Rates: *Doubles $60-70 (B&B), Suite $125 (B&B)*
Payment: *AE, MC, and VISA*
Children: *Welcome on a "limited basis"*
Dogs: *Welcome, if the dog is under two years of age it must be crated*
Open: *All year*

Portland, Maine has undergone quite a transformation in the last decade. The historic waterfront and downtown areas have been nicely revitalized and an assortment of noteworthy new shops and restaurants have sprung up. Those who are interested in visiting Portland, but do not necessarily need to be in the center of it, will enjoy the Andrews Lodging Bed and Breakfast. Situated about ten minutes from downtown Portland, this handsome, white clapboard Colonial-style home, is surrounded by mature plantings, lovely gardens, and a small lawn. We were greeted by the very congenial Elizabeth and her entourage of cats and a dog.

A side entrance opens to reveal a hallway and a back staircase that leads up to the guest bedrooms. Most of these chambers occupy the back wing of the house, and the suite is set off by itself, just opposite the upstairs common area. The common area is well laid out, and offers more than just a television and comfortable chairs. There is also a kitchenette and a washer/dryer, which is especially convenient for long-term guests. Aside from these conveniences though, we felt comfortable relaxing in the soft sofa and sidechairs and watching the large screen television. Just around the corner, there is an intimate sitting room, looking quite club-like with its golf motif wallpaper and navy blue sofa set across from a group of windows. A bookshelf is packed with paperbacks that guests often borrow during their stay. Just across the hall is the expansive suite. An Oriental rug covers the hardwood floors in here, and is topped with Shaker reproduction furnishings. The separate sitting room provides extra space to spread out, although all of this is almost secondary to the whirlpool tub set under skylights in the modern bathroom.

As guests walk back through the common room, and past a portable telephone for their use, they will enter the wing of other bedrooms. While these are obviously not as spacious as the suite, they are nicely decorated with patterned wallpapers that set the decorative theme for each chamber. Some are furnished with a pair of finial twin beds, while others have brass, maple, or wicker queen-size bedsteads. A variety of folk art fits in well with the country quilts in all the bedrooms. Guests usually appreciate the convenience of a clock radio and brass reading lamps, as well. Our favorite room is the golf room which, true to its name, is wallpapered in a golf motif. An old set of clubs hangs from a hook on the wall, and an assortment of golf books, prints, and memorabilia can be found throughout this chamber. The only potential drawback is the fact that all the bedrooms in this wing share one bathroom, which is located just down the hall.

Each morning, breakfast is served in the Andrews' lovely dining room. This bright chamber is decorated with soft, gray patterned wallpaper and a painted wainscoting. The long rectangular table is covered with a French Provincial fabric and coordinated placemats. The hearty affair consists of assorted homemade muffins and breads, fresh fruit, whole grain cereals, and gourmet coffee. Anyone who wants a little more, or something entirely different, can request it. With children of her own, and a husband who is usually off early to tend to his veterinary practice, this can be an especially hectic time of the day. But even with all there is to do, Elizabeth likes talking with her guests about local activities that might be of interest to them.

Elizabeth seems to know about all the interesting walks, tours, sights, and attractions available in Portland. On the property, they have badminton, croquet, and bocce along with a small ice skating rink in the winter months. Within Portland, there are a number of huge parks where Bowser can stretch his legs. Bradbury Mountain, consisting of 270 acres, is just north of Portland and west of Freeport. Others may prefer heading south to scenic Cape Elizabeth. Here, in Fort Williams State Park, visitors can explore the Portland Head Light, which has been in continuous operation since 1791. There are a few paths to walk along here, as well as a museum and a host of picnic spots. The Two Lights State Park offers additional walks, but even more spectacular views of Casco Bay and the islands.

Oceanside Meadows Bed and Breakfast

P.O. Box 90
Route 195
Prospect Harbor, Maine   04669
(207) 963-5557, Fax (207) 963-5928

Hostess: *Sonja J. Sundaram*
Rooms: *6 doubles, 1 suite*
Rates: *$65-85 (B&B)*
Payment: *AE, DC, MC, and VISA*
Children: *Welcome (cribs, cots, and highchairs are available)*
Dogs: *Well-behaved dogs are welcome with advance notice*
Open: All year.

Anyone who has ever visited Mount Desert Island, or has heard about the magnificent countryside and spectacular ocean views throughout this picturesque region, will certainly want to investigate this majestic promontory. Sometimes, it can be a bit crowded (by Maine standards); however, there is a peninsula just to the east of Mount Desert Island that proves to be almost as appealing and less traveled. Visitors will discover small coastal Maine towns like Winter Harbor and Prospect Harbor, as well as the renowned Schoodic Point, that are about as "Downeast" as you are likely to find. Schoodic Point is at the southern most tip of this peninsula, where visitors will come across an amazing headland that rises 500 feet above the ocean and offers commanding views of passing vessels with Mount Desert Island and the Bay of Fundy as the backdrops. Visitors who do make the extra effort to visit the Schoodic Point will enjoy a relatively unspoiled perspective of "life as it should be," in a region that is reminiscent of a bygone era.

As travelers meander along winding backcountry roads, they will eventually emerge in the small town of Prospect Harbor. A short distance away, lies a charming cove where a lovely sand beach can be found just beyond the marsh grass, a rarity in Maine. Overlooking this bucolic scene is an old captain's home, dating back to 1860, that rests on a small knoll. As guests follow the gravel drive, they will pass a split-rail fence and an old dory filled with lobster traps. Upon arriving at the house, the spacious lawn, assorted perennial gardens, and a small storage barn round out the rural scene. Most enter the B&B by way of the back door, which leads into a bright and open breakfast room, where several tables are covered with green and white tablecloths. In addition to the lovely views, guests will also enjoy a hearty country breakfast in here each morning.

The spacious living room is another comfortable congregating spot in the house. In here, couches and sidechairs center on an Oriental rug which lies in front of the fireplace. A ship's model and assorted collectibles are placed upon a windowed alcove, which also happens to bring in ample amounts of natural light. The guest bedrooms are all located upstairs. The suite is the nicest of these spaces, and is furnished with a queen bed, and two twin beds tucked into an alcove. The second- and third-floor guest chambers are Spartan but are very pleasant, with casual furnishings and a charming decor. The pastel yellow and blue bedrooms are set under the eaves and have wonderful views of the cove. It is the views, quite frankly, that make the Oceanside Meadows so appealing. One small chamber on the rear of the house, has a walk through closet that leads into the front bedroom, an ideal configuration for families. Most of these bedrooms have a common bathroom, although this will soon change as Sonja is planning to transform some of the large closets into private bathrooms during the winter months.

In addition to the terrific sandy beach and the fresh water marsh and pond, many visitors also enjoy taking a leisurely hike with Bowser along the rocky coast to the lighthouse. There are also an assortment of sights nearby, ranging from Bartlett's Maine Estate Winery and a U.S. Bells foundry to the nearby town of Corea (one of the most photographed towns in the region). During the summer months, there are also countless festivals and fairs that are fun to attend, especially with your canine cohort in tow.

Country Club Inn

P.O. Box 680
Rangeley, Maine 04970
(207) 864-3831

Hosts: Sue Crory and Margery Jamison
Rooms: 19 doubles
Rates: $108 (B&B), $144-160 (MAP)
Payment: AE, MC, and VISA
Children: Welcome (cribs, cots, and highchairs are available)
Dogs: Welcome with a charge of $10 per dog
Open: December 26 - March 31, May 15 - October 10

The Country Club Inn is most memorable for its incredible panoramic views of Rangeley Lake and the distant mountains from atop the inn's 2,000-foot hillside location. The inn was built in the 1920s by a group of wealthy sportsmen, who discovered the lakes were ideal for fly-fishing and vacationing. Some years later, Sue Crory and Margery Jamison also recognized the appeal of the area and felt the Country Club Inn would be an ideal place for an intimate, family-style resort.

People with a love of the outdoors still frequent the Country Club Inn, but the inn has also developed quite a reputation for its golf facilities. Guests enter the property by way of one of two roads that wend past an 18-hole golf course. New arrivals quickly discover that the center of activity is in the main lodge. Our favorite place is the cavernous living room, with its cathedral ceiling, comfortable sofas and armchairs, and moosehead mounted over the enormous fieldstone fireplace. When the corner television is turned on, it is usually switched to a golf tournament. There are also a number of other videos to watch, including golf (of course), and a stack of games to play at any of the sitting areas in the room. Once guests walk through the front door, they suddenly feel they could be anywhere in the world, possibly even in the Lake District of Scotland. This feeling continues in the pub, where tall stools line the old-fashioned bar. We have to admit, the golf cleat marks *do* give this room all the more character.

Another spot at the inn of which Sue and Margery are justifiably proud is the dining room. Here, every table is privy to spectacular lake and mountain views through the walls of plate glass windows. The delicious entrées are almost secondary to the 180-degree views. The menu is constantly changing, with selections such as roast duck montmorency, New York sirloin steak, and filet mignon complemented with a variety of pasta, chicken, and fish dishes. This is an extremely filling meal, as it is also accompanied by bread, salad, vegetables, rice or potato, and dessert. Everything is homemade, adding to the intimate family ambiance.

As we mentioned earlier, the same impressive views found in the dining room are duplicated in many of the bedrooms. These are located in three separate, one-story buildings and are simply, yet attractively decorated with delicate floral wallpapers, quilted bedspreads, and wall-to-wall carpeting. A few of the rooms are somewhat dated in decor but exude the same overall appeal. The bathrooms are on the small side, but they are private and well appointed. Comfortable armchairs are set in front of the small picture windows to take advantage of the lovely views. In warmer weather, many enjoy relaxing on their flagstone terraces, which overlook the lower blueberry fields, woods, and Rangeley Lakes.

The Country Club Inn is just the right vacation destination for anyone wanting a variety of activities. Most of the grassy areas are dedicated to golf; however, there are also expansive lawns that are perfect for bocci, horseshoes, and croquet. Swimming is popular at the pool, which is also easily accessible from the guest rooms. In the winter, many people take to the slopes at nearby Saddleback and Sugarloaf. The inn also gets a large number of cross-country skiers and snowmobilers who utilize the 100 miles of groomed trails that wend through the area. At the end of a busy day, guests look forward to a crackling fire and plenty of good company at the main lodge.

Bowser will enjoy his time at the Country Club Inn. A long, winding road leads from the inn down to the lake. A bit further afield is the Rangeley State Park, which offers wonderful beaches and nature trails for exploring. The Appalachian Mountain Trail runs through the area and can be used for day hikes through these scenic mountains. A short drive will bring visitors to downtown Rangeley, where there are shops and additional access to the lake.

We have been writing about the Country Club Inn for years. While the rooms could probably use a little updating, the warmth and hospitality guests feel from Sue and Margery and their extended family, is truly special. This is a family-run inn that usually exceeds the expectations of most guests, yet in the subtlest of ways.

Crown 'n' Anchor Inn

P.O. Box 228
121 North Street
Saco, Maine 04072-0228
(207) 282-3829

Innkeepers: *John Barclay and Martha Forester*
Rooms: *5 doubles, 1 suite*
Rates: *Doubles $50-85 (B&B), Suite $85 (B&B)*
Payment: *MC and VISA*
Children: *Welcome*
Dogs: *Welcome with advance notice and prior approval in the larger guest rooms*
Open: *All year*

The southern Maine coast has always attracted visitors, who are usually drawn to the picturesque towns and magnificent ocean views. Some of the more well-known places along the coast include Kennebunkport, Kittery, Ogunquit, and Wells; however, those who want to be slightly off the beaten path might want to consider Saco. It is located between Kennebunkport and Portland, offers a small town atmosphere, and fewer tourists. Granted, it does not have the seaside charms found in the other aforementioned communities, but it is convenient to just about everything a visitor might want to do. When staying in Saco, one of the best options is the Crown 'n' Anchor Inn, a graceful, two-story Greek Revival mansion that dates back to 1827.

An elegant two-story portico, supported by Doric columns, marks the entrance to the inn, The Greek Revival architecture actually has a bit of a Federal-style incorporated into its design as well. This is especially apparent when looking at the front door, which is flanked by sidelights and topped with a semi-circular, decorative wooden fan. Just inside the foyer, the elegant main staircase rises to the second floor bedrooms, and a double living room can be seen off to the side. We were drawn to a series of framed prints of the renowned glass flowers that are displayed in the botanical section of Harvard University's Museum of Natural History. It turns out that these are reflective of the house's history as well, as one of its owners was Stephen L. Goodale. Although Mr. Goodale was a respected chemist, botanist, and horticulturist, it was his son, Dr. George Lincoln Goodale, who not only became the director of the Harvard Botanical Garden, but eventually had these magnificently detailed glass flower models produced for one of the University's museums. Anyone who has not seen the collection, should do so, as it is truly amazing and one of a kind.

The common areas of the Crown 'n' Anchor Inn are the most impressive part of the house. It is easy to understand why the double living room is a popular site for weddings and other formal occasions. The high ceilings in here are enhanced by thick moldings and elaborate wainscotings. The walls are covered in a formal gold patterned wallpaper, while a lovely blue fabric is used in the floor-to-ceiling window treatments. An array of intricately carved Victorian antiques, including straight-back chairs and marble-topped tables, is quite impressive. A pair of six-foot-high, gilt-edged mirrors appear at opposite ends of these rooms, making them appear even more spacious. Portraits appear on the wall above the fireplace, while antique crystal candlesticks and a small collection of decorative china is placed on the mantels. Around the corner, behind the staircase, is the surprisingly intimate dining room, which is furnished with Chippendale and Queen Anne-style antiques that reflect a rich patina. Each morning, a "bountiful" country breakfast is presented.

As John was escorting us up the stairs, he told us that he had formerly been an innkeeper at a New Castle establishment for nine years, before coming to the Crown 'n' Anchor Inn. Over the last four years, he explained, sounding a little overwhelmed, business has been virtually nonstop with weddings and overnight guests. As we explored the upstairs bedrooms, it was easy to see why the inn was so popular. The guest rooms are all nicely appointed with yet more antiques and period furnishings. These included such pieces as a Queen Anne wing chair and a Sheraton-style chest of drawers. In one corner, a tiny barrel table was topped with a lamp created from an Oriental vase. The configurations are all quite different, with the intimate twin-bedded Nettie Chase and Lincoln rooms, or the more spacious Normandy Suite. The latter offers a double bed, but even more enticing are the pair of fireplaces and the bathroom with a boxed-in Jacuzzi tub. Most of the chambers have double beds, adorned with either Bates spreads or handmade quilts. The intrinsic architectural features in these chambers, such as the lustrous hardwood floors, detailed moldings, and wainscotings, make them truly outstanding. The Indian shuttered windows are edged by attractive valances that are nicely coordinated with the colors in the handsome wallpapers. Most of the good-size bathrooms have black and white tile floors, ample showers, and a pleasant array of bath accoutrements.

While most people are comfortable enjoying the inn's lovely setting, others will want to explore the neighboring communities. Bowser will probably want to romp on the beach or visit some of the local state parks. One of the most convenient, is the Ferry Beach State Park, which consists of over 100 acres. Here, visitors will find nature trails, picnic sites, and even swimming (for those who like invigorating water temperatures). Further north, there is Cape Elizabeth, which is not only quite scenic but also near Two Lights State Park and the Portland Head Light. Kennebunkport also has many beaches and coastal walks that are great fun for Bowser. Drive south to Ogunquit, where there is a interesting artists' colony and a yet another terrific walk wending along the cliffs.

The Craignair Inn

533 Clark Island Road
Spruce Head, Maine 04859
(207) 594-7644

Innkeeper: Theresa E. Smith
Rooms: 2 singles, 20 doubles
Rates: Doubles $42-91 (B&B)
Payment: AE, MC, and VISA
Children: Welcome (cribs, cots, highchairs, and babysitters are available)
Dogs: Welcome; but the owners must be aware of the leash law
Open: All year

One of the many wonderful things about the Craignair Inn is its proximity to civilization, yet its overall feeling of remoteness. The natural setting allows visitors to thoroughly relax and focus on the picturesque Maine coastline. The inn is set on four acres of shore-front property at the end of Spruce Head, which is connected to Clark Island by a narrow spit of land. The inn was built in 1928 and formerly served as a residence for granite quarry workers. Some of the granite extracted from Clark Island was used to build two Central Park bridges and the Brooklyn Battery Tunnel located in New York, as well the Library of Congress in Washington D.C. Today, the old boarding house has been nicely refurbished and accommodates guests who, rather than working the quarries, prefer to enjoy the picturesque surroundings and swim in the invigorating waters.

The road to the inn passes by the old Union Hall, General Store, Post Office, and a few of the old quarry workers' homes. We have been to The Craignair Inn many times over the years, and the wonderful old, three-story main building is still surrounded by lawns and framed with flower gardens. A newer building, the Vestry Annex, is tucked just behind it. Guests register at the main inn, which is delightfully informal and inviting. As they walk through the first floor, guests will find the parlor, which is warmed by a woodstove. In here, visitors can often be found playing the piano, a game of chess, or just quietly reading in one of the well-worn sofas or sidechairs.

Just across from the parlor is the good-sized dining room, with a wall of windows overlooking the water. This room is often considered the heart of the inn, where many guests are inclined to linger over their meals, not only enjoying the conversation, but also the beautiful views of the ocean and Clark Island, just across the way. Each morning, a full breakfast consisting of eggs, pancakes, sausage, breads, fruits, and juices is served.

The dinner menu offers a New England seafood chowder, vegetable tempura, and sautéed mussels in white wine. The entrées range from a seafood paella and bouillabaisse to herbed rabbit and chicken roulade (the inn's specialty). One of the perennial favorites is a traditional Maine shore dinner. This is a feast of chowder, boiled lobster, steamers, and corn-on-the-cob. After dinner, some like to gather in the kitchen around the cast iron cook stove and exchange stories about their day, while others might choose to take a walk beneath the starry skies and enjoy the refreshing ocean breezes.

When it is time to retire for the evening, guests will find the bedrooms are located both in the main inn and the Vestry Annex. Those in the former are simply furnished, with colorful quilts covering brass or iron frame beds. There are always pretty wall hangings, and braided rugs scattered about the hardwood floors. Room 2 is a particularly cozy corner chamber, that has wonderful views from the windows. Whether one has chosen this bedroom or another water view room, guests will want to listen for the distant sounds of the channel buoys and hum of the fishing and lobster boats. It should be noted that there are three shared bathrooms per floor; but that doesn't seem to concern most of the house guests.

The Vestry Annex consists of five guest rooms that are decidedly more contemporary in flavor than the original inn rooms. A pair of queen-size beds covered with Bates spreads are set amid baskets of flowers, while pastoral and seaside scenes are reflected in the framed pictures on the walls. Although these bedrooms have private bathrooms, ceiling fans, plush carpeting, and decks accessible through French doors, they do not offer the same unobstructed waterviews that many of the rooms at the main inn provide.

Clark Island is reached by way of a tiny footbridge and causeway. Once on this mini-oasis, guests will discover it is a wonderful place for walks and for observing both the waterfowl and ocean life in their natural environment. Those who want to adventure beyond the boundaries of the inn can borrow a bicycle and explore the backcountry roads. Many also take a day trip and drive over to Camden (and its state park) or possibly catch the ferry to Monhegan Island. Owl's

Head Lighthouse and State Park is another favorite destination for an outing with one's canine cohort. We think that most people will be content to rest with Bowser amidst the inn's picturesque lawns, while listening to the distant wind chimes, smelling the salt air, and taking in the panoramic views.

The East Wind Inn

P.O. Box 149
Tenants Harbor, Maine 04860
(800) 241-VIEW, (207) 372-6366, Fax (207) 372-6320

Innkeeper: *Tim Watts*
Rooms: *26 doubles*
Rates: *$48-110 (B&B)*
Payment: *AE, MC and VISA*
Children: *Welcome*
Dogs: *Welcome with prior approval*
Open: *All year*

Tenants Harbor is an unassuming hamlet nestled near the end of St. George's peninsula. Anyone who has ever caught the ferry to Monhegan Island has passed by Tenants Harbor. Others may have made this a stop during their trip along the craggy peninsulas that line the coast of Maine. We found this quaint, little fishing village quite by chance, and while we were here, we also investigated the East Wind Inn. The building that houses the inn was built as a sail loft in 1890; however, in 1974 the building was bought by Tim Watts, a native of Tenants Harbor. Situated on the harbor's edge, the inn has wonderful views of the bay from most of its guest bedrooms and common areas, as well as from its large, wraparound porch.

A lovely perennial garden, lined with cobblestones, edges the base of the wraparound porch. Once inside, guests are drawn to the expansive living room, where white wainscoting stands out against the crimson Colonial-style wallpaper. Comfortable furnishings are well placed around the piano and television or facing the wall of windows looking out towards the water.

The bedrooms are located either at the main inn, or a few hundred feet up the road in a separate antique sea captain's house. Those at the inn are accessible by a main staircase, which leads to a variety of simply decorated chambers. Subtle floral or striped wallpapers are the backdrop for the maple or brass and white iron bedsteads. A rocking chair often provides a comfortable place to enjoy the views. Modern conveniences include telephones and televisions. Room One is the most requested chamber, as much for its corner location and water views, as for its adjoining sitting room. The latter has an attractive camelback sofa and sidechairs. A queen-size brass bed and assorted comfortable furnishings are placed upon soft carpeting. Most of the rooms in the main inn have shared bathrooms, while those in the Meeting House have private bathrooms. The bedrooms at the Meeting House are decorated and furnished just like those at the main inn. This house was more recently renovated, however, and is often used as a conference center, therefore the bedrooms in here are usually reserved by groups attending meetings.

Everyone is welcome to enjoy a Continental breakfast in the main dining room each morning. This elongated space is set just off the living room and in the evening also offers a traditional menu that specializes in local Maine products. We thought the harbor views through the wall of windows were just as enticing as the food. Tables are covered with white tablecloths and fine china, which sets the mood for the meal to follow. Appetizers range from sautéed Maine crabcakes and mussels to a hearty New England fish chowder. Entrées feature the East Wind seafood stew with scallops, shrimp, mussels and haddock or the salmon filet on a bed of spinach with a chive and garlic butter sauce. The boiled lobster, grilled country lamb with garden vegetables, and medallions of tenderloin are also worth sampling. All of the pies, cakes, and desserts are prepared at the inn.

During the day, there is much to be found while exploring the area. For those at a loss for something to do, there is a small alcove located toward the rear of the building that contains a rack of brochures giving overviews of the area's activities and attractions. Less structured excursions might include walking Bowser around the waterfront and harbor areas, or driving along the back roads of this rural peninsula. During the last weeks of June and the first weeks of September, sailors of all ability levels may register to take week-long seminars to further improve their sailing skills. Warren Island is a 70-acre recreation area in the Penobscot Bay. This is certainly worth a trip with your canine companion, particularly if you have your own boat. Monhegan Island is another popular daytrip, especially with its array of trails and abundance of flora and fauna. The picturesque town of Camden also has a great state park, which offers magnificent views of the surrounding area and is a great place for both hiking in the summer, and cross-country skiing during the winter months.

Kedarburn Inn

Box 61
Route 35
Waterford, Maine 04088
(207) 583-6182

Innkeepers: Margaret and Derek Gibson
Rooms: 5 doubles, 1 suite
Rates: Doubles $69-88 (B&), Suite $88 (B&B)
Payment: MC and VISA
Children: Welcome, children under four years of age are free of charge
Dogs: Welcome with advance notice
Open: All year

We have always been intrigued with the historic village of Waterford, Maine. Its pristine white clapboard houses located next to tree-lined Lake Keoka, are as appealing as the town common, general store, and intimate restaurant. One of the town's antique houses belongs to Margaret and Derek Gibson, who, after living all over the world, have settled (for now) in Waterford. Actually, they have been residents here for quite some time, although Margaret still retains her British accent and citizenship, along with a strong sense of pride for her homeland.

As a result of Margaret's ties to England, guests are treated to an authentic English B&B experience. Anyone who has stayed in an English B&B, tends to have fond memories of their "holiday" — a stay at the Kedarburn Inn will rekindle memories of those past joys. When we arrived, Margaret was kneeling on the living room floor, carefully blocking one of her handmade quilts. We soon learned that she had been trained at one of the premier sewing schools in England and was quite adept at her craft. The beautiful quilts that can be found hanging from the walls and over the banister result from her mastery of intricate quilting techniques. Margaret also has a small craft shop on the main floor, displaying her handmade items along with others produced by Maine craftspeople.

It would be rather difficult to miss this huge, white frame house when driving through Waterford. It is set into a hill, with a picturesque stream running along the side of it. Originally built in 1858, the house has an interesting history. It was constructed by a local man, who soon thereafter died, leaving it to his daughter. She lived there alone for years, and eventually sold the house to a carpenter. Strangely enough, this large home, which has numerous bedrooms, has never had a family living in it. Now that the Gibsons' daughters are all grown and living on their own, their idea of a family includes the many guests who enjoy staying at the B&B.

The Kedarburn Inn truly feels like home, albeit a stately one. The foyer has a rich, blue carpeting lining the halls and the central staircase. To the rear of the house, there is a sizable living room. Here, comfortable sofas and chairs are intermixed with antiques and more contemporary pieces. A pale blue and white color scheme has been chosen for this sunny chamber, which makes it appear all the more open. Guests can either read, play cards, or watch television in here, but more often than not, people like to talk with Margaret. She has an engaging personality and enjoys discussing the various political and moral issues of the day.

The sunny breakfast room lies just off the living room. During the day there are a variety of English teas set out on a sidetable, so that guests may fix themselves a cup at their convenience. In the afternoon, however, a full English tea with finger sandwiches and sweets is presented between 3:00 and 4:30. Those who miss it, will be able to sample another English tradition the following morning, that of a full English breakfast. This hearty repast consists of hot porridge or cereal, eggs, a meat dish, fresh breads, fruit, and even fried tomatoes. Of course, those interested in a lighter fare can certainly pick and choose from any of these items.

The wonderful aroma emanating from the kitchen each morning is probably the one thing that lulls guests out of a deep sleep. The guest rooms are very appealing, with cozy beds and attractive appointments. At the top of the stairs, off to the left, is one of the larger bedrooms complete with a small sitting area. Draped tables and overstuffed chairs are merely the backdrop for the king-size bed covered with one of Margaret's beautiful quilts. This is also the only bedroom to have a private bathroom. Just across the hall is a yellow room with high ceilings that contains a huge secretary and an antique brass bed draped with a coordinated handmade quilt. Down the hall, past more quilts and stuffed patchwork animals, we arrived at two more rooms that were furnished in a similar fashion. Combinations of either blue and yellow or yellow and pink are very appealing color schemes. After seeing some of the oversized furnishings, we wondered just how they had fared during the Gibsons' numerous moves. Margaret informed us that even though their furniture had made a handful of trans-Atlantic crossings, nothing had ever been damaged.

As tempted as some might be to stay and chat, there are plenty of activities in the area. Bowser will want to say hello to the two resident dogs, a Bichon Frisée and an English Cocker Spaniel. Bowser might also enjoy a walk up the hill next to the stream, or possibly down the hill to the village and lake. Some guests like to rent a boat and spend the day either fishing or exploring Lake Keoka. There are also plenty of popular hiking trails nearby and guests might want to check with Margaret for the exact location of the trail heads. In the winter months, the emphasis turns to cross-country and downhill skiing. Waterford remains a relatively undiscovered area for travelers, and we are certain that its quiet country charm will be greatly enjoyed from the Kedarburn Inn.

The Waterford Inne

Box 49
Chadbourne Road
Waterford, Maine   04088
(207) 583-4037

Innkeepers: Barbara and Rosalie Vanderzanden
Rooms: 9 doubles, 1 suite
Rates: Doubles $74-99 (B&B), Suite $99 (B&B)
Payment: AE
Children: Accepted but not encouraged as there are no special facilities available for them
Dogs: Welcome with prior approval and a nightly fee of $10
Open: All year except April

The Waterford Inne is an 1825 farmhouse located along an old stagecoach route in Maine's Oxford Hills. The inn, situated on 25 acres of woods and fields, is an idyllic setting for those in search of a true country inn experience. The restored farmhouse has an especially refined feeling to it, thanks to the extensive efforts of Barbara and her mother, Rosalie. Rosalie has owned the inn for 17 years, and with each visit we find her even more gracious and hospitable than we previously remembered.

A sense of the 1800s is rekindled as guests wander through the house, with its wide pumpkin pine board floors, beamed ceilings, narrow staircases, and old-fashioned hearths. These architectural features are accented with brass fixtures, period furniture, and intricate stenciling on the walls. There are two common rooms filled to capacity with handsome furnishings, including Queen Anne-style tables, a tall secretary, a harvest table, and an inviting rocking chair all set upon braided rugs. Our favorite chamber is the common room with the barn board walls and an array of dried herbs and flowers hanging from the beamed ceiling. The mix of primitive art and formal antiques is particularly attractive.

The five upstairs bedrooms and four chambers in the old converted woodshed are each decorated using a different theme. The bedrooms that are the most appropriate for guests traveling with dogs are those located in the converted woodshed. These rooms not only allow easy access to the outdoors, but also have small decks overlooking the grounds. Those who want an especially romantic setting, might request the soothing pale blue bedroom with a four-poster bed. Another favorite chamber has a distinct African safari theme (which Bowser might find appealing). The wallpaper in here has lions on it and an imitation animal fur is draped over the bed. Those looking for additional space may request the suite, which also has a fireplace and a private porch. This chamber, and many of the others, have lovely stenciled wallpapers and antiques, which are more in keeping with the house's antique feeling. During the summer months, guests will find fresh bouquets of flowers, picked from the Vanderzanden's extensive gardens, displayed in both the guest and common rooms.

The inn has always been well-known for the superb dinners that Barbara and Rosalie prepare. These gourmet, home-cooked meals are especially notable because they are accompanied by fresh vegetables which are also gathered from their garden. Each of the courses is artfully arranged on beautiful porcelain plates. When we asked about a typical menu, Barbara and Rosalie were quick to point out that they enjoy catering to their guests' palettes and their personal whims. Each night one entrée is presented, along with various side dishes. They will certainly take into account any special dietary needs, but for the most part, they treat their guests as one of the family — whatever is created in the kitchen is that evening's meal. Of course, it is the personal touches and extra attention to detail that bring guests back year after year. Rosalie told us a story about a British couple who had booked two nights at the Waterford Inne and then planned to stay at a variety of other inns in Maine. Two days after their departure they came back to the inn stating that this was going to be their "home" for the rest of their visit.

Bowser, and his human companions, should find the rural locale to be a welcome treat, as there are a number of truly quiet country roads that are ideal for long walks. From high on one hillside, guests can wander over to a white birch grove or down to the base of the road, where there is a stream and waterfall. In the warmer months, many head out to the nearby lakes for swimming and boating; while the colder months bring out an array of cross-country skiers. A short drive away is the hidden village of Waterford, which is listed on the National Register of Historic Places. Bordered by a lake and the surrounding mountains, Waterford is nestled in the heart of rural Maine, far from anything that is remotely commercial. When the Vanderzandens say that Waterford is located in a secret and undiscovered part of Maine, they are sharing with us a piece of their unique understanding of the area. It is for these insights, and more, that The Waterford Inne has become such a wonderful tradition for many people.

Olde Rowley Inn

Route 35
North Waterford, Maine   04267
(800) LOVE-INN, (207) 583-4143

Innkeeper: Ray Peterson
Rooms: 1 single, 4 doubles, 3 suites
Rates: Single $29 (B&B), Doubles $59 (B&B), Suites $69-110 (B&B)
Payment: AE, MC, and VISA
Children: Welcome (highchairs, cots, and babysitters are available)
Dogs: Welcome in certain rooms with a $10 fee
Open: All year

The Olde Rowley Inn stands today as it did over 200 years ago. When it was built in 1790, it was known as the Forest House and used primarily as a stagecoach stop. Visitors will find that it still caters to travelers by offering authentic antique surroundings, unusual rooms, and great food. The tiny village of North Waterford is comprised of the inn, a general store, and a handful of other buildings. Even in these progressive times, the village center has managed to maintain its sense of history. It would be difficult to miss the rambling inn, as it is made up of three connected buildings: the original barn, carriage house, and farmhouse. It has been painted a rich barn-red with yellow trim and black shutters.

Over the years, the buildings have been refurbished many times. During our most recent visit, there had been some additional changes, although nothing too dramatic. The ever-popular restaurant has expanded into most of the former common rooms on the first floor. Where there once had been a cozy parlor with a sofa and chairs, there are now tables. The walls are stenciled and the simple, wooden tables are adorned with neatly folded napkins, floral tablecloths, and tin lanterns. Meandering through the inn, one finds that each room is situated on a slightly different level. The wide king pine and hemlock floors, the exposed beam ceilings, and the 200-year-old fireplaces, some containing the original baking ovens and warming cupboards, lend an additional air of antiquity to the establishment.

Dining patrons have long enjoyed sitting in these rooms and sampling the extensive, seasonally changing menu. During our most recent visit, there had been an interesting addition to the choice of appetizers. This dish was prepared for the second son of the Emperor of Japan who certainly must have enjoyed the scallops in a lobster sauce served on a shell with a fancy potato border. The escargots en croûte with Roquefort cheese is also a notable choice. Entrées range from the delicious Black Angus strip steak and salmon sautéed with lemon, garlic, and white wine, to the more innovative chicken strudel rolled up in ham and Vermont cheddar and then wrapped in a thin pastry. Maui prawns, although a long way from home, are another excellent selection. These are wrapped in a thin Oriental pastry with a honey rum tartar sauce. After such a memorable dinner, many like to linger over their dessert or drinks in front of a crackling fire.

Our two favorite guest chambers are on the first floor. The Hannibal Hamlin Room is at the back of the building, and offers the most privacy. The country antique furnishings in oak nicely complement the hand-hewn exposed beams (both round and square). The bed is covered in a lovely, pastel patchwork quilt. The fresh, clean look extends to the white walls, which are stenciled in a variety of bright colors. The adjacent Blue Room is reminiscent of springtime with its blue and yellow stenciling coordinating with the handmade quilt covering the brass bed. The huge bathroom has a reversed color scheme with white and yellow stenciling. None of these bedrooms are overdone with knickknacks, just a few well-placed pieces of furniture. A narrow staircase leads to the upstairs chambers, where guests quickly discover the other intimate guest rooms. These have also been furnished with pretty period furniture and antique bedsteads, each of which rests upon canted, creaky floorboards.

After a restful night's sleep, guests are offered a full breakfast. The selections vary, and include such dishes as blueberry pancakes, eggs (any style), fruit, and juice. After a filling meal, most people are anxious to explore the area. Although the inn is not set on acres of land, Bowser will still enjoy walking the quiet country lanes which lead from the inn. The local Crooked River is close to the inn, where anglers can fly-fish while Bowser explores the river bank. We suggest that guests inquire at the inn for recommendations on local hiking trails, these vary greatly in difficulty, but will undoubtedly prove appealing to Bowser. Many also decide to rent a boat and spend a quiet day exploring one of the many lakes that dot this region. In the winter, the pace is a bit slower, although there is great cross-country skiing available locally. There is always the option of driving an hour to excellent downhill skiing at Sunday River.

Kawanhee Inn Lakeside Lodge

Box 119
Mt. Blue - Webb Lake
Weld, Maine 04285
Winter Address: 7 High Street, Farmington, Maine 04938
Summer Number: (207) 585-2000, Winter Numbers: (207) 778-4306 or 778-3809

Hostess: Martha Strunk
Rooms: 13 doubles, 1 suite, 11 cottages
Rates: Doubles $75 (EP), Suite $125 (EP), Cottages $550-750 per week (EP)
Payment: MC and VISA
Children: Welcome (cribs, cots, and babysitters are available)
Dogs: Welcome May, June, and October and in one cottage at any time during the season
Open: May 15 through October 15th

It is always a treat to find a place that has maintained its simplicity, avoiding the trappings of modernization. The Kawanhee Inn is one such spot. The main lodge was originally built in 1930 to accommodate the parents of the children attending a nearby boys camp. Set on a knoll overlooking the crystal-clear waters of Lake Webb, little about the lodge has changed over the years. Hunter green window trim set against the dark weathered shingles of the main lodge and cabins enables them to blend in nicely with the dense woods and the cathedral pines surrounding them.

The cabins are located below the main lodge, along the edge of the lake, and offer a great deal of privacy. They are simply constructed and nicely furnished, in a rustic sort of way. Handmade calico curtains frame the windows, while old-fashioned bureaus, beds, and small birch tables fill the rooms. Natural board walls and hand-hewn beams complete the effect. Most of them are considered to be housekeeping units, so guests have the option of preparing their own meals, often choosing to eat them on the screened-in porch. On cool evenings, and there are plenty of these, the warmth from the stone fireplaces merely adds to the rustic aura of these accommodations.

Those who are lucky enough to squeeze in during the in-season months, will be able to enjoy the excellent food served at the main lodge in either the old-fashioned main dining room or on one of the screened-in porches. The menu changes every two weeks. Dinners are substantial, with appetizers such as the crabcakes with lemon dill sauce, vegetable platters with hot crab dip, and stuffed mushroom caps with a crumb seafood stuffing topping the list. The entrée selections include roast prime rib, baked stuffed scallops or trout, and roast duck served with an orange sauce. Those with a penchant for chicken will find many varieties on the menu, ranging from chicken Dijon to a grilled Cajun chicken.

Everything is accompanied by fresh vegetables, rolls, salads, and a choice of potato or rice. Guests will find an equally appealing menu in the morning, and box lunches are available for those planning to be away for the day.

Anyone with a love of the outdoors, particularly for pristine forests and lakes, will want to think about spending some time at the Kawanhee Inn. It is located in a beautifully unique region, where loons can be heard calling to each other over the still waters of Lake Webb and moose can often be seen on its sandy shores. In some ways, it is unfortunate that people traveling with a dog are relegated to the "shoulder" season; however, in many other ways this is really the best time to be here. There is a wonderful sandy swimming beach at the lodge, or the more adventurous can spend hours fishing, canoeing, or hiking on or around Lake Webb. Bowser might be interested in investigating the multitude of hiking trails around the lodge. A short drive will lead to Blueberry Mountain, where a three and a half mile trail leads to a rock summit with incredible views. The Mount Blue State Park offers a great trail that heads up one and a half miles to the top of Mount Blue. Halfway up, hikers will find a fresh water spring for quenching their thirst. For those who are interested in a more leisurely climb, there is one ideal trail up Bald Mountain. In the evening, many choose to congregate in the large beamed-ceiling living room of the main lodge, where they can enjoy the warmth emanating from the huge fieldstone fireplace. Here, there is also a small television, although most prefer playing billiards, cards, or trying their hand at the various board games. The moose head mounted over the fireplace is a subtle reminder, as if it were needed, that this truly is in the wilds of Maine.

As often as we visit the Kawanhee Inn, we find that very little seems to change. We like that, and so do most of the other guests who book rooms year after year, with many trying to visit twice during the season. The combination of a helpful, but unobtrusive staff, comraderie among the guests, and secluded lakeside location make it an ideal vacation for anyone wanting to truly get away from it all.

State Maps

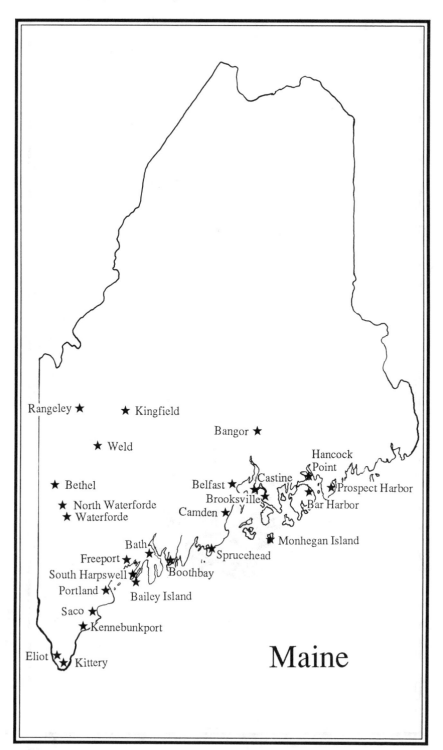

Rangeley ★   ★ Kingfield

Bangor ★

★ Weld

Hancock
Point

★ Bethel   Belfast ★   Castine   Prospect Harbor
                                    Brooksville ★   Bar Harbor
★ North Waterforde   Camden ★
★ Waterforde

                                                Monhegan Island

        Bath
Freeport ★   Sprucehead
South Harpswell   Boothbay
Portland ★
            Bailey Island
    Saco ★
    ★ Kennebunkport

Eliot   Maine
    ★ Kittery

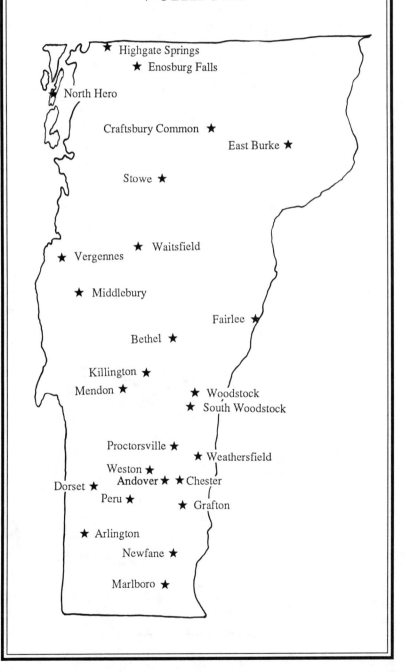

Vermont

★ Highgate Springs
★ Enosburg Falls
★ North Hero
Craftsbury Common ★
East Burke ★
Stowe ★
★ Waitsfield
★ Vergennes
★ Middlebury
Fairlee ★
Bethel ★
Killington ★
Mendon ★
★ Woodstock
★ South Woodstock
Proctorsville ★
★ Weathersfield
Weston ★
Andover ★ ★ Chester
Dorset ★
Peru ★
★ Grafton
★ Arlington
Newfane ★
Marlboro ★

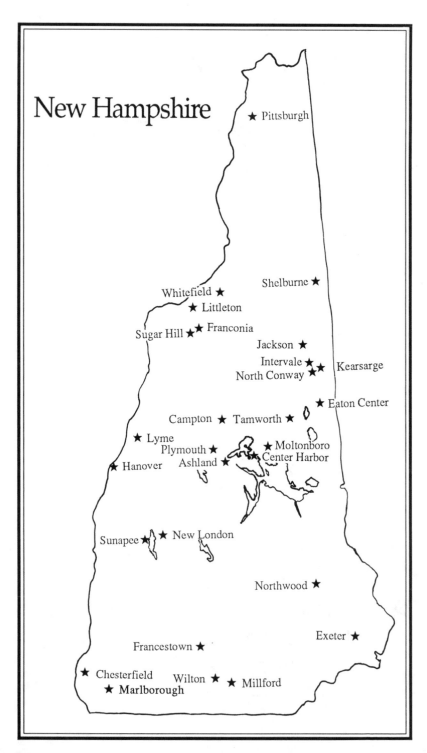

New Hampshire

★ Pittsburgh

★ Shelburne

Whitefield ★
★ Littleton

Sugar Hill ★★ Franconia

Jackson ★

Intervale ★★
North Conway ★★ Kearsarge

★ Eaton Center

Campton ★ Tamworth ★

Lyme ★
Plymouth ★ Moltonboro ★
Ashland ★ Center Harbor ★

Hanover ★

Sunapee ★★ New London

Northwood ★

Exeter ★

Francestown ★

Chesterfield ★
★ Marlborough
Wilton ★ ★ Millford

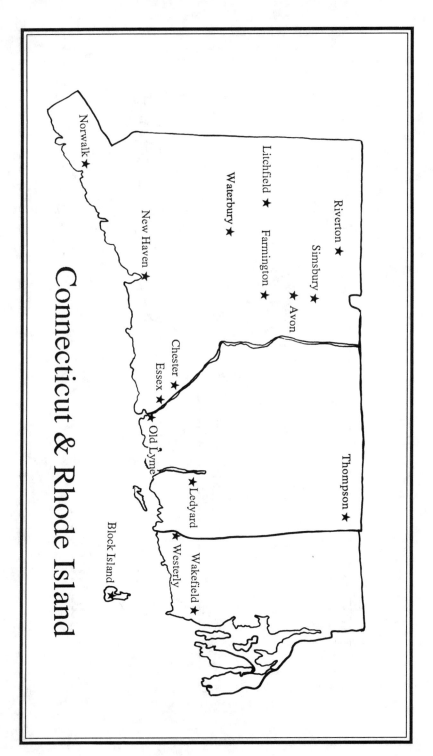

Connecticut & Rhode Island

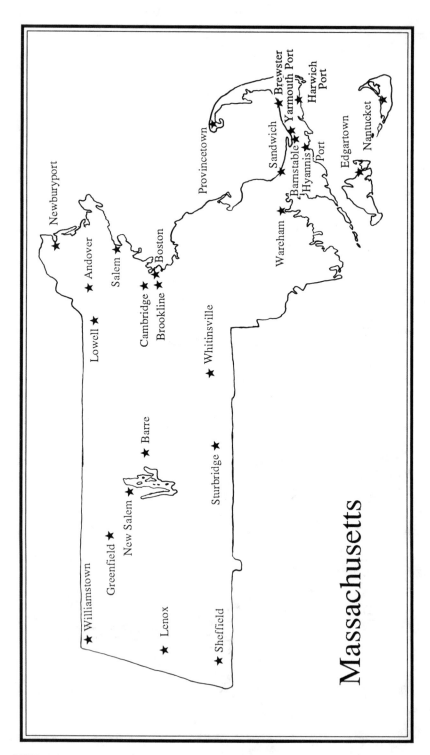

Massachusetts

The Best of the Rest

B&Bs, Inns, Motels, and Hotels

Connecticut

BRANFORD	Branford Motor Inn	(203) 488-8314
	375 East Main St.	
BRIDGEPORT	Days Inn	(203) 366-5421
	815 Lafayette Blvd.	
	Holiday Inn	(203) 334-1234
	1070 Main St	
CROMWELL	Comfort Inn	(203) 635-4100
	111 Berlin Road	
	Holiday Inn	(203) 635-1001
	4 Sebethe Drive	
	Radisson Hotel	(203) 635-2000
	100 Berlin Road	
	Super 8 Motel	(203) 632-8888
	1 Industrial Park Rd	
DANBURY	Danbury Hilton	(203) 794-0600
	18 Old Ridgebury Rd.	
	Ethan Allen Inn	(203) 744-1776
	21 Lake Ave (Extension)	
	Hilton	(203) 794-0600
	18 Old Ridgebury Rd.	
	Holiday Inn	(203) 792-4000
	80 Newtown Rd.	
	Ramada Inn	(203) 792-3800
	(exit 8 off I-84)	
DARIEN	Comfort Inn	(203) 655-8211
	50 Ledge Rd.	
EAST HARTFORD	Holiday Inn	(203) 528-9611
	363 Roberts St.	
	Ramada Hotel	(203) 528-9703
	100 East River Dr.	
	Wellesley Inn	(203) 289-4950
	333 Roberts St	
EAST WINDSOR	Ramada Inn	(203) 623-9411
	161 Bridge St.	
ENFIELD	Red Roof Inn	(203) 741-2571
	5 Hazard Rd.	
FARMINGTON	Farmington Inn	(203) 677-2821
	827 Farmington Ave	
GROTON	Best Western	(203) 445-8000
	360 Route 12	

	Gold Star Inn	(203) 446-0660
	156 King's Highway	
	Trails Corner Lodge	(203) 445-0220
	580 Poquonnock Road	
HARTFORD	Hilton Hotel	(203) 249-5611
	1 Hilton Plaza	
	Holiday Inn Downtown	(203) 549-2400
	50 Morgan St.	
	Ramada Hotel Downtown	(203) 528-9703
	100 East River Dr.	
	Ramada Inn Capitol Hill	(203) 246-6591
	440 Asylum St	
	Sheraton Hartford Hotel	(203) 728-5151
	315 Trumbull St.	
	Super 8 Motel	(203) 246-8888
	57 West Service Rd	
LAKEVILLE	Interlaken Inn Resort	(203) 345-9878
	74 Interlaken Rd	
	Iron Masters	(203) 435-9844
	229 Main St.	
	Wake Robin Inn	(203) 435-2515
	Rte 41	
MANCHESTER	Clarion Inn	(203) 643-5811
	191 Spencer St	
MERIDEN	Hampton Inn	(203) 235-5154
	10 Bee St	
	Ramada Inn	(203) 238-2380
	275 Research Pkwy	
	Residence Inn	(203) 634-7770
	390 Bee St	
MILFORD	Hampton Inn	(203) 874-4400
	129 Plans Rd	
	Red Roof Inn	(203) 877-6060
	10 Rowe Ave.	
	Holiday Inn	(203) 878-6561
	1212 Boston Post Rd.	
MYSTIC	Harbour Inn & Cottages	(203) 572-9253
	RFD#1, Box398	
	Hilton Hotel	(203) 572-0731
	20 Coogan Rd	
	Howard Johnson's	(203) 536-2654
	176 Greemanville Rd	
	Ramada Inn	(203) 536-4281
	Route 27	

NEW BRITAIN	Ramada Inn 65 Columbus Blvd.	(203) 224-9161
NEW HAVEN	Residence Inn 3 Long Wharf Dr.	(203) 777-5337
NEW LONDON	Radisson Hotel 35 Gov. Winthrop Bvd.	(203) 443-7000
	Red Roof Inn 707 Colman St.	(203) 444-0001
NEW PRESTON	Atha House Wheaton Rd	(203) 355-7387
NORTH HAVEN	Holiday Inn 201 Washington Ave	(203) 239-4225
NORWALK	Holiday Inn 789 Connecticut Ave.	(203) 853-3477
NORWICH	Ramada Inn 10 Laura Blvd.	(203) 889-5201
	Sheraton 1 Sheraton Plaza	(203) 889-5201
OLD SAYBROOK	Heritage Inn 1500 Boston Post Rd	(203) 388-3743
	Sandpiper Motor Inn 1750 Boston Post Rd.	(203) 399-7973
PLAINVILLE	Howard Johnson's Lodge 400 New Britian Ave	(203) 747-6876
PUTNAM	King's Inn 5 Heritage Rd	(203) 928-7961
SHELTON	Ramada Inn 780 Bridgeport Ave	(203) 929-1500
	Residence Inn 1001 Bridgeport Ave.	(203) 926-9000
SOUTHBURY	Ramada Inn 1284 Strongtown Rd	(203) 598-7600
STAMFORD	Raddison Tara Hotel 2701 Summer St	(800) 777-1700
	Ramada Inn 19 Clark's Hill Dr.	(203) 327-4300
STRATFORD	Ramada Inn 225 Lordship Blvd.	(203) 375-8866
VERNON	Howard Johnson's 451 Hartford Turnpike	(203) 875-0781
WATERBURY	Best Western Schrafft's Drive	(203) 597-8000
	Holiday Inn 63 Grand St	(203) 596-1000

	Howard Johnson's	(203) 756-7961
	2636 South Main St	
	Seventy Hillside B&B	(203) 596-7070
	70 Hillside Ave	
	Super 8 Motel	(203) 757-0888
	91 Scott Rd	
WEST BROOK	Maple's Motel	(203) 399-9345
	1935 Boston Post Rd	
WEST HAVEN	Days Hotel	(203) 933-0344
	490 Saw Mill Rd	
WETHERSFIELD	Ramada Inn	(203) 563-2311
	1330 Silas Deane Highway	
WINDSOR	Residence Inn	(203) 688-7474
	100 Dunfey Lane	
WINDSOR LOCKS	Budgetel Inn	(203) 623-3336
	64 Ella T. Crasso Tpke	
	Howard Johnson's	(203) 623-9811
	Center St.	
	Homewood Suites	(203) 627-8463
	65 Ella T. Grasso Tpke.	
	Sheraton Hotel (Bradley)	(203) 627-5311
	1 Bradley International Airport	

Rhode Island

GREENHILL	Fairfield by the Sea	(401) 789-4717
	527 Greenhill Rd	
KINGSTOWN	Holiday Inn	(401) 789-1051
	3009 Tower Hill Rd	
MIDDLETOWN	Budget Inn	(401) 849-4700
	1185 West Main Rd	
	Comfort Inn of Newport	(401) 846-7600
	936 West Main Rd	
	Howard Johnson's	(401) 849-2000
	351 West Main Rd.	
NEWPORT	Marriott Hotel	(401) 849-1000
	25 America Cup Ave.	
	Motel 6	(401) 848-0600
	249 J.T. Connell Hwy	
PORTSMOUTH	Founder's Brook Motel/Stes	(401) 683-1244
	314 Boyd's Lane	
PROVIDENCE	Holiday Inn Downtown	(401) 831-3900
	21 Atwells Ave.	
	Marriott	(401) 272-2400
	Charles and Orms Sts.	
WARWICK	Comfort Inn (Airport)	(401) 732-0470
	1940 Post Rd	
	Econo Lodge	(401) 737-7400
	2138 Post Rd	
	Holiday Inn	(401) 732-6000
	800 Greenwich Ave	
	Residence Inn	(401) 737-7100
	500 Kilbert St	
	Sheraton Tara Hotel	(401) 738-4000
	1850 Post Rd.	

Massachusetts

AMHERST	Howard Johnson 401 Russell St.	(413) 586-0114
	University Motor Lodge 345- North Pleasant St.	(413) 256-8111
ANDOVER	Boston Marriott Andover 123 Old River Rd.	(508) 975-3600
ATTLEBORO	Emma C's B&B 18 French Farm Rd	(508) 226-6365
BEDFORD	Stouffer Bedford Glen Hotel 44 Middlesex Tpk.	(617) 275-5500
	Travel Lodge 285 Great Rd.	(617) 275-6120
BOSTON	Boston Back Bay Hilton 40 Dalton St.	(617) 236-1100
	Boston Park Plaza Hotel One Park Plaza/Arington St.	(617) 426-2000
	Hilton-Back Bay 40 Dalton St.	(617) 236-1100
	Hilton-Logan Airport 75 Service Rd.-Logan Airport	(617) 569-9300
	Marriott Hotel Copley Place 110 Huntington Ave	(617) 236-5800
	Sheraton Boston Hotel 39 Dalton St.	(617) 236-2000
	Swissotel 1 Ave. de Lafayette	(617) 451-2600
	Westin Hotel, Copley Place 10 Huntington Ave.	(617) 262-9600
BURLINGTON	Day's Inn 30 Wheeler Rd.	(617) 270-9834
	Howard Johnson 98 Middlesex Turnpike	(617) 272-6550
	Marriott 1 Mall Rd.	(617) 229-6565
CAMBRIDGE:	Howard Johnson's 777 Memorial Drive	(617) 492-7777
	Marriott 2 Cambridge Center	(617) 494-6600
CENTERVILLE	Centerville Corner's Mtr Crt. 369 South Main St	(508) 775-7223
CHELMSFORD	Howard Johnson's 187 Chelmsford St	(508) 256-7511

CHICOPEE	Best Western	(413) 592-6171
	463 Memorial Dr	
CONCORD	Howard Johnson's	(508)369-6100
	740 Elm St.	
DANVERS	Econo Lodge	(508) 777-1700
	50 Dayton St	
	Residence Inn	(508)777-7171
	51 Newbury St	
EASTHAM	Town Crier Motel	(508)255-4000
	Rte. 6	
FALL RIVER	Days Inn	(508) 676-1991
	332 Milliken Blvd	
	Holiday Inn	(508) 672-9011
	360 Airport Rd	
FALMOUTH	Falmouth Inn	(508) 540-2500
	824 Main St	
	Mariner Motel	(508) 548-1331
	555 Main St	
	Quality Inn	(508) 540-2000
	291 Jones Rd	
FITCHBURG	Royal Plaza Hotel	(508) 342-7100
	150 Royal Plaza Dr	
FRAMINGHAM	Red Roof Inn	(508) 872-4499
	650 Cochituate Dr	
GREENFIELD	Candle Light Motor Inn	(413) 772-0101
	208 Mohawk Trail	
	Hitchcock House	(413) 774-7452
	15 Congress St	
HADLEY	Howard Johnson's	(413) 516-0114
	401 Russell St	
HAVERHILL	Best Western	(508) 373-1511
	401 Lowel Ave	
	Comfort Suites	(508) 374-7755
	106 Bank Rd	
HOLYOKE	Holiday Inn	(413) 534-3311
	245 Whiting Farms Rd.	
HYANNIS	Sheraton-Hyannis	(617) 771-3000
	Rte. 132	
HYANNIS PORT	Sea Breeze Cottages	(508) 775-4269
	397 Sea St (rear)	
KINGSTON	Howard Johnsn's	(617) 585-3831
	Rte 3, exit 9	
LAWRENCE	Hampton Inn	(508) 975-4050
	224 Winthrop Ave	
LEE	Hunter's Motel	(413) 243-0101
	Rte 10	

LOWELL	Sheraton Inn	(508) 452-1200
	50 Warren St.	
MANSFIELD	Holiday Inn	(508) 339-2200
	31 Hampshire St	
	Motel 6	(508) 339-2323
	60 ForbesBlvd	
MARLBORO	Best Western	(508) 460-0700
	181 Boston Post Rd West	
	Super 8	(508) 460-1000
	880 Donald J. Lynch Blvd	
MIDDLEBORO	Days Inn	(508) 946-4400
	Clark St East	
METHUEN:	Methuen Inn	(617) 686-2971
	159 Pelham St.	
MILFORD	Sheraton Inn	(508) 478-7010
	11 Beaver St	
NANTUCKET	Nantucket Inn	(508) 228-6900
	27 Macy's Lane	
	10 Hussey Street	(800)245-9552
	10 Hussey St	
NATICK	Holiday Inn	(508) 653-8800
	1360 Worcester Rd	
NEEDHAM	Sheraton Hotel	(617) 444-1110
	100 Cabott St	
NEW BEDFORD	Days Inn	(508)997-1231
	500 Hathaway Rd	
NEWTON	Days Inn	(617) 969-5300
	399 Grove St	
NORTH HAMPTON	Quality Hotel	(413) 586-1211
	1 Atwood Dr	
ORLEANS	Holiday Motel	(508) 255-1514
	Route 6A	
	Skaket Beach Motel	(508)255-1020
	203 Cranberry Hwy	
PEABODY	Marriott	(508) 977-9700
	8 Centennial Dr	
PERU	Chalet d'Alicia	(413) 655-8292
	East Windsor Rd	
PITTSFIELD	The White Horse Inn	(413) 443-0961
	378 South St	
PROVINCETOWN	Holiday Inn	(508) 487-1711
	Route 6A	
RANDOLPH	Holiday Inn	(617) 961-1000
	1374 North Main St	
RICHMOND	A B&B in the Berkshires	(413) 698-2817
	1666 Dublin Rd	

	Middle Rise B&B Route 41	(413) 698-2687
SANDWICH	Dillingham Housen B&B 71 Main St	(508) 833-0065
	Earl Sandwich Motor Manor 378 Route 6A	(508) 888-1415
	Sandwich Motor Lodge 54 Route 6A	(508) 888-2275
SAUGUS	Days Inn 999 Broadway	(617) 233-1800
SCITUATE	Raspberry Ink 748 Country Way	(508) 545-6629
	Clipper Ship Lodge 7 Beaver Dam Rd	(617) 545-5550
SHEFFIELD	Depot Guest House Route 7A	(413) 229-2908
SHREWSBURY	Days Inn Route 9	(508) 842-8500
SOMERSET	Quality Inn 1878 Wilbur Ave	(508) 678-4545
SOUTH HARWICH	Handkerchief Shoals Motel Route 28	(508) 432-2200
SOUTH YARMOUTH	Windjammer Motor Inn 192 South Shore Dr	(508) 396-2370
SPRINGFIELD	Holiday Inn 711 Dwight St	(413) 781-0900
	Marriott Inn Boland Way	(413) 781-7111
	Ramada Inn 1080 Riverdale St.	(413) 781-8750
STURBRIDGE	American Motor Lodge Route 20	(508) 347-9121
	Econo Lodge Route 20	(508) 347-2324
	Sturbridge Host Hotel 366 Main St	(508) 347-7393
	Sturbridge Motor Inn Route 131	(508) 347-3391
TEWKSBURY	Holiday Inn 4 Highwood Dr.	(508) 640-900
	Residence Inn 1775 Andover St	(508) 640-1003
WAKEFIELD	Lord Wakefield Hotel 595 North Ave.	(617) 245-6100

WALTHAM	Westin Hotel	(617) 290-5600
	73rd Ave	
WESTBOROUGH	Ramada Inn	(508) 366-0202
	399 Tpke Rd	
	Residence Inn	(508) 366-7700
	25 Connector Rd	
	Westborough Marriott Hotel	(508) 366-5511
	5400 Computer Dr	
WESTFORD	Regency Inn	(508) 692-8200
	219 Littleton Rd	
WESTMINSTER	Westminster Village Inn	(508) 874-5351
	Route 2	
WESTPORT	Hampton Inn	(508) 675-8500
	53 Old Bedford Rd	
WEST SPRINGFIELD	Econo Lodge	(413) 734-8278
	1533 Elm St	
	Goodlife Inn	(413) 781-2300
	21 Baldwin St	
	Hampton Inn	(413) 732-1300
	1011 Riverdale St	
	Howard Johnson B&B	(413) 739-7261
	1150 Riverdale St	
	Ramada Hotel	(413) 781-8750
	1080 Riverdale St	
	Red Roof Inn	(413) 731-1010
	1254 Riverdale St	
WEST TISBURY	Pondside B&B	(508) 693-4613
	Lambert Cove Rd	
WILLIAMSTOWN	Cozy Corner Motel	(413) 458-8006
	284 Sand Springs Rd	
	The Willows	(413) 458-5768
	480 Main St	
WOBURN	Comfort Inn	(617) 935-7666
	315 Mishawum Rd	
	Days Inn	(617) 935-7110
	19 Commerce Way	
WORCESTER	Hampton Inn	(508) 757-0400
	110 Summer St	
	Marriott	(508)791-1600
	10 Lincoln Square	
YARMOUTH	Colonial House Inn	(508) 362-4348
	Old Kings Highway	

Vermont

ALBURG	Ye Olde Graystone B&B	(802) 796-3911
	Route2	
ARLINGTON	Cut Leaf Maples	(802) 375-2725
	Route 7A	
	ValhallaMotel	(802) 258-2212
	Route 7A	
BARRE	Hollow Inn and Motel	(802) 476-5242
	278 South Main St.	
BELLOWS FALLS	Whippowil Cottages	(802) 463-3442
	Route 5	
BENNINGTON	Fife N' Drum	(802) 442-4074
	Route 7	
	Knotty Pine Motel	(802) 442-5487
	130 Northside Drive	
	Southgate Motel	(802) 447-7525
	Route 7	
	Vermonter Motor Lodge	(802) 442-2529
	Route 7	
BRADFORD	Bradford Motel	(802) 222-4467
	Route 5	
BRANDON	Brandon Motor Lodge	(802) 247-3802
	Route 7	
	Hivue B&B	(802) 247-3042
	Box 1023	
	Old Mill Inn	(802) 247-8002
	Stone Mill Rd	
BRATTLEBORO	Colonial Motel	(802) 257-7733
	Route 9	
	Quality Inn	(802) 254-8701
	Putney Rd.	
BROWNSVILLE	Millbrook B&B	(802) 484-7283
	Route 44	
BURLINGTON	Anchorage	(802) 863-7000
	108 Dorset St.	
	Bel-Aire Motel	(802) 863-3116
	111 Shelburne Rd.	
	Friendship Lakeview Inn	(802) 862-0230
	1860 Shelburne Rd.	
	Holiday Inn	(802) 863-6363
	1068 Williston Rd.	

	Howard Johnson's	(802) 863-5541
	Route 2 and I-89	
	Town & Country Motel	(802) 862-5786
	490 Shelburne Rd.	
COLCHESTER	Days Inn	(802) 655-0900
	Route 15	
	Hampton Inn	(802) 655-6177
	8 Mountain View Dr.	
EAST DORSET	Christmas Tree B&B	(802) 362-4889
	Box 582	
ESSEX JUNCTION	The Wilson Inn	(802) 879-1515
	10 Kellogg Rd.	
FRANKLIN	Fair Meadows Farm	(802) 285-2132
	Route 235	
ISLAND POND	Lakefront Motel	(802) 723-6507
	Route 105	
JEFFERSONVILLE	Highlander Motel	(802) 644-2725
	Route 108	
JERICHO	Homeplace B&B	(802) 899-4694
	Box 367	
KILLINGTON	Butternut On the Mountain	(802) 422-2000
	Weathervane Rd.	
	Cascades Lodge	(802) 422-3731
	Killington Rd.	
	Cedarbrook Motor Inn	(802) 422-9666
	Route 100S	
	Edelweiss	(802) 775-5577
	Route 4	
	Mendon Mountain Resort	(802) 773-4311
	Route 4	
	Val Roc	(802) 422-3881
	Route 4	
LONDONDERRY	Coombes Family Inn	(802) 228-8799
	Route 100	
LUDLOW	Timber Inn Motel	(802) 228-8666
	Main St.	
MANCHESTER	Brittany Inn	(802) 362-1033
	Route 7A	
	Stamford Motel	(802) 362-2342
	Route 7A	
	Wedgewood North Motel	(802) 362-2145
	Route 7A	
NEWPORT	Top Of the Hills Motel	(802) 334-6748
	Route 105	

NORTH SPRINGFIELD	The Abby Lyn Motel Route 106	(802) 886-2223
NORWICH	Inn at Norwich 225 Main St.	(802) 649-1143
PUTNEY	Tails up Inn RR#1, Box 958	(802) 387-5673
	Putney Inn Depot Rd.	(802) 387-5517
QUECHEE	Quality Inn Rout e 4	(802) 295-7600
RICHMOND	The Richmond Victorian Inn Box 652	(802) 434-4440
RUTLAND	Econo Lodge Route 4	(802) 773-6644
	Highlander Motel 203 North Main St.	(802) 773-6069
	Holiday Inn 411 South Main St.	(802) 775-1911
ST. JOHNSBURY	Aime's Motel Route 18	(802) 748-3194
SHAFTSBURY	Bayberry Motel Route 7A	(802) 447-7180
	Hillbrook Motel Route 7A	(802) 472-7201
SHELBURNE	Countryside Motel 2222 Shelburne Rd.	(802) 985-2839
	Econo Lodge 1961 Shelburne Rd.	(802) 985-3377
SOUTH BURLINGTON	Econo Lodge 1076 Williston Rd.	(802) 863-1125
	Ethan Allen Motel 1611 Williston Rd.	(802) 863-4573
	Ramada Inn 1117 Williston Rd.	(802) 658-0250
	Sheraton Hotel 870 Williston Rd.	(802) 865-6600
SPRINGFIELD	Howard Johnson's Route 5 and Rte 1	(802) 885-4516
	Pa-lo-mar Motel 2 Linhele Drive	(802) 885-4142
STOWE	Commodore's Inn Route 100	(802) 253-7131
	1820 House Box 276	(800) 248-1860

	Hobknob Inn	(802) 253-8549
	2364 Mountain Rd.	
	Innsbruck Inn	(802) 253-8582
	4361 Mountain Rd.	
	Mountaineeer Inn	(802) 253-7525
	3343 Mountain Rd.	
	Snowdrift Motel	(802) 253-7305
	2135 Mountain Rd.	
	Ye Olde England Inne	(802) 253-7558
	433 Mountain Rd.	
WARREN	Bridges Resort	(802) 583-2922
	Sugarbush Access Rd.	
	Powderhound Resort	(802) 496-5100
	Route 100	
WATERBURY	Holiday Inn	(802) 244-7822
	Blush Hill Rd.	
WHITE RIVER	Holiday Inn	(802) 295-3000
JUNCTION	Holiday Inn Dr.	
	Howard Johnson	(802) 295-3015
	Route 5	
WILLIAMSTOWN	Autumn Crest Inn	(802) 433-6627
	Clark Rd.	
WOODSTOCK	Braeside Motel	(802) 457-1366
	Route 4	
	Winslow House	(802) 457-1820
	38 Route 4	

New Hampshire

ALTON	Eye Joy Cottages Roberts Cove Rd.	(603) 569-4973
ANTRIM	Maplehurst Inn 155 Main St.	(603) 588-8000
BARTLETT	North Colony Motel Route 302	(603) 374-6679
	Villager Motel Route 302	(603) 374-2742
BRADFORD	Bradford Inn Main St.	(603) 938-5309
CONCORD	Brick Tower Motor Inn 414 South Main St.	(603)224-9565
	Comfort Inn 71 Hall St.	(603) 226-4100
	Econo Lodge Gulf St.	(603) 224-4011
	Holiday Inn 172 North Main St.	(603) 224-9534
CONWAY	Sunny Brook Route 16	(603) 447-3922
	Tanglewood Motel Route 16	(603) 447-5932
EXETER	Best Western 137 Portsmouth Ave.	(603) 772-3794
GLEN	Red Apple Inn Route 16	(603) 383-9680
GORHAM	Gorham Motor Inn 324 Main St.	(603) 466-3381
	Royalty Inn 130 Main St.	(603) 466-3312
	Topnotch Motor Inn 265 Main St.	(603) 466-5496
	Town and Country Route 2	(603) 466-3315
HAMPTON	Hampton Village Resort 660 Lafayette Rd.	(603) 926-6775
	The Inn of Hampton 815 Lafayette Rd.	(603) 926-6771
	Villager Motor Inn 308 Lafayette Rd.	(603) 926-3964
HANOVER	Chieftain Route 10	(603) 643-2550

HENNIKER	Henniker Motel Flanders Rd.	(603) 428-3536
HOLDERNESS	Olde Colonial Eagle Route 3	(603) 968-3233
INTERVALE	Swiss Chalets Route 16A	(603) 356-2232
JAFFREY	Woodbound Inn Woodbound Rd.	(603) 532-8341
JEFFERSON	Evergreen Motel Route 2	(603) 586-4449
KEENE	Best Western Hotel 401 Winchester	(603) 357-3038
	Days Inn 175 Key Rd.	(603) 352-7616
	Winding Brook Lodge 631 Park Ave	(603) 352-3111
LEBANON	Airport Economy Inn 7 Airport Rd.	(603) 298-8888
	Days Inn Route 20	(603) 448-5070
LINCOLN	Mount Coolidge Motel Route 3	(603) 745-8052
LITTLETON	Eastgate Motor Inn Cottage St.	(603) 444-3971
	Maple Leaf Motel 297 West Main St.	(603) 444-5101
MANCHESTER	Days Hotel 55 John E. Divine Dr.	(603) 668-6110
	Holiday Inn 700 Elm St.	(603) 625-1000
	Howard Johnson's 298 Queen City Ave.	(603) 668-2600
	Manchester Travel Lodge 21 Front St.	(603) 669-2660
MERRIMACK	Ramada Hotel Everett Trnpk	(603) 424-6181
	Residence Inn 246 Daniel Webster Hwy.	(603) 424-8100
MOULTONBORO	Matterhorn Motor Lodge Route 25	(603) 253-4314
	Rob Roy Motor Lodge Route 25	(603) 476-5571
NASHUA	Marriott Hotel 2200 South Wood Drive	(603) 880-9100

	Red Roof Inn 77 Spitbrook Rd.	(603) 888-1893
	Sheraton Tara Hotel Tara Blvd.	(603) 888-9970
NORTHWOOD	Meadow Farm B&B Jenness Pond Rd	(603) 942-8619
OSSIPEE	Pine Cove Motel Route 16	(603) 539-4491
	Windsong Motor Inn Route 25	(603) 539-4536
PLYMOUTH	Days Inn Route 3	(603) 536-3520
	Susse Chalet Route 3	(603) 536-2330
PORTSMOUTH	Anchorage Inn 417 Woodbury Ave.	(603) 431-8111
	The Port Motor Inn Portsmouth Circle	(603) 436-4373
	Susse Chalet 650 Borthwick Ave.	(603) 436-6363
	Wren's Nest Motel 3548 Lafayette Rd.	(603) 436-2481
SALEM	Red Roof Inn 15 Red Roof Lane	(603) 898-6422
SEABROOK	Best Western Route 107	(603) 474-3078
SUNAPEE	Burkehaven 179 Burkehaven Hill Rd.	(603) 763-2788
TROY	The Inn at East Hill Farm Mountain Rd.	(603) 242-6495
TWIN MOUNTAIN	Charlmont Motor Inn Route 302	(603) 846-5549
WILTON	Auk's Nest East Rd	(603) 878-3443

Maine

AUGUSTA	Best Western Senator Inn 284 Western Ave.	(207) 622-5804
BANGOR	Best Western White House 155 Littlefield Ave.	(207) 862-3737
	Comfort Inn 750 Hogan Rd.	(207) 942-7899
	Days Inn 250 Odlin Rd.	(207) 942-8272
	Econo Lodge 482 Oldin Rd.	(207) 942-6301
	Holiday Inn 500 Main St.	(207) 947-8651
	Holiday Inn 404 Oldin Rd.	(207) 947-0101
	Motel 6 1100 Hammond St.	(207) 947-6921
	Ramada Inn 357 Oldin Rd.	(207) 947-6961
	Marriott 308 Godfrey Blvd.	(207) 947-6721
BAR HARBOR	Balance Rock Inn 21 Albert Meadow	(207) 288-9900
BELFAST	Belfast Motor Inn Searsport Ave.	(207) 338-2740
	Colonial Gables Route 1	(207) 338-4000
BELGRADE	Woodland Camps Point Rd.	(207) 495-2251
BETHEL	L'Auberge Mill Hill Rd.	(207) 824-2774
BOOTHBAY HARBOR	Lawnmeer Inn Route 27	(207) 633-2544
	Pines Motel Sunset Rd.	(207) 633-4555
	Welch House B&B 36 McKown St.	(207) 633-3431
	West Harbor Resort Route 27	(207) 633-5381
BREWER	The New Stable Inn 448 Wilson St.	(207) 989-3200
BROOKSVILLE	Breezemere B&B Box 90	(207) 326-8628

BRUNSWICK	AtriumMotel	(207) 729-5555
	Route 24	
	Comfort Inn	(207) 729-1129
	199 Pleasant St.	
	Viking Motor Inn	(207) 729-6661
	287 Bath Rd.	
BUCKSPORT	Best Western	(207) 469-3113
	Route 15	
	L'ermitage	(207) 469-3361
	Box 418	
CAMDEN	Lodge at Camden Hills	(207) 236-8478
	Route 1	
	Pine Grove Cottages	(207) 236-2929
	Route 1	
DAMARISCOTTA	Brannon Bunker Inn	(207) 563-5941
	Route 129	
EAST BOOTHBAY	Leeward Village	(207) 633-3681
	Ocean Point Rd.	
	Smuggler's Cove Motor Inn	(207) 633-2800
	Route 96	
EASTPORT	Todd House	(207) 853-2328
	Moose Island	
EDGECOMB	Edgecomb Inn	(207) 882-6343
	Route 1	
ELLSWORTH	Holiday Inn	(207) 667-9341
	High St.	
	Jasper's Motel	(207) 667-5318
	200 High St.	
	White Birches	(207) 667-3621
	Route 1	
FREEPORT	Freeport Inn	(207) 865-3106
	Route 1	
GREENVILLE	Greenwood Motel	(207) 695-3321
	Route 6	
	Chesnook Lake House	(207) 745-5330
	Route 76	
GRAND LAKE STREAM	Leen's Cottages	(207) 796-5575
	Route 1	
JACKMAN	Tuckaway Shores	(207) 668-3351
	Forest St.	
KENNEBUNK	Friendship Inn	(207) 985-6525
	Route 35	
	Arundel Meadows Inn	(207) 985-3770
	Box 1129	

KENNEBUNKPORT	1820 School House B&B School St	(207) 967-4813
	English Robin B&B 99 Western Ave	(207) 967-3505
KITTERY	Kittery Motor Inn Route 1	(207) 439-2000
LEWISTON	Chalet Motel 1243 Lisbon St.	(207) 784-0600
	Motel 6 516 Pleasant St.	(207) 782-6558
LINCOLN	Briarwood Motor Inn West Broadway	(207) 794-6731
	Lincoln House 85 Main St.	(207) 794-3096
MACHIAS	Bluebird Motel Route 1	(207) 255-3332
	Machias Motor Inn 26 East Main St.	(207) 255-4861
MILLINOCKET	Atrium Inn 740 Central St.	(207) 723-4555
	Best Western 935 Central St.	(207) 723-9777
NAPLES	Augustus Bove House Route 302	(207) 693-6365
NORTH ANSON	Embden Lake Resorts West Shore Drive	(207) 566-7501
NORTH WINDHAM	SebagoLodge White's Bridge Rd	(207) 892-2698
OGUNQUIT	Beachmere Inn 12 Beachmere Pl.	(207) 646-2021
	Studio East Motor Inn 43 Main St.	(207) 646-7297
OLD ORCHARD BCH	Waves Motor Inn 87 West Grand Ave.	(207) 934-4949
ORONO	Best Western 4 Godfrey Dr.	(207) 866-7120
	University Motor Inn 5 College Ave.	(207) 866-4921
PORTLAND	Best Western 700 Main St.	(207) 774-6151
	Hampton Inn 171 Philbrook Ave.	(207) 773-4400
	Howard Johnsons 155 Riverside St.	(207) 774-5861

	Ramada Inn	(207) 774-5611
	1230 Congress St.	
	Sonesta Hotel	(207) 775-5411
	157 High St.	
RANGELEY	Mallory's B&B	(207) 864-2121
	Hyatt Rd.	
	Rangeley Inn	(207) 864-3341
	Main St.	
RAYMOND	Segbago Inn	(207) 655-3345
	1262 Roosevelt Terr.	
	Northern Pines	(207) 655-7624
	559 Route 85	
ROCKLAND	Navigator Motor Inn	(207) 594-2131
	520 Main St.	
	Oakland Seashore Motel	(207) 594-8104
	Route 1	
	Seaview Motel	(207) 594-8479
	Route 1	
	Tradewinds Motor Inn	(207) 596-6661
	2 Parkview Dr.	
ROCKWOOD	Salmon Run Camps	(207) 534-8880
	Route 15	
RUMFORD	Linnell Motel	(207) 364-4511
	Route 2	
	Madison Motor Inn	(207) 364-7973
	Route 2	
SACO	Tourist Haven Motel	(207) 284-7251
	757 Portland Rd.	
SANFORD	Bar-H-Motel	(207) 324-4662
	581 Main St.	
SKOHEGAN	Somerset Motor Lodge	(207) 474-2227
	422 Madison Ave.	
	Belmont	(207) 474-8315
	425 Madison Ave.	
SOUTH HARPSWELL	Vicarage East	(207) 833-5480
	Box 368	
SOUTH PORTLAND	Best Western	(207) 774-6151
	700 Main St.	
	Comfort Inn	(207) 775-0409
	90 Main Mall Rd.	
	Howard Johnsons	(207) 775-5343
	675 Main St.	
	Marriott Hotel	(207) 871-8000
	200 Sable Oaks Dr.	

	Sheraton Tara Hotel	(207) 775-6161
	363 Main Mall Rd.	
SULLIVAN HARBOR	Sullivan Harbor Farm B&B	(207) 422-3735
	Rte 1	
STRATTON	Spillover Motel	(207) 246-6571
	Route 27	
WATERVILLE	Anchorage Inn	(207) 872-5577
	Main St.	
	AtriumMotel	(207) 873-2777
	332 Main St.	
	Budget Host	(207) 873-3366
	400 Kennedy Mem. Dr.	
	Econo Lodge	(207) 872-5577
	455 Kennedy Mem. Dr.	
	Holiday Inn	(207) 873-0111
	375 Main St.	
	Waterville Motor Lodge	(207) 873-0141
	320 Kennedy Mem. Dr.	
WELLS	Ne'r Beach Motel	(207) 646-2636
	Route 1	
	Tatnick B&B	(207) 676-2209
	Tatnick Road	
WEST PARIS	Mollyockett Motel	(207) 674-2345
	Route 26	
WILSON MILLS	Bosebuck Camps	(207) 422-3735
	Rte 16	
WILTON	Whispering Pines Motel	(207) 645-3721
	Route 2	
WINTERPORT	Colonial Winterport Inn	(207) 223-5307
	Route 1A	
YORK	York Commons Inn	(207) 363-8903
	Route 1	

Chain Hotels/Motels-800 Numbers

Best Western: (800) 528-1234

Budgetel Inns: (800) 4-BUDGET

Clarion Hotels: (800) CLARION

Comfort Inns: (800) 228-5150

Days Inn: (800) 325-2525

Econo Lodge: (800) 446-6900

Embassy Suites: (800) 362-2779

Fairmont Hotels: (800) 527-4727

Four Seasons Hotels: (800) 332-3442

Guest Quarters: (800) 424-2900

Hampton Inn: (800) HAMPTON

Hilton Hotels: (800) HILTON

Holiday Inn: (800) HOLIDAY

Howard Johnson: (800) 654-2000

Hyatt Corp: (800) 228-9000

Marriott Hotels: (800) 228-9290

Meridien: (800) 543-4300

Omni Hotels: (800) 843-6664

Quality Inns: (800) 228-5151

Radison Hotels: (800) 333-3333

Ramada Inns: (800) 2-RAMADA

Ritz-Carlton: (800) 241-3333

Sheraton Hotels: (800) 325-3535

Sonesta Hotels: (800) 343-7170

Stouffer Hotels: (800) HOTELS-1

Travelodge: (800) 255-3050

Helpful Telephone Numbers

American Animal Hospital Association .... (303) 986-2800
American Humane Association .... (800) 227-4645
A.S.P.C.A .... (212) 876-7700
Assistance Dogs International .... (303) 234-9512
Dog Camp ("Camp Gone to the Dogs") .... (802) 387-5673
Guide Dog Foundation for the Blind .... (800) 548-4337
Humane Society for the U.S. .... (202) 452-1100
National Animal Poison Control Center .... (800) 548-2423
Pet Loss Support Hot line .... (916) 752-4200
Pet Finders .... (800) 666-5678
Tattoo-A-Pet International .... (800) TAT-TOOS

State Forests, Parks, and Recreation Areas

Rules and Regulations

Regulations for State Parks, Forests, and Recreation Areas

Connecticut State Park Regulations:

Pets and riding animals, including but not limited to dogs and horses, are prohibited in the following areas of state parks and forests at all times: all buildings, swimming areas and other areas so posted. No pet or riding animals shall enter a water body in which there is a DEP swimming area from anywhere on the DEP property containing that swimming area or from any contiguous DEP property. Riding animals are permitted in all other areas, and pets are permitted in all other areas provided they are on a leash no longer than seven feet and are under the control of their owner or keeper. Pets are permitted in state forest campgrounds, no more than one pet shall be allowed per campsite. Pets are prohibited from state park campgrounds. For more information, please telephone (203) 566-2304.

Rhode Island State Park Regulations:

Pets are allowed in all state parks; however, they are not allowed on the beaches in season during the peak hours. Pets are allowed on the beaches, in season, either early in the morning or late in the evening. During the off-season pets are allowed on the beach any time of day. For more information, please telephone (401) 277-2601

Massachusetts State Park Regulations:

Leashed pets are welcome in all state forests and parks except those listed below. For more information, please telephone (800) 831-0569 or (617) 727-3180.

Parks where dogs are NOT allowed:

Brimfield State Forest
Chicopee Memorial State Park
Demarest Lloyd State Park
Ellisville Harbor State Park
Gardner Heritage State Park
Hampston Ponds State Park
Lake Lorraine State Park
Moore State Park
Mt. Sugarloaf State Reserve
Myles Standish Monument State Reservation
Pilgrim Memorial (Plymouth Rock) State Park
Roxbury Heritage State Park
South Cape Beach State Park
Spencer State Forest
Western Gateway Heritage State Park
Whitehall State Park

New Hamsphire State Park Regulations:

General Guidelines:
Pets are never allowed on the beach or in the water
Dogs must be on a leash at all times
If any pet creates a disturbance or threatens park patrons, it will be removed
from the park. For more information , please telephone (603) 271-3254.

Parks where dogs ARE allowed:

Androscoggin
Annett
Bedell Bridge
Bear Brook (campground areas)
Cardigan
Chesterfield (dog walk areas)
Coleman
Crawford Notch (campgrounds and
dog walk areas)
Dixville Notch
Franconia (dog walk areas, not in camp
grounds)
Gardner

Greenfield (campground areas)
Honey Brook
Kearsarge: Rollins & Winslow
Lake Francis
Milan Hill
Moose Brook (campground areas)
Nansen
Pillsbury
Pisgah
Rollins
Mt. Sunapee (not at beach or shelters)
Mt. Washington
Winslow

Vermont State Park Regulations:

For the comfort and safety of our human visitors, pets are not allowed in day
use areas (beaches or picnic areas) or parking lots unless they are guide animals.
For more information, please telephone (802) 241-3655.

General Guidelines:
Owners must have, and show upon entering any park, a proof of rabies
vaccination for each pet.
Quiet hours for everyone, including pets, are between 10 PM and 7AM.
Domesticated or trained animals must be kept on a leash no longer than ten
feet and must be attended at all times.
Pets are not allowed in any day use areas.
Pet owners are responsible for repairing damage caused by their animal and
cleaming up after them.
Note: Vermont is at the turning point where they may potentially ban pets in their
parks unless visitors begin to comply with their rules and regulations.

Maine State Park Regulations:

No pets are allowed on the beaches or in Sebago Lake State Park campground. Pets
are allowed only under suitable restraint and must not be left unattended. Pets
must be on a leash not exceeding four feet in length. Pet owners must immediately
clean up any fecal deposits left by their pets. Pet owners may be assigned picnic
or campsites in a less congested area of the park. For more information telephone
(207) 287-3821.

Index